SOVEREIGNTY AND SOCIETY IN COLONIAL BRAZIL

SOVEREIGNTY AND SOCIETY IN COLONIAL BRAZIL

THE HIGH COURT OF BAHIA AND ITS JUDGES, 1609–1751

STUART B. SCHWARTZ

UNIVERSITY OF CALIFORNIA PRESS
BERKELEY, LOS ANGELES, LONDON

UNIVERSITY OF CALIFORNIA PRESS
BERKELEY AND LOS ANGELES, CALIFORNIA
UNIVERSITY OF CALIFORNIA PRESS, LTD.
LONDON, ENGLAND

ISBN: 0-520-02195-9
LIBRARY OF CONGRESS CATALOG CARD NUMBER: 76-186112
PRINTED IN THE UNITED STATES OF AMERICA
DESIGNED BY LLOYD LINFORD

TO
MY PARENTS

TO
CHARLES K. WARNER
BAILEY W. DIFFIE
HISTORIANS, MENTORS, FRIENDS

CONTENTS

ILLUSTRATIONS

PLATES (following p. 228)

FIGURES

MAPS

TABLES

PREFACE

Three fingers with pen in hand is the boldest of human ventures. How many sins are embellished by a pen's flourish? How many virtues obscured by a stroke? How much fame darkened by a blot?

Padre Antônio Vierra

Vasco da Gama on the quay at Calicut, Hernán Cortes beholding the splendors of Tenochtitlán, Francis Drake on the Spanish Main, and other images of swashbuckling soldiers and bold mariners have long been prominent in the history of European expansion. But in the wake of these adventurers other more mundane types followed —merchants, midwives, priests, servant girls, and bureaucrats. In the areas of America settled by these men and women, a complex society arose, a society which blended the racial and cultural elements of Europe, Africa, and America, but which always maintained a strong European flavor in its government and in the social organization of its elites. The creation of overseas empires was undoubtedly one of the most significant processes of European and world history in the period after 1450, and its effects are still felt today.

At about the time overseas expansion began, yet another historical process commenced to shape the societies of Western Europe: strong centralized states emerged under the aegis of royal authority. As monarchs sought to establish their authority and to diminish the powers of various groups, corporations, and estates, they came to depend increasingly on the services of a professional bureaucracy whose interests became intimately bound to those of the crown. The "New Monarchies" faced the tasks of collecting taxes, maintaining military strength, and enforcing law. The various branches of administration (to which in some cases the Church hierarchy can be added) represented the State's attempt to meet the challenge of government. It is perhaps unnecessary to speak of an "administrative revolution," as G. R. Elton has done in the case of Tudor England, because much of the new style of government had medieval precedents and the changes were not always in the direction of increasing centralization; but change there was, nevertheless. Prussia, Scandinavia, France, England, and the Iberian peninsula all witnessed this process in the sixteenth and seventeenth centuries, and although the tempo and style differed from country to country, the movement was general. By the mid-seventeenth century, bureaucracy and the State had become synonymous and the machinery of government had grown to enormous size and complexity.[1]

Iberia presents a special case. In Castile, Ferdinand and Isabella created a Renaissance State by breaking the power of the magnates, pitting the towns against the nobility, and then developing a professional bureaucracy to control both.[2] In Portugal, the House of Aviz depended on mercantile and lower-class support in its struggle to establish a centralized monarchy, but like Castile it also turned to bureaucratic administration to formalize its achievement. This is not to say that the nobility withdrew from government. Both kingdoms reserved places of distinction and service for the

---

1. G. R. Elton, *The Tudor Revolution in Government* (Cambridge, 1962). For an excellent general statement see Hans Rosenberg, *Bureaucracy, Aristocracy, and Autocracy: The Prussian Experience, 1660–1815* (Cambridge, 1958), pp. 1–26.

2. J. Beneyto, "La gestación de la magistratura moderna," *Anuario de la Historia de Derecho Español*, XXIII (1953), 55–82; José Antonio Maravall, "Los 'Hombres de Saber' o letrados y la formación de su consciencia estamental," *Estudios de historia de pensamiento español* (Madrid, 1967), 345–380.

titled nobility so long as they tied their fortunes to the rising star of the crown. The counts and marquises who served in royal councils, represented the king at foreign courts, or ruled as viceroys attest to the continuing role of the nobility in government. But in both Spain and Portugal the professional bureaucrats, that quasi-estate of royal servants and officers, were commonly nonnoble lawyers or judges whose training in, emphasis on, and respect for legal procedure and the Roman Law tradition eventually pervaded society as a whole.

The precocious overseas expansion of Portugal and Spain was not unrelated to the rise of monarchical power. In both cases and especially in Portugal, royal investment and sponsorship had played a significant role in the discovery and exploitation of new sources of wealth, which could in turn be used to support the State's growing administrative and military responsibilities. The roughly contemporaneous processes of overseas expansion and state bureaucratization stamped the American colonies with a well-developed administrative structure and a curiously legalistic approach to government and life. The Roman Law tradition embodied in judges, clerks, notaries, and law itself was transferred to the New World. The king's primary responsibility to his subjects, both colonial and metropolitan, lay in the just enforcement of the law. Individual statutes might be unjust, lawyers dishonest, and the courts corrupt, but the law, society's very foundation, was by definition a positive good. Even today, Brazilians say "*É legal* (It's legal)" for anything that is very good.

Modern Brazilians also retain another tradition from their colonial past which can best be illustrated by the following anecdote about an incident which was the initial stimulus for this study. While studying the Portuguese language at Columbia University in the summer of 1963, our class was asked to memorize a number of dialogues in Portuguese which reflected everyday situations in Brazil. One dialogue went something like this. João: "Pedro, I hear you have a good new job in the Ministry of Finance." Pedro: "Yes, my brother-in-law is now the undersecretary." This open admission of nepotism brought peals of laughter from the North American students in the class, but the fine Brazilian woman who was teaching the course saw nothing humorous in it at all. How else could one get a job in the Ministry of Finance? This incident brought into focus for me a vital question: how did the Portuguese empire, a highly rationalized system of bureaucratic organization, accommodate the personal relations of kinship, friendship, and interest which have always characterized Iberian society? The answer to this question provides not only a deeper understanding of Brazil's social and political heritage, but also some explanation of its historical development, over three hundred years, as the colony of a nation far inferior to it in size, population, and wealth.

My basic premise throughout this study is that government and society in colonial Brazil were structured by two interlocking systems of organization. On one level, a metropolitan controlled and directed administration, characterized by bureaucratic norms and impersonal relations, tied individuals and groups to the political institutions of formal government. Parallel to this, there existed a network of interpersonal primary relations based on interest, kinship, and common goals, which while no less formal in one sense, nevertheless lacked official recognition. This book is an attempt to examine the dynamic relationship between these two systems of human organization within the context of two hundred and fifty years of Brazilian history, the period of that nation's creation as an overseas colony of Portugal.

The men who filled the offices of government in the Portuguese empire came from a wide range of social and occupational backgrounds. Titled nobles, churchmen, and accountants all held administrative positions and all could be fairly called bureaucrats, but it should be remembered that the crown's claim to sovereignty lay in its role as the guardian of justice. Despite its military, fiscal, and administrative responsibilities, the bureaucracy of the Portuguese empire had at its heart a judicial organization staffed by professional magistrates whose life, status, and prospects were inextricably tied to government. I have placed these magistrates at the core of my study by concentrating on the development and operation of the High Court (Relação) of Bahia, a judicial and administrative institution established in Brazil in 1609. The Relação served as a principal link between the desires of the colonial population and the dictates of royal government. Special emphasis has been placed on the administrative functions of the High Court and on the nature and performance of its personnel rather than on its judicial role.

Throughout this study, my intention has been to emphasize the human nature of bureaucracy and to examine the historical dimensions which a human relations approach to government can provide. Formal tables of organization have not been ignored, and the reader will find many references to institutional conflicts, as is traditionally the case in administrative histories; but in order to understand the operation of government and society in colonial Brazil, we must look beyond it to the complex web of other social and economic relationships which constituted the fabric of colonial existence. It is in this area that I hope the present study has something new to offer.

The book is divided into three parts. Part One examines the nature of the Portuguese bureaucracy and the rise of the magistrates as a political power both in Portugal and in its colonies. In 1580 the union of Spain and Portugal resulted in a general reform of Portuguese judicial structure and during this reform the Relação of Bahia was born. Part One closes with an examination of the Portuguese magistracy and a detailed description of the personal and professional lives of the first ten magistrates (desembargadores) of the High Court of Bahia. In Part Two, I have used the first Relação of Bahia (1609–1626) as a vehicle for the examination of the structure, functions, procedures, and actions of the Relação. This section analyzes the social milieu in Bahia, the seat of the Relação, and attempts to show the impact of the Relação on local conditions. Conflicts of jurisdiction and interest which arose between the Relação and other institutions are set forth with an eye to broader questions, such as the nature and effectiveness of colonial government. Then, by showing the various links of family, friendship, and business interest I have attempted an analysis of bureaucracy within the context of colonial society. Finally, Chapter Nine demonstrates how wartime measures and private pressures brought about the temporary abolition of the Relação.

Part Three reviews the reasons for the Relação's rebirth and traces the outline of its history down to 1751. Then, using the biographies of all one hundred and sixty-eight magistrates of the Relação of Bahia (1609–1759), I have attempted a general analysis of magisterial government in colonial Brazil with special emphasis on the primary relations established between magistrates and colonial society.

Although this volume comments on the nature of both bureaucracy and society in colonial Brazil, it does not pretend to be an exhaustive study of either. It is principally a study of elites: on one hand, the highest level of the professional bureaucracy, the desembargadores; and on the other, the sugar planters and cattle ranchers who dominated colonial institutions and often monopolized the available social and economic resources. This emphasis on the upper strata of colonial government and society does not reflect any lack of interest on my part in the vast majority of the population. Instead, it recognizes that the social and political institutions of colonial Brazil often operated to the detriment of that majority, and it attempts to examine how that system came into being, and more important, how and why it was perpetuated.

In preparing this book I have used many works on Portuguese and Brazilian history, but very few dealt directly wtih my subject. As a result, this study is based primarily on printed and unpublished documents from a wide variety of sources, small bits and pieces which I have attempted to weave together. The professional magistrates of the Portuguese empire are not an easy group for the historian to treat. The Portuguese have rarely felt the need to memorialize themselves in prose or portraiture. The diary is not a Portuguese genre, and in an age when every Dutch burgher sat for an artist, Portuguese iconography is limited in the main to kings and clerics. Five years of searching failed to uncover any personal papers or private correspondence of the magistrates. Thus, many aspects of their private lives which would have proven invaluable to this study remain unknown. The reader may lament my failure in this area, but I can assure him that the absence of this type of information was not due to disinterest or oversight.

Whereas studies of the Portuguese magistracy are virtually nonexistent, the literature on bureaucracy in general is enormous. Fine historical studies have traced the development of state bureaucracies in many nations, and a whole range of works in political science and sociology has developed around such themes as public administration, organization theory, and bureaucracy.[3] I have read widely but by no means exhaustively in this literature, and although I make no sociological claims for this study, I have learned some lessons and borrowed a variety of concepts from that discipline. Although I would avoid the label "functionalist," my approach would basically fall under the heading of a post-Weberian, human relations model.[4]

Undoubtedly, Max Weber's classic studies of bureaucracy have served as the starting point for modern historical and sociological analysis of that phenomenon.[5] Scholars like John L. Phelan have

---

3. An excellent summary and analysis of this literature is presented in Nicos Mouzelis, *Organisation and Bureaucracy* (Chicago, 1968). Richard Hall, "The Concept of Bureaucracy: An Empirical Assessment," *American Journal of Sociology*, LXIX (July 1963), 32–40, evaluates a large body of literature in comparative terms.

4. Mouzelis, *Organisation*, 55–75; Eugene Litwak, "Models of Bureaucracy Which Permit Conflict," *American Journal of Sociology*, LXVII (September 1961), 177–184. I have found Peter Blau, *The Dynamics of Bureaucracy*, 2nd ed. (Chicago, 1963); Michel Crozier, *The Bureaucratic Phenomenon* (Chicago, 1964); and Robert K. Merton, *et al.*, *Reader in Bureaucracy* (New York, 1952), particularly suggestive and helpful.

5. Max Weber, *The Theory of Social and Economic Organization*, trans. A. M. Henderson and Talcott Parsons (New York, 1947); *From Max Weber*, trans. and ed. H. H. Gerth and C. Wright Mills (New York, 1946); Julien Freund, *The Sociology of Max Weber* (New York, 1969), especially pp. 229–267.

demonstrated the continuing utility of Weber's model of bureaucratic development and its applicability in the context of a colonial empire.[6] There is a great deal in Weber's approach which I have found useful, but I have avoided his model for two basic reasons.

First, Weber was principally concerned with stages of administrative development. His ideal stages of patriarchal, patrimonial, and bureaucratic authority are particularly unsuited to an analysis of the Portuguese empire, which developed in a historical age of transition and therefore contained elements of at least two Weberian stages and fit neither of them comfortably. Weber, of course, realized that these were "ideal types" in need of historical description, analysis, and refinement, but the problem of moving from one type to the next is the weakest part of his model. It is this process of change which is difficult to accommodate in Weber's theory, and this book makes clear that colonial Brazilian administration was characterized by constant changes and great flexibility. Moreover, patrimonial and bureaucratic forms of organization do not appear in the Brazilian case to have been mutually exclusive stages, but rather variant types which could exist simultaneously within the same organization. Second, Weber's emphasis on the "rational" aspects of bureaucracy—those features designed for the direct accomplishment of administrative tasks—detracts from his usefulness in an analysis which stresses the non-categorical and personal relations of bureaucrats as opposed to the categorical and impersonal ones of the bureaucracy.

Although I have eschewed Weber's model, I have incorporated some of the concepts he developed, particularly the concept of patrimonial control in which the ruler embodied legitimacy and authority, and bestowed offices on the basis of particularistic criteria, not merit. In such a system, the private interests of the officer and the public interests of the office were often blurred, and offices

---

6. John Leddy Phelan, *The Kingdom of Quito in the Seventeenth Century* (Madison, 1967).

were commonly owned by their holders.[7] Many elements of this form of control characterized the lower levels of the Portuguese bureaucracy long after some move had been made toward establishing the hierarchy, specialization, and task-orientation of "rational" bureaucratic administration. That the desembargadores, the most professional element of the bureaucracy, continued to hold values and pursue goals contrary to those of rational administration displays the difficulty of applying Weber's model. Moreover, implicit throughout this book is my belief that the frequency of non-bureaucratic behavior increased as one moved down the echelons of office. Thus, whatever evidence of this non-rational behavior exists among the desembargadores would be many times greater among minor local officials; and while I have admittedly concentrated on only one sector of the bureaucracy, I believe that much of my analysis is applicable to other levels.

The work of S. N. Eisenstadt has been especially helpful to me in defining elements of the historical process of bureaucratic formation and in seeing that process as one of constant change.[8] Following him, I have tried to differentiate between the goals and values of the bureaucracy (as defined by the crown) and those of the bureaucrats, both personal and professional. My basic approach has been to view the bureaucracy as a social system as well as a form of administration, and to examine the relationship between it and the society in general. It is in the dynamic pattern of these relations that the story of colonial bureaucracy is to be found.

---

7. A cogent argument in Weber's defense is presented by William Delany in "The Development and Decline of Patrimonial and Bureaucratic Administrations," *Administrative Science Quarterly*, VII (March 1963), 458–501.

8. Eisenstadt's bibliography on this subject is very large but his major ideas are drawn together in *The Political Systems of Empires* (New York, 1963).

ACKNOWLEDGMENTS

Many friends and colleagues gave me assistance, advice, and encouragement in writing this book. Aside from the directors and staff members of the various archives and libraries cited in the Bibliography, all of whom extended me the usual privileges, I owe a special debt of thanks to Alberto Iria, Carlos de Azevedo, and Father Antônio da Silva Rêgo of Lisbon; to Manuel Lopes de Almeida, Américo da Costa Ramalho, and Jorge Peixoto of Coimbra; and to Armando Nobre Gusmão of Evora. Three distinguished scholars took the time to answer my queries on more than one occasion: C. R. Boxer of Yale University, José Antônio Gonçalves de Mello of the Federal University of Recife, and Engel Sluiter of the University of California at Berkeley. John Russell-Wood allowed me to see his fine manuscript on the Misericórdia of Bahia prior to its publication. Francis A. Dutra of the University of California at Santa Barbara spent long hours seated next to me in the great Iberian archives and pointed the way to many an interesting document. In Brazil, the kindness and interest of many people made this book possible. José Honório Rodrigues read an early version of the manuscript and gave me the benefit of his excellent criticism. José Gabriel da Costa Pinto facilitated my work at the Arquivo Nacional. In Bahia my good friend Luís Henrique Dias Tavares placed the Arquivo Público at my disposal, and I shall always be thankful for the friendship and aid of Neusa Esteves.

The criticism and comments of colleagues and friends in the United States helped to eliminate at least some of the errors and flaws in this book. Frederick Holden Hall of the Newberry

Library, John Phelan and Thomas Skidmore of the University of Wisconsin, and my friend Kinley Brauer of the University of Minnesota all underwent the ordeal of reading various versions of the manuscript. Dauril Alden of the University of Washington deserves my special thanks. His example, encouragement, suggestions, and companionship all contributed to the completion of this volume. To him, and to Professor Lewis Hanke, who gave of his time and expertise without reservation as my doctoral adviser, and who continued to take an interest in this project after the termination of that relationship, I shall always be grateful.

The research and writing of this book took place between 1965 and 1971. The project could not have been completed without the generous aid of a number of institutions. Research was carried out with the aid of a National Defense Foreign Language Fellowship to Portugal (1965); a grant from the Calouste Gulbenkian Foundation of Lisbon (Summer 1966); a fellowship of the Organization of American States to Brazil (Summer 1967); and a grant from the Organization of International Programs of the University of Minnesota for research in Brazil (Summer 1970). Two Junior Fellowships from the Newberry Library of Chicago (Summer 1965, 1966–67) enabled me to write under ideal conditions.

ABBREVIATIONS AND EDITORIAL CONVENTIONS

Archival

ACL	Academia das Ciências de Lisboa
ACMB	Arquivo da Câmara Municipal da Bahia
ACML	Arquivo da Câmara Municipal de Lisboa
AGI	Archivo General de Indias (Seville)
AGS	Archivo General de Simancas
AHI	Arquivo Histórico do Itamaraty
AHNM	Archivo Histórico Nacional Madrid
AHNRJ	Arquivo Histórico Nacional de Rio de Janeiro
AHU	Arquivo Histórico Ultramarino
AMC	Arquivo Municipal de Coimbra
ANTT	Arquivo Nacional da Torre do Tombo (Lisbon)
APB	Arquivo Público do Estado da Bahia
ASCMB	Arquivo da Santa Casa da Misericórdia da Bahia
AUC	Arquivo da Universidade de Coimbra
BA	Biblioteca da Ajuda (Lisbon)
BGUC	Biblioteca Geral da Universidade de Coimbra
BM	British Museum (London)
BNL	Biblioteca Nacional de Lisboa
BNM	Biblioteca Nacional de Madrid
BNRJ	Biblioteca Nacional do Rio de Janeiro
BPE	Biblioteca Pública de Evora
BPMP	Biblioteca Pública Municipal do Porto

IHGB	Instituto Histórico e Geográfico do Brasil
PRO	Public Record Office (London)
RAHM	Real Academia de la Historia (Madrid)
SGL	Sociedade de Geografia de Lisboa

Printed

ABNR	*Anais da Biblioteca Nacional do Rio de Janeiro*
ACVSP	*Actas da Câmara da Villa de São Paulo*
AMP	*Anais do Museu Paulista*
Arquivo Cadaval	*Os manuscritos do Arquivo da Casa de Cadaval repeitantes ao Brasil*
CIELB	*Colóquio internacional de estudos Luso-brasileiros*
Col. chron.	*Collecção chronologica da legislação portugueza*
CSPF	*Calendar of State Papers Foreign Series*
DHBNR	*Documentos históricos da Biblioteca Nacional de Rio de Janeiro*
HAHR	*Hispanic American Historical Review*
HAJEI	*História da administração da justiça no Estado da Índia*
HCJB	*História da Companhia de Jesus no Brasil*
HCPB	*História da colonização portuguesa do Brasil*
Livro Primeiro	*Livro Primeiro do govêrno do Brasil*
Livro Segundo	"Livro Segundo do governo do Brasil," *AMP*, III (1927), 5–128
Ord. fil.	*Ordenações filipinas*
Ord. man.	*Ordenações manuelinas*

A number of editorial problems and conventions deserve some mention here. Portuguese orthography is a particularly thorny matter. Its rules have changed a number of times in the last century and there is no reason to believe that they will not change again. Moreover, despite attempts at standardization, differences still exist between Portuguese and Brazilian usage. In general, I have followed modern Brazilian usage (for example, Antônio not António, Bahia not Baía), although this has led me to supply accent marks which people of the seventeenth and eighteenth centuries usually left "in the inkwell." I have given the titles of publications as they appear on the title page. Variant spellings of proper names (Affonso for Afonso, Ruy for Rui) have been standardized. As a matter of personal taste, I have used the old and distinctively Portuguese "Manoel," not the modern "Manuel." Place names are usually given in the common English form (Lisbon not Lisboa, Oporto not Porto) when such exists. The city of Salvador da Bahia de Todos os Santos was, and still is, commonly called simply Bahia, which was also the name of the captaincy where it was located. In geographical references, I have used Salvador for the city and Bahia for the captaincy. When for stylistic reasons this was impossible, the context should indicate which is being discussed.

With the exception of the term "desembargador" (high court magistrate), which is central to this study, I have italicized all foreign terms. Those which appear repeatedly are placed in the Glossary for the reader's reference. The titles of institutions have been left in the original language. This may seem strange since Conselho da Índia could very well be rendered as India Council, but Desembargo do Paço would be difficult to translate, and Treasury Council would not indicate whether the Spanish Consejo de Hacienda or the Portuguese Conselho da Fazenda was the original. Because much of this study concentrates on the period between 1580 and 1640, when the crowns of Spain and Portugal were united, there is yet another problem. Philip II, III, and IV of Spain were Philip I, II, and III of Portugal. I have used the Spanish numeration more familiar to English-speaking readers, but this has led to the seeming inconsistency of a textual reference to Philip II supported by a Portuguese archival citation to a document of Philip I. If in all this there are lapses of uniformity, I can only point to the hallowed precedent of centuries of confusion in these matters.

PART ONE: JUSTICE AND BUREAUCRACY

I. THE KING'S JUSTICE: PORTUGAL, AFRICA AND ASIA

But one bad judge in a city
destroys the community;
Look well at the harm they do,
the many of this quality;
God and the king are not served,
the people destroyed,
the police damned,
the republic robbed,
and the poor oppressed.
Garcia de Resende, *Miscelania*
(c. 1534)

The pillory (*pelourinho*), a symbol of justice and royal authority, stood at the center of most Portuguese towns of the sixteenth century. Within its shadow, civil authorities read proclamations and punished criminals. Its location at the core of the community signified the Iberian belief that the administration of justice was the most important attribute of government. Sixteenth- and seventeenth-century Portuguese and Spaniards thought that the impartial application of the law and the honest performance of public duty insured the well-being and progress of the realm; conversely, circumvention of justice by avaricious officials or powerful groups and individuals brought ruin and provoked divine retribution. In Portugal royal concern with justice had reached a draconic height during the reign of Dom Pedro I (1357–1397), in whom the dispensation of justice to high-born and low-born alike became a psychotic fixation.[1] Time and time again, learned treatises and the laws themselves spoke of justice as the formost responsibility of the king. From the thirteenth to the seventeenth centuries the Portuguese saw a close relationship between the king and his law.[2]

Overseas, the colonial sons of Spain and Portugal were no less aware of the value of justice and law. Frei Vicente do Salvador, a native of Brazil and one of its first historians, recounted in his *História do Brasil* an illuminating anecdote. An earthquake in Portuguese India had leveled the entire city of Bassein except for its *pelourinho* and a wall where the whips for judicial punishment were hung. Frei Vicente extracted from this incident the moral that God preferred the loss of cities and peoples to the suspension of punishment for crimes.[3] The administration of justice, therefore, is one key to an understanding of the empires of Spain and Portugal in the sixteenth and seventeenth centuries.

The Portuguese maritime empire, of which Brazil was but a part, has been called a "thalassocracy" and a commercial empire in a military and religious mold.[4] It was an organized state for which a complex machinery of control had been developed. The patterns of government and the official institutions of Brazil were based on forms that had originated in Portugal or in those areas of the Atlantic, Africa, and Asia into which the Portuguese had expanded.

---

1. H. V. Livermore, *A History of Portugal* (Cambridge, 1947), pp. 161–163; Fernão Lopes, *Crónica de D. Pedro I*, in *Classicos portugueses: Trechos escolhidos* (Lisbon, 1943).

2. Martim de Albuquerque, *O poder político no renascimento portugues* (Lisbon, 1968), 146, 152.

3. Frei Vicente do Salvador, *História do Brasil, 1500–1627*, João Capistrano de Abreu, Rodolfo Garcia, Frei Venáncio Willike, ed., 5th ed. (São Paulo, 1965), liv. IV, cap. 40, p. 346. All future citations are from this edition.

4. C. R. Boxer, *The Portuguese Seabourne Empire* (London, 1969).

Brazilian development both before and after 1580 was often prefaced or paralleled by developments in Portugal or elsewhere in the empire. Hence an understanding of the organization of the Portuguese judicial structure in 1580 is necessary if the subsequent period is to be understood. Moreover, as we shall see, the judicial structure became the skeletal outline of the colonial bureaucracy.

The basic unit of the Portuguese judicial and administrative structure was the township, the *conselho*. Each township maintained a number of officials who exercised the administrative and judicial functions necessary for urban life. These included the *almotacel* (market inspector), *alcaide* (constable), *meirinho* (bailiff), and *tabelião* (notary), but the most important local justice officer was the *juiz ordinário*, sometimes called the *juiz da terra* (municipal mgaistrate).[5] Each town council usually included two of these elected municipal magistrates. Not usually trained in the law, they were ordinary citizens who were willing to serve the community for a year.[6] A red staff symbolized the authority of the municipal magistrate. He was responsible for the maintenance of law and order within the township, but he was often hindered in the accomplishment of this goal; as an elected official and a member of the community, the *juiz ordinário* and his family were subject to the threats and pressures of nobles (*fidalgos*) and other powerful individuals or groups. On the other hand, a municipal

5. C. R. Boxer, *Portuguese Society in the Tropics: The Municipal Councils of Goa, Macao, Bahia, and Luanda* (Madison, 1965), p. 5. Smaller communities of from twenty to two hundred people that had no *juiz ordinário* had a local magistrate, the *juiz de vintena*. This description of the Portuguese judicial system (c. 1580) is based primarily on a manuscript in the Biblioteca Nacional de Madrid (Códice 2292, folios 5–21) entitled "Descripción de Portugal." The manuscript is dated 1599 by the BNM but internal evidence indicates that its true date is probably 1579.

6. *Ordenações do Senhor Rey D. Manuel*, 5 vols. in 4 (Coimbra, 1797), I, tit. xlii (cited hereafter as *Ord. man.*); W. Ferreira, *História do direito brasileiro*, 4 vols. (São Paulo, 1951–1956), I, 189 (the author has used the 2nd ed. of vol. I which bears the subtitle *As capitanias coloniais de juro e herdade*, São Paulo, 1962); Fortunato de Almeida, *História de Portugal*, 6 vols. (Coimbra, 1925), III, 331.

magistrate could abuse his authority to favor friends and relatives.

These shortcomings moved the crown to create as early as 1352 the office of *juiz de fóra* (literally, judges from afar) to supplant the municipal judges in some communities.[7] As royal appointees, the *juizes de fóra* were theoretically less subject to local pressures. Moreover, it was the crown's policy that its magistrates should have no personal connections within the areas of their jurisdiction. Like the municipal justices, the royal magistrates could hear civil and criminal cases in the first instance, except those which involved royal prerogatives. By 1580 royal and central authority—symbolized by the white staff of the *juiz de fóra*—had supplanted the municipal control of justice in over fifty towns and cities of Portugal.[8]

The next higher level of justice in the administrative structure was the *comarca* or *correição*, of which there were twenty-one, divided among the six Portuguese provinces of Beira, Entre Douro e Minho, Tras-os-Montes, Alentejo, Extremadura, and Algarve. To each *correição* was assigned a *corregedor* (superior crown magistrate), whose functions were primarily of an investigatory and appellate nature. In addition, the *corregedor*, whose title literally

---

7. Duarte Nunez de Leao, *Descripção do Reino de Portugal* (Lisbon, 1610), pp. 4–10, provides a full listing of the administrative and judicial division of Portugal. The seats of the *juizes de fóra* were changed from time to time. BNM, *Cod.* 2292, reports *juizes de fóra* in the following communities. (1) Extremadura: Abrantes, Alemquer, Coimbra, Leiria, Óbidos, Santarém, Sintra, Tomar, Torres Vedras. (2) Beira: Castelo Branco, Castelo Rodrigo, Covilhã, Conselho de Fonis (?), Guarda, Lamego, Penamaior, Pinhel, Sea, Trancoso, Viseu. (3) Entre Douro e Minho: Guimarães, Ponte do Lima, Oporto, Monção, Viana. (4) Tras-os-Montes: Freixo de Espada à Cinta, Miranda. (5) Alentejo: Arronches, Beja, Campomaior, Castelo de Vide, Elvas, Estremoz, Evora, Mertola, Montemor-O-Novo, Moura, Mourão, Olivença, Portalegre, Serpa. (6) Algarve: Faro, Lagos, Loulé, Silves, Tavira. There were also *juizes de fóra* in towns located within the territories under the jurisdiction of the Military Orders of Santiago (Alcacer do Sal, Setúbal) and Aviz (Fronteira, Aviz).

8. *Ord. man.*, tit. xxxvii, attempted to eliminate abuses by forbidding all judicial officials to buy, sell, rent, or engage in any kind of commerce in the area of their jurisdiction. This was aimed specifically at crown magistrates.

meant corrector, was required to prosecute criminals, supervise public works, review municipal elections, enforce royal ordinances and safeguard royal prerogatives. During the course of each year the *corregedor* was expected to visit all the towns and villages under his jurisdiction to ascertain the state of justice, to review the procedure of lesser magistrates, and to hear those cases in which the lesser magistrates were implicated or suspect. To make this tour was to *fazer correição;* hence the title *corregedor.*[9]

The presence of the *juiz de fóra* and the *corregedor* in the towns and villages of Portugal signaled an attempt by the monarchy to limit the control of local elements of power. One contemporary observer of Portugal noted that it was also the duty of the *corregedor* to "quiet factions and dissension and to restrain the powerful of the province." [10] Both the *corregedor* and the *juiz de fóra* were mainstays of royal government on the local level.

Within the Portuguese judicial and administrative system matters pertaining to orphans, charitable institutions, probate and surrogate were assigned to another group of officials. On the municipal level there was a *juiz dos órfãos* (judge of orphans), with duties limited to the guardianship of orphans and of their inheritance.[11] His im-

---

9. *Ord. man.*, tit. xxxix, 247–269. Although similar in origin, name, and certain functions, the *corregedor* of Castile cannot be equated with that of Portugal. The Spanish *corregedores* exercised greater political control over municipal government than did their Portuguese counterparts. Moreover, certain fiscal functions of the Spanish *corregedor* were not exercised by the *corregedor* in Portugal, but were rather the concern of of the *provedor.* Portuguese *corregedores* were almost always judges, while in Spain military men were sometimes employed, especially in frontier areas. But there were marked similarities and in both countries the *corregedor* represented the extension of royal and central authority. See Jerónimo Castillo de Bovadilla, *Política para corregedores y señores de vassallos en tiempo de pas y guerra,* 2 vols. (Barcelona, 1616), and the article based on it, Robert S. Chamberlain, "The Corregedor in Castile in the Sixteenth Century and the Residência as applied to the Corregedor," *HAHR,* XXIII (1943), 222–247.

10. BNM, Cód. 2292, "Descripción de Portugal," f. 10.

11. *Ord. fil.*, I, tit. lxii; *Ord. man.*, I, tit. lxvii, provided that all towns over four hundred inhabitants would have a separate *juiz dos órfãos.* In smaller towns the *juiz ordinário* performed this duty. Two editions of the *Ordenações filipinas* have been used for this study: *Codigo philippino ou*

mediate superior on the *comarca* level was the *provedor*, who was in charge of orphans, hospitals, lay brotherhoods, and matters of probate, as well as the supervision of the collection of certain rents and taxes. By the end of the sixteenth century the *juiz de fóra* and *corregedor* had assumed these offices in many places, with the result that power was concentrated in the hands of the royal magistrates far in excess of their warrant.

There were many exceptions to the general pattern outlined above. Most of these originated in various medieval concessions and privileges that had been given by the Portuguese monarchs to groups, institutions, and individuals. The areas belonging to the military-religious orders of Christ, Aviz, and Santiago were not under the regular system of administration, and in them law was enforced by a *ouvidor* rather than a *corregedor*. The powers of a *ouvidor* were roughly equivalent to those of the superior crown magistrates, but he was appointed by the military order rather than by the crown. The University of Coimbra also enjoyed a distinct position since justice there was administered by a *conservador da justiça*, who exercised the same jurisdiction over faculty and students on or off campus that a *corregedor* normally had in a *comarca*.[12] The Archbishop of Braga—Primate of the Spains—exercised temporal as well as ecclesiastical control over a large territory. Moreover, lands belonging to certain magnates such as the Prior of Crato, the Duke of Bragança, the Duke of Aveiro, and the Marquis of Vila Real were exempt from the visitation of *corregedores* and were subject to only limited royal control in matters of administration and justice.[13]

Ordenações e leis do reino de Portugal, Candido Mendes de Almeida, ed., 24th ed. (Rio de Janeiro, 1870) is an excellent annotated edition; but because of its rarity textual citations, unless otherwise noted, refer to *Ordenações e leis do reino de Portugal*, 5 vols. in 4 (Coimbra, 1833).

12. For a description of the duties of the *conservador* of the University of Coimbra, see Serafim Leite, ed., *Estatutos da Universidade de Coimbra* (1550), (Coimbra, 1963), cap. 49, p. 146.

13. BNM, Cód. 2292; *Ord. man.*, II, tit. xxvi, art. 15. states that lands of the nobility were subject to visitation by the *corregedor*. It also stated that

The High Courts of Appeal were the next level in the judicial structure. The High Court was known in the Portuguese world as the Relação, or sometimes as the Casa da Relação. In 1580 there were three High Courts in operation in the Portuguese empire: two subordinate tribunals, the Casa do Cível in Lisbon and the Relação da India in Goa; and the superior Casa da Suplicação, which owed its position to its proximity to the king's person.

The Casa do Cível had been fixed in Lisbon since 1434. All civil cases in Portugal, if entitled to appeal, were heard by this tribunal, which exercised final jurisdiction in disputes involving small sums. Actions involving larger amounts could be appealed to the Casa da Suplicação. The Casa do Cível also had jurisdiction in all criminal cases from the province of Extremadura and the city of Lisbon without recourse of appeal from its decisions. The Casa do Cível had a general reputation for a badly overburdened docket and an extremely slow process of litigation.

The Casa da Suplicação was also a High Court of Appeal, but it held a position above the other tribunals. It had begun as a court for the king's retinue and had originally been joined with the Casa do Cível, but by 1392 it had been permanently separated.[14] After that date the Casa da Suplicação accompanied the monarch and thus usually sat in Alentejo, Extremadura, and the city of Lisbon. Criminal cases originating outside the province of Extremadura and entitled to appeal were heard by the Casa da Suplicação, as were those civil cases which were beyond the jurisdiction of the Casa do Cível. Appeals from judicial decisions in the colonies were also heard by the Casa da Suplicação. As tribunal for the royal court, the Casa da Suplicação maintained two magistrates (*corregedores de*

---

there might be no exceptions save in the case of those exemptions expressly granted by Dom Fernando (1388–1421) or any of his successors. In such cases the *ouvidor* exercised the right of *correição*. It is interesting to note that this was exactly the exemption that characterized the proprietary jurisdiction granted to the *donatários* of Brazil in the 1530's.

14. Henrique da Gama Barros, *História da administração pública em Portugal*, 2nd ed., 11 vols. (Lisbon, 1945), III, 272. Cited hereafter as *HAPP*.

corte) to adjudicate the suits of courtiers and the king's household.

The internal organization and procedures of the Casa da Suplicação served as a model for all other tribunals in the Portuguese empire. Each position within the court's structure carried with its functions certain perquisites and prestige which the magistrates were anxious to acquire. The main body of the court consisted of high court magistrates (desembargadores), who were divided into the *desembargadores extravagantes* (unassigned judges) and the *desembargadores dos agravos* (appelate judges). The former were junior members, usually younger and less experienced men who were assigned as the need arose to those cases presided over by the *desembargadores dos agravos.* By 1580 there were over twenty magistrates entitled to serve in the Casa da Suplicação.[15] The desembargadores were divided into two chambers (*mesas*), one for civil and one for criminal cases, each directed by a *desembargador dos agravos* who bore the title *corregedor.*[16] A plenary session, the *mesa grande*, was summoned only for matters of great importance.

As in all the Portuguese High Courts, the senior officer was usually a great noble, high churchman, or in the colonies, the resident governor or viceroy. His rank and lineage added prestige to the tribunal and was supposed to set him above the quarrels of its members.[17] In the Casa da Suplicação, as in the Casa do Cível and the later tribunals of the empire, the role of the president (*regidor, governador*) was more honorific than functional and real leader-

---

15. The confusion over numbers of members of the High Courts stems from the custom of granting the title of desembargador to the magistrate before he was installed. This was often the case when a crown magistrate was sent to the colonies on a special mission which called for the use of extraordinary powers. Hence it is not unusual to find a magistrate in Angola or Brazil mentioned as *desembargador da Relação do Porto*, or *da Casa da Suplicação* although it is obvious that he was not a resident member of that tribunal.

16. José Gomes B. Camara, *Subsídios para a História do Direito Patrio*, 3 vols. (Rio de Janeiro, 1954–1965), I, 79.

17. *Ord. man.* I, tit. i.

ship fell to the chancellor, who was in effect the chief justice. Experience and a distinguished legal career prepared a magistrate for the position of chancellor, which carried great responsibility. The chancellor's duties included assigning judges to hear litigation, issuing sentences, reviewing decisions to avoid conflict with existing statutes, and affixing the seal of the tribunal. In Lisbon, Goa, Bahia, and Oporto, the seats of High Courts within the empire, the personality and performance of the chancellor generally set the tenor and style of each tribunal.

Although not usually considered part of the apparatus of colonial administration, the Casa da Suplicação did exercise some influence on Brazil. Not only did its structure serve as a model for later Brazilian tribunals, but as the highest court of appeals it sometimes heard cases appealed from the colonies. Thus, some of the most important decisions affecting the life of the colonists were made in the chambers of the Casa da Suplicação. Unfortunately, almost nothing is known about the possible political influence of this tribunal on the decision-making process of the crown.

At the apex of the judicial system stood the Desembargo do Paço, a body that had developed from an advisory committee to Dom João II (1481–1495) into a board of governmental fully institutionalized by the Ordenações manuelinas of 1514. Although cases of special merit that had exhausted all other means of settlement could be appealed to this body, its primary function was not as a tribunal, but rather as a council and advisory board on all matters of justice and legal administration. In fact, the Desembargo do Paço became the central organ in the bureaucratic structure of the Portuguese empire.

It was the custom of the Desembargo do Paço to accompany the king and to meet with him each Friday afternoon to discuss the formulation and amendment of laws, the appointment of magistrates, and the general political and legal condition of the country.[18]

---

18. During the Hapsburg period the Desembargo do Paço sat in Lisbon and made its contact with the king through the Conselho de Portugal that remained in Spain.

The Desembargo do Paço appointed royal magistrates, promoted them, and evaluated their performance by means of the *residência* (investigation) held at the end of their tour of duty. When occasion arose, the Desembargo do Paço also conducted special examinations (*devassas*) or reviews, and it sometimes settled conflicts of jurisdiction between subordinate tribunals or magistrates. The various ranks of the royal magistracy, from the youngest *juiz de fóra* to the most experienced magistrate in the realm, were subject to the scrutiny, review, and examination of the Desembargo do Paço. This was as true in the colonies as in the metropolis; and unlike the Spanish empire, in which the Council of the Indies appointed royal magistrates for the colonies, this function remained unified in the control of the Desembargo do Paço.[19]

The size of the Desembargo do Paço was not fixed, although custom had kept the number of magistrates at about six. By 1580 there were thirteen *desembargadores do paço* serving or entitled to do so. One member was always an ecclesiastic trained in canon law so that the rights and privileges of the Church would be guarded. Membership in the Desembargo do Paço represented the pinnacle of promotion in the judicial system, and all magistrates aspired to the prestige, influence, and high salary of this position.[20]

A system of ecclesiastical courts and officers who enforced canon law paralleled the civil judicial organization outlined above. Clerics were entitled to trial in the religious courts where, as a rule, the penalties were light and the court lenient.[21] A special tribunal, the

---

19. In the Spanish empire, control of the peninsular and the American bureaucracy was divided between the Consejo de Indias and the Cámara de Castilla. On the Hapsburg bureaucracy, see Richard L. Kagan, "Education and the State in Hapsburg Spain," unpublished Ph.D. thesis (Cambridge University, 1968).

20. PRO, State Papers 9/207, ff. 1163–65; BNM, Cod. 2292; Camara, *Subsídios*, I, 85.

21. A famous incident in the reign of Dom Pedro I, who disliked the leniency of the ecclesiastical courts, is recounted by Edgar Prestage, *The Chronicles of Fernão Lopes and Gomes Eannes de Zurara* (Watford, 1928), pp. 10–13.

Inquisition or Holy Office, maintained its own organization and exercised jurisdiction over laity and clergy in matters of morality, heresy, and sexual deviation. The Inquisition in Portugal operated from the cities of Lisbon, Coimbra, and Evora.

Analogous to the Desembargo do Paço was a board created by Dom João III in 1532 to advise him on matters pertaining to the Church and the royal conscience. This Mesa da Consciência e Ordens was composed of churchmen and civil lawyers who advised the crown on questions affecting the Church, the military orders, and the University of Coimbra. It was also the responsibility of the Mesa da Consciência to provide all benefices and bishoprics, to ransom captives, to administer the property of persons who died intestate, and to see generally to the state of the royal conscience. The Mesa da Consciência nominated the *provedores dos defuntos e residuos* and collected the tithe in Brazil and in the other conquests by a system of tax farming.

Like the Desembargo do Paço, the Mesa da Consciência also exercised certain judicial functions. Members of the military orders were exempt from civil jurisdiction and were entitled to be tried before a special judge who was always a member of one of the orders. This *juiz dos cavaleiros* (judge of knights) took cognizance of all cases involving knights of the military orders, and from his decisions appeal could be made only to the Mesa da Consciência. Likewise, this was the only recourse from decisions of the *conservador* of the University of Coimbra. Most important, however, it was the Mesa da Consciência that debated and resolved the moral problems of Portuguese rule in Brazil: the position and nature of the Indian, the legality and morality of the African and Indian slave trade, and the problem of a "just war." These moral problems and their resolution exercised considerable influence on the formation of the society and mentality of colonial Brazil.[22]

---

22. PRO, State Papers 9/207, f. 1164; Mathias Kieman, O.F.M., *The Indian Policy of Portugal in the Amazon Region, 1614–1693* (Washington, 1954), p. 4; Camara, *Subsídios*, I, 83–85. Most of the documentation concerning the Mesa da Consciência is now kept in the Torre do Tombo in

The system of royal and ecclesiastical courts was apparently a highly rationalized mechanism of judicial administration, a system predicated on the concept that the king's obligation to provide for the legal means to right various wrongs lay at the core of his authority. But the observer is struck, especially in the royal judicial organization, by the multiple concerns of the magistrates and their tendency to assume non-judicial functions. In the process of centralization the Portuguese crown had found in the judicial system an expedient and effective tool for the extension of royal power, and in the corps of professional magistrates that staffed the judicial system the crown not only found but also created an able ally.

The *letrados*, or university graduates, had risen to prominence in the fourteenth century after the Cortes of Coimbra of 1385. By the mid-fifteenth century their position was one of approximate equality with the knights and the *fidalgo* class, although the latter were unwilling to recognize this fact.[23] By the middle of the next century the *letrados* began to assume some of the aspects of a caste in that by marriage and family relationships they became a self-perpetuating group occupying most of the judicial and many of the administrative positions of government. The sons of *letrados* followed in their father's footsteps, going from a course in canon or civil law (usually at the University of Coimbra but sometimes at Salamanca) into the royal service. After that, promotion depended not only on seniority, university degrees achieved, and performance, but also on whether one's father had also served.[24]

Although the *letrado* class had sprung from humble origins in

---

Lisbon. The records used for this study were the *Livros de registro das consultas*, which are the minutes of the deliberations of that body.

23. Gama Barros, *HAPP*, III, 256–258; Edgar Prestage, *The Royal Power and the Cortes in Portugal*, (Watford, 1927), pp. 12–20; and on the *letrados* in the Cortes of Coimbra of 1385 see Marcello Caetano, "As Cortes de 1385," *Revista Portuguesa de História*, V, vol. ii (1951), 5–86.

24. BGUC, Cod. 460, "Consulta do Desembargo do Paço," (Lisbon, 26 Jan. 1636), ff. 59–61, in which Pero Nogueira Coelho of the Relação do Porto noted that "costumava fazer em semelhantes occasiões a pessoas de qualidade E principalmente filhos de desembargadores."

the fourteenth century, three hundred years later its importance and prestige were institutionalized by grants of knighthood and membership in the military orders. Thus the magistracy began to adopt the attitudes and attributes of the military aristocracy. But whereas the magnates and lesser military nobility struggled against the infringement of their traditional immunities and privileges inherent in royal centralization, the *letrados* owed their very existence to the expansion of royal power. In Portugal as in Spain, the *letrados* were a group closely tied to the Crown, deeply respectful of law and order, and anxious to find legal solutions to the practical problems of government.[25]

The crown judges aspired to promotion in the judicial hierarchy from *juiz de fóra* or *juiz dos órfãos* to *corregedor* or *provedor* and successively through the various positions of the High Courts. Eventually the most able *letrados*, or those with the best connections, would be appointed to one of the king's councils, such as the Desembargo do Paço, or occasionally to one of the advisory bodies on colonial or financial matters. Each promotion brought increased prestige, salary, and privilege. The well-being of the university-trained *letrados* depended to a large extent on royal favor.[26] In the struggle of the Portuguese kings to impose a centralized monarchy, the *letrados* had become a natural ally. Once the administration of the overseas empire became an abiding concern, the crown turned again to the magisterial class. Who could check the centrifugal forces of empire generated by Brazilian sugar magnates and soldiers-of-fortune in Goa better than the sober royal magistrates? And who would have more to gain than they by compliance with the king's will and protection of his interests? In theory, the magistrates represented the crown and could be depended upon because of bureaucratic controls and their professional desire to achieve certain career goals.

Portugal's overseas possessions, although distinguished by their

---

25. Cf. John H. Parry, *The Audiencia of New Galicia in the Sixteenth Century* (Cambridge, Mass., 1948), pp. 3–4.

26. The financial and juridical exemptions and privileges enjoyed by the members of the High Courts are stated in *Ord. man.*, II, xliii.

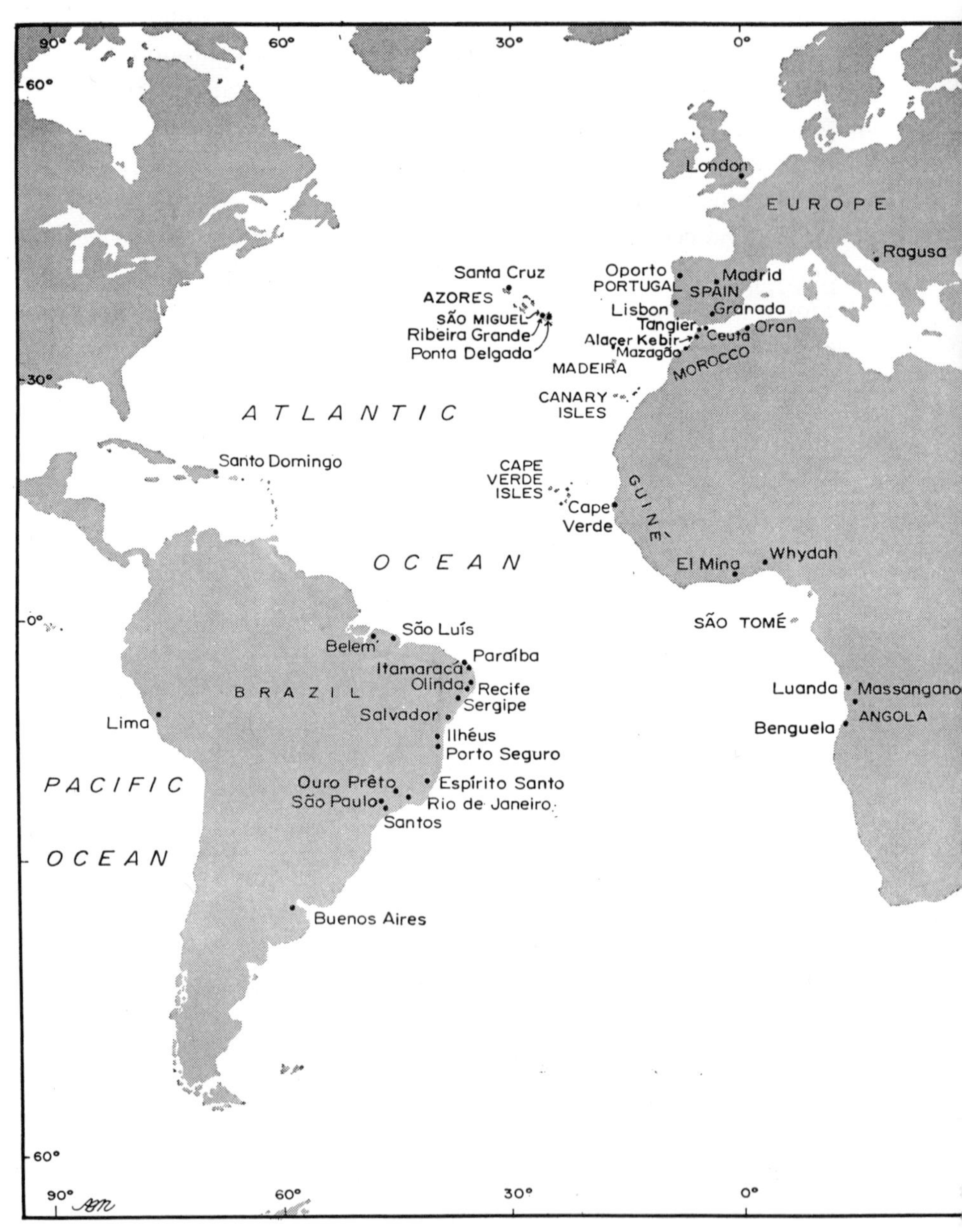

Map 1. The Portuguese Empire

60°
90°
120°
150°
60°
30°
0°
30°
60°
Hormuz
INDIA
BENGAL
Damao
Diu
Bassein
Chaul
Goa
Mangalore
Cannanore
Calicut
Cranganore
CEYLON
Aden
Nagasaki
Macao
PACIFIC
OCEAN
Manila
Malacca
INDIAN
OCEAN
Mombasa
Mozambique
MADAGASCAR

peculiar conditions and geographic locations, were subordinated to the judicial system of the metropolis. Portuguese law became the law of territories newly brought under control, and ministers of justice similar to those in Portugal took up posts in the colonies to enforce this law. Local conditions and the particular relationship of a colony to the crown, however, did determine to some extent the nature of judicial administration.

The outposts of North Africa—Ceuta, Tangier, Mazagão, and Arzila—were first and foremost military establishments whose captains were invested with summary judicial powers. In cases involving treason, desertion, theft, piracy, and sodomy, and in all other cases not involving death or dismemberment as the penalty, the captains had final jurisdiction.[27] Other cases could be appealed to Portugal.

In the Azores, as in Brazil, the various captains were allowed to appoint a *ouvidor*, but the crown periodically sent a *corregedor* to inspect the administration of justice. Royal interest in judicial control was also signified by the presence of a *juiz de fóra* in the town of Ponta Delgada on the island of São Miguel. On the island of Madeira, where the captaincy system was first applied, the captain was entitled to appoint a *ouvidor* to administer justice. The crown, however, exercised the right of nominating the *provedor dos órfãos*.[28]

In their conquest along the west coast of Africa the Portuguese had developed no one formula for the administration of justice. In Angola the problem was first effectively dealt with in the donation made to Paulo Dias de Novais in 1571. Dias de Novais was made captain and *donatário* of Angola with judicial powers equivalent to those previously granted the Brazilian *donatários* in the early 1530's.[29] He was allowed to appoint *ouvidores* and to review and

---

27. *Ord. man.*, II, tit. xxvii.

28. *Ord. man.*, I, tit. viii, states that appeals from the decisions of magistrates in the Atlantic islands could be heard in the Casa da Suplicação. There were three *desembargadores das Ilhas* for the adjudication of the appeals which could only be made in civil actions.

29. See below, pp. 24–29.

confirm judicial appointments made by municipal officials.[30] In the islands of São Tomé, Cabo Verde, and those off Guiné, proprietors were given jurisdiction of a final nature except in cases involving a punishment by death or loss of limb.[31] But such wide private powers were found to be detrimental to royal interests and by 1516 royal *corregedores* were appointed to invesigate the performance of the *ouvidores* who represented the captains.[32] The proprietors, therefore, continued to appoint judges but the crown used its corregedores to exercise surveillance of them and the local municipal councils.[33]

In the Indian Ocean, Portugal had begun to create a maritime empire across the trade routes from China to Malacca to Goa. Swashbuckling Portuguese soldiers, proud prelates, and avaricious officials mixed with the local peoples and created serious administrative and judicial problems. Nowhere was this more apparent than in "Golden Goa," the seat of Portuguese power in Asia, where luxury, concubinage, and malfeasance flourished. To provide an adequate justice beyond the Cape of Good Hope was perhaps an

30. Alfredo de Albuquerque Felner, *Angola: Apontamentos sobre a ocupaçao e início do estabelecimento dos portugueses no Congo, Angola e Benguela* (Coimbra, 1933), doc. 17, "Carta de Doação a Paulo Dias de Novais," pp. 407–412.

31. António Brásio, ed., *Monumenta missionaria africana: África ocidental*, 2nd ser., 3 vols. (Lisbon, 1963), I, doc. 87, "Doação das Ilhas de Cabo Verde ao Duque de Beja," (30 May 1489), 568–569.

32. *Ibid.*, II, doc. 41, "Carta régia ao Corregedor do Fogo," (8 Nov. 1516), 135–136.

33. *Ibid.*, II, doc. 65, "Carta da Capitania da Ilha do Fogo ao Conde de Penela," (20 April 1528), 208–209; doc. 69, "Carta régia ao Corregedor de Cabo Verde," (25 Nov. 1530), 216–217; doc. 108, "Carta de Corregedor a Pero de Araújo," (1 Oct. 1542), 36–3; doc. 116, Primeiro juiz dos órfãos em Cabo Verde" (28 Nov. 1545), 384–385; doc. 118, "Carta de Corregedor de Cabo Verde ao Doutor Pedro Moniz," (20 Dec. 1546), 388–389. The proprietary system was superseded in Guiné in 1550 with the appointment of a *capitão-mór* for Cabo Verde and Guiné. At the time of Philip II's acquisition of Portugal, desembargador Gaspar de Andrade was serving as *corregedor, provedor dos defuntos,* and captain of the city of Ribeira Grande on the island of Santiago—that is, for Cabo Verde e Guiné. See Christiano José de Senna Barcellos, *Subsídios para a história de Cabo Verde e Guiné*, 3 vols. (Lisbon, 1899–1911), I, 153.

impossible task given the nature of that area and the problems that its geography presented.

First, the component parts of the State of India (Estado da India) spread from Macao to Mozambique and were separated by the vastness of the Indian Ocean.[34] Moreover, the diversity of organization caused confusion. Cities like Goa and Macao possessed elected municipal councils with the usual local judges, while in the military establishments, the *fortalezas da Índia*, the captain of the garrison appointed the *ouvidor* and his baliffs. Dom Francisco de Almeida, the first Viceroy of India, had been granted some judicial powers in his instructions of 1505, but for the most part judicial authority was vested in a superior judge or *ouvidor geral*, usually a member of the royal magistracy. The powers of this office were expanded somewhat in the orders given to João de Osorio, who came out in the company of Vasco da Gama in 1524, and from that time forward the *ouvidor geral* maintained appelate jurisdiction over subordinate magistrates throughout the State of India.[35]

As a royal appointee, his wide jurisdiction and power often brought the *ouvidor geral* into conflict with the viceroy and with the local inhabitants.[36] The sheer quantity of litigation and the difficulty imposed by geographical distance diminished the effectiveness of the *ouvidor geral* and finally led in 1544 to the creation of a high court of appeal in Goa modeled on the Casa do Cível and the Casa da Suplicação.[37]

The Relação da India created in 1544 was the first of the high courts of appeal to be established beyond the boundaries of continental Portugal. Although created to reduce the volume of litigation and to mediate disputes, it was constantly involved in internal

---

34. See Boxer, *Portuguese Society*, Chaps. 1, 2.

35. Gonçalves Pereira, *HAJEI*, I, 14–15, 39. A list of the lesser justice officials in the Estado da Índia in the year 1545 is on pp. 85–86.

36. *Ibid.*, Chaps. 3, 5; *Archivo Portuguez-Oriental* (Nova Goa, 1857), fas. i, doc. 18 (King to the *Câmara* of Goa, 1552), 34.

37. The *regimento* of the Relação da India of 1554 is printed in full in Carlos Renato Gonçalves Pereira, *Tribunal da Relação da Goa* (Lisbon, 1964).

bickering and open clashes with other sources of authority. Within three years of its establishment, complaints were being made against the avarice and incompetence of the magistrates of the Relação. Simão Botelho wrote from India in 1547 that since the establishment of the Relação, "matters are dispatched now worse than ever, for everything increases and litigation more than anything else."[38] Such charges of inefficiency, sloth, and incompetence characterized the history of the Goan tribunal from its creation to its short-lived abolition by the Marquis of Pombal in 1774.[39] Various projects for reform failed to achieve much improvement, and if we can believe Diogo do Couto and other eyewitness observers, the magistracy in the State of India accomplished little aside from lining the pockets of magistrates. Certainly, the fluid social and economic conditions of Portuguese India contributed to this situation, but the similarity of complaint registered against magistrates in Lisbon, India, and Brazil indicates a general pattern—if not of judicial abuses then at least of society's perception of the magistracy.

Portuguese soldiers, merchants, clerics, and commoners saw the administration of justice as the core of royal government and the primary justification of royal power. Thus they came to expect the highest level of performance from the magistrates who enforced the king's justice, and when a judge failed to meet these expectations complaints were often loud and continuous. What most people failed to see, however, was the way in which judicial organization had become the structural outline of the empire. That organization, rationalized and systematized since the fourteenth century, provided the crown with a bureaucratic means of control and almost imperceptibly the royal magistracy had been extended to the colonies. How and why the colonial situation turned judges into bureaucrats can be seen quite clearly in the early history of Brazil.

---

38. Gonçalves Pereira, *HAJEI*, I, 93, 95.

39. *Ibid.*, p. 80, Pombal criticized the Relação of Goa for being a "congresso de bacharéis."

II. JUSTICE AND JUDGES IN BRAZIL, 1500-1580

There is no peace, but all is hate, rumors, and slander, robbery and pillage, tricks and lies; there is no obedience of, nor do they observe even one commandment of God, much less those of the Church.

Father Manoel da Nóbrega
(Bahia, 5 July 1549)

A land of dyewood, naked Indians, and parrots, there was little in Brazil to attract much royal concern or many Portuguese colonists in the first thirty years after the colony's discovery in 1500. The few tiny settlements and trading posts on the Brazilian coast were a far cry from golden Goa, and royal control, like everything else in this colonial backwash, developed slowly. Until the 1530's there was no attempt to legislate for the new land in any systematic manner. Ship captains and the leaders of military and exploratory expeditions exercised their traditional prerogatives as the arbiters of shipboard disputes. For those few Europeans who remained for any length of time on that inhospitable coast, justice was of the frontier variety, personally dispensed by sword-thrust and musket-ball.

During the early years of Brazil's history, the colony was viewed principally as a commercial enterprise and its integration into the existing colonial structure was effected by means of the maritime-commercial organs of government. Thus the provisioning of Brazil and the ships that traded there, as well as the settlement of disputes that arose from the commerce and navigation with it, were matters for the Casa da Guiné, Minas e Indias and for the Juiz da Guiné e India.[1] But, so long as there were few Europeans permanently settled in Brazil, there was no attempt or need to establish a regular system of judicial administration in the colony.

The expedition of Martim Afonso de Sousa that sailed from Lisbon in 1530 marked an important transition from a loose administration of justice imposed by military necessity to a more concrete form predicated on the establishment of permanent colonization and recognizing the need for a regularization of society. Fearing French designs on the area, Dom João III sponsored this expedition to secure the new colony for Portugal. To that end, Martim Afonso de Sousa was instructed to carry out military actions against any foreign interlopers found on the coast and to reconnoiter the littoral in preparation for exploration inland. At the same time, however, he carried with him the men and materials for a permanent settlement.

The broad judicial powers granted to Martim Afonso de Sousa as Capitão-Mór of the fleet reflect the transitional nature and dual objectives of his expedition. As military commander he was given full legal authority in all civil and criminal cases and there was to be no appeal from his decisions except for *fidalgos*. His judicial power extended to all members of the expedition and to all persons in Brazil. These extensive powers were in the tradition of the military authority accorded to a supreme commander; but in recognition of the colonizing aims of the expedition, a separate charter was issued to Martim Afonso which entitled him to create offices of justice and government necessary for the proper administration

---

1. The *Juiz da Guiné* decided all overseas matters relating to trade or shipboard incident. The office was filled by a *letrado*. Appeals from his decisions were made directly to the Casa de Suplicação.

of the new colony.[2] This new formula recognized the summary powers of a military commander and the nominating powers of a governor as two aspects of judicial administration. Within five years, and even before Martim Afonso's return to Portugal, the crown applied this formula in its next attempt to secure undisputed Portuguese possession of Brazil.

Convinced that permanent settlement was the only way to hold Brazil against foreign rivals. Dom João III divided the new conquest into fifteen parcels, and between 1533 and 1535 he granted them to twelve Portuguese *fidalgos*. This was an attempt to use the donatary system of the Azores and Madeira to spread the burden of colonization among a number of private individuals and thus lighten royal obligations.[3] The grants were made by means of two instruments, the *carta de doação* which delineated the powers and privileges of the recipient, and the *foral* which stated his obligations to the crown and to the inhabitants of his territory. The judicial powers granted to the proprietors underlined the colonizing objective. The crown recognized that the distribution of lands in *sesmarias*, or land grants, and the establishment of towns along traditional Portuguese lines would require a judicial structure. The jurisdiction of the proprietors almost exactly paralleled that of Martim Afonso de Sousa.

The *carta de doação* gave the proprietor extensive civil and

---

2. The judicial powers granted to Martim Afonso de Sousa are found in two documents: ANTT, *Chan. D. João, III*, liv. 41, f. 103 and f. 105. Both documents, and others relating to the voyage, are printed in Carlos Malheiro Dias, ed., *História da Colonização Portuguesa do Brasil*, 3 vols. (Oporto, 1924–1926), III, 159–164. (Cited hereafter as *HCPB*). For an adequate account of the expedition, see Francisco Adolfo de Varnhagen, *História geral do Brasil*, 7th ed., 6 vols. in 3 (São Paulo, 1962), I, 124–150.

3. The continuing question of the feudal or capitalistic nature of the *donatário* system can be traced in the pertinent articles of the *HCPB*, especially Paulo Mera, "A solução do Brasil," III, 167–188; C. Malheiro Dias, "O regimen feudal dos donatários," III, 190–216. Their views are refuted in the important article by Alexander Marchant, "Feudal and Capitalistic Elements in the Portuguese Settlement of Brazil," *HAHR*, XXII (1942), 493–512. A summary of other bibliography is given by Bailey W. Diffie, *Latin American Civilization* (Harrisburg, 1945), p. 643n.

criminal jurisdiction to be exercised by his own appointees: a superior magistrate (*ouvidor*) and other necessary justice officials; clerks (*escrivães*), notaries (*tabeliães*), and bailiffs (*meirinhos*). When the growth of population warranted it, a second *ouvidor* could be appointed. The superior magistrate could hear cases in the first instance coming from a ten-league radius around his abode and all appeals from lower judges. The *donatário* and the *ouvidor* had jurisdiction in civil cases up to amounts of 100 *milreis* without appeal and in criminal cases entailing the death penalty. As in the case of Martim Afonso de Sousa, their jurisdiction over *fidalgos* was more limited. *Fidalgos* could be tried without appeal in civil cases involving less than 100 *cruzados* and, in criminal cases, sentenced to as much as ten years of exile.[4] In cases of blasphemy, heresy, sodomy, and counterfeiting even *fidalgos* could not appeal the death penalty.

Being allowed to review the roll of citizens considered eligible to serve on the municipal council, the *donatário* and the *ouvidor* exercised considerable control over the selection and confirmation of municipal officers. Since the *juiz ordinário* was normally one of these, the proprietary lord controlled justice from top to bottom. This was especially true since the *donatário* was also granted exemption from the visitation of any superior crown magistrate (*corregedor*) in his captaincy, even if the *donatário* himself was charged with a crime.[5] The crown did expect, however, that rather than attempting any radical legal innovations, the proprietors would

4. The term actually used is "*gente da mór qualidade*." This probably included not only those who were legally *fidalgos* but also officials and royal functionaries who were not so entitled.

5. The *capitania* or area controlled by a *donatário* also enjoyed a privileged position as a refuge for those fleeing from justice or retribution. The extension of the Portuguese legal concepts of asylum (*couto*, *homizio*) to the captaincies in Brazil was done in an effort to stimulate immigration to those areas. The same had been done in India where the cities of Pangim, Cannanore, and Damão enjoyed the privilege of *couto* as a means of fostering colonization. In Brazil those fleeing punishment for heresy, sodomy, treason, and counterfeiting were not entitled to *couto*. See W. Ferreira, *História do direito brasileiro,* I, 117–122; Gonçalves Pereira, *HAJEI,* I, 126; PRO, State Papers 9/207, n. 24.

follow the laws of Portugal and would enforce subsequent uncodified legislation (*leis extravagantes*).[6]

The judicial privileges and exemptions extended to the proprietors recall those which in Portugal had been extended to magnates such as the Duke of Aveiro and the Prior of Crato. Certain lands belonging to these great lords enjoyed exemption from the investigations of *corregedores* and the magnates were able to appoint their own magistrates. The title *ouvidor*, selected for the judicial representatives of the proprietors, had been connected most closely in Portugal with the areas under control of the military orders and the territories of the magnates—areas normally beyond the jurisdiction of royal magistrates. Thus, the judicial powers granted to the proprietors harkened back to earlier royal concessions to certain nobles and were in opposition to the then dominant royal concern with centralization. While the judicial powers granted to the *donatários* were not in themselves feudal, they were retrograde and did not contribute to the growth of royal power. The crown's lapse, however, was short-lived and although captaincies were granted in Brazil as late as 1685, the crown never surrendered judicial powers as it had done in the original Brazilian proprietary grants.

By and large, the proprietary system in Brazil proved as inefficient in the administration of justice as it was ineffectual in the promotion of colonization. Generally, the *donatários* or their representatives assumed the powers of *ouvidor* unto themselves in addition to their other roles as captain and governor. Being lesser nobility with only military experience, the majority of the proprietors lacked both the training and the inclination to discharge their judicial duties. The results were apparently disastrous. Although little information has survived from the period prior to 1550, retrospective reports indicate widespread abuses and a general laxity in law enforcement.

---

6. Marchant, "Feudal and Capitalistic Elements," 505; W. Ferreira, *História do direito*, I, 130–241, for a detailed but often irrelevant discussion of the judicial aspects of the captaincies.

Map 2. Colonial Brazil

Disturbed by these conditions, the failures of the proprietors, and the constant pressure of foreign interlopers, Dom João III resolved to centralize the government of Brazil under a governor-general and to provide this new form of government with the necessary officers of justice. This decision altered the captaincy system but did not abolish it. Tomé de Sousa, the first governor-general, was sent to Bahia with a large expedition and specific instructions to colonize and to establish a central government for the colony. In his company were a number of men assigned to various administrative positions such as captain of the coast guard, treasurer (*provedor mór*), and most important, *ouvidor geral* (superior crown magistrate). For the next sixty years justice in Brazil would be administred by the *ouvidor geral* and his subordinates, and in the problems that confronted these men we can see not only the difficulties of judicial administration, but also how and why justice officers eventually assumed administrative and bureaucratic powers.

The arrival of Pero Borges as *ouvidor geral* in 1549 marked a significant departure from the structure of the Brazilian judiciary in use before that date.[7] It was a change, however, entirely in keeping with the overall alteration of royal policy toward Brazil. Instead of simply abolishing the entire proprietary system and creating a fully centralized royal administration, the *ouvidor geral* was superimposed on the existing structure of municipal magistrates and proprietor-appointed *ouvidores*. The result was a confused and sometimes inoperative system of royal and proprietary control.

Although the instructions given to Pero Borges have not been discovered, supplementary materials indicate that he was given extensive appelate jurisdiction as well as investigative functions and obligations.[8] Borges was to hear appeals from the sentences of the proprietor-appointed *ouvidores* and was himself to serve as local magistrate for the captaincy of Bahia. Moreover, he was expected to visit each captaincy to review the state of justice there.

7. Pero Borges had served as *corregedor* in Loulé and Elvas. His record was not without blemish, for in Elvas he had been implicated in the misappropriation of public funds in the early 1540's. See Pedro de Azevedo, "A institutição do governo geral," *HCPB*, III, 341.

8. *DHBNR*, XXXV (1937), 23–26. Varnhagen, *História geral*, I, 234, feels that the regimento issued to Borges was analogous to that given in 1628 to Paulo Leitão de Abreu. Although Varnhagen gives no citation, his opinion was probably based on a *consulta* of the Desembargo do Paço, AGS, *Sec. Prov.* 1475.

This duty conflicted with the exemption from royal review granted previously to the proprietors and visitation by the *ouvidor geral* now extended the power of the crown over the various captaincies. The previous judicial structure thus became subordinate to the crown's magistrate who stood as an intermediary between the *ouvidores* and the Casa da Suplicação in Lisbon. This was a structure parallel to that which had developed in Portuguese India prior to 1544.

The conditions that Pero Borges discovered in Brazil in the 1550's can be taken as indicative of the whole period from 1535 and they clearly showed that for a conscientious royal official, Brazil was no bed of roses. Administrative abuse and incompetence abounded. For example, in the absence of the proprietor of Ilhéus, a Castillian named Francisco Romero was serving as captain and *ouvidor*. Although a good man and an experienced soldier, Romero was unfit to be a judge, being "ignorant and very poor, conditions that often cause men to do what they ought not." [9] Borges urged the crown to force the *donatários* to select their *ouvidores* from men with at least some legal training. He noted that in Lisbon, a highly trained and experienced magistrate on the High Court might hear only a few cases, while in Brazil an illiterate could pass many sentences, all in total disregard of legal principles.[10]

Borges' report also noted that the proliferation of government employees, a characteristic phenomenon of Iberian administration, had already begun by the 1550's. Borges stated that since almost all men eligible for public office had already gained some post in royal service, the municipal offices were filled by allegedly unfit exiles (*degredados*)—some of whom had lost their ears as punishment in Portugal.[11] Others served as notaries and clerks without the slightest heed for the regulations prescribing their duties. Borges' observations on this matter are confirmed by the perceptive Jesuit Father Manoel da Nóbrega who urged the crown to send farmers to

9. The letter of Pero Borges is printed in full in *HCPB*, III, 267–269.
10. *Ibid.*
11. *Ibid.*

Brazil rather than "so many officials with such great salaries who want nothing more than to finish their term of office and collect their pay . . . and as this is their principal goal they do not love the land and all their affection is for Portugal." [12] Nóbrega was speaking of conditions in the newly founded city of Salvador, but his remarks could be applied to other areas of settlement as well.

Judicial incompetence contributed to the turbulent conditions in Brazil, but the many opportunities for license and excess lay at the root of these conditions. The arm of the law could not reach into remote areas, and the sparse settlement resulted in a lack of community pressures in support of accepted morality and respect for the law. Blasphemy was common among high- and low-born alike and a matter of concern for both civil and ecclesiastical authorities.[13] Large numbers of Indian women whose concept of sexual morality differed considerably from Portuguese norms were an understandable attraction to the early colonists. More than any other factor, the lack of European women drove the settlers into the arms of their Indian counterparts. The scandalous sexual license of the early colony stimulated constant clerical censure. The Jesuit fathers who had first arrived in the expedition of Tomé de Sousa of 1549 poured forth a constant stream of criticism and numerous suggestions to remedy the moral situation of the colonists. Father Nóbrega and others felt that the best solution lay in the shipment of more Portuguese girls to the colony, where they could all find good husbands.[14] Despite such measures and infrequent marriages

---

12. Serafim Leite, ed., *Cartas e mais escritos do P. Manuel da Nóbrega* (*opera omnia*) (Coimbra, 1955), p. 114. Cited hereafter as *Cartas Nóbrega.*

13. *Ibid.*, Nóbrega to P. Simão Rodrigues (Bahia, 9 August 1549), p. 31, notes that he has brought the matter of widespread blasphemy to the attention of Pero Borges. The most famous blasphemer in early colonial Brazil was Pero do Campo Tourinho, the *donatário* of Porto Seguro, who was sent back for trial by the Inquisition of Lisbon. See *DHBNR*, XXXVIII, p. 224, and the description in João Capistrano de Abreu, *Caminhos antigos e povoamento do Brasil* (Rio de Janeiro, 1930), pp. 37–52.

14. Leite, *Cartas Nóbrega,* pp. 31–79. Nóbrega stated that it was usually the poorer Portuguese who married the Indian women. He suggested that

between Portuguese settlers and Indian women, concubinage was the rule and the squeak of the hammock was heard in the land. This particular abuse, however, remained the concern of the clergy rather than the civil magistrates.

It should be kept in mind that Portuguese statute law in Brazil applied almost exclusively to Europeans. The Indian population remained largely beyond the scope of civil government and was consequently deprived of recourse to the normal channels of justice. Even those laws specifically designed to regulate Portuguese-Indian relations were seldom enforced. Father Nóbrega provides us with one example of how the Portuguese administered justice to the indigenous population. An Indian who had slain a Portuguese was apprehended and by the governor's order placed over the mouth of a canon and literally blown to bits.[15] No doubt the execution had the desired effect of impressing the Indians. Another Jesuit, Father Fernão Cardim wrote caustically about the judicial abuse of the Indians and warned of divine retribution:

> Against the Indians was always a rigorous justice. They have already been hanged, hewn in pieces, quartered, their hands cut, nipped with hot pinchers, and set in the mouth of *pieces*, and shot away for killing . . . some Portuguese (who probably had well deserved it at their hands). But having persons, not a few in Brazil, as always there were, and yet there are, notoriously infamous for robbing, stealing, branding, selling, and killing many Indians, never until this time was there any show of punishment, and it is to be feared, seeing it lacks on earth, that it will come from heaven on all the inhabitants of Brazil.[16]

Those Indians who sought the protection of justice officials found the scales of justice weighted against them. The testimony of one Portuguese, for example, was considered equal to that of

---

all kinds of women be sent, even prostitutes. Orphans of respectable families could hope to marry the better class of colonists, the "good and rich men."

15. *Ibid.*, Nóbrega to P. Martin de Azpilcueta (Bahia, 10 August 1549), p. 54.

16. Samuel Purchas, *Hakluytus Posthumous or His Pilgrims*, 5 vols. (London, 1625), IV, 1324. (Spelling and punctuation have been modernized.)

three or four Indians.[17] Colonists had little to fear from judicial reprisal when they abused or committed crimes against the Indians. Those Indians who lived in Jesuit controlled villages (*aldeias*), however, had some protection from mistreatment by colonists. The Jesuits provided a paternalistic legal system in which punishments were not severe and Indian baliffs were allowed to apprehend and punish minor offenders. These baliffs were especially disliked by the colonists. After 1580 there were a number of attempts by colonists to remove the administration of justice in the *aldeias* from the hands of the Jesuits and their Indian helpers, but this was part of the larger question of the control of Indian labor.[18]

Obviously, the prevailing conditions in the colony and the existence of so many injustices and abuses presented Pero Borges and his successors with a herculean task. The failure of these men to improve the quality of law and order resulted not only from frontier conditions, but also from the accumulation of additional responsibilities to the office of *ouvidor geral.* It must be recalled that the introduction of the *ouvidor geral* in Brazil reflected not only the crown's desire to improve the state of justice, but also its desire to increase royal centralized control. After 1550 the crown's interest in this area grew steadily and the *ouvidor geral,* as a dependable royal official, increasingly assumed new functions and responsibility for royal interests. Figure 1 demonstrates Brazil's place within the context of the imperial judicial structure.

Based perhaps on Roman precedents, Portuguese administrative

17. Serafim Leite, *História da Companhia de Jesús no Brasil,* 10 vols. (Lisbon, 1938–50), II, 61–64. (Cited hereafter as *HCJB*). In Spanish America according to the famed jurist Juan Solórzano Pereira, *Política Indiana,* 2 vols. (Madrid [1647–1648]), I, cap. 28, 234–235, the testimony of six Indians was considered equal to that of one white man.

18. The law code of the *aldeias* is printed in Serafim Leite, *Monumenta Brasiliae,* 4 vols. to date (Rome, 1960), IV, doc. 44 (Bahia, 30 July 1566). On the problem of Indian judicial administration, see the same author's "As raças do Brazil perante a ordem teológica moral e juridica portuguêsa nos séculos XVI a XVIII," *Actas, V Colóquio internacional de estudos Luso-brasileiros,* III, 18; "Os 'Capítulos' de Gabriel Soares de Sousa," *Ethnos,* II (1941), 31.

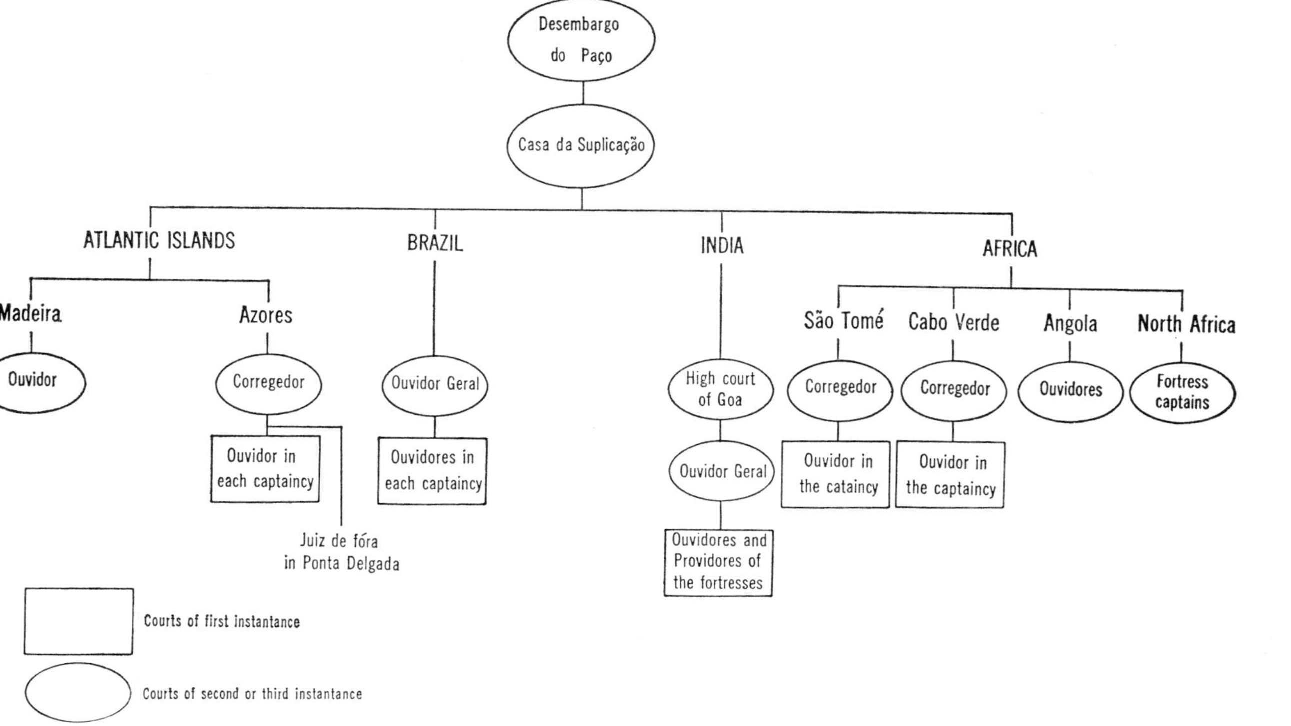

Fig. 1. The Hierarchy of Royal Justice in the Portuguese Overseas Empire, ca. 1580.

practice in the Middle Ages had maintained a division between the fiscal and judicial branches of the bureaucracy.[19] As we have seen, however, the lines of division were blurred considerably in the sixteenth and seventeenth centuries as royal magistrates in Portugal began to assume fiscal responsibilities. A similar phenomenon occurred in Brazil. In 1554, in addition to his duties as *ouvidor geral*, Pero Borges was given those of *provedor mór da fazenda* (superintendant of the treasury). This was one of the three most important offices in the colony, along with those of *ouvidor geral* and governor-general, and the exercise of two of these offices gave Borges extensive powers.[20] Later *ouvidores gerais* also assumed these fiscal responsibilities, especially on an interim basis. The theoretical distinction between the two branches of the bureaucracy was maintained, but in poorer and frontier regions royal magistrates often performed the duties of treasury officers.

During Borges' incumbency other problems first appeared that would later plague the royal magistracy in Brazil. Magisterial possession of power generated conflict with other sources of authority. During his term of office Borges supported Duarte da Costa, the second and highly unpopular governor-general, against the Bishop of Brazil, Dom Pedro Sardinha.[21] It was probably more because of his affiliation with the hated governor-general than for any misdeed of his own that Borges was so harshly criticized by the members of the municipal council of Salvador in 1556. They claimed that:

> there is no one who for the tranquility of his life and the security of his honor would not choose to be captive of the Sheriff [of

---

19. A. Jones, *Studies in Roman Law and Administration* (Oxford, 1960).

20. *DHBNR*, XXXV (1937), pp. 237–239, 277–278. The union of the two offices had been suggested by Tomé de Sousa but was implemented by governor-general Duarte da Costa after his removal of Antônio Cardoso de Barros from the office of *provedor-mór*. Da Costa removed Barros from office ostensibly because of negligence but more probably because Barros had supported Bishop Sardinha's faction in that prelate's struggle with the governor.

21. Frei Vicente do Salvador, *História do Brasil*, liv. iii, caps. 2–6, pp. 163–170.

Morocco] than a citizen of *morador* of this city so long as it is governed by Dom Duarte and ruled by Pero Borges, who are such absolute and dissolute masters of it that no one now has property or honor secure.[22]

There was probably considerable exaggeration in the *câmara's* accusation since it was a partisan in the dispute, but the same letter also stated that the governor and the *ouvidor geral* were abusing their power to revise the list of candidates for municipal offices in order to install their own supporters. This charge has the ring of truth, for that abuse was a common one, as we have already seen. Contemporary opinion of Borges, however, was not always unfavorable, and according to Frei Vicente do Salvador, Pero Borges worked admirably in conjunction with the third governor-general, Mem de Sá, in the administration of justice.[23]

It was, in fact, the arrival of Mem de Sá in 1557 that marked the opening of a new period of royal concern for the administration of justice and the enforcement of law. Best remembered for his expulsion of the French from Rio de Janeiro and his military exploits against hostile Indians, Mem de Sá also deserves praise as an able administrator. Unlike his predecessors, Mem de Sá was by training a *letrado* who had risen in the royal service to a position on the Casa da Suplicação and had been granted the honorific title Councilor of the King.[24] He was, therefore, well-equipped to exercise the judicial powers and prerogatives pertaining to his office.

It was probably in recognition of Mem de Sá's abilities in this field that his powers in matters of justice were specifically expanded at the expense of the proprietors. The privilege of exemption from the visitation by royal officials enjoyed by the *donatários* was now explicitly revoked. This was not a wholly new departure since the

---

22. *HCPB*, III, Letter of the officials of the *câmara* of Salvador (11 December 1556), 381.

23. Frei Vicente do Salvador, *História do Brasil*, liv, iii, cap. 6, p. 172.

24. On the background and exploits of Mem de Sá, see the succinct article by Ruth L. Butler, "Mem de Sá, Third Governor-General of Brasil, 1557–1572," *Mid-America*, XXVI (April 1944), 111–137, and the sources cited therein.

ouvidor geral had been able to inspect the state of justice in the captaincies, but the explicit statement regarding the governor's ability to visit the captaincies underlined the crown's determination to extend royal control.[25] Mem de Sá, however, desired even greater powers because, as he pointed out to the king, "this land is populated with exiles, evil-doers, most of whom deserved the death penalty and who have no other occupation than to plot evil." [26] The governor felt that he should be given the power to punish and pardon, for he distrusted the competence of the *ouvidor geral.* Mem de Sá's complaint was prompted by the arrival in the previous year of a new *ouvidor geral,* Bras Fragoso, whose instructions conflicted with and diminished the powers of the governor. The complaint was justified because suits, litigation, and crime began to increase after Bras Fragoso's arrival.[27]

The governorship of Mem de Sá from 1557 to 1572 was an important period for the development of Brazilian judicial administration. When not occupied with military matters the governor-general devoted much time and energy to the suppression of vice, usury, neglect of duty, and mismanagement. His success must be ascribed not only to his particular talents and personality, but also to the fact that he was able to work effectively with his subordinates. Moreover, Mem de Sá mustered considerable support from the Jesuits, who were becoming a dominant force in the spiritual and socio-political life of the colony. His alliance with the Jesuits to protect the Indian population from the depredations of the colonists was necessary for the preservation of law and order, or at least he so believed. After 1560 the governor's pro-Indian policy was supported by a new official, the *mamposteiro,* who was a civil officer appointed in each captaincy to guard the liberty of the Indians. The creation of these *mamposteiros* in Brazil was one of the

25. *ABNR,* XXVII, 219–223.

26. *Ibid.,* XXVI, 228.

27. Fragoso arrived in the company of the new Bishop Pedro Leitão on 9 December 1559. The increase in litigation is noted in Frei Vicente do Salvador, *História do Brasil,* liv. iii, cap. 6, p. 172.

first attempts to bring the Indian problem under secular control and it reflected a growing desire of the crown to protect the indigenous population of Brazil.[28]

Mem de Sá's efficiency was affected in his last years by sickness and before that by military concerns. Bras Fragoso, whose primary concern was judicial, found that other obligations increasingly impaired his effectiveness. He was called upon to lead a punitive expedition against the warlike Aimoré Indians in Porto Seguro, and like his predecessor he was also given the duties of *provedor mór*. These new obligations made it increasingly difficult for him to perform his judicial duties.[29] By 1562 it had become apparent at least to his subordinates in the treasury that the duties of *ouvidor geral* and *provedor mór* were incompatible. The minor officials complained that both posts required special talents and the full-time attention of separate administrators. Moreover, and herein seems to lie their basic complaint, the *ouvidor geral* was required to visit the captaincies each year and his absence from Bahia left the treasury neglected. Without his signature and approval his subordinates were unable to perform their duties.[30] Despite such remarks the crown remained unconvinced and the two offices remained united into the seventeenth century.

28. Varnhagen, *História geral*, I, 307–308. Neither Kieman, *Indian Policy*, nor A. Marchant, *From Barter to Slavery* (Baltimore, 1942) makes any reference to the role of the *mamposteiro* and his contact with the Indians. In Portugal the *mamposteiro* was in charge of the collection of funds for the ransom of prisoners, especially those held by the North African pirates. This office was often held by a layman and was administered by the Mesa da Consciência. In Brazil the office took on a different function. In each captaincy there was to be at least one *mamposteiro* to guard against the illegal enslavement of the Indians. Cf. BNL, *Col. Pomb.* 741, "Regimento dos Memposteiros-mores," ff. 1–29.

29. Varnhagen, *História geral*, I, 277.

30. *ABNR*, XXVII, 239–241. ". . . que as ocupações que tem na judicatura nam lhe daa lugar a emtemder nem pode ir a ela com he neçesaryo por esta ocupação que tem e por que tambem o sentido que tem nas cousas da judicatura lhe faz remoto das da fazenda . . . e indo ele a fazer correiçam nelas fiqua qua o negocio da fazenda desfeito e o contador atado que nam pode dar fim a conta alguma nem outro algum negocio."

Increasing bureaucratic, fiscal, and military responsibilities fell upon the men who served as *ouvidor geral* between 1549 and 1609.[31] Judicial administration undoubtedly suffered from these distractions. This development is easily explained. As the highest ranking royal officer in Brazil after the governor-general, the *ouvidor geral* appeared to offer skill and devotion to the crown in a region where literacy and loyalty were at a premium. The metropolitan tendency for the judicial hierarchy to become an administrative bureaucracy was intensified in the loose frontier conditions of the colony.

The non-judicial activities of the magistrates already cited could be greatly expanded. Pero Borges, Bras Fragoso, and Fernão da Silva (who succeeded Fragoso in 1566) were all called upon to serve as *provedor mór*. Fernão da Silva and his successor, Cosme Rangel, also served as interim governors. Then, too, there were military obligations. Fragoso and da Silva both captained punitive expeditions against hostile Indians, and Cosme Rangel led troops against marauding bands of escaped slaves. Later, and perhaps most noteworthy of all, Martim Leitão captained the conquest of Paraíba, and although his exploits made him the subject of honorific poetry, the administration of justice did not benefit from his military preoccupations.[32] In general, the crown magistrates' military and fiscal responsibilities, although often of undoubted benefit to the colony, distracted them from the performance of their primary

31. The men who served as *ouvidor geral* in Brazil between 1549 and 1609 were Pero Borges (1549–1558), Bras Fragoso (1559–1565), Fernão da Silva (1566–1575), Cosme Rangel (1577–1587), Martim Leitão (1583–?), Diogo Roiz Cardoso (1586–1588), Gaspar de Figueiredo Homem (1591–159?), Diogo Dias Cardoso (1597–1598), Bras de Almeida (1599–1604), and Ambrosio de Siqueira (1604–1608).

32. BPE, CXVI, 1–26, "Sumario das armadas. . . ." For example:

> Martim Leitan se nombra este excellente
> que tanto illustra aquestra noble tierra
> Con su valor iscientia tan sabrada
> Ques diole Dios tan dilicandame'te
> que a todos sobre puja en pax y e'guerra
> no Embotando su pluma lança y espada

role as judges. Part of the failure of judicial administration in Brazil lay in this constant use of magistrates for a variety of other tasks.

Another obstacle, and perhaps one inherent in the nature of Portuguese colonial government, although certainly exacerbated by personalities, was constant jurisdictional dispute. There is no doubt that the crown magistrates moved into the vortex of colonial feuds and rivalries where their powerful position made them valued allies or hated opponents. The Jesuits in disputes with the Governors Luís Brito de Almeida (1573–78) and Manuel Telles Barreto (1583–87) were accused of currying the favor and support of the *ouvidor geral*, an accusation they never denied.[33] Such conflicts undermined the dignity and authority of the *ouvidor geral*. Colonists retained little respect for a crown judge when, as in the cases of Fernão da Silva, Martim Leitão, and Cosme Rangel, he was sent off in chains for trial in Portugal.

Whether the feuds between magistrates and other officials were the result of ill-defined jurisdictions intentionally fostered by the crown to prevent excessive autonomy, or whether they were accidental flaws in the administrative system, is a question still open to debate. Whatever their cause, these conflicts sometimes erupted into wide-open personal and institutional battles.

In administrative disputes governors often aligned themselves with the crown judges, but when such was not the case the conflict could reach virulent extremes. The career of *ouvidor geral* Fernão da Silva provides an excellent case in point. Fernão da Silva had risen through the ranks of the professional magistracy in Portugal before his appointment as *ouvidor geral* and *provedor-mór* of Brazil in 1566.[34] With the death of Mem de Sá, da Silva also temporarily assumed the duties of governor-general, but on the arrival of the new governor, Luís de Brito Almeida, a dispute developed. The cause of the conflict is open to conjecture. Although the historian Gabriel Soares de Sousa felt that the governor

---

33. Leite, "Os Capítulos," p. 17.

34. Fernão da Silva had been *juiz de fóra* of Silves and *juiz dos órfãos* of Santarém. See note 35.

had moved against da Silva for malfeasance, there is a strong possibility that da Silva's lackluster expedition against hostile Potiguar Indians in Pernambuco lay behind their differences. In any case, the governor seized his estate and remanded da Silva to Portugal. Due to the intercession of the Jesuits, however, da Silva was exonerated by the Desembargo do Paço, and he returned to Brazil to regain his property, undergo a *residência*, and gather his family together for the trip back to Portugal. On this return voyage from Brazil, his ship foundered off the bar at Bahia and da Silva, his wife, four daughters, a son, and three grandchildren were lost at sea. Only one son, Roche da Silva, survived the disaster and he continued the feud with the descendants of Luís de Brito. Such hatreds died hard in old Brazil.[35]

More common but no less ardent were disputes between the magistrates and other sources of authority like the municipal councils and the ecclesiastical establishment. Martim Leitão, although he could produce a certificate from Cristóvão de Gouvea, the noted Jesuit supervisor, stating that he was one of the best justice officials ever to serve in the colony, ran afoul of Bishop Dom Antônio Barrieiros. The specific points of the conflict remain unclear, but Leitão was eventually arrested and suspended from all offices.[36]

35. *Ibid.;* Varnhagen, *História geral,* I, 362. Much of the information in this paragraph is provided by a petition of Bartolomeu Cunha, the husband of da Silva's granddaughter, submitted in 1624 to the Conselho de Portugal and now registered as AGS, *Sec. Prov.* 1467 (Madrid, 30 April 1624), ff. 3–41. On da Silva's connection with the Jesuits, see *ABNR,* XIX (1897), 119.

36. Viceroy Cardinal Alberto to king (Lisbon, 18 October 1586), AGS, *Sec. Prov.* 1550, ff. 536–537. Leitão claimed that in the performance of duty in Brazil he had gained many enemies and that due to their false accusations he was imprisoned. Since Leitão had been granted a habit in the Order of Christ at the time of his appointment as *ouvidor geral,* his case was heard by the *juiz dos cavaleiros.* In 1596 he appealed to the Desembargo do Paço to be restored to office, but, although he regained most of his financial privileges, he was still out of a job in 1598. See AGS, *Sec. Prov.* 1460, n. 29; Viceroy Pedro de Castilho to king (Lisbon, 17 January 1597), BA, 51-VII-17, ff. 10–11v.; BA, 44-XIV-18, f. 77.

The story of Cosme Rangel is another one which shows how personality often entered into political questions. Rangel arrived in Brazil in the company of governor Lourenço da Veiga in 1578. When in 1581 da Veiga died, Rangel, the bishop, and the *câmara* of Salvador served as a ruling junta until a new governor could be sent from Portugal. Rangel soon proved himself an ambitious and power-hungry official by usurping complete control of the government. The *câmara* refused to legalize Rangel's position and both the *câmara* and the bishop left the city in protest against the *ouvidor geral*'s actions. Rangel immediately took advantage of their absence by imposing his followers as city councilors and by creating new positions on the council for his supporters from the artisan class. The next governor, Manuel Telles Barreto, deposed Rangel in 1583 and arrested him.[37]

By 1580 Brazil had moved from the loose judicial administration of privately appointed *ouvidores* to a more centralized system based on the royal *ouvidor geral*. This change underscored the increasing royal control of the colony that marked the period beginning in 1549. These administrative changes, however, only partially reveal other and more important modifications in the colony's life. The sugar industry had begun to flourish in the coastal areas of Pernambuco and Bahia during the 1570's. As the green cane fields began to spread over the northeastern coast, the size of the population and the amount of litigation grew apace. By the early 1580's it was clear that a single *ouvidor geral* was simply not capable of providing an adequate and equitable administration of justice. But, as a colony, Brazil's political and administrative pulse was not wholly determined by its own needs. The year 1580 brought a dynastic crisis in Portugal and the claimant who emerged victorious was Philip II, King of Spain. Philip II viewed the judicial deficiencies of Brazil as part of a general breakdown of law in the Portuguese empire and it was exactly to this problem that he first turned in 1581.

---

37. Leite, "Os Capitulos," 20; Varnhagen, *História geral*, I, 379.

III. SPANISH REFORM AND THE BRAZILIAN HIGH COURT

The science of the laws is like a fountain of justice and the world benefits from it more than from any other science.

Las Siete Partidas

Philip II, King of the Spains, was a paper-pusher; he was a monarch with an eye for detail, a penchant for bureaucratic nicety, and a deep sense of his administrative responsibilities. He had inherited the Spanish bureaucratic system from Ferdinand and Isabella and from his father, Charles V, but Philip displayed a personal interest in the expansion of that bureaucracy and in the improvement of the empire's judicial system. The period of the 1580's brought a number of important administrative and bureaucratic changes in Castile. Chief among these was the creation in 1588 of the Cámara de Castilla, a body somewhat analogous to the Desembargo do Paço, which exercised extensive powers over the recruitment and control of the Spanish professional bureaucracy. It was with the same interest that during this period Philip II turned to his newly acquired Portuguese inheritance.[1]

1. Philip II's interest in this matter is apparent in "Advertimento de mano de Su Mag[d] sobre el neg[o] de la justicia de portugal en Lisboa xy de enero de 1582," AGS, *Estado, Negociaciones de Portugal*, 428, in which the king stated: "aunque tengo por ver quasi todo lo que vino ayer assi de Madrid, como de Flandres, Francia, y Inglatierra he querido ver primero

The crown of Portugal and with it the far-flung Portuguese empire became a Hapsburg possession after a curious and turbulent two years.[2] In 1578 Dom Sebastião, the young and reckless king of Portugal, led a crusade into Morocco. It was a disaster. Before the walls of Alcácer-kebir, Dom Sebastião and the flower of Portugal's arms fell to the Moor. Many of those who survived were held for ransom, so that in a single battle Portugal lost her king and most of her nobility. Cardinal Henry, Dom Sebastião's great-uncle, took control of the kingdom as regent, but he was an old man without ability and it was soon apparent that the Aviz dynasty could no longer control the Portuguese throne. Between 1578 and 1580 claimants began to push forward their title to the prize. Although Dom Antônio, the Prior do Crato, an illegitimate son of King Manoel I, had much support from the populace, Philip II, whose mother was a legitimate child of Manoel, had better legal claims. Moreover, he had the Spanish army.

Philip II is supposed to have justified his title to the Portuguese crown by stating "I bought it, I inherited it, I conquered it." To accomplish the first part of that formula Philip called upon a number of Portuguese sympathizers and sycophants to press Spanish silver into the hands of the Portuguese high clergy and nobility, many of whom wished to use the money to ransom their relatives from the infidel in Morocco. At the same time he put the Spanish (and some Portuguese) jurists to work composing legal defenses of the Hapsburg claim. When, after the death of Cardinal Henry in 1580, Dom Antônio with the support of the Portuguese lower classes tried to seize the throne, Philip sent the Duke of Alba and his Spanish regulars into Lisbon to settle the issue.[3] For the next

---

esto de la justicia por lo que importa la brevidad." For the advice of Charles V to Philip II on matters of justice, see Francisco Caeiro, *O Arquiduque Alberto de Austria* (Lisbon, 1961), p. 63.

2. I have listed the major sources on the union of Spain and Portugal in "Luso-Spanish Relations in Hapsburg Brazil, 1580–1640," *The Americas*, XXV (July 1968), 33–48. See also the excellent summary in John Lynch, *Spain under the Hapsburgs*, 2 vols. (New York, 1964–1969), I, 304–311.

3. For a modern defense of Dom Antônio, see Joaquim Veríssimo Serrão,

sixty years the Hapsburg rulers of Spain also wore the crown of Portugal, but the two nations and their empires were never united. Instead, a liberal solution emerged in which the king ruled both lands but each maintained its distinctive customs, laws, administration, and its national integrity. This solution, formalized by Philip II and the Portuguese estates at the Cortes of Tomar (April 1581), remained the guiding set of principles while the Spanish Hapsburgs ruled Portugal. Although there were violations of this agreement from the outset, Philip II generally adhered to it and only in the reign of Philip IV was it seriously threatened. A Council of Portugal was created to advise the king on Portuguese affairs and a viceroy ruled in Lisbon in the king's name. With these changes Portugal and her empire passed into the hands of the Spanish Hapsburgs.

Although geopolitical and imperial concerns lay behind Philip II's desire to wear the Portuguese crown, it is curious to note that even before 1580 Philip was planning a judicial and administrative reform of Portugal. To aid him in this matter, Philip created a small junta which included the Duke of Alba, Philip's best soldier, and Dom João da Silva, a Spanish noble connected by blood and marriage to the Portuguese nobility and who thus bore the Spanish title of Count of Salinas and the Portuguese rank of Count of Portalegre. Da Silva, in fact, had served as Philip's ambassador to the Portuguese court in the reign of Dom Sebastião and had accompanied that unhappy monarch on his abortive crusade. Because of his family ties, experience, and expertise, Dom João da Silva became, along with Cristóvão de Moura, Philip's specialist on Portuguese affairs.[4]

O reinado de D. António, Prior do Crato 1580–1582, 1 vol. to date (Coimbra, 1956).

4. A most interesting figure, D. João da Silva, became fourth Count of Portalegre by his marriage in 1577 to Filipa da Silva. João da Silva, soldier, diplomat, and author, was born in Toledo in 1528, son of a Spanish father and a Portuguese mother. He served in military campaigns in Oran before assuming his diplomatic post in Portugal as Philip II's ambassador. Wounded and captured at Alcácer-Kebir, he was ransomed by Philip II and ap-

The man selected to report to the junta on Portugal's judicial and administrative structure was Rodrigo Vázquez de Arce, a noted Spanish jurist and a firm supporter of Philip II's claim.[5] Vázquez was sent to win adherents to the Hapsburg cause, but he also received instructions ordering him to make a thorough examination of the Portuguese legal system and to report his findings to the junta. Rodrigo Vázquez proved to be an astute observer and his reports included a detailed description of Portuguese administrative organization, legal procedure, common abuses, and suggestions for improvement. He bluntly concluded, "that there is a lack of justice in this kingdom and a necessity to remedy it, everyone confesses." [6]

The first problem was that of legal codification. The corpus of Portuguese law was complex. It had developed from Roman and Visigothic codes enriched and complicated by royal concessions and grants and by a dominant strain of consuetudinary law. Codification had begun in the fifteenth century with the *Ordenações afonsinas* (1446) which had been revised in the sixteenth century

---

pointed majordomo of Portugal, a position in which he served during the Cortes of Tomar. From 1593–1600 he was a member of the board of governors that ruled Portugal. He died in Toledo in 1601. He wrote some poetry, letters, and is usually held to be the author or the source of *Dell' Unione del regno de Portogallo alla corona di Castiglia.* Diogo Barbosa Machado, *Biblioteca Lusitana,* 4 vols., 2nd ed. (Lisbon, 1933), II, 689–691; *Nobreza de Portugal,* 3 vols. (Lisbon, 1960–61), III, 160.

5. The decision to send Rodrigo Vázquez had been made by 14 April 1579. See Carlos Riba Garcia, *Correspondencia privada de Filipe II con su secretário Mateo Vázquez,* p. 204. Rodrigo Vázquez de Arce was born in 1529 in a family of noted jurists. He attended the University of Valladolid and served in the High Court of the chancery of Granada. After his service in Portugal, he returned to Spain and in 1584 became President of the Consejo de Hacienda. In 1592 he was made President of the Consejo Real. After the death of Philip II, Vázquez fell from power and was banished from the court, apparently because of his intransigence against any sort of pardon for the crypto-Jews. He died in 1599. See *Diccionario de Historia de España: desde sus orígenes hasta el fin del reinado de Alfonso XIII,* 2 vols. Madrid, 1952).

6. "Advertencias dadas a Philip II para la buena administración de la justicia en Portugal," BNM, Codice 8686, f. 63.

by Dom Manoel in his *Ordenações manuelinas* (1514, 1521).[7] Since that time, however, a considerable body of subsequent legislation had been issued. Then too, local custom and usage sometimes differed from the prescribed legal forms. Vázquez noted that some laws were antiquated or unjust while others were good but disregarded in practice. But, Vázquez claimed, "the truth is that the lack is not in the laws but in the little force they have here and the disinclination of the judges to enforce them with integrity."[8] He went on to claim that the *letrados* and royal magistrates were poorly trained, poorly paid, and ill-disposed toward their duties.

In many instances, powerful individuals acted with impunity in the face of judicial leniency and the impotence of the law. Taking advantage of their wealth, status, and privileges, the *fidalgos* often placed their retainers in local judicial and administrative posts, where they acted as advocates for their masters. The remedy suggested by Vázquez was the appointment of judges on a strict basis of merit and the equal enforcement of the law. High Churchmen and *fidalgos* enjoyed a privileged exemption from search of their homes and estates by justice officials. Vázquez felt that without the end of that exemption "there was no cause to even think of reform."[9]

Other proposals for reform were also made. The great delays of appeal caused by presenting all such cases before the Casa do Cível and the Casa da Suplicação in Lisbon clogged the channels of justice. Rodrigo Vázquez suggested that the local *juiz de fóra* and *corregedor* in the provinces be given wider appelate jurisdiction in order to diminish the need for appeal to Lisbon. Vázquez, in fact, looked with a skeptical eye at the high courts of Portugal. He noted—with some exaggeration—that the two Lisbon high courts were staffed by over seventy magistrates and that the large number

---

7. *Ordenações do Senhor Rey D. Manuel*, 5 vols. in 4 (Coimbra, 1797). All future citations are to this edition. For a discussion of the development of Portuguese law, see Gama Barros, *HAPP*, I, 5–136.

8. AGS, *Estado, Negociaciones de Portugal*, 428 (10 October 1581).

9. *Ibid.*

Map 3. Portugal in the sixteenth to eighteenth centuries

of judges, clerks, lawyers, and hangers-on at these tribunals increased litigation and generated unnecessary pleas and appeals. He suggested, in fact, that the Casa do Cível be abolished. Such suggestions and the others cited above indicate quite clearly that Rodrigo Vázquez de Arce must be considered the architect of the Hapsburg judicial and administrative reform of Portugal which took place in the decade of the 1580's. Philip II and his Spanish advisers, however, cannot be given total credit for these reforms.[10]

During the fifteenth and sixteenth centuries there had been considerable agitation in Portugal for judicial reform. At the Cortes of Tomar (April 1581) all three estates—but especially the third estate—had asked for reform in procedure, selection of judges, reduction of the number of desembargadores, and an increase in the salaries of the judiciary. The last request was made in the hopes that an adequate salary would place the magistrates beyond the temptations of bribery. Philip II was disposed to comply in this matter, but he had to proceed carefully. The agreement between the Portuguese Cortes and Philip centered on a liberal solution in which the Spanish king abjured any interference with the norms and customs of Portugal or the introduction of any foreign, especially Castilian, laws or ministers.

But although Philip II proceeded carefully neither he nor his advisers could divest themselves of their own backgrounds in Castilian law and tradition, and they expressed a natural inclination to introduce Castilian forms in Portugal. The king thought of

10. Almeida, *História de Portugal*, III, 328–335, 341–344; Helmut Koenigsberger, *The Government of Sicily under Philip II of Spain* (London, 1951), p. 116, agrees with this view of Philip II's preoccupation with justice, as does J. M. González de Echávarri y Vivanco, *La justicia y Felipe II: Estudio historico-crítico en vista de diez y siete reales cédulas y cartas acordadas del Consejo inéditas* (Valladolid, 1917). Candido Mendes de Almeida, *Codigo philippino*, pp. xxiii-iv argues that the motive of the judicial reform in Portugal was Philip II's desire to revise the relationship between civil and ecclesiastical law imposed by unquestioned acceptance of the Council of Trent in Portugal. This view does not take into account Philip II's judicial reforms in Spain, the reports of Rodrigo Vázquez, nor the desire of the Portuguese themselves for reform.

introducing the *hermandad* for the "good execution of justice and the punishment of delinquents." [11] Rodrigo Vázquez felt that in view of the mercantile nature of Portugal, a commercial law code like that of Burgos should be instituted.[12] The voice of moderation, however, was that of the Count of Portalegre, Philip's pro-Portuguese adviser, who felt that although nothing should impede justice, caution was necessary for:

> any change in government should be made with the greatest consideration in states newly acquired . . . for each province has its own style which experience has introduced and established, and although to foreigners it may seem inconvenient, they should proceed with prudence because this stems from the fact that they are accustomed to other uses. . . . The states of Your Magesty offer better proof than those of any other Prince . . . for in Spain there are many different customs because there were many rulers, and in you other possessions the customs are also quite unlike those of Spain, but that is not to say that the contradictions of usage are directly opposed to the administration of justice.[13]

Such moderate advice and Philip II's own inclination to comply with the agreement of Tomar resulted in a cautious and basically Portuguese approach to the reform of justice. Portuguese forms

---

11. "Advertimiento," AGS, *Estado, Negociaciones de Portugal,* 428 (Lisbon, 15 January 1582). The *santa hermandad* was a constabulary and judicial force for the maintenance of order in rural areas and on roadways. Organized at first by the individual Castilian municipalities, after 1496 it was sponsored by the Spanish crown.

12. "Advertencias," BNM, Cod. 8686. The reference to the commercial code of Burgos is to the *consulado* or merchant guild of Burgos established in 1494. See Robert S. Smith, *The Spanish Guild Merchant: A History of the Consulado, 1250–1700* (Durham, 1940). This suggestion bore fruit in 1592 with the creation of the Tribunal e Mesa do Consulado of Lisbon based on Spanish models. See Eulália Maria Lehmeyer Lobo, *Aspectos da influência dos homens do negocio na política comercial Ibero-Americano* (Rio de Janeiro, 1963). On a later unsuccessful project see Hermann Kellenbenz, "O projecto duma 'Casa da Contratação' em Lisboa," *Actas: Congresso internacional de história dos descobrimentos,* V, part 2, 233–249.

13. "Lo que parece al Conde de Portalegre del escripto q. ha hecho Rodrigo Vázquez," AGS, *Estado, Negociaciones de Portugal,* 428.

and usage were employed and Portuguese legal experts performed the necessary review of statute law. Philip established a commission in Portugal composed of prominent lawyers and presided over by Damião de Aguiar, a Portuguese jurist and a staunch supporter of the Hapsburg cause. In other words, although Philip II displayed a willingness to allow the Portuguese some autonomy in their judicial reform, he refused to risk any political autonomy or infringement of his royal prerogative. Damião de Aguiar would be Philip's insurance against any such risk.

The commission completed the revision of the *Ordenações manuelinas* by 1595 adding, deleting, and amending as necessary. Publication of the new code, the *Ordenações filipinas*, was delayed until 1603 but in the interim the crown instituted many of the projected reforms. The period from 1581 to 1590 was one of intense activity in the reformation of Portugal's judicial and administrative structure.[14] These reforms would have important effects not only on Portugal, but on her colonies as well.

The general reform law of 27 July 1582 abolished the Casa do Cível and permanently established the Casa de Suplicação in Lisbon. A new high court was established in Oporto to serve as a tribunal for appeals from the northern provinces and thus take pressure off the docket of the Casa da Suplicação in Lisbon. The former difficulties of communication between northern Portugal and Lisbon were thus eliminated. On 27 July 1582 both the Casa da Suplicação and the newly created Relação do Pôrto received their *regimentos*.[15] The ideas planted by Rodrigo Vázquez had borne first fruit.

The new High Court at Oporto, the Relação do Casa do Pôrto, served as the appelate court for the provinces of Tras-os-Montes, Entre Douro e Minho, and Beira, areas that because of distance found appeal to Lisbon a hardship. The Relação do Pôrto consisted of a large body of over twenty magistrates and lesser officials.

14. Much of the documentation of this reform is presently in the Archivo General de Simancas in the section *Estado, Negociaciones de Portugal.*

15. *Codigo philippino,* 242–253.

Those magistrates assigned to it were assured preference in promotion to the Casa da Suplicação, and thus the Relação do Pôrto became an important rung in the promotional ladder of the professional magistracy.[16]

Following the first initiatives of 1582, the crown continued to press for further reforms. In 1585 an investigation of the Desembargo do Paço and the Casa da Suplicação weeded out those magistrates who had failed in their duties or had abused their authority. During this same period the reform began to reach into the colonies. In Africa changes and reforms were attempted in Angola and Guiné. Between 1583 and 1584 a general inspection of the state of justice and the judiciary was made in Angola while in 1587 royal magistrates in Guiné received new instructions which increased their power and jurisdiction.[17]

Conditions beyond the Cape of Good Hope also called for reform. In the fortresses of India captains obstructed the *ouvidores* from the successful performance of their duties. In response to this situation, the crown issued in February 1586, a new *regimento* to the ouvidores, designed to increase their power vis-à-vis the

---

16. The *alvará* concerning promotional preference in BGUC, Codice 713, f. 62. A study of the Relação do Pôrto has not been written. The first fifty years of its history are difficult to reconstruct because a fire in 1631 destroyed the High Court building and most of its records (AGS, *Sec. Prov.* 1527, n. 182). There is a large body of material concerning the court from the late seventeenth century to the present. Modern court records are presently housed in the archive of the Tribunal da Relação do Pôrto, which due to the kindness of the officials of that institution, I was able to scan in 1966. Papers of the Relação do Pôrto from the eighteenth and nineteenth centuries are now in the Arquivo Distrital do Pôrto. The following manuscript sources also contain information concerning the Relação do Pôrto: Cartório do Relação do Porto, BGUC, Codice 695, pp. xvi, 335; José Luís Ferreira Nobre, "Compendio da Antiguidade e establicimento da Relação do Porto e Lisboa, BPMP, ms. 1. 114, ff. 1–36; Antônio de Sousa Coelho Caldas," Colecam doq. mais essentialmente contem os Libros da Esfera e dos Assentos da Relaçam do Porto (1733)," BPMP, ms. 795; Historia abreviada da Relação do Porto e Casa da Suplicação," ACL, ms. 185.

17. Caeiro, *O Arquiduque*, 66–69; Felner, *Angola*, docs. 18, 19, 20, pp. 412–417; Senna Barcellos, *Subsídios*, I, 161–167.

captains. During this period the Desembargo do Paço also drafted new instructions for the High Court of Goa in order to bring that tribunal's procedure and organization in line with the newly reformed metropolitan courts.[18]

While jurists discussed these reforms and applied new remedies in Portugal and its Asian and African colonies, the problem of justice in Brazil also demanded attention. In view of the trend of judicial reform in Portugal represented by the reorganization of the metropolitan and Goan tribunals, it is not surprising that these councilors now considered the creation of a High Court for Brazil. Although few documents survive concerning the deliberations and decisions of the councils of government in creating a Brazilian tribunal, apparently by September 1586 Philip II had decided to consider this possibility.[19] The king ordered the Desembargo do Paço to offer suggestions, and he solicited opinions from Bras Fragoso and Cosme Rangel, both of whom had firsthand experience as former magistrates in Brazil. Generally, they responded favorably and most felt like the viceroy of Portugal, that a High Court would administer justice with more equality than had been possible under the *ouvidor geral*.[20]

In Brazil legal conditions had not improved. The successors of Mem de Sá did not duplicate his administrative achievements. For a while it seemed as though the success of Mem de Sá, a *letrado*, had instigated the crown to turn toward this group for governors of the colony. Thus Luís de Brito Almeida and Antônio de Salema

18. Gonçalves Pereira, *HAJEI*, I, 83, 153–154; Viceroy Cardinal to king, AGS, *Sec. Prov.* 1550, f. 115 (Lisbon, 1 March 1586). The *regimento* of the High Court of Goa is published in *HAJEI*, I, 364–381.

19. Viceroy Cardinal Alberto to king (Lisbon, 11 October 1586), AGS, *Sec. Prov.* 1550, f. 525. The lack of material is due to the fact that many of the original papers were submitted to the Conselho da India in 1606 and remained in the Casa da India, which was later destroyed in the Lisbon earthquake of 1755 and the aftermath of fires and flood. See Mendes da Luz, *O Conselho da India*, 117–118.

20. AGS, Sec. Prov. 1550, f. 52, "porque se deve correr melhor e co' mais igoaldade na administraçao da iust[ça] nesta orden q. por hu soo ouvidor como tequi foy."

were both *letrados* rather than important nobles or accomplished soldiers. This trend, however, ended shortly.[21] Meanwhile, the growth of population and commerce and the concurrent increase in litigation underlined the need for reform. The size of the task simply became too great for one man, and as we have seen, the *ouvidor geral* was unable to devote his full attention to matters of justice because of his other bureaucratic and military responsibilities. Nor did the crown always find it easy to fill positions in Brazil with able and willing *letrados*. In fact, it was just at this time that Diogo Dias Cardoso excused himself from service as *ouvidor geral* in Brazil, claiming that his wife in Portugal was "stark raving mad" and that he could not in good conscience leave her.[22] *Letrados* unwilling to accept a post sometimes reached imaginative heights in their excuses. Although some royal councilors felt that the selection of more experienced magistrates would improve the notorious conditions in Brazil, most generally agreed that the system itself needed structural modification.

The reform of the Brazilian judicial structure projected between 1586 and 1588 reflected the previously described situation in Brazil and the general pattern of judicial reform enacted by Philip II in Portugal. Most authors who have concerned themselves with the development of Brazilian institutions in the colonial period have viewed the creation of the High Court of Brazil as the result of purely Brazilian factors. This interpretation ignores Brazil's posi-

21. There is some evidence that displacement in the high offices of colonial government of the military and landed nobility by the magisterial class was resented by the former and contributed toward their acceptance of Philip II. Chapter XI of the petition of the Nobility made at Tomar asks that "the captaincies of Mina, São Tome, Cabo Verde, Brazil, . . . be given in the old manner to *fidalgos*—for they won them and defend them —and not to *letrados* as has been done recently against the ancient and good custom of past kings." See *Patente das merces, graças, e privilegios* . . . (Lisbon, 1582).

22. AGS, *Sec. Prov.* 1550, f. 443. Some thought was also given to improving and strengthening the office of *ouvidor geral* at this time. See Viceroy Cardinal Alberto to King (Lisbon, 7 June 1586), AGS, *Sec. Prov.* 1550, f. 261.

tion as merely one of a number of colonial areas under Portuguese control, and in this period certainly not the most important of them. The fact that the new tribunal was to be created according to Portuguese models should not disguise the presence of Spanish initiative in the original reform, even though Philip II's compliance with the agreement of Tomar forced this presence into the background.[23] Present Portuguese nationalists would have us believe that the Spanish reforms were minimal in their accomplishments and results, but the continued use of the *Ordenações filipinas* after the separation of Portugal from Spain in 1640 and the perisistence of the Relação do Pôrto to this day attest to the durability and effectiveness of the Philippine judicial and administrative reforms of the 1580's.

Conversely, it is only fair to note that many of the reforms suggested by Philip II's advisers had been previously sought by the Portuguese themselves both in Portugal and in the colonies. This perhaps explains the ready acceptance of these changes. The Relação do Pôrto, for example, was welcomed by many as a long-needed reform.[24] In Brazil, as early as 1562 minor treasury officials had suggested the administration of justice by a board of magistrates rather than by just an *ouvidor geral*.[25] This suggestion most

---

23. The attention of judicial reform within Portugal itself was still a matter of concern to the Spanish monarch in 1586. In that year the crown had submitted a thirty-five point outline of judicial problems to the Viceroy of Portugal, Cardinal Alberto, and to the Desembargo do Paço for their review and opinion. The viceroy's opinions on each point can be seen in Viceroy Cardinal Alberto to king (Lisbon, 1 March 1586), AGS, *Sec. Prov.* 1550, ff. 109–112v.

24. ACL, Ms. 185, f. 3, where the High Court of Oporto is referred to as "couza tão desejada, e tantas vezes pedida ao Sen. Rey D. João 3º nas Cortes que fez em Torres Vedras . . . 1525 e nas de Évora de 1538."

25. *ABNR*, XXVII, "Carta dos Officiaes da fazenda do Salvador . . ." (24 July 1562), 240; "tambem achamos que o ouvydor jeral per sy soo tem gramde alçada e cabendo nela tao gramdes casos como cabem podese causer alguma presunção e sendo devertida em tais pessoas nam fica causa pelo que nos parece nam devia ter mais alçada nesta capitania que ha que tem os capitães e que passando dela os feitos se despachessem per desembargo com o govenador e juizes ordinarios com o veador mais velho desta cydade no

certainly foreshadowed the creation of a Brazilian high court of appeal. But, whatever the reasons, these long-standing Portuguese desires received little satisfaction until a Spanish Hapsburg sat on the throne of Portugal.

Well-planned reforms designed in Portugal did not always coincide with Brazilian realities. It was one thing to issue a *regimento* for a new Brazilian tribunal and to select ten magistrates for its bench, but it was quite another matter to establish this body in the colony. The Relação da Bahia, created in 1588 as part of the general administrative and judicial reform, never reached the colony. But it was wind and tide rather than any political or administrative conflict that caused the court's failure. The story is simple. Most of the ten magistrates chosen to serve in the Relação da Bahia embarked in 1588 in the company of the newly appointed governor Francisco Giraldes.[26] His ship, the galleon *São Lucas*, battled winds and currents without being able to cross the equator and finally made a forced landing at Santo Domingo in the Caribbean. Giraldes and his companions, unable to sail southward along the coast because of the contrary currents of the season, re-embarked for Portugal. Four desembargadores did, by one means or another, reach Brazil, where they served in various offices, but the high court as such was not instituted.[27]

---

qual vosa alteza podera acresemtar a alçada que lhe bem parecer porque sendo cinquo juizes fica fora toda sospeta e sospeiçam e sera menos trabalhos custas aos omens que mandarem ou forem com seus feitos ao reino especialmente os que ficão em prisam."

26. On Francisco Giraldes and his Florentine connections, see Sérgio Buarque de Holanda, "Os projectos de colonização e comércio toscanos no Brasil ao tempo de Grão Duque Fernando I (1587–1609)," *Revista de História*, XXXV (1967), n. 71, 61–84.

27. Of the ten *letrados* chosen to serve in Brazil, the author has been able to identify nine: Antônio Coelho de Aguiar, Ignácio Bandeira, Balthesar Ferraz, Custódio de Figuereido, Gaspar de Figuereido Homem, Luís Machado Gouveia, Jácome Ribeiro de Leiva, Ambrósio Peixoto, and André Martins Rollo. Of the ten appointed, Varnhagen, *História geral*, II, 31, lists three as having arrived in Brazil (Aguiar, Ferraz, Figuereido Homem). It is apparent, however, that Custódio de Figuereido also reached Brazil. See

The attempt was not without some result. The *regimento* issued in 1588 was not destroyed but merely shelved. This set of statutes, which outlined the functions of the tribunal and specified the duties of its magistrates and functionaries, indicated clearly that the newly reformed Casa da Suplicação was the model for the High Court's organization and procedure. When, in 1609, the Relação do Brasil began to operate, it employed the same *regimento* with only minor additions.[28]

Within two years after the failure of 1588, the Desembargo do Paço returned to the problem of judicial administration in Brazil.[29] The state of justice—or rather the lack of justice—was a continuing problem and the conditions that had stimulated the attempt to establish a High Court in 1588 persisted in 1590. In fact, the number of appeals from the decisions of the *ouvidores* increased steadily and the metropolitan organs were unable to deal effectively with them.[30]

To the crown there seemed to be three basic alternatives: (1) the establishment of a High Court according to the original plan of 1588; (2) the continuation of the prevailing system based on the office of the *ouvidor geral;* (3) the institution of some new organization of justice other than that of a High Court. The Desembargo do Paço discussed this problem and reported its findings to the crown. Although one member of the Desembargo do Paço favored a judicial status quo in Brazil, the majority felt the need for change.

BA, 44-XIV-5, f. 186; BA, 44-XIV-6; f. 101; Frei Vicente do Salvador, *História do Brasil*, liv. iv, cap. 34, p. 331. See also king to Balthesar Ferraz (Lisbon, 22 October 1588), BNRJ, 7, 3, 1 on Ferraz' failure to reach Brazil.

28. The titles Relação da Bahia and Relação do Estado do Brasil were used interchangeably, although the latter was the official title used in the *regimento* of 1609.

29. The debates concerning judicial reform in Brazil in 1590 are embodied in a series of documents in the Biblioteca da Ajuda, 44-XIV-4, ff. 43v., 64, 66v.–67. These have been printed in Joaquim Veríssimo Serrao, *O Rio de Janeiro ao seculo XVI*, 2 vols. (Lisbon, 1965), II, 147–50. The date of the *consulta* of the Desembargo do Paço printed on p. 148 as 9 July 1590 should read 5 July.

30. BA, 44-XIV-4, f. 67.

They did not believe that the *regimento* of 1588 suited Brazilian conditions, because it called for the presence of ten royal magistrates whose residence in the colony would result in increased litigation, disputes, dissension, and chaos. The councilors stated, "the land of Brazil is not capable of supporting so many lawyers." [31]

Herein lay an underlying cause for much of the opposition to the High Court of Brazil. As in India, many observers feared that the establishment of a high court with ten judges would stimulate an influx of advocates and pettifoggers, stimulate unnecessary litigation, and bring the process of justice to a standstill. It is tempting to accept at face value this complaint so often brought against the High Court of Goa and the Spanish American *audiencias,* especially since the knowledgeable Desembargo do Paço had made the charge. That council and its contemporaries overlooked, however, the multiple functions of the magistracy and the extra duties assigned to colonial justices. The presence of a court of appeals in Brazil might stimulate litigation, but an increase in the number of magistrates might also allow for the prompt and proper hearing of disputes. The Desembargo do Paço tried a middle course. Instead of sending the full tribunal, it voted to send five *letrados* with circuit duties.[32]

The Viceroy of Portugal, Cardinal Alberto, submitted an alternate plan suggesting the placement of three crown magistrates in Brazil: an *ouvidor geral* in Bahia and crown-appointed *ouvidores* in Pernambuco and Rio de Janeiro. Realizing that the appointment by the crown of *ouvidores* in these captaincies violated the original donations, the viceroy suggested that the new officials be called *provedores* and that they proceed as did their counterparts in Portugal. The viceroy's recommendation obviously attempted to extend royal power at the expense of the proprietors and was, in fact, such a blatant effort that he felt compelled to disguise it in

---

31. *Consulta* of Desembargo do Paço (Lisbon, 15 February 1590), BA, 44-XIV-4, f. 43v.

32. *Consulta* of Desembargo do Paço (Lisbon, 5 July 1590), BA, 44-XIV-4, f. 66v.

complex terminology. The interest of the Hapsburg rulers of Portugal in continuing the trend toward centralization initiated by the House of Aviz was already apparent, although it did not become a dominant concern until the reign of Philip IV. In this context, however, the ultimate decision of the Desembargo do Paço is more comprehensible.

One faction of the Desembargo do Paço approved the extension of royal control but felt that the powers of the *provedores* of Portugal were insufficient to cope with the existing Brazilian situation. They advocated an expansion of the jurisdiction of these *provedores* to enable them to hear appeals from the decision of those justice officials appointed by the proprietors. This would create in both Rio de Janeiro and Pernambuco the equivalent of an *ouvidor geral.* The opposing faction based its contrary opinion on three arguments. First, a *provedor* on the Portuguese model limited to probate matters could accomplish very little and would be useless in Brazil. Second, the creation of a de facto *ouvidor geral* would bring great difficulties, especially in terms of conflicting jurisdictions. Third, the whole plan was contrary to those privileges granted to the proprietors. Instead, the opposing faction suggested that five *letrados* be sent as a tribunal, and that if this could not be done the whole matter be dropped.

These conflicting opinions left the crown in a quandary, for since the principal objective of the creation of the High Court in 1588 had been to eliminate the number of actions appealed to Portugal, it now seemed strange that with litigation increasing, the original number of magistrates assigned to that tribunal was considered execessive. If a High Court with ten judges was too heavy a burden for Brazil, then the crown felt no need to alter the existing system. The crown formalized this decision in a letter to the Desembargo do Paço dated 26 November 1590.[33]

---

33. Joaquím Veríssimo Serrão, *Do Brasil filipino ao Brasil de 1640* (São Paulo, 1968) pp. 52–54, analyzes these discussions well. He claims, however, that the king ordered the Relação established in Brazil in 1590 but that for some reason the order was not obeyed. The document he cites in support of this contention he has transcribed and published in *O Rio de Janeiro*

Thus in 1590 a negative decision of the crown settled the question of establishing a High Court of Appeal in Brazil. For fifteen years the matter remained in abeyance, although conditions in the colony increasingly warranted some modification of the existing system. The flurry of interests in 1590, however, indicated not only the major functional and administrative difficulties involved in a reorganization of the Brazilian judicial system, but also an implicit royal desire to bring this colony, now growing in size and importance, under royal bureaucratic control. Moreover, the ideas put forward in 1590 were not completely sterile, and when in 1609 a High Court did begin to function in Brazil, there would also be an *ouvidor geral* in Rio de Janeiro, as had been suggested by the Viceroy of Portugal, Cardinal Alberto.

Philip II died in 1598. To his young son, Philip III, fell the patrimony of the Spanish Hapsburgs, an inheritance which included Portugal and its empire. But this legacy also included a smoldering war in the Low Countries, a problem of internal security in the only partially hispanized Moriscos, and above all a budget which ran increasingly in the red. Philip III, weak, irresolute, and easily influenced by his advisers, simply lacked his father's interest in matters of administration and justice and he found in the pressing political and financial problems of his era more than enough to occupy his limited personal resources. Nevertheless, during this period the High Court was finally established in Brazil, probably as a result of local conditions.

As early as January 1605, Philip III ordered the then recently created Portuguese colonial council, the Conselho da India, to review the question to determine the wisdom of sending a High Court to Brazil.[34] The king's primary considerations, or at least

---

no século XVI. My reading of this letter of 26 November 1590 does not support Veríssimo Serrão's claim and rather indicates that the crown left the matter to the Viceroy of Portugal and the Desembargo do Paço, but the crown did intimate that the High Court with ten *letrados* should not be sent.

34. The short-lived Conselho da Índia (1604–1614) was to some extent created as the colonial council. Rivalry with the Conselho da Fazenda and the Desembargo do Paço eventually resulted in its demise. Francisco Paulo

those he stated explicitly, centered on his interest in effective administration and the state of the royal treasury in that colony. There is strong evidence, however, that other considerations also existed. For example, a letter from the *câmara* of Bahia to the king (27 January 1610) noted that before 1609 the governor and the *ouvidor geral* had joined forces to eliminate their political opponents from the municipal council.[35] This was the same complaint of collusion that Pero Borges had registered against the proprietors and their *ouvidores*.[36] Moreover, in the later years of the sixteenth century the *ouvidores* and the *ouvidor geral* were failing in their duties and abusing their authority. Domingos de Abreu e Brito, a royal investigator who visited Brazil in 1591, reported that the justice officials were easily subverted by planters and merchants. He claimed that since the time of Cosme Rangel justice had faltered in the colony.[37]

Although such conditions may have stimulated new interest in reform, the conflict between colonial institutions also provided a compelling reason for reorganization. The traditional conflict of interests between the secular and ecclesiastical officials in Brazil stimulated an appeal by the former requesting that the crown send a special judge to adjudicate these disputes in the colony. This request, made in February 1604, drew a negative response from the crown, but the conflicts did not abate and when the High Court reached Brazil in 1609 one judge was specifically assigned to hear these disputes.[38]

Whatever the underlying factors that moved the crown to action

---

Mendes da Luz, *O Conselho da India* (Lisbon, 1952) is an adequate study which reproduces a number of important documents.

35. King to Conselho da Índia (? 31 January 1605), BA, 51-VIII-48, f. 17–17v. Cf. ANTT, *Sala da Livraria*, Livro das Cartas de Felipe III, f. 47, as cited by Mendes da Luz, *O Conselho da India*.

36. ANTT, *Corp. cron.*, pt. 11, maço 115, doc. 102.

37. Domingos de Abreu e Brito, *Um inquérito a vida administrativa e económica de Angloa e do Brasil (1591)* (Coimbra, 1931), pp. 76–79.

38. King to Viceroy of Portugal (Valladolid, 22 March 1604), AGS, *Sec. Prov.* 1487, f. 88.

in 1605, the stated cause for the creation of the Relação do Brasil was the growth in size and importance of Portuguese America. The colony was burgeoning and becoming increasingly important both strategically as a line of military defense and economically as a source of sugar. By 1605 the Conselho da India favored the establishment of a permanent tribunal in Brazil and within a year the crown ordered Dom Pedro de Castilho, Viceroy of Portugal, to take action to this end. The order stated:

> Because of the discovery and conquest of new lands, that state has expanded and grown in the number of vassals as well as in the quantity of its *fazendas,* which have caused an increase of the suits and suspicions that each day aret set in motion. And in that Justice can not be administered fully by an *ouvidor geral.* I agree with that which was proposed to me by a *consulta* of the Conselho da India and your written opinion. And desiring to attend to a matter of such particular importance to me as it is most convenient to God's service, my own, and the common good of my vassals, I deem it good to approve that once again the said High Court be organized to go to the said parts with the greatest possible speed.[39]

Once the crown decided to revive the High Court of Brazil, the first tasks were the selection of a suitable group of trained *letrados* and the drafting of a revised *regimento.* The former problem was extremely important. Poorly trained or inexperienced magistrates in a situation as difficult as that presented by the frontier conditions of Brazil and the combative spirit of its inhabitants could disrupt the community and create more difficulties than they resolved. Thus the crown desired the selection of able and experienced men.[40] Originally, the Conselho da India assumed the task of nominating men for positions on the High Court, but the council

---

39. BA, 51-VII-8, ff. 116v–117.

40. *Ibid.* The crown wanted "pessoas mui benemeritas de cuias letras einteireza se tenha conhecida noticia E experiencia E q' de nenhua' man^ra^ serao' de prim^ra^ instancia em meu ser^co^ por quanto importa muito q' assi plo q' toca a bom governo e administracão da justica como por exemplos e consequencias Seautorize e califique nestes principios com sogeitos de muita confianca."

which the Spanish Hapsburgs maintained in Spain as the highest advisory board on Portuguese matters, the Conselho de Portugal, realized that technical problems of law and the judiciary pertained to the Desembargo do Paço. On the suggestion of the Conselho de Portugal, the king sent the *regimento* of 1588 and the nominations made by the Conselho da India to the Viceroy of Portugal, instructing him to meet with the Desembargo do Paço and in "all secrecy" to nominate candidates for office and note any necessary amendments in the *regimento*.[41] Thus, three sets of papers served as a basis for the final decision of the Conselho de Portugal: the opinion and nominations of the Desembargo do Paço; the comments of the viceroy; and the *regimento* and nominations of the Conselho da India.[42]

All officers and institutions in the Portuguese administrative structure operated under a specific written set of by-laws. This instruction or *regimento* may be taken as the crown's ideal for the proper behavior of the individual bureaucrat or bureaucratic institution. Actual and expected behavior, however, often deviated considerably from the bureaucratic ideal expressed in the *regimento*. Nevertheless, these instructions present the theoretical basis of the tribunal's performance and the standards expected by the crown. An analysis of the *regimento* seems, therefore, a proper means of concluding this discussion.

The new Brazilian High Court was subordinate to, and modeled on, the Casa da Suplicação. Its members enjoyed the same rights and privileges as the desembargadores of other High Courts and their salaries were to be equal to those of the members of the Relação do Pôrto.[43] Voting and seating in the court proceeded

41. Cf. Ferreira, *Inventário*, n. 200.

42. The viceroy's opinions exist as BA, 51-VII-21, ff. 41–41v., 69–69v. The opinions of the Conselho da India and the Desembargo do Paço must be gleaned from the *consultas* of the Conselho de Portugal in AGS, *Sec. Prov.* 1476 (Valladolid, 19 January 1606), ff. 42–44; (Madrid, 29 November 1606), ff. 202–204.

43. Viceroy Cardinal Alberto to king, AGS, *Sec. Prov.* 1550, (Lisbon, 14 November 1586), f. 627. The *regimento* is published in José Justino de

according to a strict hierarchy. To represent the dignity of their office, the desembargadores were to wear dark robes both in court and in the city and the use of foppish attire was forbidden. Unlike the Oporto magistrates, however, the law did not require them to wear long beards to represent the authority of Roman senators.[44] The *regimento* also specified that the desembargadores were to be housed and maintained with as little cost and inconvenience as possible to the inhabitants of Bahia and the rest of the colony.[45] This This attempted to mitigate friction between the court and the colonists. Court costs were to be paid by the financial penalties levied by the tribunal and this source was also to provide the salaries of a chaplain and a physician to care for the spiritual and physical needs of the magistrates.

Unlike the Casa da Suplicação, the High Court had no *regidor* designated to preside over it; instead, the governor-general of Brazil was ordered to serve in this capacity. This formula had developed in India, where the viceroy performed these functions. The relationship of the governor-general of Brazil to the Relação paralleled that of the viceroy of Peru to the Audiencia of Lima. As president of the Relação, the governor could attend the sessions of the court when he so desired, but he could neither vote nor sentence. It was the governor's duty to see that the magistrates of the court were paid promptly, and although he could not make permanent appointments, he could assign members on an ad hoc basis. Every third year the governor was expected to appoint a desembargador to make a circuit tour of the other captaincies in order to conduct a *residência* of their captains and the *ouvidores*.

Andrade e Silva, *Colleção chronologica da legislação portugueza*, 12 vols. (Lisbon, 1854), I, 258–265. For the salaries of the members of the Relação, see Engel Sluiter, ed., "Report on the State of Brazil, 1612," *HAHR*, XXIX, No. 4 (1949), 538–539.

44. ACL, Ms. 185 (13 January 1584), f. 3v.

45. The desembargadores were also ordered not to requisition goods or to pay for them at a price below market value. These attempts to eliminate possible causes of dispute had only limited success. See Andrade e Silva, *Col. chron.*, I, 260.

If he discovered infractions, he was to submit the matter to the crown's attorney for prosecution. A similar but separate investigation was also to be held every three years in Bahia.[46] As the supreme civil authority in Brazil, the governor had to preserve the royal prerogatives of justice in the face of ecclesiastical encroachment. In this matter the governor was to proceed according to the *regimento* of the Relação da India.[47]

As in the other Portuguese High Courts, the chancellor was designated as chief magistrate. It was his duty to register the laws and ordinances issued by the governor and to annotate or amend them when necessary. Like his counterparts in Goa, Lisbon, and Oporto, the chancellor reviewed decrees and sentences to insure that they were not contrary to existing statutes. As the highest magistrate of the court, he also had jurisdiction in complaints and accusations brought against the governor-general. During the adjudication of these charges the governor was not allowed to attend the court. The other magistrates of the High Court and the various lesser functionaries when charged with some offense fell within the jurisdiction of the chancellor. Then, too, the chancellor served as *juiz dos cavaleiros* for Brazil and the members of the military orders were, therefore, directly subject to him in matters of law. This duty made it necessary for him to belong to one of the military orders.

In reality, the chancellor was the second highest official in the administrative organization of Brazil, a fact reflected by his salary as well as his power and prestige. In case of the governor's absence, the chancellor served as the head of government, and between 1609

46. The governor-general also had the power to suspend desembargadores for minor offenses and to prosecute them for more serious crimes, but final sentence had to be passed in Portugal. *RIHGB*, LXVII, pt. 1 (1906), "Regimento de Francisco Giraldes," 226.

47. The lengthy and explicit order included in the *regimento* of the Relação da Índia of 1587 regarding civil-ecclesiastical jurisdictional disputes was entitled "Determinacoes q. se tomarão per mandado del Rei nosso s^or^ sobre as duvidas q avia Entre os perlad^os^ E Just^as^ Ecleziasticas E seculares." See Gonçalves Pereira, *HAJEI*, I, 397–410.

and 1625 the governors were often absent from Bahia. Hence, the chancellor of the High Court of Brazil often governed the capital of that colony.[48]

The Brazilian High Court had three *desembargadores dos agravos* who passed judgment on civil suits involving amounts of up to two *milréis* in real property and three *milréis* in personal property. In cases involving larger amounts appeal could be made to the Casa da Suplicação. In Brazil, desembargadores heard appeals from the decisions of the lesser officials of justice such as the *ouvidores* in the captaincies, as well as those emanating from the decisions of the *ouvidor geral* and *provedor mór dos defuntos*. All civil cases were dispatched by *tenções* (depositions), as was the custom in Portuguese law. Whereas in the Casa da Suplicação three concurring votes decided a case involving ten *milréis* or more, the remoteness of the colony and the difficulties of appeal made necessary a change in this procedure. Hence, in Brazil only two votes settled a dispute involving amounts up to twenty *milréis*, and for greater amounts three votes. A majority vote of the desembargadores at the *mesa grande*, a plenary session, decided permission to appeal to the Casa da Suplicação.

The office of *ouvidor geral* was not abolished by the creation of the new tribunal but incorporated into the structure of the court. The functions of the *ouvidor geral* as a member of the High Court of Brazil resembled those of the *corregedor da corte* of the Casa da Suplicação.[49] Three times a week, on Monday, Wednesday, and Friday, the *ouvidor geral* sat, hearing both civil and criminal cases. In civil disputes he could hear suits in the first instance and adjudicate them by himself without appeal in amounts up to fifteen *milréis* in real property and twenty *milréis* in personal property.

---

48. This power derived from article 16 of the *regimento* of the *regidor* of the Casa da Suplicação. In Brazil the lengthy and frequent absences of the governors-general in Pernambuco during the period prior to 1630 put this provision into effect.

49. *Ord. fil.*, I, tit. vii, viii, pp. 48–61. Actually, in the Casa da Suplicação there were two *corregedores*, one for civil and one for criminal cases, but in Brazil their functions were joined in the office of *ouvidor geral*.

In criminal actions he had original jurisdiction in the captaincy of Bahia or the place of his temporary residence if he so desired, and he had appellate jurisdiction over the rest of Brazil. To the *ouvidor geral* was also assigned legal jurisdiction over civil and criminal actions involving troop detachments and the men and officers of the garrisons.

Disputes that directly affected the interests of the crown were the province of the crown judge or *juiz dos feitos da coroa e fazenda*. He adjudicated these cases in the first instance if they originated in the captaincy of Bahia, and on appeal if they came from another captaincy. Since the royal treasury was also his concern, he heard appeals from the decisions of the *provedores* of the captaincies in which there was an aggrieved party if he happened to be closer to the scene of the dispute than was the *provedor mór*. Moreover, those cases that involved amounts beyond the jurisdiction of the *provedor mór* could be appealed to the *juiz dos feitos da coroa*.[50]

A crown's attorney or *procurador da coroa* represented the king in those cases heard by the *juiz dos feitos da coroa* and also served as prosecuting attorney in criminal cases. Like the governor, the crown's attorney guarded the prerogatives of the king, especially against usurpation by the Church. One of the younger men of the court usually filled this position.

The *provedor dos defuntos e residuos* was in charge of estates and orphans. Generally, he proceeded as did the *provedores* of Portugal. In those cases in which the deceased had died testate and had named an executor of the estate, the *provedor* had no power to interfere. When, however, the heirs were absent or unknown, the *provedor* was in charge of probate and the disposal of the estate. Unlike the *provedores* of Portugal, the *provedor dos defuntos* could not hear appeals from the decisions of the *juizes dos órfãos*, and in Brazil those appeals came instead to the *desembargadores dos agravos*.

50. The *alçada* of the *provedor-mór* was 20 *milréis* in personal property and 15 *milréis* in real property.

Aside from the offices enumerated by the *regimento*, there were also two *desembargadores extravagantes* selected to aid in the work of the court, often joining the other magistrates in those cases that called for the decision of more than one judge. The *regimento* also provided for a number of lesser functionaries. They included six secretaries: two for appeals, two for the *ouvidor geral*, one for the *juiz da coroa*, and for the chancellor. These clerks prepared the evidence for presentation, recorded depositions and interrogations, wrote out charges, and registered laws. The Relação also maintained its own physician and chaplain to administer to its physical and moral needs and thus make the judges less dependent on the community. In the courthouse a bailiff and a custodian (*guarda-mór* also collected the fines levied by the High Court.

With only slight modification, the structure of the Relação described above remained the basic form of Brazilian High Courts for the next two hundred years. As an institution the Relação changed very little over the course of those two centuries. What changed constantly, however, was its membership, the magistrates who filled the seats of the bench. Men and not laws made the Relação a dynamic institution.

IV. THE MAGISTRATES

Choose ministers regarded highly not only for their knowledge but for their honesty, for this last feature is most important for those who go to administer justice in overseas positions.

Consulta of the Conselho
Ultramarino (9 July 1725)

The creation of a Brazilian High Court of Appeals marked a significant point in the administrative and social history of the colony. Before 1609 the extra-legal duties of the *ouvidores gerais* had limited their success as judges, and their position in the colony as the sole representatives of the professional magistracy had reduced the impact and extent of their personal relations. After 1609 the presence of ten desembargadores in Brazil not only increased the probability of better judicial performance but also multiplied the opportunities for social contacts. The judges who composed the first Brazilian tribunal were in many ways typical representatives of their profession. The degree of continuity between them and their successors in terms of social origins, career patterns, education, and experience is striking. The arrival of the first desembargadores can be seen as the beginning of magisterial government in Brazil, the full-fledged extension of royal bureaucracy to the colony at a time when Brazil was entering a period of economic prosperity brought on by the sugar boom. To explain fully the operation of royal government in Brazil both the bureaucracy and the bureaucrats must be understood. A table of organization can tell us a great deal, but as an expression of reality it is meaningless without some knowledge of the human qualities of the men who filled its various positions.

It should be made clear that magisterial bureaucrats were a small specialized group. Of the thousands of major and minor bureaucratic positions, perhaps only four hundred were reserved for the *letrado* bureaucracy throughout most of the sixteenth and seventeenth centuries. Actually, there were three types of bureaucratic posts, each filled to some extent by a distinct group. At the top, the old military and landed aristocracy continued to serve the crown in various positions, usually of an executive or conciliar nature. They served as viceroys in India, governors in Brazil, and ambassadors to the courts of Europe. These traditional nobles took great pride in their lineages, believed they were born to command, and never surrendered their role in government. The crown hoped to use the prestige of these men to reinforce its own authority and to enhance their effectiveness as its representatives. From these noblemen also came many of the royal councilors who staffed and headed the various organs of government described in Chapter One. After all, in a sense the titled nobility were the relatives and social equals of the king, and their heritage of command and outlook made them suitable advisers to him.

The various royal councils were not, however, the exclusive domain of the traditional nobility. In these bodies the crown called increasingly on the *letrado* bureaucracy throughout the course of the sixteenth century. Opinions varied as to the effectiveness of the two types of men as advisers to the king. One seventeenth-century observer stated that a mixture of *letrados* and titled nobles would produce the best conciliar decisions. He felt that *letrados* knew too much and intellectualized things so far as to make action impossible; the aristocrats or "*idiotas*" could act with speed but usually did so without wisdom. Thus the best solution was a mix of the two. The crown apparently agreed with this approach and a combination of professional bureaucrats and titled nobility continued to fill the seats of the king's councils.[1]

1. [Antônio Vieira], *Arte de Furtar* (Amsterdam, 1657). This seventeenth-century critique of venality in all its forms is among the most

As we have already seen, the magistrates were professional bureaucrats whose existence as a group was inextricably bound to the extension of royal authority at the expense of various corporate entities. Each increase in royal power created new duties and powers for the magistracy. The obligations of the magistracy remained judicial only in the broadest sense of that term, since the king's justice could be equated with the general welfare of the realm. The magistracy had become the spinal column of royal government, both in the colonies and in the metropolis, and as such it is the subject of this study. Not all bureaucratic ranks were filled by university-trained professionals, however, and before proceeding with our analysis of the magistracy it will be necessary to describe the myriad of lesser bureaucratic offices.

Beneath the magistracy lay the third layer of bureaucracy, a vast array of minor positions from notaries and clerks to port inspectors and paymasters. There were literally hundreds of these posts and their presence on the royal payroll indicated their position within the royal employ.[2] Some of these offices required absolutely no ability or experience, or if they did so, such criteria were often not applied in making an assignment. Many positions in the non-professional bureacracy could be bought or acquired as a reward from the crown. The phrase "some office of justice or the treasury" usually constituted the crown's response to a petitioner who pointed to his meritorious service or military exploits as grounds for reward. Such offices were not only assigned directly to prospective holders but were sometimes given to widows and orphaned girls as dowries. Obviously, these minor offices constituted a royal patrimony, a resource which enabled the crown to secure loyalty and

---

trenchant and damning books of its kind. The authorship is hotly disputed and Father Antônio Vieira, Tomé Pinheiro da Veiga, and Francisco Manuel de Mello have all been suggested by various scholars. To date, the most complete discussion of the problem is presented by Afonso Pena, *A Arte de furtar e o seu autor*, 2 vols. (Rio de Janeiro, 1946) in which he argues for the authorship of Antônio de Sousa de Macedo.

2. See the discussion in Alden, *Royal Government*, pp. 279–311, on the offices in the treasury.

reward service. Their function, therefore, was not purely bureaucratic. At this level of administration, pluralism (the holding of more than one office) was common and the use of deputies a common practice.

Distinctions did exist between lesser offices which required little or no skill and those posts which called for at least some ability. Notarial offices were the most important in this latter category. Clerking offices called for at least a minimum of literacy and usually the award of a notarial office included the provision calling for proof of aptitude. Notarial ability, however, seems to have decreased in direct ratio to the distance from the throne, so that if the existing manuscripts can be used as an index, the best scribes sat at the court in Lisbon and the worst scribbled half-literate Portuguese in poor colonial towns. Generally, *letrados* refrained from service as notaries and such posts went to men with only a rudimentary education.

In the sixteenth century, continental Portuguese filled most offices in the lesser bureaucracy of Brazil. By the Hapsburg period, however, colonials had acquired many of these positions and were anxiously competing to become a "child of the payroll (*filho da folha*)." Minor bureaucratic positions with their perquisites, fees, and salaries seemed a godsend to destitute *fidalgos,* indigent Indian-fighters, and geriatric widows. The general interest in becoming a government employee gave the crown considerable political leverage, since the granting or withholding of these posts constituted royal control of an important "free-floating resource," to use Eisenstadt's phrase.[3] At this level of employment, opportunities existed for both nobles and commoners. The recruitment and advancement of low-born subjects within the bureaucracy should be kept in view alongside those offices reserved exclusively for the aristocracy. The presence of high-born and low-born in bureaucratic posts indicated the crown's desire to mobilize contending sources of power and to balance them to its ultimate advantage. Between

3. S. N. Eisenstadt, *The Political Systems of Empires* (New York, 1963).

the second and third estates, however, some neutral group had to serve as the mediators of power and guardians of the system. This was the role which the crown envisioned for the professional magistracy.

By the late sixteenth century the magistracy had become a semi-autonomous and somewhat self-perpetuating class in which generation followed generation into royal service. Persons from other strata of society, however, continued to enter the *letrado* ranks and although the sons of magistrates served in the first Brazilian tribunal, so too did judges of *fidalgo* origin. Both the requirements for university matriculation and for entry into the royal employ operated to exclude men of certain backgrounds. In both cases "New Christians" (the euphemism for crypto-Jews) were prevented from entry in an attempt to assure the crown of officials who would be racially "pure," religiously orthodox, and politically loyal. Such an exclusion was impossible to enforce in every case, but a magistrate with the "taint" of "New Christian" background probably found his career somewhat limited. With this one factor of limitation, magistrates seem to have come from a wide range of social origins, which included *fidalgos* and farmers but which drew most heavily on non-titled gentry and bureaucrats. There is no way of determining from the present state of research the extent to which younger sons of the landed gentry sought their livelihood in the magisterial bureaucracy as an alternative to the Church or the army, but such a possibility certainly existed.

The key to a career in the royal service lay in a university law degree. Social origins or place of birth might vary considerably, but almost without exception the magistrates shared the common experience of graduation from the faculties of canon or civil law at the University of Coimbra. Since 1537, when King João III permanently established the university at Coimbra, legal studies had become increasingly important. Canon law was a particular favorite since it prepared the student for both the civil and ecclesiastical bureaucracies. In both civil and canon law, however, study centered on a number of prescribed courses which emphasized the corpus of Roman and ecclesiastical laws, the medieval glossators, and the commentaries of such jurists as the greatly esteemed Bartolus of Sassoferato.[4] As in most European universities of the age, instructors placed a premium on rote memory and on the ability of a student to dot the margins of his argument or treatise with learned citations and classical references. Nevertheless, from the few remaining written arguments of lawyers in Brazil and elsewhere, it is clear that sound legal reasoning and precedent also had their impact on judicial decisions.

There were three academic degrees in civil (*Leis*) or canon (*Canones*) law that the student could earn. The bachelor's degree (*bacharelado*) was by far the most common and it became almost synonomous with the magistracy. More valued until the seventeenth century was the licenciate (*licenciado*), a degree which required four additional years of study beyond the bachelor's degree. After the reform of Coimbra in 1612, the licenciate decreased in importance and became an adjunct to the bachelor's degree.[5] The doctorate (*doutorado*) was an honorific degree which did not really indicate superior qualities or learning and was pursued chiefly by men who joined the university faculty. Such men might, however, enter the royal service after a university career and former university professors could be found in the higher positions of the professional bureaucracy.

University degrees did serve as marks of distinction and status but never to the extent which they did in Spain and Spanish America, where the titles of *licenciado* and *doctor* were proudly displayed and jealously preserved.[6] Portuguese magistrates, unlike their Spanish counterparts, preferred their functional title (such as

4. On Bartolus, see Mario Julio de Almeida Costa, "Romanisme et Bartolisme dans le droit portugais," *Bartolo da Sassoferato: Studi e documenti per il VI Centenario*, 2 vols. (Milan, 1962), I, 314–345; Cecil N. S. Woolf, *Bartolus of Sassoferato: His Position in the History of Medieval Political Thought* (Cambridge, 1913); Jacques Flach, *Cujas, les glossateurs et les Bartolistes* (Paris, 1883).

5. Joel Serrão, ed., *Dicionário de História de Portugal*, 4 vols. (Lisbon, 1963–1971), II, 677–693. The excellent section "Leis, canones, Direito" is the work of Mario Julio de Almeida Costa.

6. James Lockhart, *Spanish Peru* (Madison, 1968), pp. 60–61, 225–226.

desembargador) to their university degree as means of status classification. Curiously, despite the small intellectual value ascribed to the doctorate, those magistrates who had obtained that degree usually insisted on the use of the title.

The demands of government and the particular goals and policies of the crown exerted an influence on the nature and content of a university education in Portugal. Legal study did more than prepare the student for the practice of law and entry into royal service in a technical sense; it also inculcated in him a complex pattern of accepted standards and actions. Legal education at Coimbra was a process of socialization which had at its core the creation of a sense of loyalty and obedience to the king. It is significant that throughout the three hundred years of the Brazilian colonial era, the only law faculty in the Portuguese empire was at Coimbra. Every magistrate in that empire, be he colonial or continental born, passed through the curriculum of that school and drank his knowledge of law and statecraft from that font. In a sense this process tied the colonial intellectual elite to the metropolis in a way quite different from Spanish America, where local universities served the colonial elite. There were Peruvian-born and Peruvian-educated magistrates who had never seen Spain, but no colonial-born magistrate in the Portuguese empire failed to study in the metropolis.

From the sixteenth century onward Coimbra became the training ground of the Portuguese clergy and the magistracy. In its halls they learned their craft and beneath the shadow of its belltower they assimilated the dominant political philosophy of the era. This is not the place to discuss in detail the major tenets of political thought in that age, since others have admirably performed that task, but at least one point must be made clear.

In the Portuguese Renaissance the relationship of the king to both the people and the law constituted the core of political thought.[7] Various authors had developed theories subordinating

7. Martim de Albuquerque, *O poder político no renascimento portugues* (Lisbon, 1968), pp. 235–277.

the king to the law and recognizing the right of the people to resist a tyrant; but few, if any, stated that the magistracy shared the right of the people to resist a bad ruler. At Coimbra, the Jesuits through their College of São Paulo came to dominate study and Jesuit thinkers emphasized that the magistracy was a royal creation and therefore totally subservient to the crown. Magistrates were royal servants, not civil servants. This doctrine found considerable support in foreign legal thought. Italian and Spanish political ideas were no strangers at Coimbra, especially during the Hapsburg era. In this period the doctrines of Spanish thinkers such as Francisco Suárez and Juan de Mariana were widely read and discussed. The Jesuit Suárez is most important in this respect, for he taught at Coimbra in the second decade of the seventeenth century and his impact was therefore direct.[8] Best known, perhaps, as an exponent of the popular will against tyranny, within Suárez' concept of the state the magistracy derived its authority from the crown and not the commonwealth. Such a position obviously constituted a sound theoretical foundation for the subservience of the bureaucracy to the king, a position that the monarch, whether Aviz, Hapsburg, or Bragança, could not fail to support.[9]

Not all students who matriculated at Coimbra entered the royal service upon graduation but those who had decided on a bureaucratic career generally began to prepare for the entrance examination during their last year at the university. To enter the magistracy the applicant petitioned the Desembargo do Paço, which then conducted a personal and academic investigation to determine the applicant's suitability for service. Of the many documents concerning the Portuguese bureaucracy none are more revealing of the recruitment procedures, criteria for selection, and social origins of

---

8. Most of Suárez' important works bore a Coimbra imprint. For example, *Defensio fidei catholicae* (Coimbra, 1613) and *De Legibus ac de Deo Legislatore* (Coimbra, 1612).

9. On this aspect of Suárez' doctrine see Mateo Laseros, *La Autoridad civil en Francisco Suárez* (Madrid, 1949); and the general discussion in Bernice Hamilton, *Political Thought in Sixteenth Century Spain* (Oxford, 1963), pp. 30–68.

the magistrates than the entry examinations conducted by the Desembargo do Paço.[10]

The Desembargo do Paço required all applicants to be graduates in law from Coimbra and to have practiced law for at least two years. Statutes also required the applicant to be at least twenty-eight years of age by the date of his appointment. At graduation most Coimbra students were between twenty-six and thirty-three years old, depending on the degree obtained, and thus the age requirement was not a serious handicap. Upon receipt of an application, the Desembargo do Paço circulated a questionnaire to the royal judge in the home town or district of the applicant's parents and grandparents. The judge then called before him a series of witnesses who testified on the background, activities, and reputation of the applicant and his family. Specifically, the questionnaire sought to establish the applicant's "purity of blood," to make certain that neither he nor his ancestors were tainted with the blood of "Moor, mulatto, Jew, New Christian, or other infected race." Moreover, the family's social origins and occupation were also important, for theoretically only those men whose parents and grandparents lived without recourse to manual labor, an artisan craft, or shopkeeping could enter the magistracy. Exceptions to this rule were made if the applicant's father or grandfather had been a member of a *senado da câmara* or the Casa de Vinte-quatro, the representative organ of the artisan guilds, since members of those institutions enjoyed a special privilege enabling their sons to enter royal service. All relevant testimony was then forwarded to Lisbon, where along with a certificate of good conduct from Coimbra it was deposited in the candidate's file. If all the testimony proved favorable, the applicant was then summoned to "read" before the Desembargo do Paço or, in other

---

10. These documents comprise the collection known as *Leitura dos Bacharéis* which is presently housed in the ANTT. The following analysis is based on a reading of over five hundred individual examinations. For some printed examples, see Luiza da Fonseca, "Bacharéis Brasileiros—Elementos biográficos (1635–1800)," *Anais: IV Congresso de História Nacional* (Rio de Janeiro, 1951), XI, 109–406.

words, to take an examination for competence in the law. A successful performance completed the application process and upon approval from the Desembargo do Paço, the applicant's name was placed upon a list of magistrates awaiting appointment.

The entire investigative and examinatory process known as the "*Leitura dos bachareis*" supposedly assured the crown of competent professional magistrates whose social origins were relatively homogeneous and whose religious and political orthodoxy could be trusted. Like any such process, it never fully achieved its goals. The magistracy was never free of its incompetents and thieves. The author of the *Arte de Furtar*, who was generally rather kind to the magistracy, claimed that educational abuses at Coimbra led to ludicrous judicial performances. He stated that there were judges who were so ignorant that they did not know "their right hand from their left, but when it [came] to pocketing fees and salaries they [knew] their right hand like Bartolus and Covarubias." [11] Conversely, the recuitment process did have relative success in assuring that at least minimum standards of competence were maintained. Although the crown did not openly sell magisterial offices, patronage and clandestine purchase undoubtedly existed within the professional bureaucracy. However, the fact that recruitment and promotion ultimately depended upon a majority vote of the Desembargo do Paço guaranteed a certain degree of competence and professional autonomy. Whatever the individual abuse, neither kings nor courtiers ever turned the Portuguese magistracy into a host of patronized sychophants.

The question of bureaucratic autonomy is crucial to our analysis, for although the crown envisioned a corps of dependent and subservient officials, the training and operational practices of the magistracy engendered actions and attitudes independent of, and at times contrary to, royal desires. Student days at Coimbra, where drinking and brawling were as normal as the rote learning of the law, were as likely to result in group cohesion and close personal

---

11. *Arte de Furtar*, 249–250.

ties as they were in acceptance of loyalty to the crown. The shared experience of university days and old school ties reinforced the autonomous tendency of the magistracy, a tendency which the Desembargo do Paço as a semi-independent and fully professional council, also fostered. Here then was a problem faced by all bureaucratic empires. The bureaucracy, created by the crown to achieve royal goals, eventually gained the autonomy and power to seek fulfillment of its own ends. It was no longer simply a tool of the crown. The magistracy, therefore, had a number of options in the use of its power. It could seek the king's objectives and act as a royal agent, or it might attempt to achieve its own goals. Moreover, the magistrates could also serve as mediators between conflicting groups or other sources of power and by doing so form an array of temporary alliances. This pattern is further complicated because individual magistrates could and did pursue programs of action that were purely personal. None of these options excluded all others and the magistracy could occasionally perform two or more roles at the same time. Thus magisterial government was a highly complex equation which allowed for considerable choice by the men who formed the professional bureaucracy.

Bureaucracies cannot exist without bureaucrats. To comprehend the actions of the magistracy we must understand not only its institutional structure and collective history but also men who served in it—how they were selected, and the nature of their personal and professional histories. This theme will be dealt with at some length in a more quantitative manner in Chapter Eleven, but at this juncture let us turn to the men who arrived in Bahia in 1609 as the magistrates of the first Brazilian tribunal.

The nomination of the first ten magistrates sheds some light on the procedure of magisterial selection. Generally, the Desembargo do Paço and the Conselho da India agreed on the nominees to the principal offices of the new tribunal, but in those cases where opinions varied the Desembargo do Paço exercised more influence. The Viceroy of Portugal, Dom Pedro de Castilho, suggested a number of alternative *letrados* who apparently enjoyed his patronage. These men received little serious consideration even though they possessed the proper qualifications. The viceroy's nominations are interesting for two reasons. First, his failure to place favorites on the new High Court indicates that patronage alone was not enough to surmount the decisions of the Desembargo do Paço. Second, to support his candidates the viceroy had emphasized the fact that they were unmarried and that this was the preferred civil status for overseas judges.[12] The Conselho de Portugal suggested that two of the High Court's positions be filled by men already serving in Brazil. Philip III agreed and he assigned Ambrósio de Siqueira and Francisco Sutil to the tribunal in reward for past services and because of the "information that they [may] provide to those who are arriving for the first time." [13] The eight other *letrados* selected in 1606 were Dr. Gaspar da Costa (*chanceler*), Gaspar Pegado (*juiz da coroa e fazenda*), Afonso Garcia Tinoco (*procurador da coroa*), Álvaro Pessoa, Manuel Pinto da Rocha, Sebastião Pinto Lobo (*desembargadores extravagantes*). Not all of them, however, actually reached Brazil.[14] As a group these men were a competent if not particularly distinguished group of university-trained lawyers. Nine of the first ten magistrates had previous judicial experience and some would later return from Brazil to occupy positions of considerable importance in metropolitan councils. Their individual backgrounds and the story of their appointment presents a revealing glimpse into the Portuguese magistracy.

The councils and individuals concerned with the selection of the magistrates had unanimously approved Gaspar da Costa as chancellor of the High Court since his previous service was distinguished. Da Costa had served as *desembargador dos agravos* on

12. BA, 51-VII-21, ff. 41–41v., 69–69v. The viceroy also nominated Jácome Ribeiro de Leiva, a member of the Casa da Suplicação and the only man appointed to the 1588 Relação to be nominated to the revived tribunal. See ANTT, *Chan. Filipe I, Doações,* liv. 18, ff. 60v., 68v.

13. AGS, *Sec. Prov.* 1476, ff. 42–44.

14. Gaspar Pegado was excused from service in Brazil with great secrecy so as to avoid similar requests from other magistrates. See Varnhagen, *História geral,* II, 106.

the High Court of Oporto and on the Casa da Suplicação. Obviously, the crown had selected an experienced and respected judge to head the new tribunal.[15]

A man of Gaspar da Costa's abilities and prospects does not eagerly leave family, friends, and a comfortable position in Lisbon for the uncertainties of colonial life.[16] Reluctance of crown magistrates to serve in the colonies was not, however, a new phenomenon and the crown had developed a policy of reward and enticement to procure officials for overseas appointments. It had become an established policy to promise financial benefits, honors, and future promotions as a means of persuading men to undertake colonial service. As the king phrased it in da Costa's case, the favors promised were "to make him more disposed to serve me." [17] Thus, da Costa received a grant of *fidalguia*, knighthood in the Order of Christ, the honorary title of Councilor of the King, and financial benefits totaling about 300 *milréis*.[18]

As the crown had suspected, da Costa was not inclined to serve in Brazil, but he had been long enough in the royal judiciary to realize the dangers in provoking the king's displeasure. Therefore, instead of refusing the position, he tried to obtain even greater concessions, asking for 80 *milréis* life insurance for his family in case of his death and requesting that his brother be allowed to assume the office of Abbot of Vila das Chãs de Tavares near Viseu.[19] These

15. Da Costa had become a member of the Relação do Pôrto on 29 March 1592. ANTT, *Chan. Filipe I, Doações*, liv. 23, f. 179. His appointment as chancellor of the Relação do Brasil stated that his office was to be administered as the analogous office on the Casa da Suplicação and the Relação do Pôrto "naquilo em que se lhe poder aplicar." See ANTT, *Chan. Filipe II, Doações*, liv. 13 (4 August 1606), fs. 74v–75.

16. Gaspar da Costa had a wife and at least three children at the time of his appointment to the Brazilian post, as can be verified in the letter of Philip II to the Marquês do Alenquer (Madrid, 17 June 1617), AGS, *Sec. Prov.* 1515, f. 41.

17. King to Viceroy Bishop Pedro de Castilho (14 February 1607), BA, 51-IV-48, f. 69.

18. AGS, *Sec. Prov.* 1476, f. 43v.

19. What da Costa actually asked was that Manoel Mascarenhas, Abbot of Vila de Chãs de Tavares in the Bishopric of Viseu, be permitted to re-

additional favors were refused, although some provision was made for his family and da Costa did not ask again, because the Conselho de Portugal had stated with obvious irritation, "with this and the other favors granted he ought to content himself and desist from further replies." [20] Although this was communicated to da Costa in July 1606, and he was urged to sail with the first favorable wind, neither he nor his colleagues arrived until three years later.[21] Such delays were common among newly appointed overseas ministers who sought exemption from colonial service.

Gaspar da Costa served only two years in Brazil and thus his influence on the new tribunal was limited. During his short term, he became a respected and highly regarded magistrate. On 7 March 1610 the *câmara* of Bahia wrote to the king noting that the success of the High Court was dependent on da Costa, for on his "zeal, interests, and diligence rests the greatest part of the judicial remedy and the reputation of the very tribunal." [22] Da Costa's work as chancellor, however, was cut short by his death in 1611.[23]

Afonso Garcia Tinoco represented the crown's interest as *procurador da coroa e fazenda.*[24] Born in 1556, Tinoco attended the University of Coimbra and received a degree as *licenciado* in 1585.[25] In 1606 Tinoco, then *juiz de fóra* of Tomar, was confidently awaiting promotion to the High Court of Oporto when the bitter news of his appointment to the Brazilian tribunal arrived.

Like most of his colleagues, Afonso Garcia Tinoco wanted no

---

nounce (sell) his office to Joseph de Souveral, da Costa's brother. AGS, *Sec. Prov.* 1476, f. 69v (Valladolid, 31 March 1606).

20. *Ibid.*

21. King to Conselho da India (25 July 1606), BA, 51-V-48, f. 93. Da Costa's *mercés* were registered between 4 August 1606 and 31 March 1609. See ANTT *Chan. Filipe II, Doações,* liv. 13, ff. 74v–75, and liv. 20, f. 135v; also ANTT, *Chan. Filipe II Privilégios,* liv. 2, f. 99v.

22. ANTT, *Corp. Cron.,* pt. II, maço 115, doc. 105.

23. His wife Dona Leonor Remalha petitioned for a *mercé* in 1623 noting his death, BNM, Codice 2845 ff. 142–3. Frei Vicente do Salvador, *História,* liv. iv, cap. 46, p. 361.

24. AUC, *verbete de matrícula;* Afonso Garcia Tinoco.

25. Letter of the Count of Vilanova to the Count of Ficalho (Lisbon, 17 July 1600), BM, Additional Ms. 28462. ff. 350–351.

part of the cultural and occupational exile that Brazilian service presented. Thus, in an attempt to be excused he submitted an informative and somewhat amusing petition summarizing his eighteen years of service in the royal employ.[26] He emphasized that his services had never been rewarded and that there were good reasons why he should be excused. First, the trip would be very dangerous to his health, since he was "very sick in the stomach" and prone to seasickness. Then too, he was fifty years old and still a bachelor looking for a wife. The enforced trip would cut off his possibilities for marriage in Portugal, and magistrates were usually forbidden to marry in Brazil.[27] Eighteen years of service had taught him to cover all possibilities, and thus in the same petition he asked, in the event that he was not excused, that a number of rewards and privileges be granted.

The favors sought by Afonso Garcia were roughly those that had been granted to Gaspar da Costa. In fact, part of Afonso Garcia's reluctance to serve stemmed from jealousy, for he had been longer in the royal service than da Costa and thus felt he was being bypassed. This kind of professional jealousy and hostility was common. Afonso Garcia also petitioned that the crown allow his return to Portugal after three or four years in Brazil without any further authorization. More important, he asked to serve as *desembargador dos agravos*, as did the *procurador da coroa* of the High Court of Oporto. With the stipulation that he serve six years, the crown granted these last two requests but pointed out it wanted no further excuses from Afonso Garcia or any of the others.[28]

---

26. The appeal and an accompanying *consulta* of the Council of Portugal (Madrid, 29 Nov. 1606) are in AGS, *Sec. Prov.* 1476, ff. 202, 203, 203v, 204.

27. Marriage of desembargadores in Brazil was forbidden in the *regimento* and the prohibition was reinforced by an *alvará* of 22 November 1610. See Andrade e Silva, *Col. cron.*, I, 295. Special permission was an occasion granted by the crown.

28. King to Conselho da India (? May 1606), BA, 51-V-58, f. 89. The privileges granted to Tinoco are registered in ANTT, *Chan. Filipe II*, *Diações*, liv. 23, f. 94 (Lisbon, 1 May 1607) and f. 147 (Lisbon, 26 Oct. 1609); ANTT, *Chan. Ordem de Christo*, liv. 17, f. 207 (Lisbon, 26 September 1608).

Afonso Garcia Tinoco proved to be one of the ablest and most conscientious of the members of the Brazilian High Court, although he found time for other interests like slave-trading. Rather than six years, he stayed fourteen in Brazil before returning to Portugal. A unanimous vote of the Conselho de Portugal elected him to the Casa da Suplicação on 12 August 1623.[29]

Manuel Pinto da Rocha and Sebastião Pinto Lobo were nominated as *desembargadores dos agravos.* Both received degrees in canon law from the University of Coimbra, Pinto Lobo in 1584 and Pinto da Rocha in 1589.[30] Information on the career of Sebastião Pinto Lobo before his service in Brazil is limited, although it can be substantiated that he was *juiz dos órfãos* of Oporto at the time of his appointment to the Relação do Brasil. His service in Brazil lacked distinction. On his return to Portugal, he served as *provedor* of Viseu before becoming a *desembargador extravagante* of the Relação do Pôrto.[31] He retired from public life in April 1636.[32]

The professional career of Manuel Pinto da Rocha is well-documented. He was a competent crown magistrate who had risen through the normal channels of the Portuguese judicial hierarchy. Beginning as *juiz de fóra* in Montemor-O-Novo in 1592, he held positions successively as *corregedor* of Almada, *ouvidor* of Setúbal, and *corregedor* of Viana.[33] Although originally nominated as a

---

29. BNM, Codice 2845, f. 157; ANTT, *Chan. Filipe III, Doações,* liv. 11, f. 170 (Lisbon, 20 April 1624).

30. Although these two *letrados* shared the family name of Pinto, they were not directly related. Manuel Pinto da Rocha was the son of Amador Pinto and was born in Mesão Frio, while Sebastiao Pinto Lobo was from Leia, the son of Pedro Pinto. AUC, *verbetes de matrícula.* Both attempted to be excused from service in Brazil but to no avail. Their petitions were refused on 31 July 1606. King to Viceroy Dom Pedro de Castilho, BA, 51-VIII-48, f. 95.

31. ANTT, *Chan. Filipe III, Doações,* liv. 13, f. 318.

32. ANTT, *Chan. Filipe III, Doações,* liv. 25, f. 331 (Lisbon, 6 April 1636).

33. ANTT, *Chan Filipe I, Doações,* liv. 23, f. 179v (Lisbon, 10 February 1592); ANTT, *Chan. Filipe II, Doações,* liv. 6, ff. 92v–93 (Lisbon, 23 October 1599), King to Viceroy Bishop D. Afonso de Castelo Branco (? 30 August 1603), AGS, *Sec. Prov.* 1487.

desembargador dos agravos, the crown appointed him *ouvidor geral* and he served in that capacity until 1620, when he became chancellor of the High Court of Brazil. Manuel Pinto da Rocha died in office 1621.[34]

Tracing the public life of Antão de Mesquita de Oliveira is a complicated task for the simple reason that a contemporary of his had the exact same name and was also a member of the legal profession.[35] Nevertheless, it can be established that the Antão de Mesquita who served in Brazil was a native of Guarda and that he had received a degree in canon law from Coimbra in 1601.[36] Upon admission into the royal service, he sought a position on the High Court in Goa by pressing his petition in person at the court in Valladolid. There was, at that time, no opening in India, but the King was disposed to grant the young lawyer an overseas post.[37] Thus, Antão de Mesquita figured from the outset in the nominations for the High Court of Brazil, and unlike his colleagues he made no attempt to be excused, although Bahia was certainly not his preference. He was appointed *desembargador dos agravos* on 26 November 1609.[38]

In Brazil, Antão de Mesquita was one of the most diligent members of the High Court and one of those most trusted by the crown. His severity was famous and did not escape notice in Potrugal.[39] Successful performance of a number of special missions led in April

---

34. Appointment as *ouvidor geral* is registered in ANTT, *Chan. Filipe II, Doações*, liv. 23, f. 90 (Lisbon, 12 March 1609); promotion to chancellor in ANTT, *Chan. Filipe III, Doações*, liv. 1, f. 130 (Lisbon, 4 September 1620). His death in 1621 is noted in *Livro Primeiro . . .* , p. 337.

35. For Antão de Mesquita de Oliveira's namesake, see AGS, *Sec. Prov.* 1487, ff. 75, 100; ANTT, *Chan. Filipe II, Doações*, liv. 3, f. 74; ANTT, *Chan. Ordem de Christo*, liv. 9, f. 14v.

36. AUC, *verbete da matrícula.*

37. King to Viceroy Pedro de Castilho (Valladolid, 11 January 1605), AGS, *Sec. Priv.* 1491, f. 79.

38. ANTT, *Chan. Filipe II, Doações*, liv. 21, f. 26v.

39. Virginia Rau and Maria Fernanda Gomes da Silva, *Os Manuscritos do Arquivo da Casa de Cadaval respeitantes ao Brasil*, 2 vols. (Coimbra, 1955), I, n. 26.

1622 to his promotion to the position of *ouvidor geral*, when that post was left vacant by Manuel Pinto da Rocha's assumption of the chancellor's duties.[40] The death of Manuel Pinto da Rocha in the following year led to Antão de Mesquita's promotion to the chancellor's chair and he was serving in that capacity when the Dutch took the city of Salvador in 1624.[41]

Immediately after the recapture of the city, Antão de Mesquita became involved in a dispute with D. Fadrique of Toledo, General of the Luso-Spanish armada, over jurisdiction in the inquest into the city's fall. The crown ordered Antão de Mesquita to conduct the investigation and considered his presence in Brazil so necessary that he was excused from a special mission to Angola.[42] From 1626 to 1630 Antão de Mesquita remained in Brazil as *ouvidor geral*. A grateful crown rewarded his twenty years of Brazilian service with a position on the Casa da Suplicação on 17 October 1630.[43] Serving in that office, he died in late 1636 or early 1637.[44]

Francisco da Fonseca (Leitão), although nominated as *extravagante*, was appointed *dos agravos* in 1609. Born in 1572, Fonseca was from a noble family and had received a legal education at Coimbra.[45] He served as *juiz de fóra* of Vouzela and the *conselho*

40. ANTT, *Chan. Filipe III, Doações*, liv. 3, f. 151.

41. See below, pp. 218–219.

42. ANTT, *Col. S. Vicente*, liv. 19, king to the Governors of Portugal (Madrid, 7 Aug. 1625), f. 366.

43. ANTT, *Chan. Filipe III, Doações*, liv. 25, f. 105.

44. Antão de Mesquita's daughter was granted entry into a convent on 24 July 1637 in reward for the services of her father "now deceased." ANTT, *Chan. Filipe III, Doações*, liv. 28, f. 72.

45. AUC, *verbete da matrícula*. Fonseca held the title of *moço fidalgo* or page; ANTT, *Chan. Filipe III, Doações*, liv. 11, ff. 105–106. This title (literally, child *fidalgo*) was often conserved even after reaching manhood. The reason for this is explained by a seventeenth-century English observer of Portugal in PRO, State Papers, 9/207, n. 24, f. 592: "There is none can be Moço Fidalgo but he whose ancestors were Fidalgos, therefore on occasion they are called Moços Fidalgos even when they are Fidalgos, because it supposes them to be of Noble descent, de sangue illustre they call it here, whereas there be many Fidalgos who are either themselves made so by the King for some good service or that are but immediate descendants from

of Lafões from 1600 to 1604 and underwent a *residência* without any damage to his reputation.[46] He next served as *juiz de fóra* of Miranda and he was employed there when nominated to the Brazilian High Court. He, too, wished to be excused and pleaded that his poor health—attested to by a doctor's certificate—and his recent marriage made service in Brazil a hardship. Fonseca, however, did not wish to give the impression that he was averse to promotion and he rather slyly suggested service on the Relação do Pôrto instead of the Relação do Brasil.[47] His petition met with the usual refusal. Appointed to the Brazilian High Court on 7 March 1609, Fonseca eventually returned to Portugal, where he served both in Oporto and, after 1629, on the Casa da Suplicação.[48]

Because two of the original nominees never reached Brazil and the plan to have two magistrates already there serve on the court could not be implemented, four men who did not figure in the original discussions were appointed to the High Court. Three of the four—Ruy Mendes de Abreu, Pero de Cascais (de Abreu), and Antônio das Póvoas—took active roles in the High Court and were involved in most of the disputes which resulted from the court's activity. The fourth man, Manoel Jácome Bravo, did not distinguish himself in Brazil but did become an important official after his return to Portugal.

Bravo was a native of Viana do Castelo. He received a bachelor's degree from Coimbra in 1598 and entered royal service as *juiz de fóra* of Monção in 1600.[49] Bravo served in Brazil as *desembargador*

---

such, who are only of no ignoble blood, de Sangue Limpio, that is, as I said before of neither Jewish or Mechanic blood and they are called Fidalgos da caza del rey, that have no other Fidalguia than what the King's book gives them; and they are very much disregarded by the others."

46. ANTT, *Chan. Filipe II, Doações,* liv. 6, f. 142; AGS, *Sec. Prov.* 1476, ff. 201–202.

47. "Memorial de Francisco da Fonseca," AGS, *Sec. Prov.* 1476, f. 201–201v.

48. ANTT, *Chan. Filipe II, Doações,* liv. 20 ff. 134–135; ANTT, *Chan. Filipe III, Doações,* liv. 17, f. 357v.

49. AUC, *verbete da matrícula;* ANTT, *Chan. Filipe II, Doações,* liv. 6.

extravagante for six years and returned to Portugal in 1617, where he served first on the High Court of Oporto and then on the Casa de Suplicação.[50]

By 1628 Bravo had proven his worth in these offices and on a number of special assignments of a judicial nature. The crown therefore placed him on the *câmara* of Lisbon as a *vereador* on 7 June 1628.[51] In 1632 Manoel Jácome Bravo was awarded a benefice in the Order of Christ and in that same year was appointed keeper (*guarda-mór*) of the Torre do Tombo.[52] Philip IV's advisers included him in a secret report drawn up in the late 1630's for the Viceroy of Portugal, Dona Margarida, but at that time he was quite sick. He was considered dependable by the Spanish faction in Portugal.[53]

Because of the failure of Gaspar Pegado to take his position in Brazil, another magistrate of equal stature had to be appointed to

---

50. Bravo could not assume his position on the Oporto High Court until a *devassa* could be made of the actions of the Relação do Brasil; king to Marquis of Alenquer (San Lorenzo, 2 Aug. 1617), AGS, *Sec. Prov.* 1515, f. 53. His appointment to the Casa da Suplicação was registered on 13 September 1621 in ANTT, *Chan. Filipe III, Doações,* liv. 9, f. 69v.

51. He had served on one of the four *juntas dos contos* created in 1627. See AGS, *Sec. Prov.* 1553, f. 295; cf. Virginia Rau, *A Casa dos Contos* (Lisbon, 1951), p. 122. Bravo also served as a special crown investigator in 1629 according to AGS, *Sec Prov.* 1522, f. 72. His appointment to the *câmara* is registered in ANTT, *Chan. Filipe III, Doações,* liv. 22, f. 129v and his service on that body is verified by ACML, liv. 64 (27 June 1630), f. 135.

52. AGS, *Sec. Prov.* 1525 (18 Feb. 1632), f. 38. His position as Keeper of the Torre do Tombo resulted from the vacancy caused by the death of Diogo Castilho Coutinho. Bravo was appointed on 3 October 1632. See AGS, *Sec. Prov.* 1587, f. 182, and ANTT *Chan. Filipe III, Doações,* liv. 25, f. 234. As Keeper of the Torre do Tombo, Bravo penned an excellent report on the state of that archive on 4 March 1634, a copy of which exists as BGUC, Cod. 705, ff. 219–222.

53. "Papel secreto q se deu a Rey de Castella em q. se lhe dá conta da qualidade partes e sufficiencia dos principais ministros de Portugal . . . em tempo da Duquesa de Mantua," BPE, CV/2–19, f. 117v. Another copy exists as "Parecer de Diogo Soares sobre officiais de Portugal," BNL, *Col. Pomb.* 647, ff. 6–7.

assume the important duties of *juiz da coroa*. The man selected was Ruy Mendes de Abreu, son of a desembargador of the Casa da Suplicação, who had been a supporter of Philip II during the crisis of 1580.[54] Ruy Mendes had served as *juiz de fóra* in Campo Maior, Portalegre, Coimbra, and Mertola.[55] His appointment to the High Court of Brazil was accompanied by a habit in the Order of Christ, the promise of a post on the Casa da Suplicação, and assurances that in case of a vacancy in the chancellor's position he would be appointed. This came about in 1611 on the death of Gaspar da Costa.[56] Returning to Portugal in 1620, Ruy Mendes occupied much of his time in an attempt to secure privileges that he felt were due his service and lineage. Although he was made *fidalgo da casa* in 1626, most of his other claims remained unsatisfied.[57]

Antônio das Póvoas and Pedro de Cascais, junior members of the High Court, served as *extravagantes*. The former eventually rose to great heights in the Portuguese administrative bureaucracy

---

54. Ruy Mendes was the son of Antão Mendes de Abreu and Dona Jerônimo Cogominha; ANTT, *Chan. Ordem de Christo*, liv. 14 f. 59v.

55. *Chan. Filipe I, Doações*, liv. 23 (5 Oct. 1591), f. 109–109v. Ruy Mendes is not listed in the *Livros da Chancelaria* of Philip III (II) as *juiz da fóra* of Coimbra, but he is mentioned in that capacity in a letter from the king of 10 March 1595 in AMC, Provisões e Capítulos das Cortes, f. 94; cf. José Branquinho de Carvalho and Armando Carneiro da Silva, *Catálogo dos Manuscritos do Arquivo Municipal* (Coimbra, 1964), p. 212. As *juiz da fóra* of Mertola, see BA, 44-XIII-52, f. 90 as cited in *Manuscritos da Ajuda* (Lisbon, 1966), I, 233.

56. ANTT, *Chan. Filipe II, Doações*, liv. 20, ff. 203v., 204, 205; ANTT, *Chan. Ordem de Christo*, liv. 9, f. 114v.; liv. 14, f. 59; liv. 17, f. 319v. He was promoted to chancellor by a royal letter, see king to Gaspar de Sousa (28 Sept. 1612), AHI, f. 119.

57. Authorized to be sworn into the Order of Christ in 1621, Ruy Mendes must have been in Portugal by that time since the oath had to be administered at the great monastery of Tomar. His struggle to secure privileges dragged on for over seven years, and although he was awarded the title of *fidalgo* his claims remained largely unsatisfied. In order to press his claim, Ruy Mendes went to Madrid, where he obtained the support of the Count-Duke of Olivares, but by 1632 the matter was still undecided. See AGS, *Sec. Prov.* 1583, ff. 287–288; BM, Egerton 1132, f. 31; Consulta del Consejo de Estado (30 May 1626), BM, Egerton 324, f. 95.

and the latter dropped into official oblivion. Born in Midoes, *moço fidalgo* of a prominent family, Antônio das Póvoas entered royal service after his graduation from Coimbra in 1608.[58] At the time of his appointment to the High Court of Brazil, the crown promised him a position in the High Court of Oporto upon his return. In Brazil, das Póvoas displayed particular skill in matters of the treasury and after seven years service he returned to the metropolis, where in 1621 he became a member of the Casa da Suplicação. He was made a member of the Conselho da Fazenda—the Colonial Board—in 1637.[59] On 12 December 1640 he also assumed the duties of *provedor* of the Lisbon Customs House on behalf of his underaged nephew.[60]

After the revolt of 1640, Dom João IV reconfirmed das Póvoas' positions and he aided in financing the early campaigns in Alemtejo

---

58. The das Póvoas family originated in Oporto. One of its early members had been Confessor to Dom João II. The family had acquired the proprietorship of the lucrative position of *provedor dalfândega de Lisboa,* through a fortunate marriage by Diogo Fernandes das Póvoas in the early sixteenth century. Diogo Fernandes das Póvoas had a considerable number of children. His eldest son, Antônio das Póvoas (the elder) went off to North Africa, where he won himself a benefice in the Order of Christ around 1546. In Tangier he married against his father's will and as a result was disinherited when his father passed the office of *provedor da alfândega* to a younger son, Francisco. Disgruntled, Antônio das Póvoas set sail for India with his wife and son. In India his son was killed while fighting in Mangallor and his wife died there or on the voyage back to Portugal. On his return to Portugal Antônio das Póvoas married the daughter of the Chancellor of the Casa da Suplicação. Because of her death, however, he was forced to remarry and it was from this last union that Antônio das Póvoas (the younger) of our story was born.

The above information is from a genealogical manuscript in BGUC, *Cod.* 666, ff. 124–126, which is faulty, however, since it lists Francisco as the father of the younger Antônio das Póvoas. As we have seen, Francisco was not the father but the uncle of Antônio das Póvoas (the younger). Cf. AUC, *Verbete da matrícula;* ANTT, *Chan. Filipe III, Doações,* liv. 29, f. 132v.

59. ANTT, *Chan. Filipe II, Doações,* liv. 20, f. 132; liv. 23, f. 92v.; ANTT, *Chan. Filipe III, Privilégios,* liv. 3, f. 21; ANTT, *Chan. Filipe III, Doações,* liv. 16 ff. 136v–137 (10 Dec. 1626); liv. 29, f. 135 (24 May 1630).

60. ANTT, *Chan. Dom João IV, Doações,* liv. 12, f. 2.

against the Spanish. Das Póvoas had risen to positions of importance in Portugal and was a trusted expert on treasury matters. In Brazil, however, he had been a particularly hotheaded and volatile magistrate who was embroiled in altercations with landowners, the Church, and even other members of the court, especially his colleague Pero de Cascais.[61]

Pero de Cascais, a native of Olivença, had received a bachelor's degree from Coimbra in 1596. Of his early career there is little information available. Appointed for service in Brazil in 1609 he eventually served not only as *extravagante* but also as *ouvidor geral*. At one point he also acted as interim *provedor mór da fazenda*. Pero de Cascais assumed a position in the High Court of Oporto after returning to Portugal, but he does not seem to have advanced in that tribunal. He retired with a pension in 1626.[62] The failure of Pero de Cascais to advance in the royal employ probably resulted from the controversial nature of his actions in Brazil and his marked penchant for argument.

The men selected to serve on the first Brazilian tribunal and those who succeeded them represented the *letrado* class. At least nine of the first ten held degrees in canon or civil law from Coimbra and most had parents, children, or other relatives in the legal profession. Only time and the course of events would tell whether their training and university experience had provided them with an esprit de corps and a common ideological outlook. One thing was certain: they were a breed of man different from the "New Christian" outcasts, the *mestiço* frontiersmen, and the haughty sugar barons who populated the Brazilian colony.

Although historians with the advantage of perspective can see sharp distinctions between the *letrados* and other groups in society, the attitudes and aspirations of the royal magistrates often paralleled

61. ANTT, *Chan. Dom João IV*, *Doações*, liv. 11, f. 135.

62. AUC, *verbete da matrícula;* ANTT, *Chan. Filipe II*, *Doações*, liv. 20, f. 138; liv. 23, f. 93; ANTT, *Chan. Filipe III*, *Doações*, liv. 1, f. 150v.; King to Governor of High Court of Oporto (Madrid, 26 Feb. 1625), AGS, *Sec. Prov.* 1519, f. 13.

those of the old military aristocracy. Some of the desembargadores, like Antônio das Póvoas and Francisco da Fonseca, claimed descent from noble lineage, while others like Ruy Mendes de Abreu and Gaspar da Costa wore the coveted cross of the Order of Christ. But, as *letrados* and royal magistrates their interests were never simply those of the old aristocracy. In many ways they remained tied inextricably to the crown and the maintenance of royal authority. Reasons of both principle and class interest differentiated the *letrados* from other elites in society.

The crown selected for Brazilian service men who had proven their ability. The biographies of these men show them as old Christian, middle-aged lawyers, moving upward in their profession, reputable but not eminent. Most feared that the Brazilian appointment would deprive them of better or more prestigious continental positions, and this fear may also lie behind some of their subsequent actions in Brazil. The magistrates of the first High Court and many of their successors displayed an acute consciousness of precedence and formal procedure which reflected the importance they placed on professional rank. Their constant insistence on respect and deference from others and their haughty demeanor raised the hackles of the less refined but no less sensitive colonials. Despite such differences, the power and prestige of the maigstrates and the favoritism shown them by the crown made alliance with the magistracy particularly attractive to colonial sugar barons, who sought to bolster their own position of economic dominance with the social status and legitimacy of the magistracy. The effect of the High Court, the influence and actions of its members, and the efforts made by other groups and institutions to incorporate this new source of power into the existing socio-political patterns constitute an important part of the history of Brazil in the opening decades of the seventeenth century. The patterns established between the magistracy and society in the period 1609 to 1625 continued into the eighteenth century and typified the nature of these relations.

PART TWO: THE RELAÇÃO IN BRAZIL, 1609-1626

V. BAHIA: THE SOCIAL MILIEU

All who steal not, very poor:
And here you have the city of Bahia.
Gregório de Matos (c. 1670)

Those by the Rio de Janeiro and in the northern captainships are not near so effeminate and corrupted as those by the Bay of All Saints, which being in a climate favorable to indolence and debauchery, the capital city, and one of the oldest settlements, is in all respects worse than any of the others.

Edmund Burke (1758)

During the first century of Brazil's existence as a European colony, various groups and institutions had established patterns of control over the social, political, and economic factors of Brazilian life. The intrusion of a new force, a powerful judicial and administrative organ, would seem certain to disrupt some of these patterns and generate opposition from the offended interests. Rather surprisingly, however, there was little colonial opposition to the creation of a High Court in 1609, and in fact the Relação was seemingly welcomed by most elements of the population.

The reasons for this attitude were complex. Certainly, the long-standing colonial desire to improve the quality of justice cannot be discounted. As we have seen, suggestions for the establishment of a Brazilian tribunal had been made as early as 1562, but accident and administrative inertia had stifled the project. Residents in the colony, however, had never abandoned the idea, and after 1580 they found in the Iberian Union new ways to justify their appeals. After Brazil's formal recognition of Hapsburg sovereignty, proclaimed by the municipal council of Salvador on Assumption Day (19 May) 1582, old Brazil-hands turned to the comparative approach as a tactic of argument.[1] Spanish America made an excellent foil and Brazilian colonists pointed to the *audiencias* of Peru and New Spain as models for Brazil to follow.[2] Whether such tactics took effect is impossible to determine, but in June 1609 the first magistrates of the Relação of Bahia arrived on the docks of Salvador. Magisterial government had come to Brazil. The world into which the magistrates stepped was an exciting and sometimes anarchic one of a European settler-colony in formation. Many of the problems faced by magisterial bureaucracy in Brazil were specifically Brazilian in nature, and in order to understand the subsequent actions of the Relação and its judges we must first examine the fabric of the society in which they operated.

If the colonial empire of Portugal had contributed in any way to Philip II's interest in the acquisition of the Portuguese throne, it was India and certainly not Brazil that stimulated his concern. Although showing signs of increasing economic importance, especially after 1570, Brazil eighty years after its discovery remained the hindquarters of an empire. Its sparse, European population was scattered along the littoral or concentrated around a few urban nodules, vulnerable to attack from hostile Indians and jealous European rivals. Unlike its Spanish American neighbors, Brazil

1. For example, see Fernão Cardim (1604) in *Hakluytus Posthumus, or His Pilgrims*, IV, 1320.

2. The matter of informing Brazil of the change of dynasty was discussed in Spain as early as September 1580. Official notification arrived at Salvador on 16 November 1581. Joaquim Veríssimo Serrão has discussed this incident in *Do Brasil filipino ao Brasil de 1640* (São Paulo, 1968) and he has published some of the pertinent documentation in *Rio de Janeiro*, I, 204–206. The actual letter of recognition is published in *As Gavetas da Torre do Tombo*, 5 vols. to date (Lisbon, 1960), III, n. 2618, 56–57.

could boast of no universities, no printing press, few noble edifices, and little apparent mineral wealth. It was a colonial dependency in the classic sense, a source of raw materials and tropical crops. At first brazilwood used for the tinting of cloth had been the major export, but although in some regions like Pernambuco the export of this dyewood remained an important economic activity through the eighteenth century, the commerce in brazilwood could not itself sustain the colony. Brazil remained until the end of the sixteenth century a deficit to the royal treasury, consuming more in salaries and defense expenditures than it yielded from taxes and imposts.[3] Commercial relations within Brazil were based on barter, not only between whites and Indians but among the Portuguese as well.[4] It was, in fact, the union with Spain that brought Peruvian specie to Brazil after 1585, and the dependence on this source of currency was underlined when, in 1640, the Luso-Spanish union ended and the Portuguese in Brazil were once again reduced to barter.[5]

The seeds of the future, however, were already sown in the form of sugar cane imported in the early sixteenth century from São Tomé. In the fertile soils of the Brazilian coast, especially in the region of Pernambuco and in the black *massapé* soils of the Bahian Recôncavo, the sugar cane began to thrive. The improvement of production techniques, favorable legislation, and a growing European market aided the development of the Brazilian sugar agro-industry and by 1570 the green cane fields had made the Brazilian northeastern coast a land of sugar. The predominance of this crop and the nature of its production exercised considerable influence on the formation of society, the patterns of life, and the administration of government in colonial Brazil.

The production of sugar provided a stimulus for a wide range

3. Roberto Simonsen, *História económica do Brasil, 1500–1820*, 4th ed. (São Paulo, 1962), p. 92.

4. Cf. Alexander Marchant, *From Barter to Slavery: The Economic Relations of Portuguese and Indians in the Settlement of Brazil, 1500–1580*, The Johns Hopkins University Studies in Historical and Political Science, ser. lx, n. 1 (Baltimore, 1942); Vivaldo Coaracy, *O Rio de Janeiro no século dezessete*, 2d ed. (Rio de Janeiro, 1965), p. 39.

5. AHU, Rio de Janeiro, *pap. avul.* caixa 1 (3 October 1642).

of other activities and services. Sugar was a plantation crop, grown on large estates (*fazendas*) and processed in mills (*engenhos*) owned by great landholders. The labor force used for much of the work of these plantations was supplied by slaves, at first by the indigenous Indian population and later by Africans brought from the coasts of West Africa and Angola. The need for slaves and for supplies from Europe promoted an active maritime commerce and ships returned to Europe laden with dyewood and agricultural produce from the colony. More than any other commodity, however, sugar was the economic core of Brazil. The major part of the revenues of Brazil derived from the taxes imposed on the commerce in sugar and slaves, and this source of income paid for the administrative structure of the colony.

Sugar influenced even the situation of the cities of Brazil to some extent. Recife, Bahia, and Rio de Janeiro were ports, urban centers located on some bay or harbor to facilitate the arrival of ships bearing the colonists, slaves, and European commodities, and the freighting of these same vessels with the sugar of the land. It was in these cities that the artisans, merchants, doctors, lawyers, and government officials provided their services to the population, and it was thus only natural that the High Court be established in one of them. For if Brazil in the seventeenth century was an agricultural and rural society, it depended fully on its coastal ports.

By the late sixteenth century the slave-sugar complex had become the motive force of the Portuguese colonies in the South Atlantic and, supplemented by the necessary commerce in European items, it made Brazil an attractive area of legal and illegal trade. Portuguese merchantmen, small overloaded caravels, carried Brazilian sugar to Lisbon, Oporto, or other Portuguese ports, usually those north of the Tagus River. Lisbon, already a major European entrepot, became the center for Brazilian products bought by English, German, or Italian merchants and then reshipped to their respective countries. A ship like the English *Sea Flower* that sailed from Lisbon to London in 1608 carried not only cork and wood from Portugal and spices from India, but also 29 "weights" of brazilwood and 36 crates of sugar from Brazil.[6] Nor was all the direct commerce with Brazil limited to Portuguese bottoms. The account book of Miguel Dias de Santiago, a merchant who shipped sugar from Bahia between 1596 and 1598, listed vessels hailing from Ragusa, Copenhagen, and Malmo carrying sugar from Brazil.[7] Dutch, English, and Hanseatic ships sailed on behalf of Portuguese merchants to carry Brazilian produce. By 1621 there were ten to fifteen ships in the United Netherlands exclusively in the Brazil trade and twenty-nine sugar refineries in Holland. At that time Dutch bottoms carried one-half to one-third of the trade to Brazil.[8]

Although the authorities in Portugal strove to keep the Brazilian trade under metropolitan control by requiring all ships to pay taxes at Lisbon, there was, nevertheless, direct trade with other European nations.[9] English merchants specializing in Iberian commerce sought to establish direct patterns of trade with Brazil and the presence of the *Minion* at Santos in 1580 or the *Merchant Royal* at Olinda in 1583 underlined this desire.[10] The reluctance of local inhabitants to trade with foreigners and the fluctuations of international relations, however, made direct commerce with Brazil virtually impossible for non-Iberians. But what could not be gained by peaceful methods could be won by force.

---

6. License issued 12 August 1608, ANTT, *Corp. cron.* pt. 1, maço 115, doc. 44.

7. PRO, State Papers, Misc. 1/104.

8. Engel Sluiter, "Dutch Maritime Power and the Colonial Status Quo, 1585–1641," *Pacific Historical Review*, XI (1942), 35.

9. Hermann Kellenbenz, "Der Brazilienhandel der Hamburger Portugiesen zur Ende des 16 und in der Ersten Halfte des 17 Jahrhunderts," *III Colóquio internacional de estudos Luso-brasileiros. Actas*, II (Lisbon, 1957), 227–286, indicates that there was direct Hanseatic-Brazil trade from 1587 to 1602, but when Spanish-Dutch hostilities halted, the Portuguese were able to enforce the required passage through Lisbon.

10. Kenneth R. Andrews, *Elizabethan Privateering; English Privateering during the Spanish War, 1585–1603* (Cambridge, 1964), p. 213; C. R. Boxer, "English Shipping in the Brazil Trade, 1640–1665," *Mariner's Mirror*, XXXVI (July 1951), 187–199; Olga Pantaleão, "Um navio ingles no Brasil em 1581: A viagem do *Minion of London*," *Estudos Históricos* (Marília), I (1963), 45–93.

Since the early 1580's English, French, and Dutch privateers sailing under the flag of Dom Antônio, the Portuguese pretender, had raided Iberian shipping. After 1585 the attacks intensified, as the English used the pretext of Spanish seizures of English goods for these maritime depredations. Between 1580 and 1600 Brazil was exporting about 6,400 tons of sugar per year and the ships engaged in this trade were an attractive and easy prey for the enemies of Spain.[11] These Brazilmen were the prize most frequently seized by the English, who between 1588 and 1591 took 34 of them.[12] Nor were the ships laden with sugar the only target. Spanish, Portuguese, and Italian ships carrying European commodities and African slaves were also fair game. For example, the *Ponte*, a Venetian merchantman, fell to the English with a cargo of wine and oil while en route to Brazil.[13] By the second decade of the seventeenth century the losses were staggering. Between 1624 and 1626 the Portuguese lost 120 vessels with 60,000 crates of sugar and other goods—about one-third of their trade with Brazil.[14] Such difficulties of commerce struck at the colonial infrastructure and the uncertainties of trade sent sugar prices spiraling downard, forcing some planters to abandon their mills. Brazilian merchants faced with the dangers of maritime loss sought to protect their position by obtaining the sugar at the lowest possible price or entering into the production phases of the commodity.

The European rivals of Spain and Portugal were not content to seize only the carriers of the trade, and corsairs constantly threatened the coast of Brazil. Freebooters like James Lancaster, who took Pernambuco for a month in 1585, and Paul Van Caarden, who raided Bahia in 1604, made life and commerce precarious for the Portuguese in Brazil. Hence a continual theme in the docu-

---

11. Frédéric Mauro, *Portugal et l'Atlantique* (Paris, 1960), p. 236.

12. Andrews, *Elizabethan Privateering*, p. 211, and the Appendix, pp. 243–273, which lists prizes taken between 1589 and 1598.

13. *CSPF, Venice*, IX, n. 859 (24 February 1599).

14. *Consulta* of Conselho do Estado (23 July 1626), *Arquivo Cadaval,* I, n. 43.

mentation of the period is the maintenance of the militia, the building of fortifications, and the supply of armaments, especially cannon for defense. Attack and fear of attack determined much of the activity of seventeenth-century Brazilians and became the concern of administrative organs such as the Relação. Moreover, the whole question of defense increasingly became a point of contention between residents in Brazil and the metropolitan government, as well as between the Spaniards who thought in strategic and imperial terms and the Portuguese whose horizons were less ample and more mercantile.[15]

The city of Salvador da Bahia de Todos os Santos, capital of Brazil, was a main terminus of the cross-Atlantic trade and a common target for the European interlopers. At the same time, Bahia was an important entrepot of the coastal trade. Sugar from peripheral Ilhéus usually arrived at Bahia and from there was later exported to Europe, while manioc and foodstuffs from Rio de Janeiro were also common items on the wharves of Salvador.[16] Miguel Dias de Santiago listed shipments of cloth, iron, and other European commodities from Bahia to Rio de Janeiro and Espírito Santo.[17] In effect, Salvador stood at the axis of the horizontal trans-Atlantic trade routes and the vertical pattern of the coastal mercantile intercourse.

---

15. Quite soon after 1580 the Portuguese began to blame the depredations of the French, Dutch, and English on the union with Spain. Maritime losses caused considerable unrest. Hieronomo Lippomano, the Venetian ambassador in Spain, reported in 1587 that "complaints of the Portuguese have reached an incredible pitch, they say that never before has a single ship of their fleet been captured and that they are now far worse off than when they had a king of their own." Although there was some cause for this complaint, French and English penetration of the Portuguese empire began before 1580 and although D. Antônio's cause and Anglo-Spanish hostilities intensified this penetration, there is little reason to believe that the Portuguese possessions would have remained inviolate. However, the circumstances of the Dutch attacks, especially after 1621, are more justly attributed to the union with Spain. See *CSPF*, *Venice*, VIII, n. 550, 296; Andrews, *Elizabethan Privateering*, p. 201.

16. Frei Vicente do Salvador, *História*, liv. iv, cap. 34, 332.

17. PRO, State Papers, Misc. 9/104, ff. 6–7.

Part of this coastal trade pattern connected Bahia with the Spanish colony in the Rio de la Plata. The Iberian union created new opportunities for trade between Brazil and the Spanish American colonies, and by 1584 Portuguese ships frequented Buenos Aires. The ability of the Portuguese to supply Negro slaves was an irresistible attraction for the Spanish colonials, who hoped to secure sufficient labor for the mines of Potosí, and even expressed some desire to relieve the Indian population from this work.[18] Portuguese contractors undertook the responsibility of supplying the labor needs of Spanish Americans. Buenos Aires secured permission for a limited commerce with Brazil, but although this legal trade was strictly controlled, the possibilities for illegal commerce continued. Between 1606 and 1626 a thriving contraband trade existed between Brazil and Buenos Aires which brought Negro slaves to the Spanish port while the silver of Peru found its way to Brazil.[19] The contraband trade avoided taxes and duties at both ends of the commerce and thus defrauded the treasury of both crowns. The Hapsburg rulers of Spain and Portugal were most interested in arresting this illegal intercourse, in which treasury officials were often implicated. Suppression of the illegal Brazil-Buenos Aires trade and other treasury abuses was, in fact, one of the duties which the Relação assumed during its existence in Bahia, and one member of the High Court, the *juiz da coroa e fazenda*, was specifically assigned to guard against these infractions.

The mercantile community of Brazil, concentrated in the ports of Recife, Rio de Janeiro, and especially Salvador was not yet the

18. Lic. Cépeda to king (1 November 1590), AGI, Charcas, leg. 17. Cépeda, President of the Audiencia of Charcas, suggested the importation of Black slaves from Brazil, "where there was a great abundance," to work in the mines and thus allow the Indians to raise foodstuffs and cattle. On the Portuguese trade to the Plate, see Rozendo Sampaio Garcia, "Contribuição ao estudo do aprovisionamento de escravos negros da America Espanhola (1580–1640)," *Anais do Museu Paulista* XVI (1962), 7–196.

19. The standard monograph of the Platine trade of Brazil is Alice P. Canabrava, *O comércio português no Rio da Prata: 1580–1640* (São Paulo, 1944). On the Spanish side, see Ricardo Zorroquín Becú, "Orígenes del comercio rioplatense 1580–1620," *Anuario de Historia Argentina*, IV (1943).

powerful political force it would become in the eighteenth century, but by 1600 their shops and warehouses formed a vital part of Brazilian life, of obvious importance in a colony so oriented toward the export of agricultural products. Whether the mercantile community possessed a collective identity in this period and was willing to pursue common goals is unclear. Certainly distinctions existed between shopkeepers and the agents of great import-export firms, but there may have existed enough community of interest to allow some cooperation between these socially disparate elements.[20] Their economic functions and their ties to commerical interests in the metropolis made the Brazilian merchants a potential source of conflict for the Relação, but mercantile opposition to the tribunal remained muted. First, although many merchants did not welcome judicial interference with their lucrative contrabanding activities, loud complaints would only call attention to the clandestine commerce. Then too, the Relação represented an extension of royal power and perhaps an increase in royal protection of the coasts and commerce of the colony. Such a position would benefit the commercial elements in the colony. The merchants, therefore, had something to gain and something to lose by the arrival of the Relação, and they could not openly complain about what they might lose.

Salvador not only housed an active mercantile community but was the administrative nerve center of Brazil and the most important urban area of the young colony. As the seat of the governor, the bishop, and eventually the Relação, Salvador merited its title, "the head of Brazil." The choice of Salvador as the colony's capital had not been haphazard. Although one chronicler believed that Dom João III, the Portuguese king, had selected Bahia because of the "fertility of the land, good airs, marvellous waters, and goodness of the produce," there were other considerations.[21]

20. A. J. R. Russell-Wood, *Fidalgos and Philanthropists: The Santa Casa da Misericórdia of Bahia, 1550–1755* (Berkeley, 1968).

21. Gabriel Soares de Sousa, *Notícia do Brasil*, Pirajá da Silva ed., 2 vols. (São Paulo, 1940), I, 245. This edition contains both the *Roteiro geral* and

The original proprietor of the captaincy, Francisco Pereira Coutinho, failed to cope with colonists' abuse of the Tupinambá Indians or the resultant retaliatory attacks. Although a small settlement was made at Vila Velha and two sugar mills were constructed, the pressure of Indian hostility and factional disputes forced Pereira Coutinho to seek refuge in Ilhéus. While attempting to return to Bahia, Pereira Coutinho and his companions were shipwrecked and subsequently devoured by Indians. Thus, after payment to Pereira Coutinho's heirs, the colony reverted to the crown.[22] Whereas in Pernambuco the Albuquerque Coelho's exercised wide powers as proprietors, and in Rio de Janeiro the Correia de Sá clan reigned, Bahia, unencumbered by a proprietor, presented fewer difficulties of jurisdiction to the crown. Hence, Tomé de Sousa arrived in 1549 with explicit instructions for the establishment of a city on the Bay of All Saints.[23] A dove of peace was selected as the city's emblem—a most inappropriate choice, since the city's history was characterized by internal dissension and foreign attack.

Contemporary opinion differed on the merits of the city's location, for Tomé de Sousa established the new settlement not at Vila Velha, Pereira Coutinho's old colony, but at a site atop a steep escarpment that overlooked the Bay of All Saints.[24] The new city, like its Portuguese and Brazilian counterparts, seemed medieval in appearance. Its winding streets, narrow alleys, and protective walls

---

the *Tratado descritivo* and all future citations are made to it. For discussion of the author and the work, see José Honório Rodrigues, *Historigrafía del Brasil, Siglo XVI* (Mexico, 1957), pp. 51–55.

22. Possession of the captaincy of Bahia was still in dispute in the 1570's between the crown and the heirs of Francisco Pereira Coutinho. See the sentence given in the Casa de Suplicação (Lisbon, 26 March 1576) in *As Gavetas da Torre do Tombo*, II, 649–652.

23. *DHBNR*, XXXV (1937), 3–6.

24. Cf. Soares de Sousa, *Notícia do Brasil*, I, 247; "Enformacion de la provincia del Brasil para Nuestra Padre," in Frédéric Mauro, *Le Brésil au siecle xvii* (Coimbra, 1961), p. 138; Robert S. Smith, "The Arts in Brazil: Baroque Architecture," in *Portugal and Brazil*, Harold Livermore, ed. (Oxford, 1963), p. 349.

resembled the fortress cities of Portugal, and although a rough grid-plan had been imposed on the site, the irregular terrain created its own design. By the end of the sixteenth century the central square contained the buildings of civil government, the governor's palace, the city hall and jail, the customs house, and a royal warehouse. Colonial Bahians had a reputation for piety, and churches and other religious edifices dotted the city. Aside from the cathedral, the See of the Bishop of Brazil, the city also contained monasteries of the Carmelites, Benedictines, Capuchins of the Province of St. Anthony, and the church and hospital of the Misericórdia, the most important lay brotherhood in Brazil. The Jesuits were there too. Most of their efforts were at this time directed toward conversion of the Indians, but their college (secondary school) in Bahia was undoubtedly the best educational institution in the colony. The religious orders supported their establishments by means of cane fields, farms, flocks, and herds in the surrounding area.[25]

Commerce, not religion, dominated the lower city. The docks of Salvador which lay at the foot of the bluff were the center of the captaincy's maritime life. Along the waterfront, sailors, slaves, and stevedores held sway and the area probably bustled with the same activity that is found there today. By 1609 Salvador was not the great and opulent city it became in the eighteenth century, but it stood as the administrative center and maritime entrepot of the colony.[26]

The size of the population of the captaincy of Bahia in the early years of the seventeenth century is difficult to calculate. Gabriel Soares de Sousa, the best contemporary chronicler, esimated 800 householders in the city alone, which with a multiple of five would produce a city population of 4,000 whites. Father Cardim calculated

---

25. AHU, *Códice do Con. da Fazenda*, 432, ff. 162–3v., which is a summary description of the holdings of the religious orders in 1614.

26. Soares de Sousa, *Notícia do Brasil*, I, 256–264, and Marchant, *Barter to Slavery*, pp. 133–135, based on it. For a more graphic idea of the city's appearance and plan, see Luís Silveira, *Ensaio de iconografia das cidades portuguesas do Ultramar*, 4 vols. (Lisbon, 1957), IV, 542–559.

2,000 householders in the captaincy, or about 10,000 whites. The number of slaves and free people of color is still impossible to ascertain, but by this time they already appear to have been a numerous and disorderly element of society.[27] Salvador's function as an administrative and religious center, however, resulted in a higher proportion of whites than in other areas of the captaincy or the colony. Then, too, members of the sugar aristocracy of the outlying districts usually maintained residences in the city. These were required by the need to administer shipping and commercial arrangements and by social custom. Since the conspicuous display of wealth was an acceptable use for riches, appearance in the city to show off jewels, horses, slaves, and finery served a social function.

The lack of suitable demographic sources makes any analysis of the composition of the Bahian population most tenuous. Studies based on the Inquisition records of 1591–1593 indicate that the largest group of Portuguese immigrants to Brazil came from northern Portugal, and that Lisbon and the province of Alentejo also provided considerable numbers.[28] This held true for Bahia where there was also a large number of immigrants from the Atlantic islands and a higher percentage of native-born Brazilians than in Pernambuco.[29] In Bahia the predominance of the north and Lisbon as the Portuguese areas of greatest human contribution was reinforced by the large amount of mercantile traffic between Bahia and Lisbon, Oporto, and Viana do Castelo. The ports of the Algarve—Faro, Tavira, Lagos—appear rarely in the contemporary account

27. Abreu e Brito, *Um inquerito*, p. 9. See the figures in Marchant, *From Barter to Slavery*, p. 125, where using a multiple of nine he calculates 35–40,000 Portuguese in Brazil at this time. Simonsen, *História económica*, p. 271, calculated 100,000 people in Brazil in 1600, of which 30,000 were European. See also Dauril Alden, "The Population of Brazil in the late Eighteenth Century: A Preliminary Survey," *HAHR*, XLIII (May 1963), 173–205.

28. Robert Ricard, "Algunos enseñanzas de los documentos inquistoriales del Brasil (1591–3)," *Anuario de Estudios Americanos*, V (1948), 705–715.

29. Tarcizio do Rêgo Quirino, *Os habitantes do Brasil no fim do século* XVI (Recife, 1966), pp. 18–19; Carlos Ott, *Formação e evolução étnica da cidade do Salvador*, 2 vols. (Salvador, 1955–1957).

books.[30] The demographic dominance of men in the Portuguese population was especially marked in Bahia, and many of those who married in Portugal were unaccompanied by their wives.[31] The numbers of female orphans sent by the crown to rectify this situation were minimal, even though some of the young ladies and strumpets destined for India were diverted to Brazil.[32] Many colonists, both male and female, were *degregados* or exiles who for various reasons had been sent to Brazil. Although many of these exiles were converted Jews who had fallen back to their old faith, not all the *degregados* were errant Semites and Brazil continued into the eighteenth century as a dumping-ground for men like Francisco Pereira, the precentor of a church in Valença, whom the courts exiled to Brazil for five years for a certain "disorder that occurred in a nunnery." [33]

It is fair to say that the Portuguese colonists came from both ends of the social spectrum and that they came predominantly from those regions of Portugal which have always supplied the bulk of immigrants: Minho, Tras-os-Montes, Extremadura, and Alentejo.[34]

---

30. For example, a listing of the sugar shipped from the *engenho* of Sergipe do Conde from 1608 to 1613 indicates the ports of the Lisbon area—Lisbon, Cascais, and Sezimbra—and of the Oporto region—Oporto and Matozinhos—as ports of destination with great frequency. ANTT, *Cart. Jes.*, maço 11, doc. 5.

31. Rêgo Quirino, *Os habitantes*, p. 79.

32. Andrade e Silva *Col. chron.*, I (23 March 1603), 9; Sérgio Buarque de Holanda, "A instituição do govérno geral," *História geral de civilização brasileira*, 5 vols. to date (São Paulo, 1960 f), I, pt. 1, 119.

33. King to Archbishop of Braga (30 April 1604), AGS, *Sec. Prov.* 1488, f. 52.

34. Artur Ramos, *Introdução a antropologia brasileira*, 2 vols. (Rio de Janeiro, 1947), I, 105; Gilberto Freyre, *The Masters and the Slaves*, Samuel Putnam, trans., 2d English language ed. rev. (New York, 1956), pp. 221–222, indicates large numbers of immigrants from southern Portugal among the inhabitants of colonial São Paulo. His inclusion of the area of Portuguese Extremadura (including Lisbon), however, detracts from the validity of this assertion. It is curious to note, however, that the racial theories of Oliveira Vianna as expressed in his *Populações Meridionais do Brasil* (São Paulo, 1938), claiming that the immigrants to southern Brazil were Nordic descendants of the Visigoths, finds some seventeenth-century support in

Like the small number of other Europeans also present in the population, the majority of Portuguese immigrants to Brazil hoped to find opportunities for economic gain and upward social mobility. This society "on the make" presented considerable problems to the institutions of law and order.

One element of the population merits special attention, for although Portuguese it formed a distinct if not always easily distinguishable part of the community. The forced conversion of all Jews in Portugal in 1497 had produced a considerable number of "New Christians," many of whom were less than fervent in their newly adopted faith.[35] Although the crown occasionally attempted to limit New Christian emigration to Brazil and the other overseas territories, these measures were halfhearted. Brazil in fact became a favorite place of banishment for back-sliding New Christians.[36] The connection with Spain after 1580 increased the number of New Christian immigrants in Brazil, but after the first visit of the Holy Office to the colony in 1591–1593, many of these secret Jews fled to Buenos Aires and from there up into Peru.[37] Much of the contraband trade between Brazil and the Rio de la Plata lay in the hands of Portuguese New Christians. In Bahia the New Christian population was well-integrated in the population and in the economic life of the captaincy, where they participated not only in the commercial but also in the agricultural aspects of sugar production.

"Descripción del Brasil," BNM, Ms. 2355, f. 55, in which the women of São Paulo are described as "beautiful, white, and blond like Germans."

35. Alexandre Herculano, *History of the Origins and the Establishment of the Inquisition in Portugal*, trans. John C. Branner, Stanford University Publications in History, Economics, and Political Science, v. i, n. 2 (Stanford, 1926), p. 253.

36. *As Gavetas da Torre do Tombo*, I, 46.

37. Letter to the Inquisitor General (20 April 1620); AGI, Charcas leg. 112; Richard Konetzke, ed., *Colección de documentos para la historia de la formación social de Hispanoamerica, 1493–1810*, 3 vols. to date (Madrid, 1953 f), II, doc. 175; Antonio Vázquez de Espinosa, *Compéndio y descripción de las Indias Occidentales*, Charles U. Clark, ed. (Washington, 1948), par. 1283.

Portuguese policy was discriminatory. It reserved membership in the military orders, grants of *fidalguia*, and most positions in government for Old Christians not tainted with "the race of Jew, Moor, or Mulatto." [38] These same prejudices existed in Brazil; for example, Francisco Lopes, a candidate for the office of *ouvidor* of Paraíba, was discounted because he was a New Christian, and the *câmara* of Rio de Janeiro illegally deposed the *ouvidor* for the same reason.[39] Exceptions to this general policy could be made, however, and were not uncommon. The taint of a Jewish background could be overlooked in return for services rendered, especially those of a financial or military nature. A good Bahian example of how the "defect" could be disregarded is the case of Manuel Serrão Botelho, the son of Lope Botelho, a New Christian who had served with Dom Sebastião in Africa. Manuel Serrão Botelho petitioned and was considered for an office in Bahia because "although a New Christian he is married to an Old Christian and he has shown desire to be considered an Old Christian and his father no longer consorts with New Christians and is an honorable man, as is the supplicant." [40] The population in general, however, despised the New Christians and looked askance at honors awarded them. A Spanish observer noted that "*fidalguia* is a nobility that is greatly esteemed in Portugal when it falls on clean blood but little on people such as these." [41] Antisemitism in Brazil, especially in times of adversity, could attain particularly virulent heights, but to the credit of Portugal in an age of religious intolerance there were always those who felt that the sins of the fathers should not fall upon the sons.[42]

---

38. Petition of Paulo Bezerra (Lisbon, 14 July 1626), AGS, *Sec. Prov.* 1468, ff. 163–166.

39. King to Viceroy Dom Pedro de Castilho (Madrid, 29 November 1612), AGS, *Sec. Prov.* 1506, f. 3; Coaracy, *O Rio de Janeiro*, p. 24.

40. Petition of Manuel Serrão Bothelho (26 June 1617), AHU, Bahia, *pap. avul.* caixa 1; AHU, Códice do Conselho da Fazenda 33, ff. 114–116.

41. Investigation of Ruy Lopez de Veyga, AGS, *Sec. Prov.* 1581, ff. 150–59.

42. *Ibid.* For Portuguese attitudes toward Jews, see J. Mendes dos Remedios, *Os judeus em Portugal* (Coimbra, 1895), 389–409, and the ex-

Generally, the New Christians were in official terms second-class citizens, disliked, distrusted, and discriminated against by their compatriots. In Bahia, however, they were an important element of society, integrated in the population, and wielding an influence beyond their numbers in some sectors of the economy. New Christians were linked to the sugar agro-industry, and Inquisition records show them involved in it as mill owners, tenant farmers, and merchants. Well-connected with their co-religionists in Portugal, the Netherlands, and the Hanseatic cities, the Brazilian New Christians who were crypto-Jews actively engaged in the trade and production of sugar. The clandestine synagogue in Bahia was located, in fact, not in the city of Salvador, but in the sugar-growing district of Matoim.[43]

To the New Christians in Bahia, and especially to the apparently large mercantile sector of that group, the Relação's establishment

---

cellent discussion in I. S. Revah, "Le Plaidoyer en favor des 'Nouveaux-Chretiens' Portugais du licencié Martín González de Cellorigo," *Revue des études juives*, CCXXI (July–December 1963), 279–398. An example of virulent Brazilian anti-semitism occasioned by the fall of Bahia in 1624 is the account left by a Portuguese Franciscan. He placed the entire responsibility of defeat on New Christian treachery and accused them not only of betraying the city but also of revealing hiding places and poisoning the bishop. See RAHM, Colleción Salazar, K-61, ff. 248–9v.

43. Arnold Wiznitzer, "The Jews in the Sugar Industry of Colonial Brazil," *Jewish Social Studies*, XVIII (1956), 189–198; Eduardo d'Oliveira França, "Engenhos colonização e cristãos-novos na Bahia Colonial," *Anais do IV Simpósio Nacional dos Professores Universitários de História* (São Paulo, 1969), 181–241. Kellenbenz, "Der Brasilienhandel," contains information on New Christian trade connections with the Hanseatic ports. On the Jews in colonial Brazil, see Arnold Wiznitzer, *Jews in Colonial Brazil* (New York, 1960); Elias Lipiner, *Os judizantes nas capitanias de cima* (São Paulo, 1969); José Gonsalves Salvador, *Cristãos-Novos, Jesuitas e Inquisição* (São Paulo, 1969). The primary sources on which almost all of the above works are based are the records of the visits of the Inquisition to Brazil in 1591–1593 and 1618. For Bahia see *Primeira visitação do Santo Officio as partes do Brasil, Denunciações da Bahia, 1591–3* (São Paulo, 1925); *Primeira visitação do Santo Officio as partes do Brasil: Confissões da Bahia 1591–3* (Rio de Janeiro, 1935); Eduardo d'Oliveira França and Sonia Siqueira, eds., "Confissões da Bahia, 1618," *Anais do Museu Paulista*, XVII (1963).

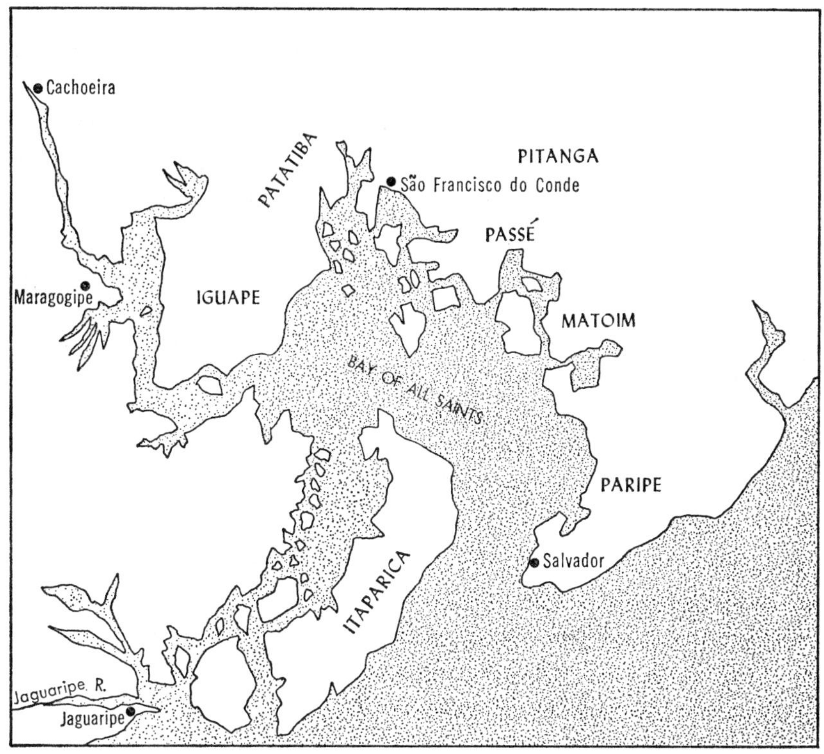

Map 4. The Bay of All Saints and Its Recôncavo

was probably an unwelcome event. Certainly, the control of the contraband trade with Buenos Aires which the Relação could enforce was a disadvantage. Moreover, the magistrates of the Relação were all Old Christians of untainted background, and no breath of scandal implicated any of the desembargadores as Jews. In fact, in 1623, the Relação was considered because of its prestige and religious purity as a possible permanent board of the Inquisition.[44] These magisterial representatives of a discriminatory royal policy,

44. *Consulta* do Con. de Portugal (20 October 1622), BM, Egerton 323, f. 97–7v. It was suggested that the desembargadores of the High Court in Bahia join with the bishop to create a permanent board of the Inquisition in Brazil.

therefore, represented to the New Christians of Bahia stricter controls and more difficult conditions. The role of the Relação in auditing the collection of the tribute levied on the New Christians in 1605 in return for a general pardon was yet another reason for their dislike of the tribunal. But the tenuous position of the New Christians in society and their desire to avoid attention muted their opposition to the Relação. It is fair to note, however, that one of the most judicious yet critical descriptions of the Relação was penned by a New Christian, Ambrósio Fernandes Brandão.[45]

Although the city of Salvador served as the focal point of the captaincy and the urban outlet of a rural society, it was economically dependent on the surrounding countryside. Encircling the Bay of All Saints were lands rich in soils suitable for the cultivation of sugar cane. The area around the Bay, the Recôncavo, stretched from Salvador to Tinharé in a great crescent, and this region provided the economic livelihood of most of the captaincy's population. In the first decade of the seventeenth century about 63 sugar mills (*engenhos*) lay scattered through the Recôncavo or on islands in the Bay. The best lands were planted in sugar, the most lucrative crop, while less suitable soils were given over to other uses. Soil type, fertility, and location determined utilization to a great extent. The best lands produced export crops—sugar if possible, and then ginger, cotton, or tobacco. Marginal lands were given over to subsistence crops, livestock grazing, and firewood. But sugar was a jealous crop, and wherever possible colonists planted the green stalks.

Sugar dominated the region, and most other economic activities were in some way connected with its production.[46] Livestock raising, for example, developed from the sugar agro-industry. The original cattle and horses brought from Cabo Verde multiplied rapidly in Bahia, but the marginal lands assigned in the Recôncavo

45. *Diálogos das Grandezas do Brasil*, José Antônio Gonsalves de Mello, ed. (Recife, 1966); Jaime Cortesão, ed., *Pauliceae Lusitana Monumenta Histórica*, 3 vols. (Lisbon, 1961), II, 16–21.

46. See Mauro, *Portugal et l'Atlantique*, pp. 180–257.

for grazing could not support herds large enough to meet the needs of the *engenhos*. Even a water-powered mill such as Sergipe do Conde had 35 oxen in service in 1591; in the seventeenth century it was calculated that an oxen-powered mill needed at least twelve to fourteen teams of oxen for clearing, cultivating, and harvesting, and three or four teams of six to eight oxen to drive the mill.[47] Horses, on the other hand, had military as well as agricultural utility. The wealthy men of the colony all aspired to a position in the militia cavalry, and horses served a social function as a symbol of status. Brazilian horses, in fact, became an item of export to Angola, where mounted troops proved effective against the Africans.[48] The increasing need for cattle and horses led to an expansion of livestock production into new areas, and the region north of Salvador toward the São Francisco River became a center of livestock raising. This region, Sergipe d'El Rey, settled by Bahian cowboys, was an economic appendage of the sugar mills of the Recôncavo.[49]

The plantation owners acquired their lands in the Recôncavo by grants of land called *sesmarias*, which delineated the parcel of land and granted rights to it in perpetuity. The crown required the recipient of each grant to construct a fortified house and supply arms for the defense of the inhabitants in his area. The size of these *sesmarias* varied, but the stipulation that no one was to receive more land than he could effectively use was often circumvented. Owners, or *sesmeiros*, were required to live on their holdings or in the

---

47. ANTT, *Cart. Jes.*, maço 13, doc. 4; André João Antonil, *Cultura e opulencia do Brasil por suas drogas e minas* (São Paulo, 1923), p. 115. An excellent new edition of this work has been published by Andrée Mansuy, ed., André João Antonil, *Cultura e opulencia do Brasil por suas drogas e minas* (Paris, 1968).

48. Memorial of Luís Mendes de Vasconcellos, 1616; AHU, Angola, *pap. avul.* caixa 1; AHU, *Códice do Con. da Fazenda* 33 (8 May 1621); Abreu e Brito, *Um inquérito*, p. 9; José Alípio Goulart, *O cavalo na formação do Brasil* (Rio de Janeiro, 1964), pp. 41–52, indicates that the import of Brazilian horses in Angola continued in the eighteenth century.

49. Rollie Poppino, "Cattle Industry in Colonial Brazil," *Mid-America*, XXXI, New Series XX (October 1949), n. 4, 224–226.

city of Salvador and the land could not be sold for three years after the original grant.[50] All these regulations, however, were usually disregarded in practice. *Sesmarias*, the extent of available land, the original scarcity of the population, and the agricultural techniques of sugar production all contributed toward the formation of latifundia. This system had important social and political implications, for the landed sugar aristocracy wielded relatively unimpeded power over its tenants, employees, and slaves. The personal relationships on the sugar plantation characterized Brazilian society at large in this era.

In the Recôncavo, the corollary of land was water. Irrigation was unnecessary in the thick rich *massapé* soil, but both livestock and humans needed fresh water. Many *engenhos* stood along the rivers leading into the Bay—the Paraguasú, the Jaguaribe, and the Sergipe—so that water power could be used to run the presses and to facilitate shipment to the city. The role of the Bay itself as an internal means of communication was vital. The sugar was usually shipped to Europe from the wharves of Salvador, and the *engenhos* of the Recôncavo transported their produce to the city in small boats. In his description of the Recôncavo, Gabriel Soares de Sousa estimated that there were over four hundred of these craft and that no *engenho* owned less than four. The Bay provided not only an easy and inexpensive means of communication but sustenance as well. Fish was a staple in the diet of the Portuguese, Indians, and Negroes, and so fishermen were regular employees of the *engenhos*. Whaling was also carried out in the Bay as a royal monopoly rented to private individuals. Based on the island of Itaparica, the whaling industry provided whale meat and oil, the former as a common item in the diet of the slaves and the latter to light the lamps of the colony. The whale fishery, a lucrative industry, tempted at least one magistrate of the Relação to invest in it.

The establishment of an *engenho* was costly. The construction of buildings, machinery, and transport facilities, as well as the purchase and maintance of a labor force, required large capital re-

50. *DHBNR*, LXVIII (1945), 108.

sources.[51] *Engenho* owners remained throughout the seventeenth century dependent on Europe for many commodities, ranging from copper and olive oil to the ubiquitous codfish (*bacalhão*), all of which were items of expense. A large *engenho* like that of Sergipe do Conde could spend up to 60 or 70 *milréis* a year on fish alone, not to mention salt, meat, and other foodstuffs.[52] An item as mundane as firewood could also be costly, to process ten measures of sugar cane the *engenho* needed fifteen measures of firewood, and as the century wore on and the forests were depleted this resource became increasingly difficult to supply.

Slaves provided the labor force of the sugar plantations and purchasing them was a major expenditure. At first, Indian captives supplied plantation labor, and in fact they continued to be used throughout the seventeenth century; but black slaves imported from Africa increasingly provided the labor force of the *engenhos.* In 1600 a female black slave sold in Bahia for about 30 *milréis* and a male for 40 to 45 *milréis.*[53] Thus an *engenho* with 150 slaves had about 6,000 *milréis* committed to its labor force. The union with Spain eventually caused a dearth of Negro slaves in Bahia and prices rose. Portuguese contractors imported cargoes of Africans into Spanish America, where they fetched handsome sums. This resulted in fewer available slaves for Brazil and consequently rising prices.[54] The shortage of Negroes in Brazil led to a return to the Indian as a captive laborer and stimulated new attacks on the indigenous populations, especially in the area of São Paulo. The unfortunate Indians who fell prey to the Paulistas were then sold to the planters of the Recôncavo and Pernambuco.

Sickness decimated the Indians and blacks employed in the

51. Simonsen, *História econômica,* p. 111.

52. ANTT, *Cart. Jes.,* maço 13, doc. 15.

53. PRO, State Papers Misc., 9/104, f. 57.

54. Walter Rodney, "Portuguese Attempts at Monopoly on the Upper Guinea Coast," *Journal of African History,* VI (1965), n. 1, 307–322, presents an excellent discussion of the conflicting European interests in the African slave trade from 1580 to 1640. See also the standard work by Georges Scelle, *La Traite négriere aux Indes de Castille: Contrats et traités d'Assiento,* 2 vols. (Paris, 1906), I, *passim.*

production of sugar. "The workings of the *engenhos* in this state," wrote Bernardo Ribeiro, factor of the *engenho* of Sergipe do Conde, "are very arduous and very expensive, for they depend on slaves that cost a great deal. The work is heavy and many die."[55] Certainly overwork and mistreatment contributed to the death rate of the slaves, but contact with unfamiliar European diseases for which the Indians and Negroes had no natural resistance was even more lethal. Epidemics could, and did, deplete the slave population, as they did in Ilhéus in 1582 and Pernambuco in 1617. The result was often a decline in the sugar production of the area.[56]

If, however, a *senhor de engenho* could survive the perils of fire, flood, drought, theft, animal damage, slave deaths and escapes, Indian attacks, and clamoring creditors, there was prestige, power, and fortune to be had as a sugar baron. The wealthy planters formed a rural aristocracy linked by kinship and common interests.[57] By wealth, status, and influence, the extended families of the sugar planters dominated the captaincies devoted to sugar. In order to protect and further their interests, the planters sought and controlled municipal offices in the coastal cities. In Bahia almost all urban institutions were dominated by the planter elite. The municipal council of Salvador was, in this period, controlled by the planters or the *lavradores de cana*, their tenants, and their retainers.[58] In institutions like the Misericórdia and the exclusive religious brotherhoods such as the Third Order of the Franciscans, the planters also held sway. Nor were they unwilling to serve in positions of royal government. For example, Pedro Viegas Giraldes,

55. ANTT, *Cart. Jes.*, maço 8, doc. 152 (27 September 1605).

56. *Livro Primeiro*, pp. 147–148; ANTT, *Cart. Jes.*, maço 9, doc. 182, which is a letter from Cristóvão Carmo Pereira to the Count of Linhares written from the *engenho* of Sergipe do Conde on 14 March 1608 reporting the death of eight out of a group of twenty-seven slaves. Pereira noted it was only "thanks to God that more did not die given the sickness with which they were afflicted." Thales de Azevedo, *Povoamento da cidade do Salvador* (Bahia, 1949), p. 122, indicates that in 1562–1563, some 30,000 Indians in the area of Bahia were killed by a plague of smallpox.

57. Azevedo, *Povoamento*, pp. 171–174.

58. Boxer, *Portuguese Society*, p. 77, refers to the period after 1625, but his conclusions seem to hold true for the earlier period as well.

who owned a *fazenda* in Pitanga served as Provedor-Mór of Bahia.[59] The examples could be easily multiplied. The Recôncavo dominated the captaincy, and the sugar aristocracy with its satellites dominated the Recôncavo.

The richness of the soils and the seemingly endless expanse of land caused the Brazilian planters to pay little attention to crop rotation, fertilization, or the search for better and cheaper techniques of production, and by the end of the seventeenth century this neglect contributed to the decline of the Brazilian sugar industry. During the first half of the century, however, the Portuguese were the recognized masters of this activity, and their proficiency was noted by the Spaniards who employed them and the English who copied them.[60] From 1580 to 1630 there were usually flush times for the sugar aristocracy, and Brazilian sugar commanded the world market to such an extent that the sugar-producing island of Madeira pleaded for the import of Brazilian sugar merely to attract ships, so that the island's sugars could be sold "under the shadow of those of Brazil." [61]

Although the sugar aristocracy dominated the Recôncavo, neither it nor its slaves were the only inhabitants of the region. The large amount of capital needed to establish an *engenho* forced many free whites to raise sugar cane on behalf of an *engenho*.[62] A large

---

59. ASCMB, *Livro I do Tombo*, 40, ff. 35–35v., 36v.–40; ANTT, *Chan. Filipe II Doações*, liv. 18, ff. 79v.–80.

60. For Portuguese employed in the Mexican sugar industry during the period of the union, see AGI, Casa de Contratación, "Autos sobre bienes de difuntos" as listed in José de la Peña y Cámara, "La participación portuguesa en la obra colonizadora de España en América según la documentación del Archivo General de Indias," *Actas: Congresso internacional de história dos descobrimentos* (Lisbon, 1961), V, 1–53. The English attention to Portuguese methods is noted in Richard Ligon, *A True and Exact History of the Island of Barbadoes* (London, 1657), p. 85.

61. *Consulta* do Con. da Fazenda (Lisbon, 31 July 1613), AGS, *Sec. Prov.* 1472, ff. 284–5.

62. I have written at length on this subject. See Stuart B. Schwartz, "Free Labor in a Slave Economy; The Lavradores de Cana of Colonial Bahia," in Dauril Alden, ed., *Colonial Roots of Modern Brazil: Papers of the Newberry Library Conference* (Berkeley and Los Angeles, 1973).

engenho might have as many as twenty cane growers (*lavradores*) who brought their cane to the *engenho* for processing. A fixed percentage of the sugar produced was divided between the *lavrador* and the *engenho;* usually one-third or one-fifth to the *lavrador* and the rest to the *engenho.*[63] Thus these tenant farmers and sharecroppers formed a numerically important stratum of society whose interests at times diverged from those of the sugar aristocracy. That friction existed between the sugar barons and the tenant farmers is beyond doubt, but the ability of the *lavradores* to own slaves, amass capital, buy land, and hold public office may have served as a check on any overt hostility between them and the great owners.[64]

There was, moreover, another group which assisted in the production of sugar. The sugar agro-industry was a complicated process that required specialized skills and techniques, and many of these were supplied by free wage-earning laborers. An observer in the 1590's noted that the great *engenho* of Sergipe do Conde employed over twenty whites who lived at the expense of the *engenho*, and that such was the case on other *engenhos* of similar size.[65]

---

63. AHU, Bahia, *pap. avul.* caixa 1 "Apontamento das cousas necessarias emmendar e acudir a Cresentamto da Faz. Real." In the late 1630's the agreement between *lavrador* and *engenho* was an equal division of the white and *muscavado* sugar produced. Lesser grades remained the property of the *engenho.* From the *lavrador*'s share of the sugar the *engenho* received one-third or one-fourth depending on the proximity of the *lavrador*'s land to water transportation. See Estevam Pereira, "Descrezão da Fazenda . . . ," *AMP,* IV (1931), 778–784. Adriaen van der Dussen, *Relatório sobre as capitanias conquistadas no Brasil pelos holandeses (1639),* José Antonio Gonçalves de Mello, trans. and ed., Instituto do Açúcar e do Alcool, série história iii (Rio de Janeiro, 1947), pp. 93–94, reported that in Dutch Brazil *lavradores* rented or owned their land and this determined their contract with the *engenho.* He also noted that about twenty slaves, four to eight carts for transport, and several teams of oxen were needed by the *lavrador.* In Bahia the estimate of carts and oxen needed was probably lower due to the availability of water transport.

64. Alice P. Canabrava, "A lavoura canaveira nas Antilhas e no Brasil," *Anais do primeiro congresso da história da Bahia* (1950), IV, 355.

65. ANTT, *Cart. Jes.* maço 13, doc. 15.

These free laborers—some of whom were apparently *mestiços* or mulattoes—served as coopers, calkers, craters, cowboys, and fishermen as well as mechanics and overseers. An overseer could earn as much as 50 *milréis* a year, which was a substantial sum.[66] The sugar master, an employee in charge of the direction of planting and processing, was so important that he was treated with "much pampering" by the *senhor do engenho* and could earn 100 *milréis* a year plus room and board.[67] Unlike the *lavradores*, there seems to have been little opportunity for the wage-earners to gain public office. Within the basic socio-economic structure of masters and slaves, therefore, there existed other important elements of society that sought to further their position through the judicial and political channels of government. To determine how responsive the Relação was to the desires of these various groups is one way to evaluate its impact on Brazil.

The sugar aristocracy was undoubtedly the most powerful element in society and hence stood to lose a great deal by the Relação's disruption of the existing socio-political patterns. Previously, the distance and difficulties of appeal to Portugal placed the wealthy individuals in Brazil in a privileged position. Ties of blood and friendship kept many cases out of court, and those that were appealed to Portugal were often accompanied by a crate of sugar to speed the wheels of justice and sweeten the disposition of venal magistrates. Those who had no crates of sugar to send or well-placed relatives in Portugal to push their interests found justice slow and expensive.[68] The presence of a High Court in Bahia, therefore, represented to the poorer inhabitants of the colony opportunities for judicial redress of grievances previously closed to them. At the same time, the Relação represented a threat to the sugar aristocracy's dominant position.

It was, nevertheless, the sugar planters and tenant farmers who

66. ANTT, *Cart. Jes.* maço 14, doc. 4, Account book of the harvest of 1612 of the *engenho* of Sergipe do Conde.

67. Antonil, *Cultura e opulencia*, 87.

68. *Diálogos dos grandezas*, 31.

were most pleased by the arrival of the Relação in Bahia. Their position, as expressed by the municipal council of Salvador, was to praise the High Court as a protector of "life, property, honor, and liberty" against the depredations of venal governors and crooked magistrates who had conspired to subvert justice. The *câmara*, in fact, wished to "kiss the royal hands" for the singular favor of establishing the Relação in Bahia. The praise of the aldermen became hyperbolic as they lauded the Relação as a work of God which brought to the king the same glory as conservator of Brazil that his ancestors merited as founders of the colony.[69] Although protection from administrative abuses contributed to the Recôncavo's favorable reception of the Relação, there appear to have been other motives which sprang from the commercial nature of colonial Brazil.

The nexus of merchant-planter relations, and conflict, lay in the nature and requirements of sugar production. Dependence on slave labor placed an extraordinary financial burden on the sugar-producing sector of the economy. Both mill owners and cane growers depended increasingly on the constant importation of African slaves for the arduous, backbreaking labor of sugar cultivation. As already noted, the importation of African slaves called for considerable expenditure. The conditions of work and the susceptibility of Africans to sickness in a new disease environment constantly depleted the labor force and created a continuing need for more slaves from Africa. Importation, sickness, overwork, and more importation formed the closed circle of Brazilian slavery. Moreover, as the production of sugar expanded in the early seventeenth century, it created an ever greater need for labor. To acquire the needed replacements, sugar barons and tenant farmers turned to the merchant houses of Salvador for loans or credit.[70] The mer-

69. *Câmara* of Salvador to king (27 January 1610), ANTT, *Corp. cron.* pt. 1, maço 115, doc. 102.

70. These two paragraphs are based on two documents: Governor Diogo de Meneses to king (Bahia, 8 May 1610) in *ABNR*, LVII, 67–71; and ANTT, *Corp. cron.*, pt. 1, maço 115, doc. 105, which is in very fragmentary condition.

chants supplied slaves or other items against the collateral of the forthcoming sugar crop. The merchants were then—at least according to the planters—"cruelly" collecting on these loans and mortgages and forcing payment at exorbitant rates.

In view of this situation, the sugar sector had pleaded to the crown for a three-year debt moratorium and a regulated system of payment with a fixed value on the price of sugar, so that merchants could not continue to manipulate the market and take the sugar at deflated prices. The planters and their retainers had sought royal intercession on their behalf and to them the Relação represented the crown's answer to their predicament. Hence, they were curiously willing and even anxious to support an institution which possessed the potential to undercut their social and political dominance. Perhaps the planter elite hoped that certain social mechanisms would operate to limit the independence of the magistrates and make the Relação receptive to the specific interests of the sugar sector. This, in fact, did come to pass in the late seventeenth century, but before such mechanisms could become fully operative a crisis arose which layed bare a weakness in planter calculations. What the sugar barons had overlooked was that the Relação represented the interests of the crown, not the local aristocracy; and although the tribunal might support planters against merchants, there was no reason to believe, in a conflict between planters and the crown that the Relação would hesitate to support the latter. Such an issue, enslavement of the Indian, arose immediately after the Relação's arrival and within a short time few planters remained willing to "kiss the King's hands" for sending the Relação to Brazil.

VI. JUDGES, JESUITS, AND INDIANS

It is my pleasure and I command that all [Indians] be placed at their liberty and that they be taken immediately from the power of anyone who holds them.

Law of 30 July 1609

Within a year after the Relação arrived in Brazil, a situation arose which threatened the position of the magistrates and the authority of the crown. The crisis revolved on the complex question of Indian slavery, a matter which involved the interests of the colonists, the missionary impulse of the Jesuits, and the moral or theological basis of Portuguese dominion. The Indian and his relationship to colonial state and society was a continuing problem in Brazil, and in 1609 conflicts over Indian enslavement lay bare the interrelationship of the coast and the interior, the colonists and the crown, labor and mineral wealth. It is clear that the arrival of the Relação was intimately linked to Hapsburg Indian policy.

Brazil presented to the Hapsburg rulers of Spain and Portugal the difficulty of reconciling two potentially conflicting goals. On one hand, since the mid-sixteenth century the kings of Spain had tried to limit the colonists' use and abuse of the indigenous population in America. To this end, laws which expressly prohibited enslavement of Indians except in certain circumstances had been promulgated as early as 1512. Perhaps an even more consistent policy of the Hapsburg monarchs was their constant search for precious metals, the be all and end all of a bullionist approach to national economics. Conditions in Brazil made the search for new sources of mineral wealth and the maintenance of Indian liberty contradictory goals, but the first decade of the seventeenth century witnessed considerable activity in both spheres. It was perhaps no accident that the arrival of the Relação in 1609 coincided with this activity.

Much of the setting for the conflict lay beyond the coastal settlements. Stretching westward toward the unknown interior of the continent, the outback, or as the Portuguese always called it, the *sertão*, remained a land of unreduced Indians and unfounded rumors of gold mines and emerald mountains. The example of Spanish Peru, where the silver mountain of Potosí had been discovered in 1545, had not been lost on the Portuguese, who were convinced that similar wealth could be found in their half of the continent. The fabled wealth of the *sertão* pulled adventurous men toward the interior, and with the examples of Potosí and the East African mines of Monomotapa in mind, Portuguese expeditions penetrated into the unknown continent. Colonists in Bahia, Espirito Santo, and especially in São Paulo, where the proximity of Peru provided an added impulse, began in the mid-sixteenth century their search for wealth in the interior.[1] Until the very end of the seventeenth century their quest proved futile, but during the period 1580–1640 the movement into the *sertão* took on a new importance. The Spanish connection created new opportunities.

Colonists in Brazil hoped to profit from the crown's interest in the discovery of new mines. The story of Gabriel Soares de Sousa is a case in point. Soares de Sousa had spent sixteen years in Brazil

---

1. *Diálogos das grandezas*, p. 5; J. Capistrano de Abreu, *Caminhos antigos e povoamento do Brasil*, 2nd ed. (Rio de Janeiro, 1960). An excellent discussion of the effect of Potosí on Brazilian exploration is presented by Sérgio Buarque de Holanda in *Visão do Paraíso* (Rio de Janeiro, 1959) especially Chapter IV, "O outro Peru," pp. 78–123.

and had become a wealthy Bahian sugar planter. Enthralled by stories of fabulous riches in the *sertão* he went directly to Madrid to plead for privileges and legal rights to the mines he was "about to discover." While lobbying on his own behalf, Soares de Sousa penned his *Tratado* as a promotional treatise aimed at securing royal support for his expedition into the *sertão* of the São Francisco River. This work is generally considered for its detail and accuracy to be the most valuable description of sixteenth-century Brazil. In 1591 the crown finally conceded wide powers to de Sousa making him governor and captain-general of the Conquest and Mines of São Francisco with broad powers to appoint officials, use convict labor, and take Indians from the Jesuit villages for use in the mines. The expedition was a total failure. Gabriel Soares died in the *sertão* and his bones were finally laid to rest in Salvador under a tombstone that said simply, "Here lies a Sinner." [2]

Although the Soares de Sousa venture had failed, neither the crown nor the Portuguese had abandoned the quest for mines. His example had shown that broad concessions could be extracted from the crown by only the promise to discover mines. Others were not slow to follow his lead. Luís Mendes de Vasconcellos, the Governor of Angola, wished to open mines in his colony and he petitioned the crown for the same privileges that had been granted to Gabriel Soares de Sousa," a native of Brazil and a person of very different [lesser] quality." [3]

More important, however, the Governor of Brazil had taken great interest in Soares de Sousa's expedition and in the exploitation of mineral wealth in the colony. In 1598 Francisco de Sousa had sailed southward from Bahia accompanied by two German mining experts. Although he stopped at Espirito Santo to send out

2. "Penetração das terras bahianas," *Annaes do Archivo Público e Museu da Bahia,* VI, VII (1920); AGS, *Sec. Prov.* 1466, ff. 288–290, which is the *alvará* and *regimento* given to Soares de Sousa. Cf. Varnhagen, *História geral,* II, note ii, 70–84.

3. Memorial of Luís Mendes de Vasconcellos, AHU, Angola *pap. avul.* caixa 1 (1616). He was mistaken. Soares de Sousa was a native of Portugal.

Diogo Martins Cão to search for precious stones, his real interests lay further to the south, in the mining possibilities near São Paulo. In 1602, while still inspecting the area around São Paulo, Francisco de Sousa received notice of his replacement by the new governor, Diogo Botelho. Returning to Portugal, Francisco de Sousa began to agitate for privileges that would enable him to exploit the mines of southern Brazil. At the same time others in Brazil were trying to extract some benefit from these rather tenuous mines.[4]

By March 1607, the councils of government were ready to hear Francisco de Sousa's plans for the mines of southern Brazil.[5] The success of his proposal in obtaining royal support reflected not only Spanish interest in new sources of mineral wealth but also the amount of administrative and judicial powers that the crown was willing to cede in order to obtain them. This willingness naturally had results which influenced the jurisdiction of the Relação in Bahia, for Francisco de Sousa's plan resulted in an administrative division of Brazil.

Like the governor of Angola, Francisco de Sousa asked for the privileges that had been extended to Gabriel Soares de Sousa. Moreover, to avoid jurisdictional and administrative conflict, de Sousa suggested that he be made governor over the southern captaincies of Espirito Santo, Rio de Janeiro, and São Vicente, and that these be separated from the rest of Brazil. He also suggested

4. During the governorship of Diogo Botelho (1603–1607) a number of men were sent to southern Brazil to ascertain the existence and value of mines in that region. Among these investigators were Francisco Sutil de Siqueira, Diogo de Quadros, who became *provedor* of the mines for six years, and Jácome de Eraso, a Biscayan expert sent from Spain. AGS, *Sec. Prov.* 1462, n. 19; 1463 (20 August 1602), (30 October 1602), (February 1603); 1466, ff. 316–317; 1467, ff. 154–159; 1489, f. 18v.

5. This petition, based on a manuscript in the Castel-Melhor collection in Brazil, has been published in Varnhagen, *História geral,* II, 124–128, with other pertinent documents. The version of this petition and the comments of the councils of government found in AGS, *Sec. Prov.* 1466, ff. 299–310, 216–217, 321–325v., is more detailed and differs slightly in form if not in substance.

that a separate tribunal be established in the southern captaincies to serve as a High Court. Such a proposal would have made these territories completely independent of Bahia. The councils of government in both Spain and Portugal rejected the judicial separation of the southern captaincies and the establishment of a High Court there. They did agree, however, that the area should have a separate *ouvidor geral,* although appeals from his decisions were to be submitted to the Relação of Bahia.

Although provided with an independent executive officer, the new government of the southern captaincies remained judicially subject to the Relação of Bahia, which had the power to review procedure and performance in the southern captaincies. The Relação of Bahia became, in effect, the only administrative control which the State of Brazil maintained over the southern captaincies, which were officially separated in 1608. Such dependence on the judiciary to maintain the lines of administrative control became a constant feature of Brazilian colonial government. By the eighteenth century viceroys often exercised little authority in subordinate areas and found their own freedom of movement circumscribed by law.[6] The royal magistracy maintained its hierarchical organization, its lines of communication, and its authority, and even though the quality of the judicial system diminished in backwater areas, the magistracy often provided the administrative bands which held the imperial structure together.

Perhaps some of Francisco de Sousa's success in obtaining his goals was due to the considerable emphasis he placed on the use of Spaniards, Spanish experience, and Spanish forms in exploiting the Brazilian mines. He advocated the use of gold miners brought from Chile, silver miners from Peru, an expert in pearls from the island of Margarita, and an iron mining expert from Viscaya to aid in the extraction of wealth from the newly created state. Francisco de Sousa wanted the statutes governing mining in his area to be those instituted in Peru by Viceroy Francisco de Toledo

6. Alden, *Royal Government,* pp. 30–44.

(1567–1581), and he wanted a tax structure similar to that in use in New Spain.[7] To supply this enterprise Governor de Sousa asked for permission to send three ships a year to Buenos Aires for wheat and for llamas (*carneiros de carga*) "to climb the mountains of gold and silver." [8] Francisco de Sousa's petition reveals some knowledge of Spanish American realities and interest in creating similar situations in Brazil by appealing to various Hapsburg interests. The Portuguese in Brazil, in fact, were not unwilling to play off these interests in hopes of attaining goals contrary to stated royal policy.

It was an explicit policy of the Spanish Hapsburgs that the Indians of the New World were free men and were not to be unjustly enslaved. The desire to procure Indian labor, however, was strong among the colonists in Brazil. Francisco de Sousa had advocated the use of Indian labor in the mines of southern Brazil according to the laws of Peru. At about the same time, two Bahians, Domingo de Araújo and Belchior Dias Moreia, had asked for similar rights to exploit mines in the São Francisco River valley, but in response to their proposal the Conselho de Portugal noted that the expeditions of Gabriel Soares de Sousa and others to discover mines had resulted in nothing more than attempts to bring Indian slaves out of the *sertão*, and that these two supplicants were rich men who could gain as much by bringing back Indians as by discovering mines. When Francisco de Sousa submitted a similar plea, Philip III noted with his own hand in the margin of the *Consulta* that "it should be made very clear that no force or violence" was to be used for the bringing in of Indians. Clearly, the crown was trying to reconcile the two goals or at least to assuage its conscience.[9] It was obvious

7. Toledo's mining code was promulgated in 1574. It regulated the wages, working conditions, and hours of the Indians. In 1584 a general mining law, the *Nuevo Caderno*, based on Toledo's code, was issued for use in the New World and was applied in New Spain. See Arthur F. Zimmerman, *Francisco de Toledo* (Caldwell, Idaho, 1938), pp. 183–185.

8. AGS, *Sec. Prov.* 1466, ff. 321–325v.

9. *Consulta* of Junta de Fazenda de Portugal, AGS, *Sec. Prov.* 1466, f. 284; *Consulta* of Conselho de Portugal and Junta da Fazenda de Portugal, AGS, *Sec. Prov.* 1466, 299–310. The king's marginal notation read "vay esto

that some Portuguese in Brazil hoped that the Hapsburg desire for mineral wealth might be used to circumvent Hapsburg Indian policy.

The quest for the mines was therefore not entirely divorced from another and far more complex matter—the freedom of the Indians. The *sertão* was not only the realm of rumor but also the domain of the unreduced Indian tribes, which continued to pose a threat to the settled regions and which as late as the 1670's raided the plantations of the Recôncavo.[10] In the area of Bahia the tribes had been in flux long before the arrival of the Portuguese and constant warfare between tribes and branches of the same tribe was the cause of continuing dislocation. The coming of the Portuguese, however, had intensified the migratory and military movements of the Indians by forcing the Tupinambá out of the Recôncavo and into the *sertão*.[11] The numbers and hostility of the Indians in the Bahian bush—and the same could be said for the rest of Brazil—deterred the expansion of the settled area, and although occasional flying-columns of missionaries, explorers, prospectors, and slave raiders ventured beyond the littoral, the dangers of nature and hostile Indians made permanent settlement almost impossible in the *sertão*. The settled frontier was, in effect, closed.

Portuguese relations with the Indians remained a principal problem with moral, theological, political, and economic ramifications in the early years of the seventeenth century.[12] It became the first

---

muy declarado de escusar toda fuerça e violencia." Also see the discussion of the project in Pedro Calmon, *O segredo das minas da prata* (Rio de Janeiro, 1950).

10. Petition of Maria de Távora and the heirs of Afonso Furtado de Mendonça (1673), ANTT, *Col. São Vivente*, liv. 13, f. 264.

11. Butler, "Mem de Sá," p. 120; Soares de Sousa, *Notícia do Brasil*, II, 290–305. On Indian migrations, see Florestan Fernandes, *A organização social dos Tupinambas* (São Paulo, 1948); A. Metraux, *Migrations historiques des Tupi-Guarani* (n.p., 1927), pp. 1–10.

12. For a succinct survey, see Dauril Alden, "Black Robes versus White Settlers: The Struggle for 'Freedom of the Indians' in Colonial Brazil," in Howard Peckham and Charles Gibson, eds., *Attitudes of Colonial Powers toward the American Indian* (Salt Lake City, 1969), pp. 19–46.

major problem with which the Relação of Bahia was forced to deal. Enslavement of the Indians in Brazil had come slowly as the original system of barter had atrophied, and the growing labor needs of the sugar plantations increased. But the enslavement of free men, no matter how savage by European standards, involved a moral problem, and in 1570 King Sebastião promulgated the first Portuguese legislation designed to regulate Portuguese-Indian relations. This law prohibited the capture and enslavement of Indians unless taken in "just war." [13] The law was reinforced in 1574 when the Governor of the North, Luís Brito de Almeida, and the Governor of the South, Antônio de Salema, met in Bahia and agreed to enforce royal Indian policy.[14]

The Jesuits consistently upheld the cause of Indian liberty and opposed enslavement, and this policy earned them the enmity of many colonists. Members of the Society of Jesus organized Indian villages along the coast and near settled areas and hoped by constant instruction and communal organization to indoctrinate their Indian charges. In 1600 there were by Jesuit count 50,000 Indians gathered in 150 *aldeias,* four of which were located near the city of Bahia.[15] The Jesuits argued that by converting these heathens to Catholicism, their control of the Indians benefited the royal conscience while it strengthened the defensive structure of the colony by providing an auxiliary force of Indian archers to be used against foreign interlopers, hostile Indians, and rebellious slaves. Colonists who advocated lay control of the Indians spoke of the civilizing

---

13. The question of "just war" or when war could be waged on the Indians is treated in Kieman, *Indian Policy,* pp. 5–7, and more fully in Lewis Hanke, *The Spanish Struggle for Justice in the Conquest of America* (Philadelphia, 1949), pp. 133–146. In Brazil the most common justification of war against the Indians was their attack on Europeans or the practice of cannibalism.

14. BPE, CXV/2–16, contains the ten-point agreement on Indian policy.

15. Petition of the Provincial and Company of Jesus of the Province of Brazil (1601), AGS, *Sec. Prov.* 1461. The *aldeias* near Salvador were named Espirito Santo, São João, Santa Cruz, Santo Antônio, and São Sebastião. Cf. Leite, *HCJB,* V, 261–269.

effect of forcing the savages to live among the Portuguese, and the colonists were no less disposed to emphasize the defensive utility argument so appealing to the Spanish kings.[16]

Labor, however, was the key to the problem. Even the Jesuits, whose primary concern was spiritual, emphasized that their *aldeias* provided pools of free-laborers which could be used by the colonists "to benefit the farms and *engenhos* of the Portuguese." [17] Bahian planters were not averse to using free Indian labor contracted in the Jesuit villages or in non-supervised Indian settlements, because this entailed neither long-term capital investment nor the hazards and responsibilities of ownership. Some of them, like Gaspar da Cunha, overseer of the *engenho* of Sergipe do Conde, felt that "Negroes are neither as necessary nor as beneficial to the *engenho* as the Indians of the land"; he wanted *aldeias* placed near the *engenho* to provide workers and protection.[18] The location of Indian villages thus became another aspect of the problem, and while the colonists agitated for the advantageous placement of these villages, the Jesuits argued against disrupting existing patterns of Indian settlement. The sugar planters were not at first dedicated to eliminating the communal villages on the periphery of their plantations which could provide a free labor force, but experience eventually demonstrated to them that this arrangement was undesirable because control of the labor force rested ultimately in the hands of the Jesuits. The planters did not treat the free Indians much differently from the slaves, and increasing Jesuit objections placed greater limitations on the planters.

Mistreatment of the Indians, and continuing misuse of the "just

---

16. Diogo de Campos Moreno, *Livro que da rezão do Estado do Brasil* (1612), Helio Vianna, ed. (Recife, 1955), pp. 113–114, for lay arguments against Jesuit control of Indians.

17. AGS, *Sec. Prov.* 1461 (1601).

18. Gaspar da Cunha to Count of Linhares (Bahia, 28 August 1585), ANTT, *Cart. Jes.* maço 8, doc. 9. Governor Diogo de Meneses wrote to the crown from Olinda on 23 August 1608 that free Indian labor was a great benefit because "this state will not need so many Negroes from Guiné, who are the greatest cause of the poverty of men since everything is spent in their purchase." *ABNR*, LVII, 39.

war" clause as a means of circumventing the law to enslave them, called forth new royal action against the colonists in 1595.[19] By that time Brazil was under Hapsburg control and Philip II was already experienced with the problems colonist-Indian relations because the question had been long and hotly debated in Spanish America for almost a century. There, despite occasional violations, the crown had come down fully in favor of Indian liberty. In formulating the law of 1595, the crown gathered opinions from Jesuit Father Gaspar Beliarte, from the former *ouvidores gerais* Cosme Rangel and Martim Leitão, and from the governors of Portugal. Their discussions resulted in the new law which defined "just war" as consisting only of actions authorized by the crown, insisted that wages be paid to Indian laborers, and commanded the governor, magistrates, and captains in the colony to enforce the statute. At the same time the crown issued an accompanying decree which gave the Jesuits the right to bring Indians from the *sertão* into villages under control of the Black Robes. Colonists could hire Indians, but they could not employ them for more than two months at a time and a special magistrate, a lay Portuguese, would adjudicate all disputes arising between Indians and whites.[20]

---

19. Agostinho Marques Perdigão Malheiro, *A escravidão no Brasil*, 3 parts in 1 volume (Rio de Janeiro, 1866), II, 44. The first Hapsburg Indian legislation in Brazil was the law of 22 August 1587, which restated the law of 1570 and provided against the enslavement of those Indians working for the Portuguese. The best summary of Portuguese-Indian relations under the Hapsburgs is found in Georg Thomas, *Die portugiesische Indianerpolitik in Brasilien, 1500–1640* (Berlin, 1968), pp. 78–158.

20. The opinions are found in BA, 44-XIV-6, ff. 179–181, 185–193v. The law and the accompanying *alvará* are printed in full in Albuquerque Felner, *Angola*, pp. 484–486. The creation of magistrates for Indian affairs did not apparently conflict with the already existing office of *mamposteiros*. By the end of the sixteenth century, the office of *mamposteiro* was usually held in conjunction with some other position such as *provedor dos difuntos*, which in turn was often filled by the *juiz ordinário*. The effectiveness of the *mamposteiro* in aiding the Indians was by the early seventeenth century doubtful. Amaro da Cruz Pôrto Carreiro, for example, applied for the position of *mamposteiro* in 1603, yet in 1591 he had been denounced to the Inquisition for stating that the Indians had no souls. Cf. Andrade e

The law of 1595 was reinforced in 1605 by a simple restatement of Indian liberty occasioned by continuing colonist disregard of existing statutes.[21]

These laws should have made clear to the Brazilian colonists that Hapsburg policy toward Indian liberty in Brazil would run parallel to, if not duplicate, the policies implemented in Spanish America. There, the crown had long since declared the freedom of the Indian in law and had moved away from awarding grants of groups of Indians who provided labor or tribute to individual colonists (a system known as the *encomienda*) toward the *repartimiento*, a type of conscripted but paid labor. The *encomienda* had reached a high point in the 1540's, and although it continued into the seventeenth century and some places beyond, the crown had made it quite clear that for political, moral, and demographic reasons it wanted this institution to wither away.[22] Nevertheless, Governor Diogo Botelho apparently had the Spanish American *encomienda* in mind in 1605 when he asked that Indians in Brazil be controlled under the same system in use in the Spanish Indies and that a copy of the proper laws be forwarded to him with haste. The *encomienda* became a highly desired but often poorly understood goal of the colonists in Brazil. It found ardent advocates in men like Bento Maciel Parente, an experienced Indian fighter and soldier in Maranhão, who wrote a number of memorials explicitly asking for the establishment of the *encomienda* in Brazil.[23]

Silva, *Col. Chron.*, I, 294; *Denunciações da Bahia*, 1591, p. 551. See also, ANTT, *Chan. Filipe II Doações*, liv. 12, ff. 193v–194v.; liv. 18 f. 329.

21. Andrade e Silva, *Col. Chron.*, I, 129. In the previous years (1604) some thought had been given to the placing of secular clergy in the *aldeias* to replace the Jesuits. The idea, generated by a letter from Governor Diogo Botelho, did not gain much support. ANTT, *Mesa da Con.* liv. 18, f. 60–60v.; AGS, *Sec. Prov.* 1488, ff. 54v–56.

22. BA, 51-VII-7, f. 37v.; *RIHGB*, LXXIII, 5; Leite, *HCJB*, V, 4. The *encomienda* was a grant of labor or tribute from a specific group of Indians given to a colonist in return for certain services, such as Christianizing his charges. This grant did not include land.

23. Bento Maciel Parente was a constant advocate of the establishment of *encomiendas* in Brazil. See AHU, Pará *pap. avul.*, caixa 1 (10 January 1635); AHU, Codice do Con. da Fazenda 41, ff. 226–229 (3 January

The idea never died and it flourished especially in the Amazon region, where in a sense it bore bitter fruit in the Directory System established in the late eighteenth century, and in São Paulo, where lay control over the Indians was established in 1696.[24] During the Hapsburg period, however, pleas for the *encomienda* fell on barren soil and displayed the colonists' lack of perception of the crown's intentions. Moreover, Jesuit advocacy of Indian freedom and Jesuit control of the *aldeias* did not abate, and hostility between the sugar planters and the Fathers continued to grow. Since royal policy favored the Jesuits, they were anxious to strengthen the crown's authority in the colony as a way of reinforcing their own position. Father Fernão Cardim, in his appeal for the establishment of a High Court in Brazil, underlined the role of such a tribunal in controlling abuses against the Indians and in interpreting the "just war" clause fairly.[25] Father Cardim and his fellow Jesuits also saw the Relação as a potential ally. The sugar planters hoped to use it against the merchants, and the Jesuits hoped to use it as a buttress against the planters.

The Indian question turned Brazil into a cauldron of conflicting interests held by the crown, the Jesuits, and the colonists. The Relação arrived at Bahia in June of 1609, and almost immediately the kettle boiled over. Portuguese colonists only superficially understood the moral and theological bases of Hapsburg Indian policy, and despite the crown's attempts to limit the *encomienda* and reform the *repartimiento* in the Spanish Indies, Brazilian sugar planters still imagined that the *encomienda* in its pristine form might be established in Brazil.[26] Such a view seemed to ignore the

---

1636); Candido Mendes de Almeida, *Memórias para a história do extinto Estado do Maranhão,* 2 vols. (Rio de Janeiro, 1860, 1874), II, "Petição dirigida pelo Capitão mór Bento Maciel Parente ao Rei de Portugal, D. Philippe III," 35–27; José Honório Rodrigues, *Historiografía del siglo XVII,* pp. 45–48.

24. Alden, "Black Robes," pp. 34–36.

25. Samuel Purchas, *Hakluytus Posthumous, or His Pilgrims,* IV, 1323.

26. On the *repartimiento,* see Lesley B. Simpson, *Studies on the Administration of the Indians of New Spain,* Ibero-Americana 13 (Berkeley, 1938).

crown's increasingly determined defense of Indian liberty as expressed in the laws of 1587, 1595, and 1605.

In 1609 Philip III considered the Indian question in both his empires. In May he issued an ordinance for the control and regulation of the *repartimiento* in New Spain, recognizing it as a necessary evil but stating that it was to be used only in activities that benefited the common good. In Mexico the *audiencia* had cautiously employed the old and established solution of acceptance but noncompliance, and the ordinance was shelved lest it provoke a hostile response from the colonists.[27] In Brazil, however, the newly arrived Relação did not exercise similar caution. In Madrid on 30 July 1609, a new law was issued designed to "close the door" to the excesses and abuses in the enslavement of the indigenous population of Brazil. This law declared that all Indians, Christian or pagan, were by nature free men and entitled to wages for their labor. The law ceded to the Jesuits permission to bring Indians from the bush to the settled areas and to maintain them in villages under Jesuit control. The Jesuits, too, were constrained to pay wages for work performed. Within each village a special magistrate was to be appointed by the governor and the chancellor of the Relação to adjudicate disputes between whites and Indians. Most important, the law declared that all Indians illegally captured were to be set free and that all bills of sale or judicial decisions which justified their enslavement were now considered contrary to law and therefore null and void.[28] No complaint or appeal of any kind against this ruling would be entertained by the crown. The law placed much of the burden of enforcement on the Relação, "which is now going to Brazil (que ora vai ao Brasil)," and it required the chancellor to insure compliance by means of an annual investigation in which all violators were to be quickly and summarily punished. The law was most likely formulated before the Relação arrived in Bahia in June 1609, and one is tempted to speculate that the crown waited for the magistrates to land in Brazil before issuing

27. *Ibid.*, pp. 11–17, 129–140.
28. Andrade e Silva, *Col. Chron.*, I, 271–273.

the controversial ordinance. This was hardly a tactic designed to win popularity for the Relação.

But it was a tactic which had been used before. On more than one occasion in the Indies, Spanish kings had correlated the publication of new and controversial laws with the arrival of high-ranking officials or the establishment of a tribunal. Royal attempts to control the *encomienda* in Mexico were made through the Audiencia which arrived in Mexico City in 1528, and upon its dismal failure with the second Audiencia of 1530.[29] The New Laws of 1542 which placed severe limitations on colonist control of the Indians called for similar measures throughout the Spanish empire in America. In Peru, promulgation of the New Laws was accompanied by the arrival of an *audiencia* and of Viceroy Blasco Nuñez de la Vela. Both the tribunal and the viceroy carried specific instructions to enforce these statutes. The establishment of the Audiencia de los Confines (Guatemala) and the visit to Mexico by a royal investigator, Francisco de Tello de Sandoval, were also intimately linked to the enforcement of the New Laws.[30] Given the past history of this tactic, the arrival of the Relação in June and the publication of the law in July seem more than coincidental. Certainly, the text of the law indicates that the Relação was to play a significant role in enforcing its provisions. After the stillborn attempt of 1588 and the fruitless discussions of 1590 the idea of sending a tribunal to Brazil had been abandoned. One is tempted to speculate that the idea was revitalized after 1605 because Philip III needed a powerful agency to enforce his Indian policy.[31]

29. For an adequate account of the role of the Mexican *audiencia* in the enforcement of royal Indian policy, see Lesley Byrd Simpson, *The Encomienda in New Spain* (Berkeley, 1950), pp. 73–110.

30. On the New Laws in general, see Mario Góngora, *El estado en el derecho indiano* (Santiago de Chile, 1951), 115–132. Cf. F. A. Kirkpatrick, *The Spanish Conquistadores* (Cleveland, 1946), which gives a brief summary of the Peruvian tribunal's arrival; William L. Sherman, "Indian Slavery and the Cerrato Reforms," *HAHR*, LI (February 1971), pp. 25–50 on Guatemala.

31. It has been pointed out in Chapter Three that plans to send the Relação to Brazil had begun in January 1605. Until more is known about

In view of previous legislation, this new and stringent law of 1609 should have come as no shock, but when the colonists learned of it, they reacted violently. In Rio de Janeiro there was an ominous threat of rioting, and in Paraíba the *câmara* of Philipéa openly charged Spanish interference, claiming that the law was "made and formulated in the kingdom of Castile," and that it had little applicability in Brazil.[32] Colonists who had repeatedly pointed to Spanish examples while trying to have the *encomienda* established, now faced with an unpopular law, did an immediate about-face and claimed that Spanish usage and precedent were inapplicable in Brazil.

The most violent reaction came in Bahia.[33] Revelation of the law by the Relação to the *câmara* precipitated a stormy meeting of the municipal council on the afternoon of 28 June 1610. A riotous demonstration led by the aldermen and magistrates took place; the *câmara*'s attorney, Gaspar Gonçalves, played a major role as an agitator. The Jesuits were considered sponsors of the law and thus the mob's wrath fell primarily on them. It was suggested that the Fathers be forcibly expelled from the city—a tactic later to be used against them in São Paulo and Maranhão. While the *câmara* made an official protest to the governor and to Gaspar da Costa, chancellor of the Relação, the mob shouted their objections in front of the government buildings. Proceeding to the Jesuit college, the crowd staged a similar demonstration, which the Jesuits tried to calm by denying any role in the formation of the law.

On the next day a representative of the *câmara*, Jorge Lopes da

---

the formulation of the Indian law of 1609, it is impossible to ascertain the extent to which the law stimulated renewed interest in the Relação, or whether the proposed dispatch of the Relação presented the crown with a new opportunity to promulgate a controversial statute.

32. *Câmara* of Paraíba to king (19 April 1610), ANTT, *Corp. cron.*, pt. 1, maço 115, doc. 108; V. Coaracy, *O Rio de Janeiro*, p. 33.

33. This account of the events in Salvador is based on the two documents printed in Leite, *HCJB*, V, 5–24. These documents, letters written by Jesuit Father Henrique Gomes, who was a participant in the events he describes, were found by Leite in the Archivum Societatis Iesu Romanum.

Costa, presented to the Jesuits for their signature a document which called the new law "a notable disservice to God and His Majesty and prejudicial to the whole state." The councilmen presented the document with a thinly veiled threat that failure to sign it would result in a general meeting of all the settlers of the Recôncavo for the purpose of expelling or punishing the Jesuits. The Fathers of the Society of Jesus refused to sign, but they were frightened enough to agree to sign a document assuring the colonists that legally captured Indians would not be set free, that free Indians employed in homes would not be taken away, and that the Jesuits had no desire to place the Indians used for personal service in the *aldeias.*

What headway, if any, the settlers made with the Relação remains unknown, but in Diogo de Meneses, the governor, they found a sympathetic supporter. He wrote to the crown on behalf of the colonists emphasizing the importance of Indian labor to the colonists and the "thousand inconveniences" of the new law.[34] He stressed that *entradas* to bring Indians to the coast were beneficial and that their prevention would result in a shrinking of the labor force, while Jesuit control of the *aldeias* would benefit only Jesuit interests and not the common good.

These protestations and the barrage of papers sent to the metropolis brought a repeal of the law of 1609 and its replacement by a statute of 10 September 1611, which reiterated the freedom of the Indians but provided for their enslavement under certain conditions. In case of hostilities, a junta was to be forced, consisting of the governor, bishop, prelates of the religious orders, and the magistrates of the Relação, to determine whether or not war in this instance was "just." Moreover, *entradas* could be permitted by the governor to ransom Indian captives and use them as indentured servants. Within the *aldeias* lay captains appointed by the governor with the approval of the Chancellor of the Relação were to govern, and these captains had full judicial powers over the In-

---

34. Diogo de Meneses to king (Bahia, 8 May 1610), *ABNR,* LVII, 68.

dians. Appeal from their decisions went to the local *ouvidor* or to the *provedor-mór dos defuntos* of the Relação, who now assumed these duties as a magistrate of Indian affairs.[35]

Although carefully worded and buttressed with legal controls, the law of 1611 was a step backward and a return to the status quo ante 1609. Local complaint in Brazil had forced the crown to modify its policy. The Relação, given the principal role in the enforcement of the law of 1611, apparently did not make extensive use of its powers in this sphere with any regularity. Another piece of important Indian legislation was not enacted until 1647, and the statute of 1611 remained the law of the land.

The role of the Relação in the promulgation of the controversial law of 1609 and the extent to which the settlers held the High Court responsible for it is unclear. The Jesuits had attempted to shift the responsibility for the law and the ire of the mob to the Relação. Henrique Gomes, a Jesuit and the major informant of the events of 28–29 June 1610, claimed that "the new law . . . came addressed to the High Court and registered by it" without consultation with the Jesuits or notification of them.[36] Whether the Relação was discredited by its promulgation of the law is impossible to determine, but to the planters of the Recôncavo it was clear that the High Court which they had accepted as an ally against the extortion of the merchants was a representative of royal policy and authority in a way that even the governor was not. The timing of the crisis of 1609 was significant, because its eruption so soon after the arrival of the magistrates gave the planters little time to make clear their position to the desembargadores or to influence them through personal contacts. Thus, the judges had no reason to hesitate in the implementation of royal policy, and they had acted in full compliance with their bureaucratically

---

35. *Livro Primeiro*, 71–75; Andrade e Silva, *Col. Chron.*, I, 309–312. The law was accompanied by a letter to the *câmara* of Bahia. See Livro Dourado, f. 170–170v.

36. Leite, *HCJB*, V, 8.

prescribed roles, giving little or no attention to conflicting standards or goals.

The crown's action in rescinding the law of 1609 also deserves some comment. Why did the crown retreat from its position and acquiesce in the wishes of the colonists? In the Spanish Indies Hapsburg monarchs had often shown a studied disregard of the colonists' position on Indian control. The answer probably lies in the nature of the Brazilian colony. Without a large, settled, tribute-paying Indian population, and with mineral wealth still a century in the future, Brazil's economic foundation was sugar. By the early seventeenth century northeastern Brazil had become the world's leading producer of sugar. Producing it depended entirely on the colonists, and despite certain tax benefits and exemptions all agricultural and industrial costs fell directly on individual colonists. The sugar planter made Brazil a colony of value, for without him there was little to sustain the area. Thus the crown took a more lenient position toward the planters' demands than it might have, both in 1609–1611 and, as we shall see, in 1626. The events of 1609–1611 did make clear, however, that the Relação which had been welcomed by the planters as an ally against the merchants was an organ of royal government and as such a potential threat to the planter elite.

VII. PROCEDURES AND FUNCTIONS

Civil or secular government consists of the proper administration of justice, management of the Royal Treasury, and the economical government of the people.

Luís dos Santos Vilhena (c. 1798)

In the spring of 1609 no pillory stood in Salvador to represent royal justice. The symbol of justice, in fact, had been removed by a former governor, Diogo Botelho, who had once been sentenced to the headman's block at the foot of a *pelourinho* in Portugal, and could not bear the sight of one.[1] The absent symbol in the capital of Brazil bespoke the lawlessness and disorder that continued to characterize Brazilian society. Avaricious officials, fortune-seekers, adventurers, social outcasts, and criminals comprised the bulk of the Portuguese population and presented to the bench a loose and lawless situation.[2] In the city of São Paulo alone, 65 of the 190

1. Frei Vicente do Salvador, *História*, liv. iv, cap. 40, p. 346. Botelho had been sentenced to death for supporting the cause of Dom Antônio, but he had been spared because of his fortunate political marriage to Maria Pereira, the sister of Philip II's Secretary of State for Portugal, Pedro Alvares Pereira.

2. Some of the crimes in Portugal that incurred exile to Brazil were resisting arrest, aiding a slave to escape, and smuggling. See *Ord. fil.* V, *passim.*

householders (*moradores*) were fugitives from justice who had found legal asylum there.[3]

Given these conditions and the traditional function of royal High Courts in Portugal, the primary duties of the Relação da Bahia centered on its role as an enforcer of statutes and a tribunal of justice. Paradoxically, it is exactly this aspect of the High Court's history which is most difficult to document. The day-to-day judicial workings of the Relação, the number of type of cases heard, and the methods and procedures of the tribunal remain, especially for the period 1609–1626, unknown. Documents have been lost or destroyed, and what little remains can only be used with caution. Although this deficiency is not crucial to the present study, which emphasizes the bureaucratic nature of the High Court, it is nevertheless a major gap in the High Court's history. What follows here is an attempt to piece together what little does exist on the procedures of the Relação da Bahia and its handling of normal judicial matters.

Procedure in the Relação of Brazil paralleled that of its metropolitan models. Books I, III, and V of the *Ordenações filipinas* dealt extensively with court structure and procedures, and a close reading of them still impresses the reader with the intricacies of the judicial process and the attempt to make the laws comprehensive. The extent to which local unauthorized variations developed in Brazil, however, cannot be ascertained, and thus a mere recounting of the regulations is of limited use, since under colonial conditions legality and reality were often in opposition. The following description is intended as a bare outline rather than a full summary of the procedure of the Relação, and emphasis had been placed on particularly Brazilian developments.[4]

3. Pedro Calmon, *Espírito da sociedade colonial* (São Paulo, 1935), p. 132.

4. An excellent summary of Hispanic appellate court procedure can be found in Parry, *Audiencia*, pp. 152–166. Although terminology and some practices differed, much of what Parry says of the procedure of the *Audiencia* can be said of the Relação.

Although the High Court was a corporate body, much of its business was performed by its members acting in their individual capacities. The *ouvidor geral*, the probate judge, and the judge of crown interests all had original as well as appellate jurisdiction and could decide actions without assistance from other magistrates of the court. When authorized by statute, and if a litigant so desired, appeal from the decision of the judge might be made to the Relação as a body and from its decision to the Casa de Suplicação in Portugal.

The probate judge's office presents a case in point and indicates how the system operated. It was incumbent on the desembargador who served as probate judge of the High Court to administer the property of those who had died intestate or en route to Brazil and to adjudicate disputes arising between heirs of an estate.[5] When heirs were absent, the property was sold at public auction and the proceeds eventually remitted to Portugal for distribution to the rightful heirs, or for the coffers of the crown should no heirs exist. Before remission to the metropolis by letter of exchange, or occasionally in gold, the money was kept in a strongbox by the probate judge, and to the impecunious governors in Brazil this fund of unclaimed money was a constant temptation.[6]

Many probate disputes originated from the custom in Brazil of making nuncupative (oral) wills, a practice that often led to fraud.[7] Estates in Brazil were often of comparatively little worth, but contested wills occasionally involved properties of great value. A famous case, and one illustrative of the process of appeal, involved claimants to the estate of the heirs of Mem de Sá, an estate that included the great *engenho* of Sergipe do Conde. The Jesuit college of Bahia, the Misericórdia of Bahia, and the Jesuit college of Santo Antão of Lisbon all had some claim to the estate. The action

---

5. *Ord. fil.* I, t. lxii; Ferreira, *História do direito*, II, 222–224.

6. Andrade e Silva, *Col chron.*, I, 213–313; ANTT, *Mesa da Con.* liv. 20, f. 12v.–13, concerning Francisco de Sousa's use of these funds.

7. *Ibid.*, liv. 24, ff. 274v.–8, *Consulta* concerning letter of probate judge Francisco da Fonseca (24 November 1618).

was first heard by the probate judge in 1622, and his decision was appealed by the Misericórdia. The Relação upheld the former sentence in 1623 and the case was then appealed to the metropolitan courts, where it dragged on until a settlement in 1669. Probate cases of this magnitude and complexity were, however, uncommon.[8]

The court transacted most of its business in writing, by deposition, or notarized testimony. Litigants could submit oral pleas only in those cases which involved less than one *milréi,* and since this was a very small sum few cases of this size ever reached the tribunal.[9] This dependence on written briefs, depositions, testimony, and questionnaires made the office of court clerk an important one. The Portuguese impulse to legalize all actions was perhaps reflected in the importance of this office. Nor can we ignore the fact that as intermediaries between the magistrates and litigants the clerks often performeed a decision-making function. They possessed the power to hasten or delay litigation and were thus far more than simple recorders of legal documents. The *regimento* of the Relação provided for the employment of five court clerks assigned to the various magistrates, but it seems certain that only four of these positions were filled at first.[10]

Unlike the magisterial positions, clerking offices in the Relação could be made proprietary and passed from one generation to the next. Appointment or award to the office of court clerk might be made in order to reward some service to the crown, but these

8. ANTT, *Cart. jes.* maço 13, doc. 21. Good descriptions of the legal battle for the *engenho* of Sergipe do Conde can be found in Leite, *HCJB*, V, 244–250. Russell-Wood, *Fidalgos*, pp. 91–92, and J. de Wanderley Pinho, "Testamento de Mem de Sá. Inventãrio de seus bens no Braisil," *III Congresso de História Nacional*, III (1941). 3–161.

9. *Ord. fil.* III t. xxx.

10. Domingos de Andrade, Jerónimo de Lemos, Antônio da Mota, and Cristóvão Vieira Ravasco were appointed to clerical positions in the Relação. Da Mota was actually the *guarda mór*, or custodian, but he sometimes performed clerical duties and was also responsible for the registry of royal orders in the Golden Book of the High Court. ANTT, *Chan. Filipe III, Doações*, liv. 39, f. 29v; liv. 23, ff. 92, 280v.

awards usually required an examination for minimum aptitude. The manner in which such an office was acquired in Brazil is well illustrated by the case of Cristóvão Vieira Ravasco, father of the great Jesuit preacher and writer, Father Antônio Vieira. Cristovão Vieira Ravasco had been a soldier and later a judicial scribe in Lisbon, but his position as appellate clerk in the Relação of Bahia came through marriage. His wife, Maria de Azevedo, had been awarded in 1604 the promise of "some office of justice or the treasury" for whomsoever she married. This was a common method by which the crown could care for honorable widows and orphans—a way, in a sense, of providing a dowry. Cristóvão Vieira Ravasco, therefore, acquired the office by marriage but he was required to prove his capability.[11]

The clerks of the Relação tended to be competent semi-professionals. Their salaries varied between twenty and forty *milréis* a year but they also collected supplementary fees for extra duties. The fact that these offices could generate considerable income made them sought-after political plums. The sale or award of such offices was, of course, in no way atypical of the general European administrative trend in which the dispensation of such offices became a primary means for obtaining revenue and fulfilling obligations.[12] In Portugal and its empire, the holder of an office often rented the office to a deputy who performed the tasks for a fixed amount of the salary drawn by the officeholder. The crown moved on occasion to eliminate these deputies (*serventuários*), and the Relação da Bahia took cognizance of disputes arising from the en-

---

11. AHU, Codice 1192, f. 161–161v.; ANTT, *Chan. Filipe III, Doações*, liv. 23, ff. 92v–93.

12. There is no adequate study of the sale of public office in Portugal or its empire. Alden, *Royal Government*, pp. 294–301, provides a beginning but the student is still forced to look with envy, for examples of what can be gleaned from the subject, at J. H. Parry, *The Sale of Public Office in the Spanish Indies Under the Hapsburgs* (Berkeley, 1963); K. W. Swart, *Sale of Offices in the Seventeenth Century* (The Hague, 1949); and Roland Mousnier, *La vénalité des offices sous Henri IV et Louis XIII* (Rouen, 1948).

forcement of these statutes and conflicting claims to the same office. The appointment of officials remained the duty of the governor.

The hearings of the court were public and litigants or their attorneys appeared before the presiding judge to submit their pleas. There was a rigid procedure to be followed in which the duties and the behavior of the contesting parties, their attorneys, and the bench were stipulated. At the hearing, prisoners, clerics, women, farmers, and those who had traveled long distances were entitled to be heard first.[13] Once a plea was entered, the defendant was given time to prepare a reply, and should any charges be added to the original plea, the defendant was then given additional time for preparation of his defense against them. This was a constant source of delay. During the court hearing, the judge could question the litigants and call witnesses, but interested parties, "capital enemies," and slaves were disqualified from giving testimony.[14] At the final hearing the judge passed sentence, assigned court costs, and heard motions for appeal. If the motion was entertained, the case was then submitted to a group of desembargadores assigned by the chancellor. Any judge or court functionary, however, could be disqualified from sitting on a case in which he was a litigant or was shown to be an interested party.[15]

At the appellate level, the ordinances of procedure required an unequal number of judges to decide a case so that stalemates on the bench could be avoided.[16] In cases involving the death penalty, however, an even number of judges were assigned—usually six—and the final decision had to be reached by a majority of two votes. In case of a deadlock, additional judges were assigned until the proper number of concurring votes was obtained. In Brazil this system proved absurd, because the limited number of judges and their constant absence from Bahia on special missions often caused interminable delay. The deficiencies of the system did not go un-

13. *Ord. fil.* III, t. xix, 4.
14. *Ibid.*, IV, t. lvi, 3, 7.
15. *Ibid.*, III, t. xxiv, 25, 26; t. i, 14.
16. *Ibid.*, I, t. vi, 1.

noticed and became almost proverbial. One loudmouthed physician who appeared before the Inquisition in 1612 was reported to have boasted that he alone had the power of life or death, while the Relação needed four votes to sentence unto death and this they could rarely accomplish.[17]

Eventually, the crown moved to rectify this situation by an *alvará* of 1616 that reduced the number of necessary concurring votes to three in capital cases and two for lesser offenses.[18] A delay of three years while prisoners rotted in the jail of Salvador was not unknown, and despite attempts at reform the wheels of justice spun slowly and painfully in Brazil. The basic problem, as we shall see, was a lack, not an excess, of desembargadores.

The deliberations of the court were secret and not even the functionaries of the court could enter the courtroom unless called by the chancellor's bell.[19] Decisions were reached by two methods —conference or opinion. In a vote by conference, the original judge of the case read the pleas and rejoinders and noted the points of law involved. Each judge then voted orally and all signed the sentence without indication of dissent. The other method, by opinion (*tenção*), was done in writing. Each judge examined the relevant documents and wrote an opinion in Latin that he then passed with the documents to the next member of the bench. When this method was used, the minority did not sign the sentence, nor did they enter a written dissent.

In criminal cases, arrest was usually made by the constabulary after a desembargador issued a proper writ.[20] In Brazil, the personal execution of a warrant of arrest was sometimes performed by the *ouvidor geral*. Prisoners were placed in the jail in Salvador. Except in capital cases fidalgos, members of the military orders, those with

---

17. Denunciation of Manoel Duarte (1612), ANTT, *Inquisição*. Senhora Anita Novinsky of São Paulo kindly provided me with this reference.

18. Livro Dourado (29 October 1616), ff. 351v.–352. *Livro Segundo*, 35–36, noted that there were only four desembargadores in Bahia who were able to vote and that the "jails are full of wrongdoers."

19. AGS, *Sec. Prov.* 1506 (Madrid, 26 July 1613).

20. *Ord. fil.* V, t. cxix.

the degree of doctor, and their wives, were, released on oath.[21] The accused was presented with the charges and given time to submit a defense. The plaintiff or attorney for the crown then submitted a response (*tréplica*). Both plaintiff and defendant were then able to submit evidence and affadavits before the court began its inquiry. During the interim, a prisoner could be released on bail (*fiança*) or by a writ of the court (*carta de seguro*).[22] The court's deliberations usually included the gathering of sworn testimony in accordance with a detailed list or questionnaire prepared from the charges and defense. Testimony, therefore, tended to be limited and repetitious. Torture could be applied to the accused to elicit a confession, although the ordinances admonished against its use and in Brazil it was rarely used, if at all, before 1652.[23]

Sentence was given in accordance with the law and the discretion of the magistrate. Statute prescribed the punishment for most crimes, but the judges could make exceptions for age, health, and social position. Although fines, confiscations, and penal banishment were the most common forms of punishment, hanging, the galleys, the stocks, and public flogging were also employed. A public whipping bore considerable disgrace, and *fidalgos*, knights, citizens of certain cities, and all citizens of the Algarve had a privileged exemption from it. As before 1609, justice for blacks and Indians was intended as an example rather than a remedy for a grievance. Thus in 1613 the crown approved the hanging and quartering of an Indian highwayman in Pernambuco and suggested that the desembargadores act with dispatch in similar cases.[24]

---

21. *Ibid.*, V, t. cxx.

22. *Ibid.*, V, t. cxxix. *Cartas de seguro* were not issued in cases involving murder, the letting of blood, or serious battery.

23. A separate *alvará* was issued by the court to permit the use of judicial torture. This court order could be appealed by the accused. I encountered no writs of this nature for the period 1609–1626 and very few indications of its use in later periods. It should be noted, however, that the absence of such writs may be due to colonial neglect of the legal form and not to the lack of judicial torture.

24. King to Gaspar de Sousa (Lisbon, 21 December 1613), AHI, Correspondencia . . . Gaspar de Sousa, ff. 281–282; *Ord fil.* V, t. cxxviii.

Although an individual could act as his own legal representative in court, the intricacies of procedure and statute created a need for a trained body of advocates, solicitors, and attorneys, who along with the notaries public became permanent fixtures of Brazilian life. The formalistic legalism, the constant need for certified documents, and the omnipresence of the public notary and the government administrator have been used to characterize the present form of government in Brazil as the *estado cartorial,* the notarized state. The roots of this phenomenon, however, reach into the colonial past. Lawyers and notaries had practiced their professions in Brazil before the arrival of the Relação, but the presence of the court created new opportunities for both groups.

The office of notary public was assigned by the crown and the number of positions limited. The desire to formalize and legitimatize all sorts of public and private actions led to constant demand for licensed legal scribes. As litigation increased, so did the need for the notaries. These fee-earning scribes, some of whom lacked the basic skills of their calling, constantly bore the brunt of colonial complaint. "Many of them," claimed one contemporary, "hardly know how to make their mark." [25] Such incompetence did not prevent these *tabelliães* from charging exorbitant fees and from using their position to exercise influence in the court's chambers. The result of this situation during the course of the seventeenth century was a tendency for colonials to transact their business by oral agreement or without the legalization of a notarized document.[26] This was especially true in rural areas, where notarial fees sometimes doubled and trebled.

Although complaints against the notaries were common, the true

---

Branding and the cutting off of ears were also used as punishment in Brazil, although they were apparently more common in the eighteenth century. See Boxer, *Portuguese Society*, pp. 197–208.

25. André de Almeida Fonseca to the Conselho da Fazenda (Olinda, 21 January 1629), AHU, Pernambuco *pap. avul.* caixa 1.

26. Câmara of Bahia to Conselho Ultramarino (10 July 1680), AHU, Bahia *pap. avul.* caixa 14. The câmara noted many oral agreements. Of course, measurement of their frequency is impossible.

villains so far as the colonists were concerned were the lawyers. Theoretically, those who served as attorneys (*procuradores*) or advocates (*advogados*) had studied eight years at Coimbra or were certified by examination before the Desembargo do Paço. Here too, the colonial situation called forth modifications of the standards. In peripheral areas the crown sometimes allowed men who lacked a Coimbra law degree to practice before the bar.[27] In Bahia, however, there were great colonial barristers like the New Christian Jorge Lopes da Costa, who, judging by the importance of his clients and the size of his fees, was the best lawyer of his day.

Lawyers had come to Brazil before the arrival of the High Court, but its presence in the colony undoubtedly created new opportunities for the legal profession. The Philippine Ordinances attempted to diminish pettifogging by regulating fees, prescribing penalties for misconduct and malpractice, and generally controlling the legal profession. But the common use of interlocutory decisions by the court led to subsequent motions and appeals with ever-increasing litigation and fees. The result was protracted suits, mountains of paper, and a painfully slow judicial process.

According to the ordinances of the Relação, a roll of all the cases heard by it during the course of a year was to be submitted to the metropolis. These lists—if in fact they were made—have not survived to the present and thus little is known of the everyday workings and decisions of the Relação. In the captaincies, the local magistrates and *ouvidores* continued to administer justice and could still arrest, sentence, and punish within the area of their jurisdiction. Only those cases involving large sums, capital crimes, or in which the Relação could exercise original jurisdiction were appealed to the proper magistrate of the tribunal. The cases that

27. Petition of Henrique de Leão (Paraíba, 2 March 1685), AHU, Bahia *pap. avul.* caixa 15. He stated: "the inhabitants of this captaincy have so little wherewithal that they can not send their sons to the university and in such circumstances men without degrees always practice law in these parts." Cf. Petition of Bernardo Mendes de Silveira (Bahia, 30 March 1688), AHU, Bahia *pap. avul.* caixa 16.

came before the Relação were varied and since there are no lists, generalization is difficult and naturally impressionistic.

What was the nature and volume of the offenses that came before the Relação? Since there is no compilation of cases for the period 1609–1626, we can only speculate on the basis of other periods. A listing of violent crimes committed in Olinda in 1671 reported 206 murders or criminal assaults in that year and the phrases "morto a punhaladas" (beaten to death), "morto à espingarda" (shot to death), or "morto à estocadas" (death by sword-thrusts) are constantly repeated.[28] The list of penal exiles reprinted by Charles Boxer, and a glance at the Books of Bail and Pardon of the Relação for the period 1652 to 1750, indicate the prevalence of blacks and mulattos among the culprits sentenced by the colonial courts.[29] Obviously, these men were socially marginal and forced beyond the outer limits of acceptable behavior by various forms of discrimination and social pressure. Moreover, slaves were often simply used to carry out the vendettas of their masters, and when caught they bore the burden of guilt. On occasion, however, masters, including desembargadores, interceded on behalf of their bondsmen; the Books of Bail and Pardon are sprinkled with such instances.[30] The general impression provided by surviving records is that of society plagued with much violence and a demi-world of highwaymen, cutpurses, and cutthroats.

The volume of litigation and of prosecution would by itself have been a cause for judicial failure. Although the Bahian notarial records for the period of the first Relação are no longer extant,

---

28. Luiza da Fonseca, "Bacharéis brasileiros-Elementos biográficos," *Anais. IV Congresso de Historia Nacional* (Rio de Janeiro, 1951), XI, 188–190.

29. Boxer, *Portuguese Society*, pp. 197–208. The *Livros de perdão e fiança* for the period 1662 to 1822 are housed in the Arquivo Público da Bahia. The entries usually state the name of the accused, his crime, and the reasons for his pardon or bail. Although they provide a selective sample, these books are a measure of crime and punishment in colonial Brazil.

30. For example, the *alvará* of pardon given to Gregório Guiné, slave of Maria de Almeida (1678), APB, Relação 495, f. 76–76v.

some idea of the number of cases heard can be inferred from a document of the late seventeenth century. In the nineteen months between October 1690 and June 1692, the Relação took cognizance of or reviewed lower court decisions in 4,035 separate cases. Of these, 41 per cent (1,645) were misdemeanors or civil suits heard by judges of the first instance (*juizo ordinário*); 41 per cent (1,662) consisted of civil disputes, probate, and treasury affairs; and 18 per cent (728) were criminal actions. Given the fact that only ten desembargadores sat in the Bahian tribunal, the workload seems extraordinarily heavy.[31]

The suppression and prosecution of crime was the duty of the *ouvidor geral*, a position not without danger. Pero de Cascais, who served as *ouvidor geral* for two years, arrested over 170 people during his term of office, and in one case he narrowly escaped death from a criminal's attack while attempting to make an arrest.[32] The frontier custom of bearing arms and the unruly nature of the colonists complicated the problems of justice. The naked blade commonly settled differences, and contending parties in land disputes were more prone to burn their opponent's holdings than to bring suit.[33]

Crimes of passion and violence arising from affronts to "honor" often drew comments from visitors to Brazil in the seventeenth and eighteenth centuries. Even today, putting the "horns" on someone (the sign of the cuckold) is in Brazil and Portugal a sure invitation to battle. The colonial Portuguese, said the Englishman Richard Ligon in the mid-seventeenth century, "are more jealous of their mistresses than Italians are of their wives." [34] Portuguese protective attitudes toward their women were almost legendary, even among the other Mediterranean peoples who shared the tra-

---

31. AHU, Bahia *pap. avul.* caixa 17 (6 November 1692).

32. Report of Pero de Cascais, AHU, Bahia *pap. avul.* caixa 1.

33. ANTT, *Cart. Jes.* maço 13, doc. 4, details one of these violent feuds between two plantations in the Recôncavo.

34. Richard Ligon, *A True and Exact History of Barbadoes* (London, 1657), p. 13.

dition of female seclusion. Not only was it expected behavior, but statute permitted the murder of an unfaithful wife and her lover by the deceived husband.[35] Pyrard de Laval, a French visitor to Salvador in 1610, reported an affair in which João de Meneses, son of Governor Diogo de Meneses, was caught in the arms of another man's wife. Both wife and lover received a number of sword wounds from the irate husband, although in this case they were not fatal. In fact, João de Meneses and his brothers had a history of molesting women at will, insulting or wounding their husbands, and then using their privileged position to avoid punishment. In 1612 the lawyer Jorge Lopes da Costa accused João de Meneses of committing adultery with da Costa's wife.[36] This charge and the other complaints about the behavior of the governor's sons led to an investigation by Desembargador Manoel Pinto da Rocha. Apparently, no charges were brought by the Relação, but the investigation may have been enough to cool the ardor of the brothers. No more complaints were heard against them.

Another scandal of this type is most interesting because of the light it casts on the possibilities for subverting justice. In 1614 Pero de Cascais as *ouvidor geral* had arrested a young blade who had lured away another man's wife and had sent her to Portugal for safe-keeping. This was a serious offense, punishable by death, and the culprit had compounded the crime by resisting arrest. The young man in question, however, was the nephew of Balthesar Ferraz, the old desembargador who had come to Brazil in 1588 as part of the ill-fated first tribunal. Ferraz had stayed in the colony and by 1614 was an influential, wealthy, admired, and well-connected member of Bahian society—a landowner and a confidant of Garcia d'Avila, one of the most powerful men in Brazil.[37]

---

35. *Ord. fil.* V, t. xxxviii.

36. Pyrard de Laval, *Voyage of François Pyrard de Laval*, Hakluyt Society LXXX, 2 vols. in 3, Albert Grey (trans. and ed.) London, 1890. King to Manoel Pinto da Rocha (Lisbon, 24 November 1612), AHI, Correspondência . . . Gaspar de Sousa, f. 179.

37. Pedro Calmon, *História da Casa de Torre*, 2nd ed. (Rio de Janeiro, 1958), p. 35. Ferraz owned land in Bahia and Sergipe. His influence on

Balthesar Ferraz worked so diligently in suppressing testimony, erecting a defense, and apparently appealing to professional connections on the bench, that the Relação released the culprit. The community reaction was strong and the clergy thundered from their pulpits against an unjust decision, warning that God would mete out his own justice. Shortly thereafter, a maritime mishap caused the death of the nephew and of Ferraz's only son; the old advocate, heartbroken at the loss, died soon after confessing on his deathbed, "Father, God punishes me by wanting my death now and my nephew has brought this to pass." [38] Divine justice, however, was not a regular part of the legal apparatus, and Ferraz's success in freeing his nephew showed what a well-connected lawyer with friends on the bench could accomplish.

The dramatic nature of such episodes should not obscure the fact that the Relação spent most of its time on the legal intricacies of property squabbles and disputed tithe contracts. Moreover, the crown specifically looked upon the legal protection of royal interests and the enforcement of statutes as a primary duty of the High Court. Matters that clearly affected the interests of the crown and in which the duties of the Relação were explicit found the magistrates ready to act with vigor and dispatch. Since evaluation of a magistrate's performance and his subsequent professional promotion would to a large extent be based on his compliance with professional norms and protection of royal interests, the judges took special care always to appear as advocates of the king's cause. In reality, the magistrates often found their actions

---

members of the legal profession was noted by one contemporary who complained that litigation in Salvador was difficult "since the lawyers here are suspect because they are friends of Balthesar Ferraz." On his death, Ferraz left 1,200 *milréis* to the Misericórdia of Bahia, a bequest three times the usual amount. Cf. Martim de Carvalho to Count of Linhares (Bahia, 25 August 1593), ANTT, *Cart. Jes.* maço 8, doc. 74; ASCMB, Livro 211, ff. 1–2; *Livro Velho do Tombo do Mosteiro de São Bento* (Bahia, 1945), xxi–xxiii.

38. Letter of Father Henrique Gomes (Bahia, 16 June 1614), printed in Leite, *HCJB*, V, 15; Frei Vicente do Salvador, *História* liv. v, cap. vi, 416–417.

constrained by social pressure in the colony or influenced by personal goals, but the need to appear as protectors of the king's business was never lost on them. Two matters, one of them a continuing problem and the other an extraordinary event, can serve as illustrations of the tribunal's actions in this sphere.

The Relação took an effective and active interest in the suppression of the illegal brazilwood trade. The period from 1602 to 1610 had witnessed not only intense activity by foreign interlopers in the dyewood trade but also many illegalities in the authorized commerce. It had been for this reason that in 1605 Sebastião de Carvalho was sent to Pernambuco to investigate these abuses and prosecute the guilty.[39] Excesses in dyewood cutting had by the opening years of the seventeenth century caused considerable deforestation along the coast, and in 1605 the crown moved to limit this process. A new ordinance for the cutting of dyewood was issued and severe penalties of death and confiscation were prescribed for violators of this law. When the Relação arrived in 1609, the body of by-laws that it carried included a special exhortation to maintain vigilance of the anti-deforestation statutes. Moreover, those still in Brazil accused in de Carvalho's investigation were turned over to the Relação for prosecution.[40]

French, English, and Dutch ships, sometimes guided by Portu-

---

39. Sebastião de Carvalho arrived in Brazil in 1608 in the company of Governor D. Diogo de Meneses. The original plan to have the Relação perform this investigation on arrival was abandoned in favor of a specially appointed *letrado*. Afonso Ruy, *História política e administrativa da cidade do Salvador* (Bahia, 1949), p. 121, argues that "under his [Sebastiao de Carvalho's] inspiration and counsel the restoration of the tribunal of the Relação of Bahia was resolved." I have seen no document to support this statement, and the fact that Carvalho was not selected for service in Brazil until after the crown's decision to re-establish the Relação argues against it. Cf. king to Viceroy Pedro de Castilho (Valladolid, 30 Sept. 1605), AGS, *Sec. Prov.* 1492, f. 44v. See also the notes by Rodolfo Garcia in Varnhagen, *História geral*, II, 99–100, 123–124.

40. King to Viceroy of Portugal Marquis of Castel Rodrigo (Madrid, 11 August 1609), AGS, *Sec. Prov* 1500, f. 81v. The best general account of the brazilwood trade is Mauro, *Portugal et l'Atlantique*, pp. 116–143.

guese pilots and often with the complicity of local residents, continued to load dyewood on the coast. The Relação took an active and effective interest in suppressing this illegal trade. In 1612 two foreign vessels were apprehended—one in Ilhéus and the other at Ilha Grande near Rio. A number of prisoners, including Englishmen, Scots, and Flemings, were sent to Bahia to await prosecution by the crown attorney, Afonso Garcia Tinoco.[41] Although a jurisdictional dispute arose between the *provedor-mór* and the Relação, it was clear that the prosecution of these violations of statute were the responsibility of the Relação. There was at this time, however, some question of the tribunal's ability to sentence foreigners, and the matter was submitted to Portugal. The crown responded that under no conditions were foreign prisoners to be sent to Portugal and that in cases not involving the death penalty they be sent to forced exile and service in Angola.[42] Four of the prisoners taken at Ilha Grande were sentenced to death by the Relação, but the judges showed some reluctance to execute the sentence and the crown, although it deplored the delay, commuted the punishment to lifetime service in the galleys.[43]

In 1616 Desembargador Manoel Jácome Bravo investigated in Paraíba and heard reports of Portuguese complicity in the Ilha Grande incident of 1612. In 1619 Antão de Mesquita took testimony from an Indian about four French ships that came to obtain wood in Porto Sequro.[44] The crown's interest in this matter was underlined by the reports of its agents in Europe forwarded to Brazil warning of recent or projected embarkations. Since many of these ventures were aided by local residents, foreigners in Brazil became highly suspect, as accomplices, and the crown

41. Chancellor Ruy Mendes de Abreu to king (Bahia, 5 September 1614), AHU, Bahia *pap. avul.* caixa 1 (1st series, non-cataloged).

42. *Carta régia* (13 July 1614), Andrade e Silva *Col. chron.*, III, 90–91; Gaspar de Sousa to Relação (14 September 1614), BGUC, Codice 708, f. 203.

43. *Livro Segundo*, 51.

44. *Livro Primeiro*, 131–133, 240–242.

ordered that all such aliens be expelled from the colony.[45] This order was never fully enforced, but when one of these resident aliens was apprehended in this illegal trade, he was prosecuted. Rodrigo Pedro, a Dutchman married to a Portuguese woman and a resident in Espirito Santo, for instance, was arrested when he guided three Dutch ships to Brazil. To the embarrassment of the Relação, however, the ships escaped.[46] After 1621, the threat of foreign interlopers became one of military attack and permanent occupation rather than clandestine and intermittent trade. The suppression, or at least control, of illegal dyewood cutting in the second decade of the seventeenth century, however, was mainly a result of the Relação's activity.

The enforcement of statutes, the protection of royal interests, and compliance with instructions were relatively easy matters for the desembargadores when the situation or event was expected. Extraordinary events, however, found the Relação, like most of the administrative organs of colonial government, temporarily paralyzed by its lack of improvisational ability and by inflexibility. The governors who exercised decision-making powers did not always act with dispatch and resolution, and the colonists reacted either by taking advantage of the situation or by refusing to face it at all.

Although the functions of the Relação can be described as judicial and administrative, it was sometimes difficult to distinguish between the two. In fact, no real concept of the division of powers existed, and often the same men would be invested with powers pertaining to more than one office or jurisdiction. There is no doubt that the Relação, like its European models, was primarily to act as a high court of appeals, but traditional functions combined with the crown's need for loyal and knowledgeable officials in the colonies expanded the scope of its actions. This often placed heavy and sometimes conflicting responsibilities on the magistrates.

---

45. *Livro Segundo*, 45, 46, 47, 60, 66. 73, 75, 109; *Livro Primeiro*, 183–185.

46. *Livro Segundo*, 75, 112.

The Relação rarely exercised extensive administrative powers independent of the governor-general's desires. The position of the governor-general as president of the Relação placed the magistrates under his control and limited the court's options in political matters. This situation paralleled the relationship of the Viceroy of India to the Relação of Goa or of the Viceroy of Peru to the Audiencia of Lima. The Relação of Bahia did participate in the political administration of the colony, since both tradition and circumstance permitted such a role, but only in exceptional circumstances did this aspect of the High Court's duties become important. Between 1604 and 1621, for example, the governors-general were often absent from Bahia and in their place the chancellor of the High Court and the *provedor-mór* usually assumed administrative leadership. This situation did give the Relação a larger role in policy formation and administration. Then too, the traditional functions of the magistrates included administrative and semi-administrative tasks which derived from their responsibility to correct abuses and faults in the judicial process.

The crown viewed the Relação as a loyal and intelligent source of information whose opinion on local matters would always take royal interests into consideration. The chancellor could correspond directly with the throne and thus play a role in policy formation. The magistrates, viewed by the crown as loyal and trusted officials, were often called upon to perform non-judicial duties. Often in Brazil, the Relação served as an advisory council on matters of common welfare. Upon returning to Portugal, both desembargadores and governors-general were asked to advise the crown on Brazilian problems or appointments.

The crown formally recognized the advisory functions of the Relação in 1611, when the Indian legislation of that year called for the Relação to participate in deliberations on the righteousness of warfare against the Indians. Political decisions made by the High Court convened under the presidency of the governor-general were called *accordões*. This formal arrangement was rarely used, however, during the seventeenth century. Instead, the governor-general or one of the royal councils would simply call upon the Relação offer an opinion. Governors-general would use the High Court as a source of accurate information and as an advisory council. In 1612 Governor Diogo de Meneses did exactly that when with the advice of the High Court he established a municipal council in Rio Grande do Norte.[47]

Both the Relação and individual magistrates sometimes were used as sources of information. In 1613 Governor Gaspar de Sousa suggested that a mint be established in Brazil to eliminate the chronic shortage of currency and free the colony of its dependence on silver imported from Spanish America. The Conselho da Fazenda wished to check the governor's report against another source of information and it turned to the Relação, which was asked to submit an opinion on the matter. The Relação reported that the coinage of copper money in Brazil would be very beneficial to the colonists because these coins would be used in everyday transactions and would lower the price of staples. The proposal was not implemented, and Brazil remained without a mint until 1694. The crown did, however, issue 6,000 *cruzados* in copper coins in Portugal to be sent to Brazil to alleviate the shortage. When certain measures could serve both king and colonists, the Relação did not hesitate to initiate reform.[48]

Individual desembargadores also proffered advice to the crown. In 1617, Antão de Mesquita, serving as crown attorney, suggested the establishment of a royal monopoly of Brazilian ginger as a measure beneficial to both the crown and the colonists. Ginger grew well in Bahia, but in 1577 Portuguese interests involved in the India trade had persuaded the crown to prohibit ginger production in Brazil as a means of maintaining the price of the Indian product. The Bahian colonists had ignored the law, and Antão

---

47. Diogo de Meneses to king (Bahia, 1 March 1612), *ABNR*, LVII, 78–81.

48. King to Aleixo de Meneses (Madrid, 13 March 1615), AGS, *Sec. Prov.* 1512; *Sec. Prov.* 1472 (Lisbon, 30 December 1613), 479–480; AHU, Bahia *pap. avul.*, caixa 1 (26 May 1614).

de Mesquita was simply suggesting that a royal monopoly would bring revenue into the treasury while at the same time allowing the colonists to grow ginger legally and thus eliminate their need to sell it in secret to the Dutch and the English. It should be recalled that Antão de Mesquita was one of the magistrates married in Brazil and was perhaps more attuned to colonial feelings than his colleagues.[49]

The use of the High Court magistrates for extrajudicial duties of a fiscal, investigative, or administrative nature increased the obligations as well as the powers of the professional jurists. The magistracy provided a pool of able, trained, and loyal officials from which the crown could draw the personnel needed for a variety of special tasks. Some of these duties were simply part of the ordinary management of government. Fiscal obligations such as the collection of the 1 per cent sales tax for church construction (*obras pias*) or administration of funds collected from New Christians as part of their ransom fell to the *juiz da coroa*, Afonso Garcia Tinoco.[50] In the late seventeenth and eighteenth centuries, the number and diversity of these extra duties seriously impeded the judicial process, as judges were increasingly called away from their normal duties.

The crown also turned to the desembargadores to staff the various ad hoc committees and investigations that became regular features of the administrative process. The earliest example of this phenomenon occurred between 1613 and 1615, and it may be taken as an example of how the magistrates could be used by the crown.

Contraband trade, fraud, tax evasion, and speculation called for

---

49. Report of Antão de Mesquita (20 August 1617), AHU, Bahia *pap. avul.* caixa 1; AGS, *Sec. Prov.* 1474, f. 108–109; Mauro, *Portugal et l'Atlantique*, p. 368. In 1604 a concession had been given for a ten-year continuance of Brazilian ginger production under strict regulation and heavy taxation.

50. The *obras pias* were instituted in Brazil as a 1 per cent surcharge on all contracts by an *alvará* of 10 April 1592. Cf. *DHBNR*, LXXVIII (1947), 325–328; AHU, Bahia *pap. avul.* caixa 1 (Fonseca 25, 31).

some remedy. In 1612 the crown appointed André Farto da Costa, a cousin of Jorge Lopes da Costa, as Secretary of the Lisbon Customs House and immediately sent him to Brazil to head a special Junta da Fazenda designed to clean up the colony. The Junta was composed of desembargadores Francisco da Fonseca and Antônio das Póvoas, Farto da Costa, and *provedor-mór* Sebastião Borges. The first session of the Junta took place in Salvador on 9 February 1613 and it proceeded to meet intermittently until 1615.[51]

The Junta concentrated on the misuse and misappropriation of funds by customs and treasury officials. The two desembargadores on the Junta took charge of making the formal accusations, which were then forwarded to the crown's attorney in the Relação. The High Court then sentenced the guilty, usually by ordering repayment of the missing funds. Ledgers were checked, back taxes collected, and the guilty reprimanded. Violators were usually given two to three years to reimburse the royal treasury.[52]

A more difficult matter and one with political implications was the elimination of contraband trade with the Rio de la Plata area of Spanish America. The Junta not only tried to eliminate illegal sailings but also complained against the practice of allowing authorized Spanish ships to freight goods in Brazil without paying duties. Acting upon a recommendation of the Junta, Governor Luís de Sousa and the Relação ordered that "any authorized goods that the Castilians load in this state for the Rio de la Plata must pay the *dízima* since they are not natives and the goods are going to a foreign country." [53]

The relations between the Junta and other organs of govern-

---

51. "Regimento da Junta da Fazenda," (19 September 1612), AHU, Bahia *pap. avul.* caixa 1; "Apontamentos das cousas q. André Farto da Costa fes," AHU, Bahia *pap. avul.* caixa 1; king to Provedor-Mór of Pernambuco (8 October 1612), AHU, Pernambuco *pap. avul.* caixa 1.

52. "Livro da Junta," AHU, Bahia *pap. avul.* caixa 1. This is the minute book of the Junta, but unfortunately the acidity of the ink has now made the ledger virtually illegible.

53. Luís de Sousa to king (8 December 1614), AHU, Bahia *pap. avul.*, caixa 1.

ment were sometimes strained. The extensive powers of the Junta were resented by both royal officials and local town councils. Governor Luís de Sousa claimed that André Farto da Costa had not bothered to present his credentials or reveal his instructions and had merely shown "closed bundles" to him. Underlying this animosity, however, lay the Junta's attack on the proliferation of unnecessary and unauthorized positions filled by the cronies and retainers of the governor and paid for by the royal treasury. Governors were usually allowed to maintain a personal guard of twenty men at the crown's expense, but the Junta found that sinecures such as "assistant to the sergeant major of Pernambuco" were totally unnecessary. Although the governor complained to Portugal of the elimination of these offices, the Conselho da Fazenda supported the Junta's action.[54]

The municipal councils in Salvador and Pernambuco were reluctant to submit their ledgers to Farto da Costa's inspection. The *câmara* of Bahia even accused him of illegally withdrawing funds from the coffers of the wine tax and using them without authorization.[55] Nor were all the members of the Relação pleased with the actions of the Junta. Desembargadores who had succumbed to the habit of placing their friends and aides in office resented the exposure of these sinecures. The appeals of the guilty desembargadores, the municipal councils, and the governor found little sympathy in Portugal, and the Conselho da Fazenda supported the Junta's actions as being of "much benefit and profit to His Majesty's treasury." [56]

The actions of the Junta obviously displeased many people, but its overall effect benefited the colony. At the conclusion of his service in Brazil in 1616, André Farto da Costa was able to produce letters of recommendation from the *câmara* of Bahia, Desembargador Francisco da Fonseca, and Vasco de Sousa Pacheco, captain of Pernambuco, who swore that "after the Junta came to this

54. "Apontamentos. . . ."
55. *Consulta* of Con. da Faz., AHU, Codice 284, ff. 115–117.
56. Antônio Villes de Cimas to King (n.d.), AGS, *Sec. Prov.* 1472, f. 443.

State, matters of the royal treasury . . . proceeded on their proper way and in a different manner than previously."[57] Conflict with the municipal councils, the governor, and even with the Relação had remained relatively muted and the Junta performed a signal service to the colony, although some of the abuses continued. The Junta da Fazenda was distinct from the Relação, but participation in it by members of the High Court linked these permanent and ad hoc organs of government. The Relação cooperated not only by prosecuting the guilty but also by acting as an advisory board. Although a few desembargadores were reprimanded for distributing sinecures, and the Relação and the Junta did not always see eye to eye on every problem, the relationship of the two bodies was complementary.

By far the most crucial task the desembargadores performed as representatives of central authority was in their role as circuit judges and special investigators in the various captaincies of Brazil. Desembargadores on mission were often instruments for the enforcement of policy and at times even created it as a result of their investigations. The power of magistrates to conduct periodic or special investigations in outlying areas of their jurisdiction or even in regions normally outside their control was not a new departure. In Portugal, *corregedores* had traditionally performed this function and desembargadores had been sent on special investigatory missions from time to time. The new departure in Brazil was the regular use of resident desembargadores as judicial investigators in outlying areas.

The administrative geography of Brazil in the seventeenth century divided the colony into four major units. The far north, the State of Maranhão, was administered directly from Lisbon and after 1621 had its own governor-general. The northeast coast was dominated by Pernambuco, the economic capital of Brazil. This captaincy and its neighbor Paraíba contained more sugar planta-

57. Certificate of Vasco de Sousa Pacheco (Bahia, 24 Feb. 1616), AHU, Bahia *pap. avul.* caixa 1.

tions and a larger brazilwood trade than any other region in Brazil. It was a highly profitable enterprise for the Albuquerque Coelho clan, the legal proprietors of the captaincy. On the central coast Bahia dominated the region and overshadowed its neighbors Ilhéus, Porto Seguro, Espirito Santo, and Sergipe d'El-Rey, the captaincy of transition between Pernambuco and Bahia. The southern captaincies, politically independent from Bahia from 1608 to 1613, were administered from Rio de Janeiro, the capital of the south, where the Correia de Sá family held sway. Further to the south, the captaincy of São Vicente contained the atypical inland city of São Paulo, a center known for its disregard of central authority and the excitable and independent nature of its heavily *mestiço* inhabitants.

The officials in each captaincy, whether appointed by king or proprietor, were subject to an investigation at the termination of their encumbency. At the end of each three-year period, the Relação conducted a review of the performance of the retiring official.[58] Such investigations were in use in Brazil before the arrival of the Relação, but as soon as establishment of a High Court for the colony was projected, its responsibility for these duties was authorized by the crown.[59]

As president of the Relação, the governor-general selected a desembargador to visit the captaincy in question and perform the necessary investigation. The governor-general—or in his absence, the chancellor—issued instructions and authorization for the inquest, and it was usually expected that the appointed magistrate would also take cognizance of any other irregularities in the area. He was expected to announce the investigation within a

58. In the southern captaincies the *ouvidor geral do sul* performed this investigation and then forwarded his findings to the Relação.

59. The governor-general's actions were also subject to review by the Relação, although through influence, chance, or subsequent appointment they were often excused from such an investigation. Cf. "Informação do procedimento illegal de Diogo Botelho," BNL, Pomb. 249, ff. 204–297; AHU, Rio de Janeiro *pap. avul.* caixa 1 (15 July 1619).

radius of six leagues around the city in question and to call for testimony or accusations. Pertinent papers were then forwarded to the Relação along with his opinion.

Normally, the desembargador reviewed the performance of a number of officials and often his tour included more than one captaincy. Manoel Pinto da Rocha was authorized in 1620 to perform a *devassa* (judicial review) of the captain and all the judicial and fiscal officers of Itamaracá, as well as the captain and the *ouvidor* of Paraíba.[60] The desembargador was accompanied at least by a clerk and a bailiff. Manoel Jácome Bravo, sent to the southern captaincies in 1614 to perform a *residência* of the *ouvidor geral do sul*, was accompanied by a clerk, a bailiff, a guard of four soldiers, and two Negro pikemen, each of whom received a daily wage at the cost of the treasury. An incentive for rigor, however, was present in the stipulation that these salaries and that of the desembargador would be increased if they could be paid from the estates of the guilty.[61]

Whereas the Relação, as a court of appeal, exercised its duties in the captaincies when called upon to do so by an aggrieved party and thus acted at the volition of the colonists, its function as an investigatory and semi-administrative institution was the cause of animosity and regional rancor. Nowhere was this more apparent than in the southern captaincies, where semi-independent judicial status and the short history of administrative separation made its

60. *ABNR*, XXXIX (1917), "Inventário dos documentos relativos ao Brasil existentes no Archivo de Marinha e Ultramar," 17. (These documents are presently in the Arquivo Histórico Ultramarino.)

61. *ACVSP*, I, 356–357; Antão de Mesquita took a guard of twelve soldiers on his circuit of the southern captaincies in 1619. See document from the AHU, Rio de Janeiro, *pap. avul.* (7 April 1619), in João Francisco de Sousa, "Documentos inéditos relativos ao Rio de Janeiro," *Revista de História*, XXX, n. 61 (1965), 442. Larger commissions were sometimes used. Afonso Garcia Tinoco was sent with two magistrates, two clerks, a bailiff and six guards for a six-month investigation in Pernambuco, Paraíba, Rio Grande, and Itamaracá in which the group was to hear cases, investigate procedure, and grant *sesmarias*. See *alvará* (28 September 1612), AHI, Correspondência . . . Gaspar de Sousa, f. 117–117v.

inhabitants sensitive to central control or interference. In 1612, 1619, and 1624, a magistrate of the Relação was sent southward on missions of investigation, inspection, and review. Each encountered hostility from some group or official and on occasion the result was defiance of the visiting desembargador.

This was certainly the case when Manoel Jácome Bravo arrived in Rio de Janeiro in 1612 for the purpose of holding a *devassa* of the *ouvidor geral do sul* and the governor of Rio de Janeiro, Afonso de Albuquerque. On behalf of the governor of Brazil, Bravo was also given the responsibility of reintegrating the southern captaincies with the rest of Brazil.[62] The situation in Rio de Janeiro was turbulent. Afonso de Albuquerque and his ally, the prelate Matius Aborim, had insulted the municipal council to the point that the alderman openly flaunted the authority of the local governor. Albuquerque, in return, had ordered the arrest of the president of the *câmara*, and when the *ouvidor* had refused to do this, he too was made prisoner. The city was up in arms and Bravo hoped to restore order and punish the guilty. He found, however, that his every move was blocked by the governor and the prelate; the governor arrested the desembargador's guard and the prelate excommunicated him, thus preventing the exercise of public office. Passions flared and at one point someone shot an arrow with a threatening note into Bravo's quarters. The situation in Rio was not brought under control until December 1613, when Constantino Meneláu was appointed to replace Afonso de Albuquerque.[63]

Manoel Jácome Bravo had received his baptism of fire, but he soon learned that his tribulations were not over. Proceeding from Rio to São Paulo, he hoped to continue his investigation into the state of justice in the southern captaincies. São Paulo, inland and remote, was not accustomed to the regular supervision of the *ouvidor geral do sul*, and the local magistrates enforced disagree-

---

62. King to Gaspar de Sousa (Lisbon, 9 November 1613), AHI, Correspondência . . . Gaspar de Sousa, f. 271–271v.

63. Coaracy, *O Rio*, pp. 36–37.

able legislation with a studied laxity.[64] Since the major occupation of many Paulistas was Indian slave-raiding, the law of 1609 had not been well received, and even after the law of 1611 the topic had remained particularly controversial and potentially explosive.

Bravo's arrival in São Paulo was the cause of local consternation, especially when he began to concern himself with "matters of the *sertão*." [65] The residents of the city held the *câmara* responsible for not protecting local interests, and the attorney for the *câmara* tried to dissuade Bravo from continuing this aspect of his investigation, because, he said, the result would be a flight of residents from the area and a depopulation of the land.[66] Paulista response was not entirely vocal, however, and attempts on Bravo's life were made on a number of occasions by arrows shot at his window. The desembargadores sent to maintain law and order in São Paulo found their task hazardous when they touched the tender nerve of the Indian question.

The hostility and opposition encountered by Manoel Jácome Bravo may have influenced his successor, Antão de Mesquita de Oliveira, to take a position less offensive to local interests. And perhaps his personal relations to the colonial elite may have made him more sensitive to their feelings. He arrived in the southern captaincies in 1619 with instructions to hold a *residência* of Constantino de Meneláu, the former governor of Rio de Janeiro. The new governor, Ruy Vaz Pinto, charged the desembargador with

64. *Ouvidor* Paulo da Rocha de Siqueira was removed from office in 1613 for participating in slave raids. The *ouvidor geral do sul* based in Rio had two paths open in regard to the Indian problem in São Paulo. A policy of intentional disregard—as in the case of Amancio Rebello Coelho who visited São Paulo in 1620—caused the least friction. A policy of vigilance brought trouble. Lázaro Fernandes, *ouvidor geral do sul* in 1624, attempted to halt the raids by confiscations and imprisonment, but he met strong resistance from the *câmara* of São Paulo, which complained to the Relação of his "insults, injustices, and criminal acts." See Afonso de E. Taunay, *História Seiscentista da Villa da S. Paulo,* 4 vols. (São Paulo, 1926–1929), I, 44, 73; *ACVSP*, III.

65. *Vereação* of 5 February 1614, *ACVSP*, II, 361.

66. *Ibid.*

failing to prosecute Constantino de Meneláu and others guilty of illegal dyewood cutting and of cooperating with them in obstructing justice. It appears that Antão de Mesquita was trying not to upset the populace even though this resulted in the accusations of the governor of Rio, Ruy Vaz Pinto.[67]

Antão de Mesquita arrived in São Paulo in 1619. He regulated the electoral process of the *câmara*, limited the original jurisdiction of the *ouvidor* to the normal ten-league radius, ordered the strengthening of the jailhouse of Santos, and instructed the *câmara* to keep the road from São Paulo to Santos in repair. As a member of the Relação, Mesquita could not ignore the question of Indian liberty. His more cautious approach was to eliminate friction caused by the problem rather than to make a frontal attack on the vested interests and the underlying causes. He ordered a heavy fine and imprisonment for anyone who took Indians from another man, and he reiterated the existing statute against farming those lands belonging to the Indians. Antão de Mesquita seemed more interested in preserving the prerogatives of royal justice than in tackling the Indian question, and he emphasized that violators of the anti-enslavement statutes were under civil, not ecclesiastical authority.[68] As a result of this approach, he encountered little opposition on this tour of inspection.

It is clear that by 1619 the periodic *devassas* of officials made by magistrates of the Relação were linked to a more general tour of inspection and correction in which the itinerant desembargador undertook the review and remedy of local conditions. The power to review the actions of local administrators and to approve or nullify their actions was in itself at least a semi-administrative function. Moreover, these magistrates sometimes performed administrative duties, such as imposing or regulating new taxes, but this power still emanated from the orders of the governor. Once on

---

67. Ruy Vaz Pinto to king (Rio de Janeiro, 8 June 1619), AHU, Rio de Janeiro *pap. avul.* caixa 1; AHU, Codice 1192, 15.

68. *Registro geral,* I, 340, 355–357; *vereação* of 23 March 1619, *ACVSP,* II, 407.

the scene, however, local conditions and the need for immediate action in an age of slow communication sometimes prompted the desembargadores to take administrative actions not specifically provided for in their instructions. This was no startling innovation. *Corregedores* in Portugal and the *ouvidores* in Brazil had exercised similar authority—a fact that in the latter case explains why the proprietors in Brazil had often united the positions of *ouvidor* and captain. For the colony as a whole, however, administrative authority remained in the hands of the governor-general.

The visit of the southern captaincies made in 1624 by desembargador João de Sousa Cardenas demonstrated his functions as a *corregedor* and elicited the typical opposition of regional and private interests to central interference in local matters.[69] Cardenas himself stated that his mission was to conduct a *residência* of the *ouvidores* and captains of the southern captaincies, but the existing record of his actions in Rio de Janeiro notes that he had come "on correction." [70] In Espirito Santo he had ordered the repair of public buildings, made arrests, eliminated violations in probate procedure, and instituted a new tax—all without difficulty.[71] In Rio, however, his actions provoked heated resistance. He ordered compliance with existing ordinances and issued others, many of them directly related to the duties and powers of the *câmara*.[72] These administrative measures made clear that the magistrate could exercise powers that were normally the prerogative of local officers and institutions.

---

69. João de Sousa Cardenas was a professional administrator, the son of Desembargador do Paço Pedro de Cardenas Sottomayor. He was one of the second group of magistrates sent to Brazil as replacements in 1621. See ANTT, *Chan. Filipe III, Doações*, liv. 38, f. 141v.; Andrade e Silva, *Col. chron.*, III, 30; *Index das notas de vários tabeliães de Lisboa. Séculos xvi–xviii*, 3 vols. (Lisbon, 1931–1944), II, 68.

70. *Autos de correições de ouvidores do Rio de Janeiro*, Eduardo Tourinho, ed., Prefeitura do Districto Federal, 3 vols. (Rio de Janeiro, 1929–1931), I, 5.

71. *Consulta* of the Desembargo do Paço (Lisbon, 29 November 1629), AGS, *Sec. Prov.* 1475, ff. 247–250.

72. *Autos de correições*, I, 5–9.

This is not surprising, however, since the separation of local and central government was never clearly defined.

Two actions, more than any others, however, estranged and embittered the citizens and authorities of Rio de Janeiro. First, Cardenas, on orders from the governor-general, Diogo Mendonça Furtado, had imposed a new tax (*avaria*) to pay for the costs of strengthening the defenses of Bahia and Pernambuco. The threat of Dutch military action against Brazil was real, and Philip IV naturally expected the Portuguese to pay for their own defense. He failed, however, to reckon with Portuguese resentment and local self-interest. In Rio de Janeiro the new tax was considered a fiscal burden that benefited only Bahia and Pernambuco, and an angry mob forced Cardenas to seek refuge in Agua de Carioca, a half-league from the city.[73]

The unlucky desembargador had also aroused a great deal of opposition by his reform of the electoral process of the *câmara.* The power to review municipal elections had been expressly granted to *corregidores, ouvidores* and desembargadores by a law of 12 November 1611, issued in Portugal and registered in the Golden Book of the Relação, but Cardenas had enforced the law by eliminating from the roll of eligible voters all those who did not reside in the city or at least maintain a residence there.[74] Inhabitants of the surrounding areas, paid employees, tavernkeepers and vendors were also excluded. The changes upset existing patterns of power and influence and were obviously detrimental to important elements of society. Pressures were brought to bear on Cardenas, complaints against him were forwarded to Portugal, and it appears that at one point he was arrested along with the local *ouvidor.* His reforms, nevertheless, were implemented.[75]

---

73. AGS, *Sec. Prov.* 1475, ff. 247–50.

74. *Autos de correições,* I, 6; Livro Dourado, ff. 336–338; Andrade e Silva, *Col. Chron.,* III, 314–316. Boxer, *Portuguese Society,* pp. 5–7, describes the electoral process of the *câmaras.*

75. Coaracy, *O Rio,* pp. 61–63, which is a letter of the governor of Rio Martim de Sá to the *câmara* (5 November 1624). King to Governors of

The use of desembargadores of the Relação as circuit court judges in the captaincies of Brazil, coupled with their common absence from Bahia in the pursuance of normal duties, had a deleterious effect on the performace of the High Court. Land surveys often called the magistrate far from the courthouse in Salvador, and the duties of the probate judge also included a yearly tour of inspection of probate matters in other areas.[76] The continual absence of the judges from Salvador and their use by the crown for non-judicial functions caused increasing delays in the dispatch of justice in the colony. The interference of the magistrates in local affairs during inspections in the captaincies was a cause of animosity, especially when the interests of central government clashed with those of the local political or socio-economic elites.

Portugal (Madrid, 14 October 1625), ANTT, *Col. S. Vicente*, liv. 19, f. 383, notes only that Martim de Sá has complained of the actions of João de Sousa Cardenas, but does not explain the nature of the complaint. Lourenço de Furtado Mendonça, later a prelate of Rio de Janeiro, claimed that Cardenas was arrested for enforcing pro-Indian legislation, but Mendonça was an interested party and his testimony must be used with care. See his printed memorial (Madrid, 1638), a copy of which exists as BNM, Cod. 2367.

76. ANTT, *Mesa de Con.*, liv. 23, f. 253v. (8 March 1614).

VIII. MAGISTRACY AND SOCIETY

The marriage of desembargadores results in two evils: the first is to become related to almost everyone in this land and therefore suspect; the second is the acquisition of properties which then cause conflicts, lawsuits, and sometimes battles.

Gov. Antônio Luís da Câmara
Coutinho (Bahia, 25 June 1691)

The sober university-trained magistrates who disembarked on the quay of Salvador in June of 1609 entered into a colonial world, a social universe based on traditional Portuguese patterns yet molded to accommodate and overcome the peculiarities of a society and economy in formation. The magistrates represented power and status to this society, not only in their aggregate as a tribunal but as individuals as well. Thus a description of the High Court's actions cannot in itself explain the impact of that body on Brazilian society. Bureaucrats are human and to overlook this truism is to lose sight of the dynamic relationships existing between bureaucracy and society. The story of the impact of bureaucracy on colonial brazil is a history of the multiple and often divergent goals of the metropolitan government, colonial interests, and the magistrates themselves, either individually or as a group. Each factor in this bureaucratic equation sought to dominate the others and to appropriate certain resources or advantages to itself. The failures and successes of each are in a sense the history of colonial Brazilian social and political formation.

The crown realized that social and economic pressures could be brought to bear on the professional magistracy and that linkages between magistrates and society could create alternate goals beyond those sanctioned by bureaucratic norms. To a large extent legislation concerning the professional magistracy was designed to organize all magisterial behavior into patterns that served royal administrative ends. Royal justice and royal bureaucracy were predicated on the honesty and impartiality of the magistracy, and, at the same time, on its obedience and loyalty to the king. Perhaps the oath which each desembargador took upon formally taking office is the best gauge of what the crown expected of its judges. The oath ran: "I gave to no one, nor will I give, nor have I promised to give or order, nor will I order anything to anybody, for having given me this office . . . I will observe and faithfully guard completely the service of God and of His Majesty and of law and justice equally to persons of all conditions." [1]

Gubernatorial reports and periodic examinations(*devassas*) present yet another measure of what the crown considered to be appropriate magisterial behavior. The repetition of such phrases as "of good understanding" (*de bom entendimento*) and "of good learning" (*de boas letras*) continually appear in laudatory evaluations of magistrates.[2] Such descriptions indicate that professional

1. "Forma de juramento que ha de tomar o governador, chanceler, e desembargadores q. de novo entrarem na Casa da Relação da Bahya," APB, Termos de Posse, 123, ff. 182v.–183. Cf. Livro da Relação, BGUC, Códice 708, f. 111–111v.

2. See for example, Governor Antônio Luís Gonçalves de Câmara Coutinho to Conselho Ultramarino (Bahia, 25 June 1691), AHU, Bahia *pap. avul.* caixa 16; and *Consulta* of Conselho Ultramarino (9 November 1692), *DH*, LXXXIX (1950), 209–211; "Devassa de Dez. Francisco de Silva Corte Real (1783)," APB, Devassas (1759–1783), 572. See the evaluation published in Ignacio Accioli de Cerqueira e Silva, *Memórias históricas e políticas da Província da Bahia*, Braz do Amaral, ed., 6 vols. (Bahia, 1931), III, 229. (Hereafter cited as Accioli, *Memórias*.)

competence was highly valued. Moreover, royal judges were expected to project a certain image. The crown expected their personal lives to be characterized by great sobriety, and adjectives such as "serious, grave, able, and prudent," were among the highest compliments a magistrate could receive. Above all, however, the one phrase which appears as a constant refrain in magisterial evaluations is "cleanliness of hands (*limpeça de maos*)." A judge with clean hands was a judge uncorrupted by graft, malfeasance, or personal interests—a man who separated himself fully from the influence of others and who lived his life guided only by the regulations of his profession and the desires of the crown as expressed in royal ordinances. Such men were few and far between.

The crown used two methods to insure the loyalty, impartiality and administrative effectiveness of the judges. First, because the disembargadores were representatives of royal authority, every effort was made to raise them above society and to give them by means of prestige, wealth, and social standing a position of unassailable respect. Colonial society placed great emphasis on ascriptive status. A wealthy landowner with pretentions of nobility would not readily acceed to law enforcement by men whom he viewed as his social inferiors. As we shall see, very few of the disembargadores came from *fidalgo* backgrounds and thus they lacked the natural social preeminence of nobility.[3] The crown did everything in its power, therefore, to insure and buttress the dignity and rank of the crown judges. Desembargadores received high salaries, financial perquisites, and exemption from certain taxes. Their persons were made inviolate. Physical attack against a desembargador was punishable by death and slander against him would result in penal exile.[4] Magistrates often received habits in the military orders, especially in the coveted Order of Christ. In the colony, the desembargadores held honorific places in various civil and religious events. The sight of the dark-robed learned judges marching closely behind the governor and the bishop sym-

3. See pp. 285–290.
4. *Ord. fil.*, V, tit. lix.

bolically demonstrated the unity of these officers and the elevated position of the judges in society. At the same time the advantages of privilege and position were not lost on the magistrates. It was clear that favors flowed from the crown and that significant rewards could be had by complying with the required bureaucratic norms.

While trying to insure their status, the crown also sought to cut off the magistrates from the society in which they lived. Desembargadores were expected to live in close residential proximity to each other and to limit their social intercourse with others in society. Marriage to women in Brazil was expressly forbidden by an *alvará* of 22 November 1610, although upon request the crown could and sometimes did grant exceptions to the law.[5] Royal ordinances also prohibited a magistrate from conducting business or owning land within the area of his jurisdiction.[6] Behind such measures lay a basic belief that the magistracy could operate in a social vacuum, devoid of the pressures of family, friends, or interest. Such an idea was utopian to say the least.

Isolating the desembargadores from society was impossible. The magistrates were no better or worse than the society in which they lived and they often sought to use their office for personal gain. Bribery and subversion of justice naturally went unrecorded, but in the records of the first Relaçáo hints of such activity do appear. In one instance, Antônio das Póvoas was disqualified from service on a financial committee because he was considered suspect in some of the questions under review. In another case, the crown ordered Governor Gaspar de Sousa to investigate the conditions surrounding the award of a certain tithe contract to determine

5. Cf. Andrade e Silva, *Coll. chron.*, I, 295; *Ord. fil.*, I, t. xcv; J. P. Ribeiro, *Indice chron.*, I, 26, and Andrade e Silva, *Col. chron.*, I, 113. In 1615, acting on the petition of his wife, the crown allowed desembargador Manoel Jácome Bravo to return to Portugal, but it took the opportunity to order that henceforth all married desembargadores sent to Brazil should be accompanied by their wives.

6. *Ord. fil.*, II, tit. lix.

"whether the contractor had an understanding with the judges of the High Court which led them to make such extraordinary and favorable decisions on his behalf." [7] Less shady but no less illegal were the economic activities of the magistrates of the first Relação. Traces of their transactions can be seen in contemporary documentation. Desembargador Francisco da Fonseca acquired a *sesmaria* in 1609 from the governor, a large grant six leagues square in the rich sugar-producing land in the Recôncavo.[8] Pero de Cascais entered into a number of business ventures such as the outfitting of ships for the whaling season of 1613. These activities brought him great debts and many jurisdictional headaches.[9]

The institution of slavery so pervaded the society of colonial Brazil that the desembargadores were not free from its effects. Most seem to have joined the ranks of the slave-owners upon arrival in Brazil, and some engaged in the business of slave trading. A ledger of the slaves received from Angola under the contract of Antônio Fernandes de Elvas lists the acquisition of African slaves by the desembargadores Ruy Mendes de Abreu and Afonso Garcia Tinoco. Ruy Mendes de Abreu purchased one adult and two children in 1618 while Afonso Garcia Tinoco acquired three slaves from Angola between 1619 and 1620.[10] This was not, however, the latter's first contact with African flesh, since in July 1612 he had sold seven Africans at public auction in Bahia on behalf of his friend or partner André Velho Fonseca, a magistrate in

7. King to Gaspar de Sousa (Lisbon, 8 October 1612); and king to Gaspar de Sousa (Lisbon, 17 August 1612), AHI, Correspondencia . . . Gaspar de Sousa.

8. ? to Count of Linhares (1609), ANTT, *Cart. Jes.*, maço 9, doc. 189. The letter runs: "it seems my duty to inform Your Lordship that governor D. Diogo de Meneses gave a *sesmaria* of three leagues of land in Sergipe on the lands of Your Lordship to a desembargador named Francisco da Fonseca who came with the tribunal." Cf. *Publicações do Arquivo Nacional*, XXVII, 34.

9. Testament of Pedro Viegas Giraldes (1637), ASCMB, Livro I do Tombo 40, ff. 125v–126; see the full discussion on pp. 212–215.

10. Account book of the contract of Antônio Fernandes de Elvas, AHU, Bahia *pap. avul.* caixa 1, ff. 7, 8.

Angola.[11] Census data from the eighteenth century and occasional references from the late seventeenth century indicate that slaves of the desembargadores were used primarily as household servants or as porters. Magistrates with large agricultural holdings employed slave labor on their estates.[12]

Critics of the Relação and the judiciary in general (and there were always plenty of these) pointed to the disregard of statutes and the wheeling and dealing of the desembargadores as sufficient reason to abolish the High Court. Defenders argued, however, that the problem was one of individual abuse and not of the judicial structure. Whatever the problems of the Relação, the presence of ten magistrates who could keep an eye on each other was surely preferable to the previous system of one relatively unchecked *ouvidor geral.* As an anonymous observer wrote in 1626: "if the sweet aroma of ambar or money or the evil stink of Negroes can accomplish so much that reaching the nostrils of one [desembargador] it subverts justice in a High Court, what would it do to one man alone?" [13]

Royal efforts to elevate the desembargadores above society and to separate them from it had exactly the opposite effect. The wealth, power, status, and position of the desembargadores made contact with them all the more desirable for important socio-economic groups or extended families. The linkages between the magistrates and society can be categorized under two basic headings: non-ritualized and ritualized. In the first category various forms of voluntary association, friendships, or partnership constituted the principal connectives. The dignity and power of the

---

11. Certification of Christóvão Vieira Ravasco (2 July 1612), AHU, Bahia *pap. avul.* caixa 1.

12. Avelino de Jesus da Costa, "População da Cidade da Baía em 1775," *Actas. V Colóquio internacional de estudos Luso-brasileiros,* 4 vols. (Coimbra, 1963), I, 191–275. Desembargador Agostinho de Azevedo Monteiro, who grew sugar cane on his properties in Bahia, was reported to have twenty-seven slaves in 1675. See *DHBNR,* LXXXVIII (1950), 48–50.

13. Razões q. darão os moradores da Bahia para não se extigirem a Relação, BNL, Pomb. 647, ff. 69–72.

desembargadores made them preferred friends and welcomed members of certain local organizations. It is not surprising to find Manoel Pinto da Rocha, chancellor of the Relação, serving in 1623 as *provedor* of the Santa Casa da Misericórdia. The Misericórdia was a charitable brotherhood which always included the most respected citizens of the city in its membership. The *provedor* was the senior officer of the Misericórdia and obviously Manoel Pinto da Rocha had been selected because of his prestige as chancellor of the Relação. In fact, in the early eighteenth century the post of *provedor* of the Misericórdia was often controlled by desembargadores of the High Court.[14]

The attempts of colonial institutions or groups to appropriate the power or prestige of desembargadores for the goals of the corporate entity were paralleled on the individual level. It is understandable why Jeronima Fernandes, an honorable old widow, made arrangements in her will for her grandson to live and study with Disembargador Antão de Mesquita so that the boy could eventually become a priest or a friar. In the learned and respected magistrate the boy would find an able teacher and a powerful protector.[15]

Of the ritually sanctioned methods of social linkage between magistrates and society, marriage was undoubtedly the most important. Although royal statute and precedent admonished against the union of crown judges and local residents, at least 17 per cent of the 168 desembargadores who served in Brazil prior to 1759 married Brazilian women.[16] Each union enmeshed the groom in an extensive web of familial ties and social obligations. Certainly, the possibility of conflict with one's in-laws was not absent from the seventeenth century, but the formal method of marriage contract and courtship—to say nothing of the family's interest in the

---

14. ASCMB, Livro I do Tombo 40 (30 June 1622), f. 25; A. J. R. Russell-Wood, *Fidalgos and Philanthropists*, pp. 372–375. Also see below, pp. 318–320.

15. Testament of Jerônima Fernandes (1 Nov. 1620), ASCMB, Livro I do Tombo 40, f. 131.

16. See pp. 338–341.

marriage arrangement—undoubtedly decreased the level or frequency of such conflict. Marriage was a business venture for both the judges and the colonial families. Aside from the fulfillment of certain social, sexual, and psychic needs, the judge sought economic position while the family hoped to incorporate the power, prestige, and status of the desembargador into the family network. There was, in other words, an exchange of resources with expectations of reciprocity and mutual hope of advantage.[17]

Of the original group of ten desembargadores, two married in Brazil and the nature of the families into which they married gives us some idea of the sort of ties such unions created. Both desembargadores wed daughters of the Pernambucan sugar aristocracy. Antão de Mesquita received royal permission to marry Antonia Bezerra, daughter of Paulo Bezerra, a sugar planter and later an alderman of the municipal council of Olinda.[18] Desembargador Manoel Pinto da Rocha also found a spouse among the Pernambucan aristocracy. He married Catherina de Frielas (Lopes) on 28 June 1612 in the cathedral of Olinda.[19] This was his wife's second marriage and it apparently placed Pinto da Rocha in a familial relationship with the Bezerra Barriga family, into which Antão de Mesquita had also married. This was one of the great lineages of Pernambuco, originating from the entail of Paredes of Viana do Castelo in northern Portugal.[20]

---

17. For an interesting study taken from the family's point of view see Marvin B. Sussman, "Some Conceptual Issues in Family-Organizational Linkages" (mimeo, 1969), a paper read to the American Sociological Association.

18. *Livro Primeiro*, pp. 148, 294.

19. ANTT, Chan. Filipe II, *Privilégios*, liv. 2, f. 196v. (29 Oct. 1611); Antônio José Victoriano Borges da Fonseca, "Nobiliarchia Pernambucana," is the great eighteenth-century genealogy of northeastern Brazil. It has been published in the *Anais da Biblioteca Nacional do Rio de Janeiro*. Sections pertinent to these marriages can be seen in *ABNR*, XLVII (1925), 164, 419, 470; and XLVIII (1926), 207, 220, 469.

20. Petition of Francisca Bezerra, AHI, ff. 297–298. Figure 2 indicates the kinship relations of Manuel Pinto da Rocha and probably Antão de Mesquita with the Bezerra Barriga family. In Figure 2 an M indicates

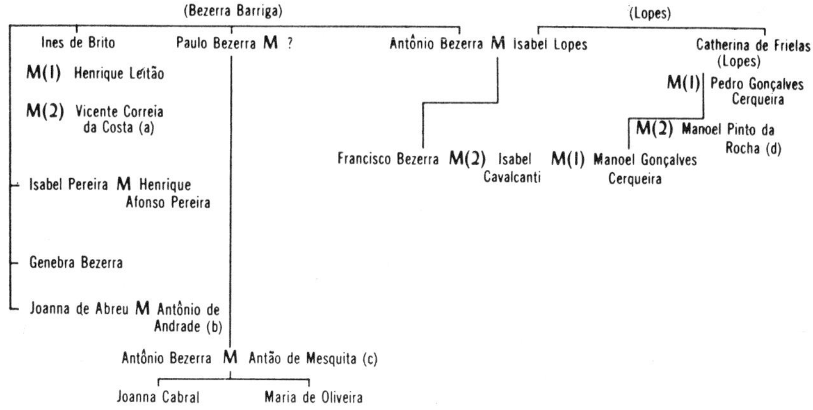

Fig. 2. Marriage Connections of Desembargadores Antão de Mesquita and Manoel Pinto da Rocha.

If, in fact, the father of Antão de Mesquita's wife was the same Paulo Bezerra who was the brother of Antônio Bezerra, the husband of the sister of Pinto da Rocha's spouse, then the two desembargadores were both connected to one of the most powerful clans in colonial Brazil. Manoel Gonçalves Cerqueira, the stepson of Desembargador Manoel Pinto da Rocha, was a knight of the Order of Christ and *familiar* of the Inquisition in Brazil. His wife, Isabel Cavalcanti, belonged to the great Cavalcanti Albuquerque family that dominated the northern captaincies of the colony. Whatever the personal sentiments involved, connection with these families presented a great attraction to the magistrates and offered them economic opportunities not usually available to High Court magis-

marriage. The two magistrates are (c) and (d). (a) held proprietary rights over the customs house of Pernambuco, and (b) may be the Antônio de Andrade mentioned on pp. 189–190 in connection with Sergipe d'El-Rey. The Bezerra Barriga clan originated from a Galician family long connected with Portugal. The predominance of northern Portuguese families in Pernambuco, especially those from Viana do Castelo, has been noted by C. R. Boxer, *The Dutch in Brazil, 1624–1654* (Oxford, 1957), p. 35. See also *ABNR*, XLVII, 164; António Machado de Faria, *Amorial lusitano* (Lisbon, 1961), p. 99.

trates. On the other hand, the great colonial families could not fail to notice the real and potential advantages of having a friend at court and perhaps eventually a relative in the councils of the king.

A second potential set of ritualized linkages between magistrates and colonial society was formed by godparentage or *compadrio*. Serving as a baptismal godparent or witness to a marriage placed mutually accepted and religiously sanctioned obligations on an individual. Such relations extended the social genealogy or sum of an individual's blood, ritual, and personal ties, far beyond the limits of biological or matrimonial kinship. In an area of intense competition for scant resources, such relations played a significant role. Unfortunately, few Bahian parish registers for the period of the first Relação are extant, but contemporary records from Portugal and the practice of desembargadores in late seventeenth-century Bahia make it safe to assume that the magistrates of the first Bahian tribunal also participated in these relations.[21]

Primary relationships tended to grow at an almost geometric rate. Once the first contact was established, be it marriage, partnership, or some other form, added relationships soon developed. Like a pebble dropped into a pool, there was no way of telling where the eddys of kinship and friendship would end. Moreover, the ritualized and non-ritualized relations seem to cluster around the same individuals. Once integrated into the kinship structure, a magistrate became an accepted member of colonial society. It is certainly no accident that Manoel Pinto da Rocha was chosen as Provedor of the Misericórdia, for he was one of the two magistrates of the first tribunal married to a Brazilian woman. In fact, all the desembargadores who held this position prior to 1755 were married to Brazilian women or were Brazilian by birth.[22] Moreover, such

---

21. On *compadrio*, see the general discussion in Charles Wagley, *The Latin American Tradition* (New York, 1968), Chapter IV, "Kinship Patterns in Brazil." For examples of magistrates involved in relations of *compadrio* in the seventeenth century see Edgar Prestage and Pedro d'Azevedo (eds.), *Registro da Freguesia da Sé desde 1563 até 1610*, 2 vols. (Coimbra, 1927), II (1582–1610).

22. See pp. 319–320.

association led almost invariably to the acquisition of property, either through dowery arrangements or by inheritance.

The considerable gap between the bureaucratic norms established for the performance of the magisterial corps and their many violations of these rules seems irreconcilable. This dichotomy did not, however, result in the breakdown of the administrative system. To understand why, we must insert a third category of "accepted behavior" somewhere between legality and actual practice. Although the law stipulated that no judge could have kinship ties within the area of his jurisdiction, the crown could and did allow a certain amount of deviation from the legal principles. But when a magistrate overstepped the bounds of accepted behavior, then the letter of the law could be strictly enforced and the violation punished. Such a pattern placed evaluation of behavior and ultimate control of bureaucratic performance in the hands of the crown yet allowed for considerable flexibility. This was perhaps the only way to reconcile the demands of royal government with the desires of the magistrates and the needs of the colonials.

Taken from a strict legalistic point of view, personal ties, business contacts, and kinship linkages were all deviant forms of behavior working against the successful operation of government. Such a definition obscures the functional aspects of primary relations and various forms of corruption. The political system of the Portuguese empire lacked well-defined mechanisms for the expression of group interests. Colonial representatives were not even included in the meetings of the Cortés (the Assembly of the Three Estates), which met rarely and only at the king's pleasure; and although individuals or groups could petition the crown directly, administrative inertia and inner-chamber politics usually carried more weight than colonial pleadings. The difficulty of influencing the formation of laws in the metropolis and the lack of representative institutions in the colony forced interest groups in Brazil to exert pressure on government officials at the local level. Corruption allowed these groups to influence the law at the level of enforcement since their influence in policy formation was restricted in a variety of ways. The ties between royal bureaucrats and colonial society allowed considerable interaction and the expression of colonial interests within the formal structure of government.[23] It should be made clear, however, that not all segments of the colonial population had access to this form of influence. The kind of social or economic resources which attracted magistrates into primary relationships could be offered in seventeenth-century Brazil only by the white planter elite, other government officials, and possibly a few wholesale export merchants. There was little chance indeed that the mulatto cobbler or the poor white farmer would become the father-in-law or business partner of a desembargador.

Using the criteria of accepted behavior, it is also fair to ask whether primary relations should be equated with graft and bribery as forms of corruption. According to bureaucratic norms such was the case, but community standards obviously permitted a different interpretation. One index of the difference is provided by the extent to which secrecy cloaked a magistrate's actions. No desembargador was likely to make public his receipt of kickbacks or his involvement in graft, whereas his kinship and friendship ties and to some extent even his business dealings might be common knowledge. Obviously, a community standard existed beyond the printed regulations of the law, and desembargadores complied with the former more often than the latter. The divergence between the bureaucratic and the colonial view of corruption may explain why colonists alternately attacked the High Court as a corrupt institution and then leaped to its defense when the crown moved against those judges who seemed by the extent of their personal relations to be the most corrupt.

The importance of family and primary relations in colonial Brazilian society would be difficult to overestimate. Whereas modern historians often ignore or depreciate the genealogical histories of colonial Brazil, these works do reflect their authors' perceptions

23. James C. Scott, "The Analysis of Corruption in Developing Nations," *Comparative Studies in Society and History*, XI (June 1969), 315–341.

of reality and underline the importance of kinship to this society. It is therefore not surprising that the professional bureaucrats hoped to utilize primary or kinship relations to supplement social and economic resources provided by their occupation. By the late seventeenth century desembargadores often arrived in Brazil accompanied by family, friends, and retainers who also constructed their own social genealogies and thus further entwined the magistrates and colonial society.

Emphasis on cooperation and friendly primary relations should not obscure the fact that non-categorical primary relations could also be hostile. A magistrate might be coerced rather than cajoled. In 1681 Cristóvão de Burgos, a desembargador in Brazil for twenty-six years, wrote that powerful men often threatened magistrates in the colony and sentences went unexecuted.[24] His statements could also be applied to the second decade of the seventeenth century. The business dealings and large debts incurred by some magistrates made them especially vulnerable to financial arm-twisting. A good example is the case of Pero de Cascais, who arrested two men for causing a public disturbance. The troublemakers were henchmen of Provedor-Mór Sebastião Borges, who brought charges against the desembargador for his involvement in a whale-fishing scheme. Obviously, the judge's effectiveness had been impaired by his vulnerability on non-bureaucratic matters. Cascais pleaded in his own behalf that he was a judge "with an open door," and that "since the discovery of Brazil, neither Your Majesty nor the people have had another who served as well; and this my King and Lord is my only crime." [25] The conflict between Cascais and Borges also points out that primary groups which had bureaucratic but non-magisterial allies or members could cause considerable difficulty for the desembargadores. Greedy officials or their relatives and friends could use their position to circumvent justice. Pero de Cascais, that

24. Memorial of Christóvão de Burgos (Bahia, 1 August 1681), AHU, Bahia *pap. avul.* caixa 14.

25. "Diz Pero de Cascais de Abreu . . . ," (1617), AHU, Bahia *pap. avul.* caixa 1.

valorous if somewhat headstrong desembargador of the first Relação, again provides a good example. On one occasion he arrested the sergeant-major, Antônio de Azevedo, for thrashing the doorkeeper of the Relação. Azevedo was a friend and retainer of Governor Gaspar de Sousa, and as a result of this incident Cascais acquired a powerful enemy in the person of the governor. The animosity between Cascais and Gaspar de Sousa probably contributed to Cascais' suspension in 1614.[26] Incidents of this nature indicate that some of the jurisdictional disputes that plagued colonial society may have emanated from personal feuds and animosity as well as from institutional conflict.

Although members of colonial society could use prestige, power, and influence to incorporate or negate the authority of the High Court and subvert the freedom of justice from outside pressure, the Relação never became the creature of any one group in Brazilian society. Professional integrity, pride, malice, and devotion to the crown contributed to the maintenance of institutional autonomy in the face of pressure from groups and individuals. Magistrates who were motivated by career considerations remained dependent on the crown for promotion and reward. It was the old story of mutual dependence between the magistracy and royal power, and it was only slightly modified in the colony. Royal interest could never be fully surrendered to personal goals if there was any hope of professional advancement. Dominant groups and individuals in Brazilian society thus found it difficult to defy the Relação.

No one was beyond the power of the court. Jorge Lopes da Costa, the rabble-rousing attorney of the *câmara*, was banished from Bahia for a short time for insulting the *ouvidor geral*. Da Costa counted among his clients and protectors the Countess of Linhares, the Jesuits, and Antônio Fernandes de Elvas, owner of

26. King to Gaspar de Sousa (1614), BI, Correspondencia . . . Gaspar de Sousa.

the Angolan slave contract, yet the Relação had taken no nonsense from him.[27] Even more representative is the case of Luís de Aguiar, twenty-seven years a resident of Brazil, pilot and captain in the coast-guard, fluent in the *lingua geral*, and a skilled legal secretary. Aguiar was an honored and respected member of the Bahian community who could produce letters of recommendation from three former governors and the town council of Salvador. Nevertheless, he had run afoul of three desembargadores who brought him before the bar of justice. Aguiar claimed that he was sentenced to ten years in the galleys, "more because of their malice than for the gravity of the crime." [28]

One way to evaluate the independence of the High Court is to examine its relationship to the sugar aristocracy. In the seventeenth century this sector more than any other exerted considerable political pressure both in the colony and in the metropolis. Whether justice officers in Brazil were admonished by the crown to avoid molesting the sugar planters, as one contemporary observer claimed, can not be ascertained.[29] There is no doubt, however, that the sugar sector could exert considerable pressure on the crown and its representatives. The development of the colony depended directly on the agricultural inputs of the sugar sector. Despite the continuing but declining dyewood trade and the constant search for minerals, sugar and Brazil had become synonymous and the sugar industry was always a creation of the private sector, a fact that the crown recognized. The planter elite controlled the municipal

---

27. Jorge Lopes da Costa was undoubtedly an important man in seventeenth-century Bahia. He not only represented important clients, but also had been treasurer of the Misericórdia in 1614, a post reserved for wealthy individuals. He was, however, denounced to the Inquisition in 1618 as a New Christian. Cf. ASCMB, Livro I do Tombo, f. 5–5v.; *ABNR,* XLIX, 180.

28. Petition of Luís de Aguiar, AGS, *Guerra Antiga,* legajo 906.

29. Memorial of Joseph Israel da Costa to the Prince of Orange, Algemein Rijksarchief (The Hague), Loketkas 6, Staten Generaal, West Indische Compagnie.

councils of northeastern Brazil and formed a significant lobby at the councils of the king, but it never fully controlled the magistrates of the Relação.

Clearly, the High Court's enforcement of the Indian protection law of 1609 had quickly dashed any hopes that the planters may have nurtured about finding the tribunal a pliant ally. From that point on it became clear that the services which the High Court could provide to the sugar planters would be more than balanced by the potential threat it presented to the dominance of the planters.

The presence of the Relação in Bahia did facilitate some matters for the planters. Disputes between equals could now be settled at less cost and in less time. At least one great absentee landowner, the Countess of Linhares, was entitled to have all suits involving her property heard by a designated magistrate, in this case Desembargador Afonso Garcia Tinoco.[30] Land survey and demarcation was another service which the tribunal provided. Statute required that such surveys be performed by a *letrado*, and throughout the history of the Relação the desembargadores often performed this task.[31] This service was a mixed blessing for the planters, however. On one hand, water and property rights were firmly established, but in the Recôncavo, where much of the land had been acquired without formal title such surveys threatened the status quo in which the planters had a vested interest. The elimination of fraud, the enforcement of regulatory legislation, and the ordering of an unruly society in which personal power had formerly settled most disputes all made the Relação a potential threat to the sugar planter elite.

The role of the Relação in adjudicating disputes between the *senhores de engenho* and their dependent tenants, sharecroppers, and copyholders (*lavradores de cana*) is one index of the High

30. Cf. *Ord. fil.*, III, t. xii; ANTT, *Cart. Jes.*, maço 16, doc. 21.

31. Examples of surveys taken by desembargadores in the seventeenth century can be seen in ANTT, *Cart. Jes.*, maço 14, n. 40; APB, Ordens regias I, n. 32; Ordens regias I, n. 63.

Court's effect on the existing patterns of dominance. Although on many issues the sugar magnates and the *lavradores de cana* shared common attitudes and interests, the relationship of tenant to landlord also brought these groups into conflict.[32] The cane growers were generally men from the same social origins as the planters, but they lacked the necessary capital to set up a sugar mill and were thus willing to supply cane to the mills in the hopes of eventually amassing enough capital or credit to become mill owners. Economic and social domination marked the relationship of the planters to the cane growers. The planters treated their tenants and sharecroppers like retainers and the tenants found appeal to the metropolitan courts too expensive or slow to be of much use. The presence of the Relação in Bahia after 1609 opened new channels of justice to the cane growers.

In 1616 Manoel de Couto, acting as representative of the Countess of Linhares, instituted a new arrangement by which the tenants of her *engenho* of Sergipe do Conde would pay to the *engenho* two-thirds of the sugar they produced each year. The cane growers vehemently opposed this new contract. Moreover, some of these *lavradores de cana* had purchased lands from former overseers of the plantation, and de Couto now claimed that the sales had been made without the authority of the Countess of Linhares. He petitioned that the present owners be removed and all such land be returned to the *engenho*. Attorneys for the *engenho* prepared a strong brief in defense of the Countess' position, but the Relação in two separate decisions ruled in favor of the cane growers.[33]

In a third case tried at the same time, Francisco de Aguilar de Araújo, a tenant farmer, had refused to accept the new one-third contract, and the representative of the Countess of Linhares had initiated a proceeding of eviction. Aguilar de Araújo claimed that he had worked the plot for thirty-three years and that he had made

32. See my paper, "Free Labor in a Slave Economy: The Lavradores de Cana of Bahia" in Dauril Alden, ed., *Colonial Roots of Modern Brazil.*

33. "Lembrança para a senhora Condessa de Linhares sobre as suas fazendas de Serigipe," ANTT, *Cart. Jes.*, maço 13, doc. 7.

considerable improvements on the property. Once again the Relação voted against the great *engenho* and the judges ruled that Aguilar de Araújo could not be evicted unless paid in full for all improvements he had made. It was a decision, said Manoel de Couto, "that we considered most unjust, but since it fell within the jurisdiction of the Relação of Brazil, we did not appeal the sentence [to Portugal]." [34]

Nor did the pressure on the great *engenho* decrease with the adverse decisions of 1616. In the following year, Antão de Mesquita, as crown's attorney, complained that the Countess of Linhares had taken far more land than was included in her original *sesmaria* of two leagues by four leagues. He emphasized that such usurped lands belonged to the crown and that these Recôncavo properties in Sergipe do Conde had never been properly surveyed. Possession of these lands by the Countess constituted a loss to the royal treasury which the crown could ill afford. Such pressures exerted on the powerful Countess of Linhares, a proprietor who held special privileges with the tribunal, indicated the ways in which the Relação impeded the high-handed activities of the sugar elite.[35] At times the Relação could and did argue in behalf of the planters and their retainers but the authority of the High Court and the independent power of the planters were destined to conflict.

The presence of the Relação in Brazil, however, did not break the power of the interlocking extended families, most of which were involved in the sugar industry, nor did it weaken their grasp on the social and economic reins of the colony. The utilization of office in the municipal councils and local judicial hierarchy enabled these kindreds to exercise control over many areas of policy and economic activity. Once again, however, the presence of the Relação at least opened new avenues of complaint and possible redress from their cavalier methods. But as long as royal interests were not at stake and royal authority was not questioned, the power of these groups and individuals remained unimpaired. For-

34. *Ibid.*

35. Report of Antão de Mesquita (20 August 1617), AHU, Bahia *pap. avul.* caixa 1.

tunately, the papers of a dispute involving one of these clans were submitted to the Relação and have survived, and from them we can get a clear view of how these interlocking families exercised political control.

The dispute centered on Miguel Maciel, the secretary of the town council of Sergipe d'El-Rey and a notary public. Maciel was not a powerful man in the community, but he was a *moço fidalgo* and his position was an important one. In 1615 Maciel became involved in an acrimonious clash with clerical representatives of the ecclesiastical courts, and while the Relação—always intent on controlling ecclesiastical judicial powers—supported him, Maciel was removed from office by the *ouvidor* of Sergipe, Antônio Andrade Caminha.

Although there were a number of charges against Maciel, he claimed that the underlying cause of his suspension lay in his refusal to surrender documents to the *ouvidor* which implicated Gaspar de Amorim, Gaspar de Oliveira, and six or seven of their friends in various thefts and frauds. Andrade Caminha, Amorim, Oliveira, and Manuel Curvello Velho had all served on the *câmara* of Sergipe and the last three were married to sisters, thus placing them in a degree of kinship that should have prevented their simultaneous service on the municipal council.[36] These were powerful men whose position rested on their wealth and family ties. Gaspar de Amorim owned herds, slaves, *sesmarias*, and probably an *engenho*.[37] Antônio Andrade Caminha was "of noble background and related to the best people of Pernambuco, where he had served as judge and alderman in the municipal council of Olinda."[38] It is interesting to note that the families of Andrade Caminha and Amorim were both of Galician origin, a fact that Miguel Maciel did not fail to point out.[39] Both Andrade Caminha

36. *Ord. fil.*, I, t. lxvii, 1.

37. Oliveira Freire, *História de Sergipe*, "cartas des sesmarias," pp. 355, 366, 394, 398.

38. *Livro Primeiro*, p. 245.

39. Carlos Xavier Paes Barreto, *Os primativos colonizadores nordestinos e seus descendentes* (Rio de Janeiro, 1960), pp. 346–347.

and Amorim defended their joint participation in the *câmara* despite their links of kinship on the ground that there were few people in the captaincy qualified to fill the positions of alderman.

Miguel Maciel did not take his suspension quietly, and he soon appeared before the home of Antônio Andrade Caminha, where he shouted that the *ouvidor* was a "dirty Galician," and that all such were "cuckolds and Jews (*cabroins e judeus*)." [40] He dared the *ouvidor* to lay down his staff of office and pick up a sword. Such scandalous insults against the person of a judge were illegal. Instead of drawing his sword, Andrade Caminha drew up charges and gathered testimony against Maciel, who along with his brother was then sentenced to four years of exile in North Africa. Significantly, among the witnesses called to testify against Maciel were Andrade Caminha's brothers-in-law Gaspar de Oliveira and Manuel Curvello Velho. Maciel and his brother fled from arrest and appealed to the Relação for justice. Maciel claimed that Andrade Caminha, Amorim, Curvello Velho, and Oliveira were "capital enemies" and thus by law excluded from giving testimony or participating in the adjudication of the charges.

How the Relação decided this appeal is unknown, but since the governor supported the *ouvidor*, it would appear that the appeal failed. Miguel Maciel was undoubtedly wrong in much of this dispute, but the ability of certain individuals to control justice on the local level and the inability, or at times unwillingness, of the Relação to alter this situation is apparent.

The relationship established between desembargadores and elements of Brazilian society during the early years of the seventeenth century set the pattern for the remainder of the colonial period, even though specific conditions changed over time. The tribunal never fully ceded its independence and authority, but individual magistrates did become linked by kinship and interest to Brazilian society.

40. *Livro Primeiro*, p. 106.

IX. THE HIGH COURT IN CONFLICT

Good counsel is very good to give, but very hard to take; many give it, few take it.

Arte de Furtar (1652)

And when this state is governed by only a governor-general and an ouvidor geral, *they are the kings, and not only them but the bishop, proprietors, and potentates as well . . . acting in all things with absolute power and Your Majesty remains king in name only.*

Anonymous defense of the Relação (1626)

The extensive corporate powers and diverse obligations of the Relação provoked jealousy, hostility, and opposition from other institutions in the colony. Such conflict was perhaps inevitable given the nature and structure of colonial government and the interplay of the powers and personalities involved. Although the legality of the High Court remained beyond question, various individuals and institutions fought vigorously to protect their specific or collective interests and spheres of authority. This chapter will analyze the relationship between the Relação and the governors-general, the municipal council of Salvador, the Bahian episcopacy, and the royal treasury office in Brazil. Accurate generalization concerning the nature of colonial administrative conflict can emerge only from close scrutiny of specific cases. Many of the incidents described in this chapter have gone unrecorded in the general histories of Brazil, for they would contribute little to a political chronology or a history filled with bugles and battles. To understand the nature of colonial government and the role of the Relação, however, such details are indispensable.

The civil administration of colonial Brazil was characterized by a tripartite delegation of powers—politico-military, fiscal, and judicial. Each branch of government maintained its own organization, membership, regulations, and standards. Although in all cases these emanated from a single source, the crown, they were at times contradictory.[1] The governor-general as political chief of state held the highest position, and in his capacity as president of the High Court he exercised some authority in judicial matters. The resident bishop headed the ecclesiastical establishment and assumed responsibility for the spiritual welfare of the colony's inhabitants. Overlapping duties, functions, and jurisdictions within various branches of government, viewed by the crown as checks and balances, became a constant source of friction and feuding within the colony. Conflicting standards and goals between and within administrative organs resulted in constant reference to Lisbon and to the king's wishes as expressed through his councils. This system often resulted in bureaucratic delay and administrative competition, but it also kept the reins of colonial government in the hands of the king and his metropolitan councilors.

The governor-general, at the apex of the colonial Brazilian bureaucracy, was the direct representative of the crown and the supreme commander of the colony. During the Hapsburg period, the men who served as governor-general were all members of the military nobility, gentlemen whose undoubted social status reinforced their political authority. The relationship of the governors-general Diogo de Meneses (1608–1612), Gaspar de Sousa (1613–

1. John L. Phelan, "Authority and Flexibility in the Spanish Imperial Bureaucracy," *Administrative Science Quarterly*, V (June 1960), 47–55.

1617), Luís de Sousa (1617–1621), Diogo de Mendonça Furtado (1621–1624), Diogo Luís de Oliveira (1627–1635) to the High Court and to its individual members varied according to circumstance, personality, and interpretation of duty. Gaspar de Sousa, for example, took a real interest in matters of justice and when in Bahia he regularly attended the sessions of the Relação, using its magistrates as an advisory council. Luís de Sousa also maintained relatively good relations with the High Court. Diogo de Mendonça Furtado, who came to Brazil in 1621 in the company of the second group of desembargadores, who were replacements for the original body, usually took a benign position toward them, although virulent disputes erupted on occasion.[2]

Generally, the governor-general and the Relação worked in harmony. The governor-general not only held the chief political, administrative, and military posts of the colony, but also served as presiding officer of the Relação with definite functions within the tribunal, albeit functions of a primarily administrative nature. Cooperation, or at least a non-interference stemming from variant obligations and concerns, characterized relations between him and the Relação. The military cast of the governors-general in the first quarter of the seventeenth century and an ever-increasing foreign threat turned the attention of these men toward defense and conquest rather than toward judicial and other civilian duties. This trend continued into the eighteenth century. Their concerns, moreover, centered at times on matters of rank, powers, prestige, and their place in the hierarchy of government. Diogo Botelho at-

2. Frei Vicente de Salvador, *História*, liv. v, cap. vii, 418–419; *ibid.*, liv. v, cap. xviii, 425. The new desembargadores that accompanied Diogo de Mendonça Furtado were Pedro Casqueiro da Rocha, João de Sousa Cardenas, Martim Afonso Coelho, Diogo de São Miguel Garces, Francisco Mendes Marrecos, João Rodrigues da Costa, and Nuno Vaz Fialho. These men came from backgrounds similar to those of their predecessors. Martim Afonso Coelho was a *moço fidalgo*. Casqueiro da Rocha, Rodrigues da Costa, and Mendes Marrecos were *juizes de fóra* at the time of their appointment to the Relação. São Miguel Garces had formerly served as *ouvidor geral* of Angola. See Andrade e Silva, *Col. chron.*, III, 24.

tempted unsuccessfully to obtain the title of Viceroy of Brazil. Diogo de Meneses complained bitterly of his loss of authority when in 1609 the captaincies of the south were separated from his jurisdiction. Gaspar de Sousa, after his return to Portugal, sought land in Maranhão along with *encomiendas* and other favors.[3]

From 1602 to 1618 the governors-general spent much of their time in Pernambuco, ostensibly for reasons of state but also for more personal concerns.[4] Diogo Botelho began the practice of sailing directly to the northern captaincy instead of to Bahia, an act that incurred the displeasure of the crown and for which Botelho was later criticized. His action became institutionalized during the administration of Gaspar de Sousa, who was authorized to remain in Pernambuco while directing the conquest of Maranhão.[5] Eventually, however, when the presence of the governor-general was no longer needed in the north, the crown found it impossible to force his return to Salvador.

High colonial office in the seventeenth-century Portuguese empire was a business venture and the governor or viceroy who did not use his office for profit was rare indeed. Opportunities were limited to some extent, however, by administrative checks, statute, and personal resources. Diogo Botelho complained:

> This state is very rich for the colonists and profitable for His Majesty . . . but for the governor it is very poor. Poor I am and poor I shall depart. I take nothing from anyone, nor could I do so in good conscience; I trade not since I lack the capital for it; there are no lands for *engenhos* that yield, nor does His Majesty permit slaving in the bush. My salary does not suffice for even half the year for this country is most expensive.[6]

---

3. *Carta régia* (Madrid, 24 April 1609), ANTT, *Corp. cron.*, pt. 1, maço 116, doc. 104; Diogo de Meneses to king (Bahia, 22 April 1609), *ABNR*, LVII, 51–59; BM, Egerton 323 (16 July 1622), f. 4.

4. King to Viceroy of Portugal Pedro de Castillo (Madrid, 19 March 1614), AGS, *Sec. Prov.*, 1511, f. 23; *Diálogos das grandezas*, p. 35.

5. King to Gaspar de Sousa (Madrid, 21 March 1615), AHI, Correspondencia . . . Gaspar de Sousa, f. 341–41v; Calmon, *História do Brasil*, II, 490.

6. Diogo Botelho to Count of Linhares (Recife, n.d.), ANTT, *Cart. Jes.*, maço 8, doc. 129.

This plaint, however, does not ring true, for Botelho was accused in 1604 of price-fixing, interfering in public auctions, tampering with the assignment of offices, venality, and a general disregard of statute.[7] Even a well-respected governor-general like Luís de Sousa was implicated in unauthorized economic activities.[8]

Despite the detrimental effects on the political direction of the colony and the defense of Bahia caused by the presence of the governors-general in Pernambuco, their absence from Bahia reduced friction with the Relação. While the governors-general remained in Pernambuco, their functions were undertaken by the chancellor of the Relação aided at times by the *provedor-mór*. These two men corresponded directly with the governor-general as well as with the crown, taking charge of local problems of government and administration. Unfortunately, the governors-general were usually accompanied to Brazil by a large retinue of soldiers, office-seekers, friends, and friends of friends, and many of these *criados* remained in Salvador while the governor-general was absent. They were an unruly and arrogant bunch, and on more than one occasion the Relação had cause to reprimand them. Moreover, to satisfy the ambition of these men, the governors-general had created unnecessary offices which drew on the royal treasury. The crown had criticized this practice as early as 1602 by an *alvará* that the Relação had duly registered.[9] But although the High Court kept a vigil in this matter, the investigation of André Farto da Costa in 1612 indicated that the abuse still existed. Hence, on the question of his friends, relations between the governor-general and the Relação were sometimes strained.

---

7. "Informação de Belchior de Amaral," BNL, Pomb. 249, ff. 204–207. Francis A. Dutra, "A New Look into Diogo Botelho's Stay in Pernambuco," *Luso-Brazilian Review*, IV (June 1967), 27–34, is a close examination of Botelho's misdeeds and suggests some reasons for the attraction of the northern captaincy.

8. *Livro primeiro*, pp. 408–409; Frei Vicente do Salvador, *História*, liv. v, cap. xix, pp. 425–426.

9. Livro Dourado, f. 305–305v. (18 December 1602); BGUC, Cod. 708, ff. 219–220.

Conflict could develop over mundane matters rather than those of state. Through the early years of the seventeenth century the governors-general and the High Court argued continually over the right to reside in the government buildings in Salvador or to draw on the royal treasury to pay for housing expenses.[10] This situation produced some ill feeling between the magistrates and the governors-general, but the construction of a new court house between 1620 and 1627 dissolved the problem without leaving any lasting scars.[11]

The underlying cause of the basically amicable relations of the governors-general and the High Court lay in the interdependence of these two institutions and in their positions of mutual control. The governors-general had the power to suspend the Relação magistrates, to make interim or committee appointments, to assign circuit tours, and to inform the crown by secret report of the actions of the judges.[12] Such was the case in 1615, when an unedifying fight between Pero de Cascais and Antônio das Póvoas erupted in the midst of a court session and resulted in the temporary suspension of both magistrates.[13] By these powers, the governor-general could exercise considerable control over the internal

---

10. *Consulta* of Conselho da Fazenda, AGS, Sec. Prov., 1472, ff. 483–485, 488; *Consulta* of Conselho de Portugal (1620), *Sec. Prov.*, 1474, ff. 416–417; Ruy Mendes de Abreu to king (Bahia, 22 April 1619), AHU, Bahia *pap. avul.*, caixa 1, Fonseca 202; "Sobre aposentadoria do G^or do Brasil," AHU, Cod. 31, f. 27–27v.

11. Andrade e Silva, *Col. Chron.*, III (21 February 1620), 5; *Livro primeiro*, 303–304; Vicente do Salvador, *História*, liv. v, cap. xix, 427. On the buildings which later housed the Relação, see Afonso Ruy, *A Relação da Bahia* (Bahia, 1968), pp. 12–13.

12. King to Viceroy of Portugal Aleixo de Meneses (Madrid, 4 April 1615) ordering Diogo de Meneses to conduct an investigation and to submit a secret report on the actions of Afonso Garcia Tinoco. The Viceroy of India was prohibited from attending sessions of the High Court of Goa, except for one meeting each month, at which time he heard criminal cases. *Archivo da Relação de Goa*, 9–10.

13. King to Viceroy of Portugal Aleixo de Meneses (Madrid, 20 May 1615), AGS, *Sec. Prov.*, 1511, 327v–328.

workings of the Relação even though he could not participate in their judicial deliberations.

On the other hand, the Relação served as a check on the governor-general through a variety of mechanisms. Orders issued by the governor-general were subject to legal review by the chancellor, and when a question of opinion arose the legality of the matter was decided by the Relação.[14] Also, the Relação took charge of the judicial review or *residência* required at the termination of each governor-general's incumbency.

The extant documents of the *residência* of Luís de Sousa, taken in 1624, provide an excellent picture of how the High Court performed this duty and they indicate the expected relationship between governor-general and High Court.[15] The chancellor of the High Court, in this case Antão de Mesquita, was ordered by the crown to conduct the investigation. He was required to post an announcement calling for all complaints and accusations against the retiring governor-general to be made within thirty days of the date of the announcement. The instructions included a list of items to be asked of the governor-general's conduct. From this list a smaller questionnaire (*interrogatório*) of pertinent matters was compiled. These questions covered a wide range and were designed to uncover venality, malfeasance, neglect of duty, or other illegal procedures, especially involvement in commerce. A number of the questions dealt with the governor-general's relation to the High Court: whether he had prevented complaints against him from

---

14. King to Governor Diogo de Meneses (20 July 1612), and *alvará* (21 July 1612), AHI, Correspondencia . . . Gaspar de Sousa, ff. 63, 65.

15. These papers are printed in *Livro primeiro*, 336–416. Governor-general Matias de Albuquerque (1625–1627) underwent a *residência* conducted by Desembargador João de Sousa Cardenas; it was lost, however, when that magistrate's ship went down off Cascais in 1628. *Consulta* of Desembargo de Paço (Lisbon, 29 November 1629), AGS, *Sec. Prov.*, 1475, ff. 247–250. The *residência* was usually conducted in more than one city. In Luís de Sousa's case, it was to have been carried out in Salvador and Recife. See *Consulta* of Conselho de Portugal, AGS, *Sec. Prov.*, 1476, ff. 714–715.

reaching the tribunal; if he had participated in a case in which he was an interested party; or "if he aided the judges and other ministers of justice in their offices and in the performance of them, or if he interfered in that which pertained to them, or impeded the execution of any sentences." [16]

In the *residência* of Luís de Sousa, Antão de Mesquita, aided by magistrates Francisco Mendes Marrecos and Nuno Vaz Fialho, then heard testimony according to the questionnaire from over fifty people. Although no desembargador testified, a number of the witnesses were connected with the High Court. The clerks Cristóvão Vieira Ravasco and Domingos de Andrade, the doorkeeper Domingos da Fonseca Pinto, and the court physician Diogo Pereira were called upon to bear witness to the governor-general's actions. These witnesses and all others were asked to comment on Luís de Sousa's observance of his obligations to the High Court and to justice in general. Most, like Cosme de Sá Peixoto, *senhor de engenho* and later an alderman in Bahia, testified that de Sousa "usually attended the sessions of the High Court and I never heard it said that he bothered any magistrates or other justice officials." [17] Of the final list of fifteen charges drawn up by the High Court, three were concerned with the governor-general's failure to cooperate with that body or to comply with its sentences.

The power of the High Court to conduct a *residência* of the governor-general served as a control of his actions toward the Relação and its members. Conversely, the regulatory and disciplinary powers exercised by the governor-general over the High Court equalized the relationship. The result was an institutional mechanism that decreased tension between the two branches of government.

This is not to say, however, that quarrels of a personal nature did not arise between the members of the Relação and individual

---

16. *Livro Primeiro*, p. 367. The instructions issued to Manuel Pinto da Rocha for the *residência* of Diogo de Meneses can be seen in AHI, ff. 107–110, 303.

17. *Ibid.*, p. 387.

governors-general. The hostility between Gaspar de Sousa and Pero de Cascais, mentioned earlier, is a case in point. Nevertheless, the presence of the Relação at least kept these quarrels at a minimum and within legal bounds. With the removal of the Relação, the governor-general, free of a strong legal opposition, could wield relatively unrestrained power. Such was the case in 1627, when Governor-General Diogo Luís de Oliveira accused Desembargador Diogo de São Miguel Garces of malpractice and overstepping his authority. Garces had been appointed *desembargador extravagante* in 1620 and had arrived in Brazil in 1621. In 1622 he had been given the position of probate judge and in 1626, after the Relação was abolished, he was commissioned to remain in Brazil in the same capacity.[18] Garces claimed that the real cause of his suspension in 1627 was certain investigations he had conducted that were embarrassing to the governor-general.

Diogo Luís de Oliveira, not content with merely suspending Garces, also prevented him from sailing for Portugal, obtaining his salary, or finding a justice official who would hear his plea. Finally, in March 1628, after a year of harassment, Garces obtained a permit to sail for Lisbon. At the last moment, his belongings were taken from the ship and impounded, ostensibly because he had stolen some silver but actually in an attempt to seize the papers of the incriminating investigation.[19] This sort of high-handed and cavalier procedure was uncommon while the Relação sat in Bahia, and one contemporary warned that in a Brazil "governed by only a governor-general and an *ouvidor geral*, they are the kings, and not only them but the bishop, proprietors, and potentates as well . . . acting in all things with absolute power and Your Majesty remains king in name only." [20]

---

18. ANTT, *Chan. Filipe II, Doações*, liv. 44, ff. 211v.–12; *Chan. Filipe III, Doações*, liv. 18, f. 77; liv. 17, f. 72–2v.

19. *Consulta* of Desembargo do Paço (Lisbon, February 1629), AGS, *Sec. Prov.*, 1475, ff. 69–70v.

20. "Rezoens q. darão os m^dores^ da Bahya para se nao estinguir a Rc^ão^," BNL, Pomb. 647, f. 69 (author unknown, probably written in 1626).

While it is not difficult to document the relations of the Relação and the governors-general, it is almost impossible to determine those of the Relação and the municipal council of Salvador. The Dutch invasion of Bahia in 1624 destroyed the minute book of the municipal council and the remaining evidence is sparse.[21] The materials that do exist, however, indicate relatively placid relations between these two bodies, a somewhat surprising fact in view of their later history of friction. Even after 1626 former members of the Relação gave favorable counsel in Portugal in behalf of the *câmara* of Salvador.[22] One factor that contributed to this cooperation was the mutual opposition of High Court and municipal council to two other institutions, the garrison and the episcopacy.

There was no love lost between the Relação and the military establishment in Brazil. The soldiers and their officers displayed a dislike and disdain for lawyers, scholars, and monks, along traditional anti-intellectual lines.[23] The magistrates, for their part, had no use for the unruly and uneducated garrison troops. As early as 1610 the Relação had arrested a number of officers of the garrison, including the son of Governor-General Diogo de Meneses and the sergeant-major. The incident caused considerable dispute between the soldiers and the magistrates; and the crown finally ruled that unless apprehended in the act, the soldiers were not to be imprisoned without previous consultation with the governor-general.[24] The grievances of the *câmara* against the military establishment, however, were basically economic, for the burden of mili-

---

21. The minute books of the municipal council of Bahia for the years 1625–1700 have been published: *Documentos históricos do Arquivo Municipal, Atas da Camara*, 6 vols. (Salvador, 1949–195?). (Hereafter cited as *ACS* for Atas da Câmara de Salvador.)

22. ANTT, *Chan. Filipe III, Doações*, liv. 31 (22 November 1628), (6 March 1630), f. 340v.

23. Campos Moreno, *Livro q. dá rezão*, p. 151; cf. Diogo de Couto, *O Soldado pratico* (Lisbon, 1937), pp. 31–32.

24. King to Viceroy of Portugal Miguel de Moura (Madrid, 31 May 1610), AGS, *Sec. Prov.* 1503, f. 9–9v.

tary expenditures fell on the shoulders of the local populace. In January 1610, shortly after the High Court's arrival, the *câmara* wrote to the crown asking that the garrison in Bahia be reduced to sixty or seventy men. The colonists complained that when there was fighting to be done it was they, not the paid soldiers, who were in the vanguard, and that it "was principally against the colonists that these troops did their soldiering." [25] This feeling worsened after 1621 and especially after 1625, when the needs of defense and fortification became an overriding royal concern and the burden of housing and provisioning the garrison became increasingly heavy. By 1626 there was a contingent of 900 Spanish and Portuguese men-at-arms in Bahia and the municipal council complained bitterly of the resultant taxes and the public quartering of the garrison.[26]

Câmara accusations of the impotence of the garrison were not without foundation, and when these charges were examined by the Relação trouble ensued. On 17 February 1614 five French corsairs appeared in the Bay of All Saints and in the absence of Governor-General Gaspar de Sousa, the local captain-major, Balthesar de Aragão, organized a small fleet to meet the enemy. "The most noble and honored young men of the country" enlisted and the fleet gave a good account of itself with the exception of the ship commanded by Bento de Araújo, captain of the garrison.[27] A freak accident marred what success the Portuguese had gained. The ship on which Balthesar de Aragão was sailing had opened her gunports to fire at the enemy and water poured through the apertures. The vessel sank like a stone and since the other ships were unable or

---

25. *Câmara* of Salvador to king, ANTT, *Corp, cron.*, pt. II, maço 115, doc. 102.

26. *ACS*, I, 25–26, 76–77. The problem of public quartering of the garrison was solved in 1630 with the building of barracks for the troops. See Luiz Monteiro da Costa, *Na Bahia colonial: Apontamentos para a história militar da cidade do Salvador* (Salvador, 1958), pp. 47–51.

27. *Câmara* of Salvador to king (13 March 1614), AHU, Bahia *pap. avul.*, caixa 1, Fonseca 58; Bento de Araújo's appointment is registered as ANTT, *Chan. Filipe II, Doações*, liv. 21 (3 February 1609), f. 24.

unwilling to rescue the company, over two hundred men perished in the Bay. This disaster caused—wrote the *câmara* of Salvador—"such great confusion and lamentation that no one knew how to console the people; and it was in truth the most notable and sorrowful loss that could have happened to this land, and it touched everyone."[28]

The distraught citizens of Bahia placed the blame on the absent governor-general and on the poor performance of Bento de Araújo and his contingent of garrison troops. An investigation of the episode was made by a member of the Relação, Desembargador Antônio das Póvoas. The magistrate set out to punish the guilty, but the investigation dragged on for more than two years and das Póvoas finally had to be removed from the case because of his quarrels with captain of the garrison, Bento de Araújo.[29]

Both the municipal council and the Relação were often at odds with the Bishop of Brazil. When the occasion arose the magistrates did not hesitate to support the municipal council—or for that matter, anyone else—against the excesses of the prelate or the ecclesiastical hierarchy. One category of incident that stimulated acrimonious disputes may today seem a matter of minor significance, but to the seventeenth-century Iberian mind it was of great importance. Precedence in a religious procession, in a society in which both civil and religious life was based on a hierarchy of status, had immediate meaning. The procession of Corpus Christi was the most important public festival of the religious calendar, and the position of the municipal alderman in it was a matter of continual contention, both before the arrival of the Relação and after its abolition.[30] While the Relação sat in Bahia, however, it provided a means of adjudicating these differences.

---

28. AHU, Bahia *pap. avul.*, caixa 1, Fonseca 58. Alternate accounts of this incident are given in Frei Vicente do Salvador, *História*, liv. v, cap. vi, pp. 415–417 and in the letter of Father Henrique Gomes (Bahia, 16 June 1614) printed in Leite, *HCJB*, V, 14.

29. Gaspar de Sousa to king (8 April 1614), AHU, Pernambuco *pap. avul.* caixa 1; *Livro Primeiro*, pp. 129–130.

30. A listing of the public processions in which the *câmara* participated can be found in Gonçalo Soares de França, "Dissertações da história ec-

In June 1623 the *câmara* of Salvador insisted on placing the municipal banner before the crosses in the procession and an altercation resulted. Bishop Marcos Teixeira submitted the case to the Relação, which returned a decision in favor of the *câmara*. The bishop then appealed the case to the Mesa de Consciência in Portugal, which unfortunately for him sought the advice of Desembargador Afonso Garcia Tinoco "who was many years in those parts." Garcia Tinoco pointed out that in a similar case in Faro, the crown had supported the municipal council.[31] The Mesa da Consciência, on the advice of the desembargador, supported the Relação's decision, but it eventually took an *alvará* in 1627 to force the religious hierarchy to comply.[32] As late as 1643 the aldermen and the bishop were still arguing this point of protocol.[33]

Relations between the Relação and the *câmara* of Salvador fluctuated between occasional alliance and uneasy hostility. The municipal council, representing the sugar elite, disliked and mistrusted the Relação, the representative of royal power. On the other hand, because individual magistrates and aldermen sometimes became linked by kinship or common interests, relations were not always hostile. But when the *câmara* felt threatened, it could and did strike out at the Relação. In 1625 the *câmara* of Salvador was partially responsible for the abolition of the Relação. In the late seventeenth century the *câmara* once again tried to have the High Court abolished.

Although much of Book II of the Philippine Ordinances define the relationship between civil and ecclesiastical authority and jurisdiction, the magistrates in Brazil found intransigent and cantankerous bishops to be among their greatest adversaries. Significantly, both Bishop Constantino Barradas (1600–1618) and Bishop Marcos

---

clesiastica do Brasil" (1724), SGL, Ms. 1-C-147. Also see Boxer, *Portuguese Society*, p. 90.

31. *Consulta* (23 Nov. 1623), ANTT, Mesa de Con. liv. 28, ff. 231v.–232v.

32. ANTT, *Chan. Filipe III, Doações*, liv. 16 (15 April 1627), ff. 110v.–11.

33. *Documentos históricos do Arquivo Municipal: Cartas do Senado*, 3 vols. (Salvador, 1950–1953), I, 18–20.

Teixeira (1622–1624) battled with both the Relação and the governors-general, which suggests the similar interests of these institutions in maintaining royal prerogatives. Whereas the High Court had little or no difficulty with the religious orders in Brazil, conflict with the bishop was almost inherent in a political structure in which the ecclesiastical establishment maintained its own judicial system. The conflict in Brazil was but a chapter in the greater struggle of Church and State in Western Europe, but the magistrates in Brazil found little consolation in this fact, nor did it temper the heat of debate.

Civil-religious jurisdictional conflicts were nothing new in Brazil, where the congruence of strong personalities in the higher positions of the two hierarchies usually resulted in a dispute of some kind. This had been the case in the conflict between the second governor-general, Duarte da Costa, and Bishop Pedro Sardinha. Even before the High Court's arrival in Brazil, Bishop Constantino Barradas had quarreled with civil authority, complaining that Governor-General Diogo Botelho had appropriated funds for the military that should have gone to orphans and widows.[34] The bishop's own actions, however, had moved *ouvidor geral* Ambrósio de Siqueira to complain.[35] Whatever difficulties Bishop Barradas had encountered in his benefice before 1608 were multiplied by the arrival in that year of the tenth governor-general of Brazil, Diogo de Meneses. The powers of office and his own personality made Barradas an especially difficult man, as the governor-general and others were soon to discover. Characteristically, the dispute between Barradas and Diogo de Meneses erupted over precedence in the Corpus Christi procession in Pernambuco in June 1608; in this dispute the *câmara* of Olinda also felt itself an aggrieved party.[36]

34. ANTT, *Mesa de Con.* liv. 19 (4 April 1605), f. 57.

35. BA, 51-VIII-20, f. 34v.

36. *ABNR*, LVII, Diogo de Meneses to king (Olinda, 12 July 1609), 34–35. It is not clear whether this suit was heard by the Relação da Bahia or the Casa da Suplicação since the document merely mentions "Relação de VM^de^." The dispute occurred in 1608, however, a year before the Brazilian tribunal's arrival in Bahia and thus a hearing in the metropolitan court seems more likely.

Underlying this incident, and the bishop's animosity, however, may have been actions taken by the governor-general against illegal economic activities of the bishop.[37]

The arrival of the Relação presented plaintiffs the opportunity to appeal the actions of the bishop. One such complaint was registered by the Brotherhood of the Holy Sacrament in Pernambuco against the continual interference of the prelate.[38] The Relação issued three writs against the bishop's actions, none of which he chose to obey. Relations between the High Court and Barradas worsened when in February 1610 he excommunciated Desembargador Pero de Cascais (at that time serving as interim *provedor-mór*) for failure to pay the ecclesiastical salaries in full. Even when the salaries were forthcoming, Barradas refused to accept part of them in sugar as was the custom, and he insisted on payment in specie. The governor-general considered this demand most unreasonable and he wrote to the crown that "in this state sugar is the same as money." [39] The High Court agreed with him and again issued three writs ordering the bishop to comply, but once again these were ignored.

By late 1610 the matter was still unresolved and the bishop once again excommunicated the *provedor-mór*, who in turn appealed to the Relação. The magistrates sentenced in his favor and ordered the bishop to lift the penalty. Again the prelate proved intransigent and the hostility deepened between the civil and ecclesiastical establishments. Bishop Barradas brandished excommunication and interdiction to force his will and obtain his goals, which according to Diogo de Meneses were wholly monetary. Said the governor-general, "there is no law, no Papal bull, no concordance, no sentence of the High Court that he [Bishop Barradas] observes but only cold cash." [40] This charge was overstated—but not much. The bishop was indeed preoccupied with the financial attributes and

37. Varnhagen, *História geral*, II, 110.

38. See Manoel Cardozo, "The Lay Brotherhoods of Colonial Bahia," *Catholic Historical Review*, XXXIII (April 1947), 3–30.

39. Diogo de Meneses to king (Bahia, 20 January 1611), *ABNR*, LVII, 62.

40. *Ibid.* (Bahia, 7 February 1611), 72.

obligations of his office. It was this concern that had caused his clash with Diogo Botelho in 1605, and as late as 1614 Barradas was still citing the "misery of the clergy" and ascribing it to the "greed of some who distribute the royal revenues." [41]

Certainly the matter of ecclesiastical salaries was a major area of contention between the civil and religious authorities. The collection of the tithe (*dízimos*) was not made directly by the Church but by the king in his office as Grandmaster of the Order of Christ.[42] From this revenue the state maintained the fiscal, military, judicial, and religious establishments in Brazil, for the justification of the colony was the extension of Christianity. Royal control of the collection of the tithe, however, placed the ecclesiastics in a disadvantageous position, because ministers of the treasury could draw tight the purse strings when they wanted to. Royal officials —the desembargadores included—were prone to assure the payment of their own salaries before those of the Church, especially since the ecclesiastical portion was large. The ill feeling over control of the tithe and prompt payment of ecclesiastical salaries had existed even before the arrival of the High Court, when the yearly costs of justice were listed at 663 *milréis*.[43] With the Relação seated in Bahia, however, judicial expenses rose to 4,954 *milréis* a year and the resultant rivalry between Relação and bishop over the priority of payment is completely understandable.[44]

In the quarrel between bishop and High Court, the crown proceeded cautiously. Although at first an *alvará* was issued calling for the return to Portugal of any ecclesiastic who refused to obey the writs of the Relação, subsequent legislation failed to support

---

41. King to Viceroy Pedro de Castilho (30 November 1605), AGS, *Sec. Prov.* 1494, f. 47–7v.; AHU, Bahia *pap. avul.* caixa 1 (17 June 1614).

42. Cardozo, "Lay Brotherhoods," p. 21. A detailed legal discussion is provided by Oscar de Oliveira, *Os dízimos eclesiásticos do Brasil nos períodos da Colonia e do Império*. 2nd ed. (Belo Horizonte, 1964).

43. Account book of the government of Brazil made by Ambrósio de Siqueira (1604), AGS, *Sec. Prov.* 1575.

44. Campos Moreno, *Livro q. da rezão*, pp. 148–149. These figures are for the captaincy of Bahia only.

the magistrates and merely admonished them to proceed with caution and just cause in disputes with the Church.[45] An attempt was made in 1616 to regularize the process of settlement in suits involving the Church. An *alvará* was issued charging the chancellor and the two eldest *desembargadores dos agravos* to hear these cases in the presence of the governor-general. Appeal from the Relação could then be made to the Desembargo do Paço.[46]

Ecclesiastical salaries were not, however, the only point of dispute between Church and High Court. The jurisdiction of the ecclesiastical courts and the relationship of these to civil justice was of far more direct interest to the magistrates. The ecclesiastical courts, directed by the vicar-general, exercised considerable regulatory and juridical authority over the population in matters of morality. Moreover, the religious community enjoyed the privilege of being judged in the notoriously lenient ecclesiastical courts. The officers of ecclesiastical justice enjoyed many of the immunities and prerogatives of their lay counterparts, such as the honor of bearing the white staff of justice. Both Bishop Barradas and his successor, Bishop Marcos Teixeira, guarded their prerogatives in this area and both had been specifically granted the right of appointing ecclesiastical bailiffs.[47]

The desembargadores were no less jealous of their prerogatives and clearly resented the encroachment of the bishop in matters they considered their own. Frei Vicente de Salvador, who as a Franciscan was not a disinterested party, accused the magistrates of excessive opposition to the ministers of ecclesiastical justice and said that "on behalf of the king's jurisdiction they totally extinguished that of the Church, something that neither God nor the king desired." [48] The High Court, in truth, had so obstructed the

---

45. King to Viceroy of Portugal Miguel de Castro (Burgos, 3 October 1615), AGS, *Sec. Prov.* 1511, ff. 358–359; Andrade e Silva, *Col. cron.*, II, 179.

46. *Alvará* (27 April 1616), Livro Dourado, ff. 293–94v.

47. ANTT, *Chan. Filipe II Doações*, liv. 29, f. 149v. (17 September 1616); *Chan. Filipe III Doações*, liv. 18, f. 44 (10 September 1622).

48. Frei Vicente do Salvador, *História*, liv. iv, cap. 45, pp. 361–362.

workings of the religious courts that the bishop was unable to find a cleric willing to serve as vicar-general.[49]

Close scrutiny indicates that in reality the Relação had no effective means of coercion against the ecclesiastical authorities. The Relação could issue writs and could interfere with the religious courts, but it exercised no ultimate authority over the bishop. Appeal to Portugal was a slow process and while it dragged on the prelate could simply refuse to obey the High Court's orders. Without any institutionalized means of direct control, the Relação resorted to extraordinary measures such as harassment or withholding ecclesiastical salaries. The bishop, however, had in excommunication and interdiction, weapons far more powerful than any the magistrates could use, and he did not hesitate to employ these weapons to achieve the goals of the Church as he saw them. The underlying problem was this: whereas the governor-general and the High Court exercised some mutual control through the *residência* and the secret report, no institutionalized check existed between High Court and bishop. In fact, the Relação and bishop were parts of different bureaucracies, each with its own goals and standards. The spheres of power, position, and protocol of bishop and Relação were never sufficiently defined despite the attempt of the Philippine Code and subsequent legislation. The result was at best uneasy peace and at worst vitriolic battle.

Bishop Marcos Teixeira, who arrived in Bahia in 1622, was no less formidable an opponent than his predecessor. From the day of his arrival in 1622 Bishop Teixeira feuded constantly with both High Court and governor-general.[50]

---

49. *Ibid.;* king to Governor Gaspar de Sousa (31 July 1612), AHI, Correspondencia . . . Gaspar de Sousa, f. 67–67v.

50. Modern historians are still unsure of the correlation between the Marcos Teixeira of the 1618 inquisitorial visit and Bishop Marcos Teixeira. José de Wanderley Pinho, *D. Marcos Teixeira quinto bispo do Brazil* (Lisbon, 1940), gives an adequate discussion of the problem but he does not incorporate the findings of Antônio Baião published in the same year in "O Bispo D. Marcos Teixeira," *I Congresso do mundo portugues*, IX, 251–260. Baião printed documents and facsimile signatures that indicate strongly that two or even three different men are involved.

On 8 December 1622, the day of his arrival in Bahia, a disagreement arose between Bishop Teixeira and Governor-General Diogo de Mendonça Furtado over the place the latter was to take in the welcoming procession. As a result of the dispute, the governor-general refused to take part at all and sent the High Court instead. The quarrel quickly expanded because of a difference of opinion concerning seating arrangements in the Cathedral of Bahia, but a low point was reached in 1624, when the bishop refused to bless the cornerstone of a new fort, stating that he would rather damn it since its construction diverted funds from the building of the cathedral.[51] Added to this was another dispute between bishop and governor-general over the tithe, in which the prelate once again threatened to excommunicate the ministers of the treasury.

With the High Court the conflict centered on a specific case. The ecclesiastical court has sentenced two colonists who, absent from their wives in Portugal, had taken up with women in Brazil. The bishop ordered them to return to Portugal and desist from the immoral life they were living with their (presumably Indian) mistresses. The two libertines were aboard ship awaiting departure when the crown's attorney, Francisco Mendes Marrecos, intervened.[52] He removed the two men from the ship and claimed that the ecclesiastical courts had no authority to order their deportation. The bishop responded quickly by excommunicating the offending desembargador. The crown mediated by a *carta régia* of 7 May 1624, but the dispute had been bitterly contested and the scars were permanent.[53] Some sort of institutionalized relationship between the bishop and the desembargadores might have mitigated their mutual hostility. In fact, this had almost been established in 1622 when the Conselho de Portugal had suggested the creation of a permanent board of the Inquisition directed by the bishop and assisted by the desembargadores. The failure of this plan to meet the approval of the Inquisitor General of Portugal and the Council

---

51. Frei Vicente de Salvador, *História*, liv. v, cap. 21, pp. 434–435; AHU, Cod. 35, ff. 233–234.
52. Ruy, *História administrativa*, p. 129.
53. Andrade e Silva, *Col. chron.*, III, 121.

of the Inquisition resulted in continuing unstable relations between Church and High Court.[54]

Opposition to the Relação came from still another quarter. The first decade of the High Court's existence in Brazil was characterized by almost continuous verbal and legal battle with the *provedor-mór da fazenda*, Sebastião Borges. At the time of the High Court's arrival in 1609, Borges had already been appointed to the position in Brazil, but he did not take up his post until 1611. Borges was not devoid of experience, having served in municipal positions in his native Oporto, but his lifetime Brazilian appointment came through the patronage of Bishop Dom Jorge de Ataide, to whom Borges had tied his political fortunes.[55]

The permanent nature of Borges' appointment and his proprietorship perhaps made him extremely sensitive to encroachment in the area of his control; in any case, he viewed the fiscal responsibilities of members of the Relação with suspicion and mistrust. Moreover, the power of the High Court to hear appeals on actions of the *provedor-mór* and to reverse his decisions was the cause of continual dispute, especially since the Relação had a tendency to exceed its authority in this area.

A dispute was not long in coming. There was natural resentment on the part of the desembargadores, who in Borges' absence had

54. *Consulta* of Conselho de (Estado) (20 October 1622), BM, Egerton 323.

55. Through the influence of his benefactor Bishop Jorge de Ataide, Sebastião Borges had held two minor positions in the municipal council of Oporto. (ANTT, *Chan. Filipe II, Doações,* liv. 6, ff. 81v–82v.) By 1604 he had attained a position as clerk of the municipal council and in that same year he was nominated for the Brazilian post. See AGS, *Sec. Prov.* 1491 (Valladolid, 7 December 1604), f. 71. His appointment was not voted on by the Conselho da India until 1607, at which time he received unanimous approval in view of his experience, performance, and the influence of the bishop. Borges received a habit in the Order of Christ in 1608, but he did not sail from Brazil until 1611 after having failed to obtain a grant for travel expenses. See AGS, *Sec. Prov.* 1476, f. 351–352; 1499, f. 10v.; ANTT, *Chan. Ordem de Christo,* liv. 17, f. 398–8v.; *Chan. Filipe II, Doações,* liv. 21, f. 143v.; ANTT, *Chan. Filipe II, Doações,* liv. 6, f. 81v–82v.

controlled financial matters in the colony but had been displaced on his arrival. The ill feeling between Borges and Pero de Cascais, who had served as *provedor-mór*, was especially acute. The first area of contention was the *dízimos* contract of 1612. In Brazil, collection of the tithe was made by private individuals or syndicates who bought the right to do so at public auction for some fraction of the expected yield. The contractor paid the crown in specie or sugar for the privilege of collecting the taxes, and his profit came from the difference between the purchase price of the contract and the amount of the tithe collected.[56] In 1612, for some reason, Borges refused to sign the contract. (It had apparently been made before his arrival.) The contractor appealed to the Relação and the tribunal issued a writ ordering Borges to comply. The *provedor-mór* claimed that he was not a lawyer and that before he obeyed the court's order, he would require legal counsel. This delay moved the Relação to suspend him from office and impose a heavy fine. Borges claimed that the Relação had no authority in matters of the treasury and he sought support for his position in Portugal. On 22 July 1612 the crown ordered that the High Court's sentence be revoked and that the Relação stop meddling in matters that did not pertain to it. "I consider this a great disservice," wrote the king.[57]

The Relação did not desist. In the following year of 1612 magistrates of the High Court charged Borges with laxity in his management of the tithe contract. This charge hardly seems justified, since the two-year contract of 1613–14 had been given to Manoel Rodrigues Sanches for 54,500 *cruzados* a year, the largest amount ever contracted up to that time. In fact, the Relação later came to the aid of Rodrigues Sanches, when because of the great drought of 1613 he was unable to meet his obligations to the royal treasury.[58]

---

56. Leite, *HCJB*, VII, 285.

57. *DHBNR*, LXXVIII, 322–323. Cf. AHU, Bahia *pap. avul.* caixa 1 (12 July 1612), Fonseca 30.

58. "Diz Manoel Roiz Sanches," AHU, Bahia *pap. avul.*, caixa 1, Fonseca 71.

It was also in 1613 that the Relação adjudicated a dispute between the *provedor-mór* and the holders of the Angolan slave contract in favor of the latter.[59] In 1614 Afonso Garcia Tinoco, with the support of his colleagues, defied an order of Sebastião Borges and unloaded a cargo of brazilwood. This was the cause of the *alvará* of 20 November 1614, once again enjoining the magistrates to desist from interference in treasury matters.[60] The High Court not only reversed decisions of the *provedor-mór* and obstructed their enforcement; it also ordered his subordinates to disobey him. This tactic was criticized by the crown, and Chancellor Ruy Mendes de Abreu was called upon to give good reason for its use.[61]

Another matter which pitted the judges against the royal treasurer was the Bahian whaling contract.[62] In 1602 a group of Basques had obtained a royal contract to hunt whales in the Bay of All Saints. The Basques believed this contract gave them monopoly rights, and when in 1608 local residents began whaling operations, the Basques brought suit.[63] The High Court ruled against them in 1609 and Desembargador Pero de Cascais stated the court's opinion: "thus it conforms with law and reason that it should not be denied to natives, Your Vassals, that which is con-

59. "Autos de aggravo q. tirarao diogo Manoel e franc° furtado mercaderes e o procurador do contrato de Angola do provedor mor Sebastião Borges." AHU, Bahia *pap. avul.* caixa 1.

60. King to Viceroy of Portugal Pedro de Castilho (Madrid, 4 June 1614), AGS, *Sec. Prov.* 1510, f. 32–32v; king to Aleixo de Meneses (San Lorenzo, 16 July 1614), ff. 48–49; king to Gaspar de Sousa (20 November 1614), AHI Correspondencia Gaspar de Sousa, f. 334; cf. *DHBNR*, LXXVIII (1947), 294.

61. King to Ruy Mendes de Abreu (24 May 1614), AHU Bahia *pap. avul.* caixa 1, Fonseca 65.

62. Soares de Sousa, *Notícia do Brasil,* II, 182. Dauril Alden, "Yankee Sperm Whalers in Brazilian Waters, and the Decline of the Portuguese Whale Fishery (1773–1801)," *The Americas,* XX (January 1964), n. 3, 269–270, includes material of the techniques of hunting and processing whales in colonial Brazil.

63. Myriam Ellis, *Aspectos da pesca da baleia no Brasil colonial* (São Paulo, 1958), is the standard work on the topic.

ceded to foreigners." [64] The magistrates had come down clearly in favor of local and Portuguese interests.

The High Court's decision opened the door, and with the way now clear a number of Bahian residents began fitting out whaling vessels. Among them was Pero de Cascais, who invested in a number of these ventures as a not-so-silent partner.[65] Trouble began, however, in 1614 when Provedor-Mór Sebastião Borges instituted a monopoly contract system for whaling similar to the contracts for tax farming. Such a system would bring the whale fishery under royal control and would exclude everyone but the contractor. When the first contract was awarded at a suspiciously low price, loud complaints were raised against the innovation and a number of men, including Cascais' partner, chose to ignore it.[66]

The battle was joined. The Relação considered Borges suspect in this case and ordered him to surrender all relevant documents. He refused and insisted that the tribunal had no authority to judge him in treasury matters, and that the desembargadores were not his superiors in the colony's table of organization.[67] Borges complained that in any suit brought against him before the Relação, he was always found in the wrong. The High Court, he said, had forgotten that they were reprimanded by the crown in 1612 after they had suspended and fined him. Borges appealed to the king, "the High Court and the Crown Judge (Afonso Garcia Tinoco) will not allow me to perform my office in the service of Your Majesty . . . and I am continually involved in conflicts of jurisdiction with them." [68]

Pero de Cascais, who as we have seen was not a disinterested party, justified his actions in a revealing memorial to the crown.

---

64. "Diz Pero de Cascais (1614)," AHU, Bahia *pap avul.*, caixa 1.
65. *Ibid.*
66. AHU, Bahia *pap. avul.* caixa 1 (3 October 1614).
67. "Precatorio do Provedor Mor," AHU, Bahia *pap. avul.*, caixa 1, Fonseca 85.
68. Borges to king (Bahia, 2 September 1614), AHU, Bahia *pap. avul.*, caixa 1.

First, Cascais claimed that Borges had instituted the new contract arrangement without specific authorization, and that such innovations, especially in taxation, were always detrimental to the "republic" when done without prior consultation with the king. Second, the whaling done by men like himself greatly benefited the commonwealth by lowering the price of oil and providing more in taxes to the coffers of the king than was possible under the monopoly contract. Cascais argued that since the discovery of Brazil, fishing was an activity open to all and this had been confirmed by a decision of the Relação of 1609. The irate desembargador also claimed that Borges held a personal grudge because Cascais had arrested some of his friends and retainers. Cascais claimed he had acted correctly. "Well, God help me if I did evil by doing that which was always done, being neither contrary to God nor to Your interest, but in profit to Your treasury and to Your subjects, the colonists." [69]

The matter was reviewed by the Conselho da Fazenda in Lisbon, and the members of the council generally supported the Relação and found no violation in its actions. Pero de Cascais was not reprimanded for his part in the episode, thus indicating that his participation and investment in the whale fishery was not considered contrary to the statutes forbidding desembargadores to engage in economic activities within the area of their jurisdiction—or at least that this was not contrary to expected behavior. A decision was made by the king on 13 January 1616, which absolved any former violators of the contract since they had acted in accordance with the ruling of the Relação. However, from this point forward the *provedor-mór* was to auction the exclusive contract to the highest bidder and if no bid was entered then a tax was to be imposed on those who hunted whales.[70]

Even with Borges out of office, the hostility between High Court and *provedor-mór* did not subside. In 1617 Chancellor Ruy

---

69. See notes 61 and 64.

70. AHU, Bahia *pap. avul.*, caixa 1, Fonseca 134; king to Viceroy of Portugal Miguel de Castro, AGS, *Sec. Prov.* 1513, f. lv., 2v–3; 1512, f. 18; AHU, Cod. 1192, ff. 169–170.

Mendes de Abreu, annoyed by delay in the receipt of his salary, ordered the arrest of the offending treasury official. The new *provedor-mór*, Pedro Gouvea de Mello, an important Bahian gentleman, complained of the chancellor's actions and notified the crown of the incident. He wrote that the previous disputes between Mendes de Abreu and Borges were due to the former's "meddling in matters of the treasury . . . without having more basis for this than his turbulent nature, ambitious to control everything." [71] Once again the crown reprimanded the High Court for interference in matters of the treasury and reminded the governor that previous orders of a similar nature had been issued in the past.[72] In this case, Ruy Mendes de Abreu was constrained to pay damages from his own pocket to the jailed official, and the High Court was directed in the future to inform the Conselho da Fazenda of abuses and await permission before interfering again in treasury affairs.[73] After 1618 the turbulent relations between the Relação and the treasury subsided into a cautious cooperation brought about by royal mediation and perhaps by a change in personnel with the retirement of Ruy Mendes de Abreu in 1621. After 1652, when the Relação again opened its doors, conflict with the officers of the royal treasury became a recurrent theme. Invariably, the magistrates would interfere with the treasury or would try to exercise jurisdiction in fiscal matters. The officers of the treasury would complain to the crown and the Relação would then be ordered to keep out of treasury business. There were royal decrees to this effect in 1670, 1674, 1684, 1694, and 1740.[74]

Undoubtedly, conflicts which pitted the Relação against other governmental institutions hindered the tribunal's performance of its normal judicial functions. Personality clash and personal feuds obviously contributed to this situation, but to explain the conflicts

71. AHU, Bahia, *pap. avul.* caixa 1 (3 May 1617), Fonseca 150.

72. *Livro Sequndo*, pp. 76–77.

73. *DHBNR*, LXXVII (1945), 295–297; BA, 49-X-10, f. 2, 3.

74. "Copia de provisoens de SMg. sobre os ministros da Relação do Brasil senão intrometerem nas materias da Faz[da] Real," AHU, Bahia *pap. avul.*, caixa 15; see also AHU, Bahia *pap. avul.*, caixa 17 (18 January 1694); APB, *Ord. reg.*, 37 (20 July 1740).

of the Relação simply in these terms would beg the question. Portuguese colonial government consisted of ill-defined and often contradictory jurisdictions and powers which ultimately depended on metropolitan decisions. Such a system prevented any one colonial institution from gaining inordinate power and forced constant reference back to Lisbon. At times, this system was reinforced by the divergent objectives of different governmental branches. The varying goals of Church and State come immediately to mind and may explain the constant struggle between the High Court and the episcopacy. The conflict between the Relação and the treasury officers indicates the existence of divisions within the civil bureaucracy. Here, if we use Phelan's model, the standards and goals of the fiscal and judicial branches were at times incongruous. It is noteworthy that in each case the crown supported the treasury office against the encroachment of the High Court.[75]

Why did the Relação repeatedly meddle in matters which did not directly pertain to it, even in the face of royal displeasure? In the answer lies the key to the High Court's role in the political structure of the colony. In the Portuguese empire the high courts had limited administrative and political duties. The use of judicial institutions for such purposes had an internal logic, for justice and the king were synonomous. The High Court's real power was negative. While there were many things it could not do, in its role as watchdog of royal interests it could prevent other institutions from taking action, or it could delay them until the king's pleasure was known. This was the court's most important political function.

The constant governmental conflicts moved some contemporaries, like Frei Vicente do Salvador, to fear divine retribution for these public sins against the commonwealth.[76] To their minds it was the hand of God that sent a Dutch fleet into the Bay of All Saints on 9 May 1624 and allowed it to capture the city shortly thereafter.

75. Phelan, "Authority and Flexibility," pp. 52–54.
76. Frei Vicente do Salvador, *História*, liv. iv, cap. xxi, 435.

X. THE SUPPRESSION OF THE RELAÇÃO

A certain donatary did not welcome desembargadores in his land, and with this interest in abolishing the Relação the said donatary joined with the officials of the town council to have his henchman chosen as attorney for the City of Bahia. On arriving in Portugal the first thing this attorney did was to ask for the abolition of the Relação.

Anonymous defense of the Relação (c. 1626)

The fall and recapture of the city of Salvador signaled the opening of a new epoch in the history of Brazil. For the next thirty years the northern areas of the Brazilian coast became a battleground in the global conflict between the Dutch and their Iberian enemies. The requirements of defense and the exigencies of war caused considerable modifications in the Portuguese colonial system. The abolition of the Relação was among them. To explain the High Court's demise as merely a response to extraordinary fiscal and military conditions would be to tell only part of the story, for powerful forces and sentiments in both the colony and the metropolis also lay behind the royal order of 5 April 1626 that abolished the Relação.[1]

The facts of the High Court's disruption can be easily stated. A powerful Dutch armada seized the city of Salvador on 10 May

1. Andrade e Silva, *Coll. cron.*, III, 158.

1626.[2] Most of the inhabitants fled to the surrounding areas in the Recôncavo, but the governor and a number of important individuals including Desembargador Pedro Casqueiro da Rocha fell captive to the invaders. The other magistrates escaped to the Recôncavo with the rest of the populace.[3] Chancellor Antão de Mesquita de Oliveira, one of the magistrates most closely connected to colonial interests through marriage, was elected temporary leader of the resistance because Matias de Albuquerque, the official successor to captured Governor Diogo de Mendonça Furtado, was absent in Pernambuco.

The election of Antão de Mesquita did not go unopposed. Contemporary accounts vary considerably on his removal as commander of the resistance forces and the assumption of this post by Bishop Marcos Teixeira. Whatever the exact sequence of events, Bishop Teixeira and his supporters wrested control from Antão de Mesquita within a few days of the desembargador's election.[4] The reason usually given for this action was the magistrate's inability to organize guerrilla operations against the Dutch because of his old age and inexperience. These claims will not bear the light of historical scrutiny, for if Antão de Mesquita was either infirm or

---

2. There are many accounts of the Dutch seizure of Bahia listed in José Honório Rodrigues, *Historiografia e Bibliografia do dominio holandês no Brasil* (Rio de Janeiro, 1949).

3. For a brief treatment, see C. R. Boxer, *The Dutch in Brazil, 1624–1654* (Oxford, 1957), pp. 17–31.

4. Antônio Vieira, "Carta anua 1624," printed in *ABNR*, XIX (1897), 177–217. The question and the sources have been discussed in Wanderley Pinho, *D. Marcos Teixeira*, pp. 45–55. Eugenio de Narbona y Zúniga, "História de la recuperación del Brasil," *ABNR*, LXIX, 189, notes the magistrate's age and unfamiliarity with military life as the reason for his replacement. The writer, however, was not a witness to these events. Serafim Leite, *HCJB*, V, 30–34, publishes the letter of Father Manuel Fernandes, which argues against any wrongdoing on the part of the bishop, but the Jesuit informant cannot be considered a disinterested party. The recognition of Antão de Mesquita's services is registered in ANTT, *Chan. Filipe III, Doações*, liv. 25, f. 105.

senile, it is strange that after the abolition of the Relação he alone was chosen to remain as a royal magistrate in Brazil. Moreover, his subsequent claims for honors and rewards and the crown's expressed satisfaction with his performance tend to refute the bishop's claims. Antão de Mesquita had been elected because he was the highest ranking magistrate of the Relação, a respected judge, and perhaps most closely linked by kinship to important elements of Bahian society. Bad blood had long existed between the High Court and the bishops, and as we have seen, civil-ecclesiastical disputes had wracked the early 1620's. The displacement of Antão de Mesquita may have been more the result of rivalry and factionalism than of the desembargador's military deficiencies. The death of Bishop Teixeira during the campaign and the aura of martyrdom that later surrounded his memory probably mitigated the bitterness of his political opponents and the incident passed forgotten. By 1626 the Portuguese banner flew once more over the city as a result of the combined efforts of the colonial irregulars and a joint Luso-Spanish fleet under the command of Don Fadrique de Toledo, an experienced Spanish admiral.

Although the capital of Brazil once again sheltered Catholic arms, the Dutch attack had marked a turning point in the colony's history. Philip IV and his ministers now became vitally concerned with the safety of the American possessions. In Spanish imperial geopolitics, Brazil had become a cornerstone of empire, not because of any intrinsic value but because of its strategic location. Military planners in Lisbon, Madrid, and Amsterdam recognized that Dutch control of the Brazilian coast could provide a base of operations against the very sinews of the Iberian empire. A hostile force entrenched at Recife or Salvador could raid the coastal ports of the Atlantic and Pacific coasts of South America, intercept the Spanish silver fleets in the Caribbean and the Portuguese Indiamen in the Atlantic, interdict the Atlantic slave trade, and in general wreak hovoc on the Hapsburg Atlantic empire. Above all, Spanish policy-makers saw the Brazilian coastline as the first barrier of defense for Peru. Peru and its silver, not Brazil and its sugar, was the heart of the empire, and no one was quite sure how far distant the mines of Potosí lay from the Brazilian littoral.[5]

Spanish realization of Brazil's strategic importance explains to a great extent the alacrity with which the crown dispatched the joint armada of 1625, giving the lie to the common saying that "help from Spain arrives late, poorly, or never." From 1625 until the separation of Spain and Portugal in 1640, the crown considered Brazil in geopolitical terms, and for its defense Philip IV and his advisers were willing to ignore the agreements of Tomar and the internal development of the colony. At one point, Philip IV even went to the extreme of ordering the settlement of Italian colonists on the Brazilian coast as a means of strengthening the colony's defenses.[6] The measure was never carried out, but it was obviously in direct violation of the agreements of Tomar.

To pay for the fortifications, troops, and artillery, new taxes were levied both in Brazil and in Portugal. Less inclined to think in political terms, the Portuguese resisted the new imposts and began to question the political theory behind them. By 1626 the governors of Portugal openly asked "if the utility of closing commerce to enemies is worth more than the damage caused by a lack of commerce." [7] This feeling intensified steadily, and after 1630 the continuing levies of men and money in support of an unpopular policy contributed to the ultimate revolt of Portugal in 1640 and its separation from Spain.

Part of the burden of Brazil's defense fell directly on the colony, and to pay for this expense the crown cut costs in other areas of government. Under the pressures of war, the judiciary was marked expendable and on the advice of the Council of State, Philip IV

---

5. I have presented this argument at some length in "Luso-Spanish Relations in Hapsburg Brazil, 1580–1640," *The Americas*, XXV (July 1968), 33–48.

6. King to Count of Monterrey, RAHM, Collectión Salazar K-72 (17 December 1631).

7. *Consulta* of Consejo de Estado, BM, Egerton 324 (16 May 1626).

ordered the abolition of the Relação of Brazil on 31 March 1626.[8] The king specifically ordered that the High Court's salaries be applied to the provisioning of the garrison of Bahia. Exactly how much money was involved in this fiscal adjustment is difficult to determine and depends on which salaries are calculated in the total. The salaries of the ten magistrates amounted to 3,460,000 *réis* a year to which must be added the salaries of the chaplain, the doorkeeper, and court secretaries. Moreover, occasional costs such as those of circuit tours, which could amount to 500,000 *réis* each, must also be taken into account.[9] These funds were now applied to support royal troops. The fiscal requirements for defense took precedence over the needs of royal justice.

Fiscal and military considerations must have influenced the crown's decision to suppress the Relação, but to explain the tribunal's demise simply in these terms is to lose sight of other factors directly related to its performance and reputation. These factors can be defined as general and specific, and they involved both local and metropolitan conditions. First, the widespread dislike of lawyers, solicitors, and pettifoggers who "bled rivers of money" from the populace was common throughout the Iberian empires.[10] It is undeniable that the presence of the Relação in Bahia had drawn these hangers-on to the tribunal's halls, where they sought to profit from the opportunities of increased litigation. Inquisition records of 1618 list six of these lawyers, some of whom were of questionable reputation.[11] Criticism was directed not only against the bar, but against the bench as well; in fact, the whole legal pro-

8. King to Governor of Portugal (Barcelona, 31 March 1626), AGS, *Sec. Prov.* 1520, ff. 35v., 47v.

9. *Livro primeiro*, 338.

10. The phrase is Antonil's, in *Cultura e Opulencia*, p. 87.

11. One of these lawyers, Manuel Pacheco de Sousa, noted it was common talk that Manuel Ferreira de Figueiredo, a lawyer, had committed sodomy with the son of Chancellor Ruy Mendes de Abreu. The originator of this tale seems to have been João Garces, who on questioning by the Inquisition, admitted that he had been thrown in jail by Ruy Mendes de Abreu. See *ABNR*, XLIX, 170, 181–182.

fession came under scrutiny in the second decade of the seventeenth century.

Along with the traditional Iberian concern with legal formalism an opposite tradition of dislike and distrust of courts and lawyers had developed. This trend had grown partly in response to real grievances against judicial corruption and shady lawyers and partly because the courts represented royal encroachment on the prerogatives of certain estates or corporations or royal control of colonial areas. More than once in the Spanish Indies, colonists petitioned that no lawyers be allowed in their province.[12] In Spain itself the growth of the *letrado* bureaucracy did not go unnoticed. Those concerned with the ills of Spanish society and the reasons for Spain's increasing economic and military difficulties often included the growth of the bureaucracy, or at least of a *letrado* class, among the major problems of the kingdom. This was a sentiment also expressed by the old military nobility. From time to time the crown made half-hearted attempts to limit bureaucratic growth. In 1624 the crown ordered that no vacancy be filled in any office created since the death of Philip II in 1598.[13] Although this order was soon ignored, the early seventeenth century was a period of increasing concern with the problems caused by the growth of the state.

Throughout metropolitan and colonial Portugal the excesses of the legal profession and the increase of *letrados* and magistrates provoked a similar concern. As the foreign threat grew ever more serious and Portuguese arms suffered a number of setbacks in Asia and America, voices rose against intellectual pursuits and the "nonproductive" legal profession. The common complaint was that: "anyone who has two sons wishes to commit one to a career of letters and from this follows the lack of people to work the fields, of artisans, of sailors, and above all of men for war and the exercise of arms with which the Kingdom of Portugal was founded, es-

12. Cf. Lockhart, *Spanish Peru*, pp. 61–62.

13. Richard L. Kagan, "Education and the State in Hapsburg Spain" (unpublished Ph.D. dissertation, Cambridge University, Trinity College, 1968), especially Chapter III.

tablished, and enlarged." [14] Here was the traditional battle of arms versus letters which Iberians had discussed since the fifteenth century.[15] The empires of Spain and Portugal, born in the valor of their soldiers, had become great mercantile structures built around bureaucratic frameworks. As these structures were beset with increasing difficulties, Spaniards and Portuguese looked back to the halcyon days of Cortes and Da Gama and idealized a simpler and more heroic age peopled with brave soldiers, not nit-picking lawyers.

From Goa to Bahia to Oporto, criticism of the magistracy, of the legal profession, and of the system of law itself rose to new levels. Diogo de Couto, in his dialogues of a soldier, noted that in Portuguese India the bending of statutes and the use of legal loopholes had become an art in the hands of the lawyers.[16] His remarks were echoed by Francisco Rodrigues de Silveira, another man who had soldiered beyond the Cape of Good Hope and who lamented the sight of lands won by the blood of soldiers being placed in the hands of venal attorneys and inexperienced nobles. In Portugal he found conditions even worse, for powerful magnates and dishonest officials made justice a farce. The comments of Rodrigues de Silveira on the Relação of Oporto are pregnant with implications for the sister tribunal of Bahia, for his complaints were also those of the American colonists. Rodrigues de Silveira claimed that the High Court of Oporto, which had been created to speed the judicial process, had in fact stimulated more litigation and thus slowed the process. In a burst of self-criticism, he placed part of the blame on "the restless and contentious nature of the Portuguese,

---

14. "Información en la causa de los estudios de Portugal," BNM, Ms. 4162. This unsigned account, apparently written by a Portuguese Jesuit, defends the utility of intellectual pursuits. Although undated, this essay is most likely from the 1630's.

15. Cf. Miguel de Cervantes Saavedra, *The Adventures of Don Quixote* (Baltimore, 1950), chapter XXXVIII, "Don Quixote's curious Discourse on Arms and Letters"; João Pinto Ribeiro, *Preferencia das Letras as Armas* (Lisbon, 1645).

16. *O soldado prático* (Lisbon, 1937), pp. 30–31.

who in their inclination to suits and swindles (*trapaças*) fabricated in the workshop of their malice, hate, envy, and ill-will, exceed all the other nations of the world." [17]

Fault-finding and malicious gossip were national characteristics that many Portuguese authors in the sixteenth and seventeenth centuries deplored.[18] For some, the most detrimental effects of these faults was that they often resulted in legal suits. In Brazil, as we have seen, there had long been a tradition of anti-judicial feelings. A good example from the second decade of the seventeenth century can be found in the *Livro que dá rezão do Estado do Brasil* (1612) of Diogo de Campos Moreno. As Sergeant-Major of Brazil, Campos Moreno expressed the normal soldier's dislike of *letrados* and clerics. He claimed that the squabbling and back-biting of the colonists had pernicious results because "from this is born so much equivocation, so much lying, and so much swindling that the news of it does nothing but bring lawyers to this poor province." The Relação, he said, "is considered in this city [Salvador] to be a heavy burden (*cousa pesado*)." [19]

The climate of anti-judicial feeling throughout the empire and an increasing clamor for reforms brought the issue squarely before the crown. The rising costs of bureaucracy and the seemingly endless multiplication of officeholders, especially in the nonprofessional offices, seemed to cause endless difficulties. In 1623 the demands of magistrates for promotion coupled with anti-judicial censure moved the crown to consider the problem in depth. A roll was prepared of all royal magistrates in Portugal and, although high court magistrates and colonial judges were not included, the list still included 214 judges serving or awaiting appointment.[20] The Desembargo do Paço, as might be expected, voted against any

---

17. A. de S. S. Costa Lobo (ed.), *Memorias de um soldado da India (1545–1634)* (Lisbon, 1877), pp. 191–193.

18. C. R. Boxer, *The Portuguese Seaborne Empire, 1415–1825* (London, 1969), p. 323.

19. Engel Sluiter, "Report on the State of Brazil, 1612," *HAHR*, XXIX (November 1949), 524–537.

20. ANTT, Convento da Graça, Tomo 3, ff. 284–285.

diminution of the magisterial ranks, but this action of 1623 and the aforementioned Spanish law of 1624 make it clear that the Hapsburg monarch of Spain and Portugal was deeply concerned with the bureaucratization of his empires and the problems that this created.

Within the context of a general dissatisfaction with the judicial system, a royal desire to thin the ranks of the magistracy, and increasing economic difficulties, it is easy to understand the appeal of an argument for the abolition of the High Court of Brazil based on fiscal considerations. We must bear in mind, however, that despite valid grievances, the general attack on the legal profession and the royal magistracy also constituted an attempt by the old military aristocracy and the new colonial elites to hold back the tide of royal centralization; this was a skirmish in the long war between royal power and corporate or class interests. In the first half of the seventeenth century the time was ripe for such a thrust. The crown, faced with the spectre of a global war, once again needed its nobles.

In Brazil specific conditions had arisen which brought new complaints against the judiciary and strengthened the hands of the magistracy's opponents. The disruption caused by the military campaign of 1625–1626 and the continued presence of military authorities in Salvador after its recapture created new conditions for conflict. Upon reentering the city, the commander-in-chief, Don Fadrique de Toledo, ordered that the Relação surrender the papers of its investigation into the debacle of the city's fall to the fleet's chief legal officer. This was an extremely touchy matter since a number of important people including the bishop had acted in a less than heroic manner. Moreover, many New Christians had been accused of collaborating with the Dutch and anti-semitism ran rampant in the city.[21] Rumors flew that a Jewish "stab in the back"

---

21. This incident is described in a deposition made before the Inquisition in 1632 which stated that the accused New Christians were "ricos e poderosos [q.] foram apadrinhados pela fidalguia dêste reino." See Anita Novinsky, "A Inquisição na Bahia (Um Relatório de 1632)," *Revista de História,* XXXVI (1968), n. 74, 417–423.

had brought about the city's capture, and even that the Jews had poisoned the bishop.[22] A number of New Christians were summarily sentenced to death by Don Fadrique de Toledo, but the Relação protested his interference in their jurisdiction. Chancellor Antão de Mesquita compained to the crown of the admiral's action and the prisoners were freed. Whether the accused were "sponsored by the nobility of the colony," as one informant claimed, is impossible to determine, but the involvement of Antão de Mesquita, the judge who had shown himself to be most closely linked to colonial interests, gives the story some credibility.[23]

The investigation into the fall of Bahia in 1624 was finally conducted by the Relação. The High Court had successfully kept Don Fadrique de Toledo and the military authorities at arm's length, but now other powerful interests were also interested in the tribunal's abolition. Both the successes and the failures of the Relação had gained it enemies, some of whom were powerful enough to sway metropolitan councils.

Who would speak for the Relação and argue for its maintenance? Certainly not the bishop and the diocesean clergy, who had struggled so bitterly with the magistrates and had at one point in the past advocated the High Court's demise. The sugar barons, less able to enforce their will on tenants and laborers, wasted no love on the Relação nor did the *câmara* of Salvador, which usually represented the sugar planters. The proprietors and *câmaras* in the other captaincies of Brazil, anxious to be free of the periodic visits and investigations of the desembargadores, would surely not plead on the Relação's behalf. In short, the Relação had made too many enemies, and chief among them stood the Albuquerque Coelho clan of Pernamubuco.

---

22. Among the first reports of the Jewish "stab in the back" was that supplied by Henrique Sinel, a Flemish merchant in Oporto. See *Consulta* Consejo de Guerra (21 August 1624), AGS, Guerra Antiga 901; *Consulta* Conselho de Portugal (2 September 1624), BM, Egerton, 1131, f. 272.

23. King to Governors of Portugal (Madrid, 7 August 1625), ANTT, Coleção São Vicente, livro 19, f. 366.

PLATES

PLATE 1. Sovereignty and justice: The king as supreme judge. (From the *Ordenações manuelinas* (1514); reproduced from Joel Serrão, ed., *Dicionário de História de Portugal*, II, Lisbon, 1965.)

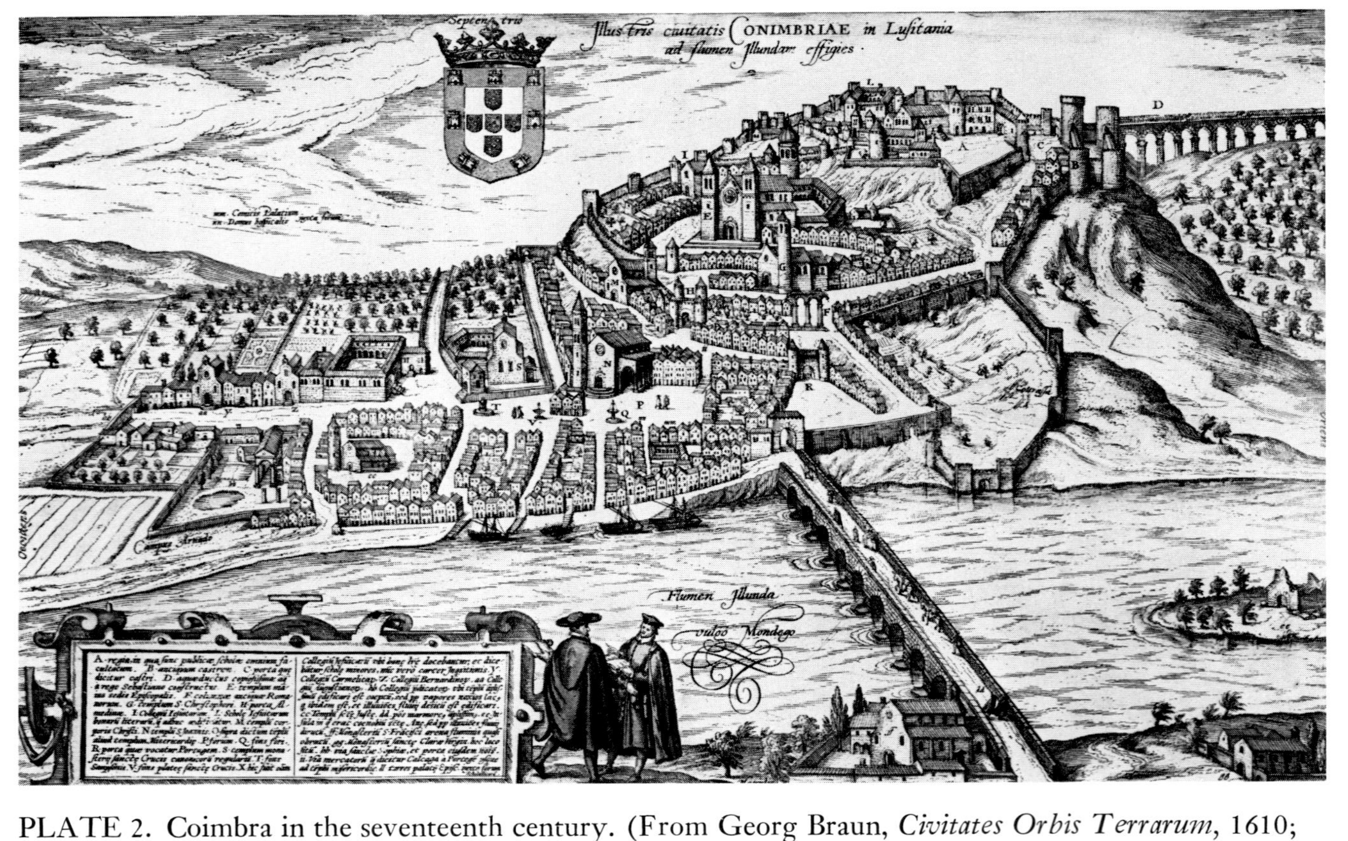

PLATE 2. Coimbra in the seventeenth century. (From Georg Braun, *Civitates Orbis Terrarum*, 1610; courtesy of the Newberry Library.)

PLATE 3. A Portuguese magistrate of the seventeenth century. (Courtesy of the Museu das Janelas Verdes, Lisbon.)

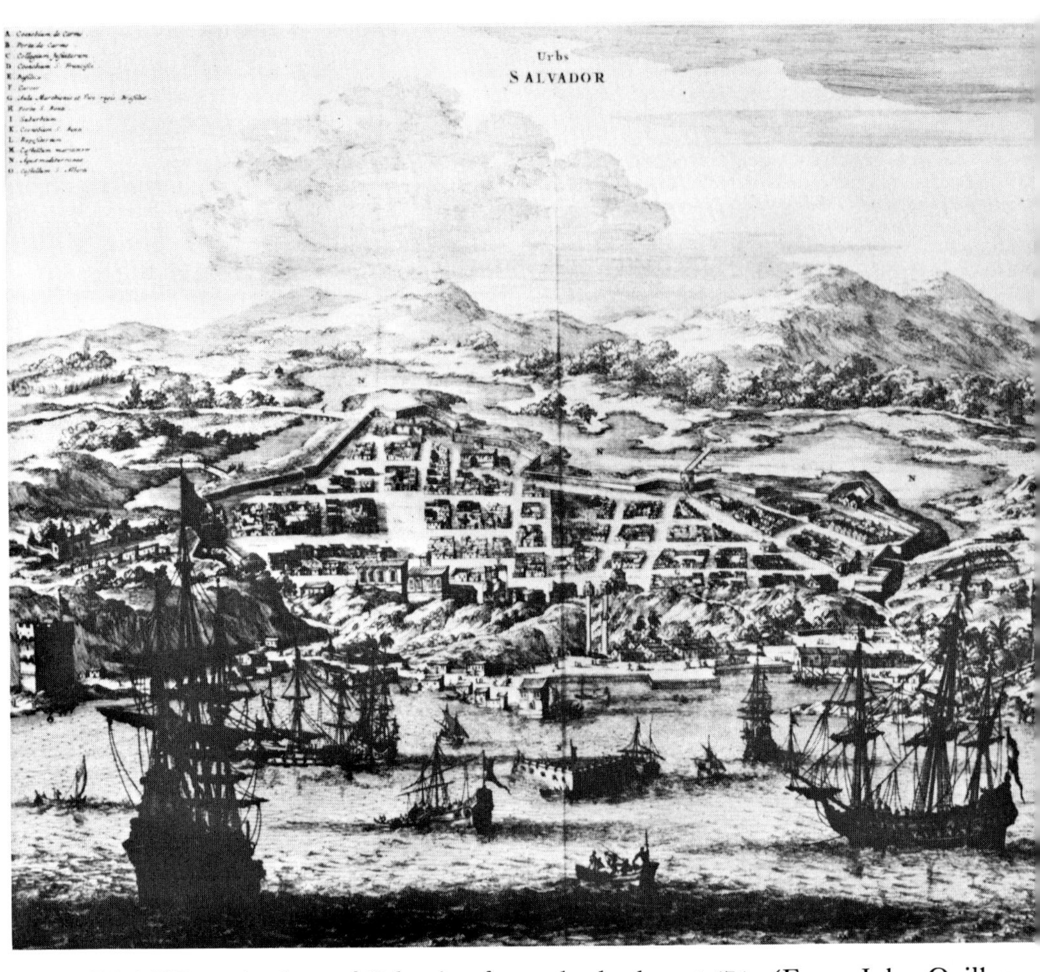

PLATE 4. A view of Salvador from the harbor, 1671. (From John Ogilby, *America: Being the Latest and Most Accurate Description of the New World* . . . , London, 1671; courtesy of the James Ford Bell Library, University of Minnesota.)

PLATE 5. Plan and prospect of Salvador, 1714. (From A. Frezier, *Relation du voyage aux côtes du Chily et du Perou*, Paris, 1716; courtesy of the James Ford Bell Library, University of Minnesota.)

PLATE 6. Portuguese officers and Jesuits captured by the Dutch in the fall of Salvad
1624. (An engraving by Claes Jansz Visscher, 1624; reproduced from Serafim Lei
História da Companhia de Jesus no Brasil, V, Lisbon, 1945.)

PLATE 7. The Solar de Unhão. (Reproduced from Luís Gardel, *Brazil*, New York, 1969.)

PLATE 8. Letter of promotion of Desembargador Bento da Costa de Oliveira e Sampaio (1740), signed by Dom João V. (Document in the author's collection.)

bem, e hão de folgar de hir servir a V. A.

Quanto a fazinda R. S. Com se encomendar ao g. que faça ajustar as contas dos devedores a faz.ª R., e que as dividas se ponhão em arrecadação com effeito e que o dr.º se recolha na arca das tres chaves na forma da ordem que para isso la tem de V. A. e que nisso ponha todo o cuidado e o faça praticar, e procure q. o apontador das obras seia home de boa Conciencia, e que ordene que na Secretaria do Est.º se nam passe patente algua de postos de milicia nem provisão de serventia de off.º algum sem q. p.º Conste por bilhete do Official a que tocar em como tem pago os novos direitos como aquy se usa e com se lhe mandar de qua o Regimento delles, se ficarão remediando os descuidos e desaminhos que tenho apontado.

Isto S.r He o que me consta do Brazil, devido a exp.ª e pratica de muitos annos. E estes sam os remedios que me parece podem aplicarse a ferida ue Ha daquelle Estado, dada tantas veses e aberta p.la impia mão da injustiça. E porq. a Justiça he a ancora sagrada dos Reys e dos Reynos utilid.e dos vassallos, e authoridade dos Ministros, em que deve haver respeito contra os delitos, e he o mesmo não castigallos que permitillos, porque quem não castiga os Reos parece que se fas parcial nos seus erros. Não tenho para que encarecer a V. A. que deve em consciencia acodir aquelle Estado com estes Remedios, porque quem os consulta os quer saber p.ª os aplicar, e tanto mais effectivos serão q.to V. A. os estuda com o seu grande zello, e exemplar Cristandade, que N. S.r conserve e augmente p.ª manter os seus Reynos e Estados em paz e Justiça. Lisboa o prim.º de Agosto de 1681.

Cristovão de Burgos

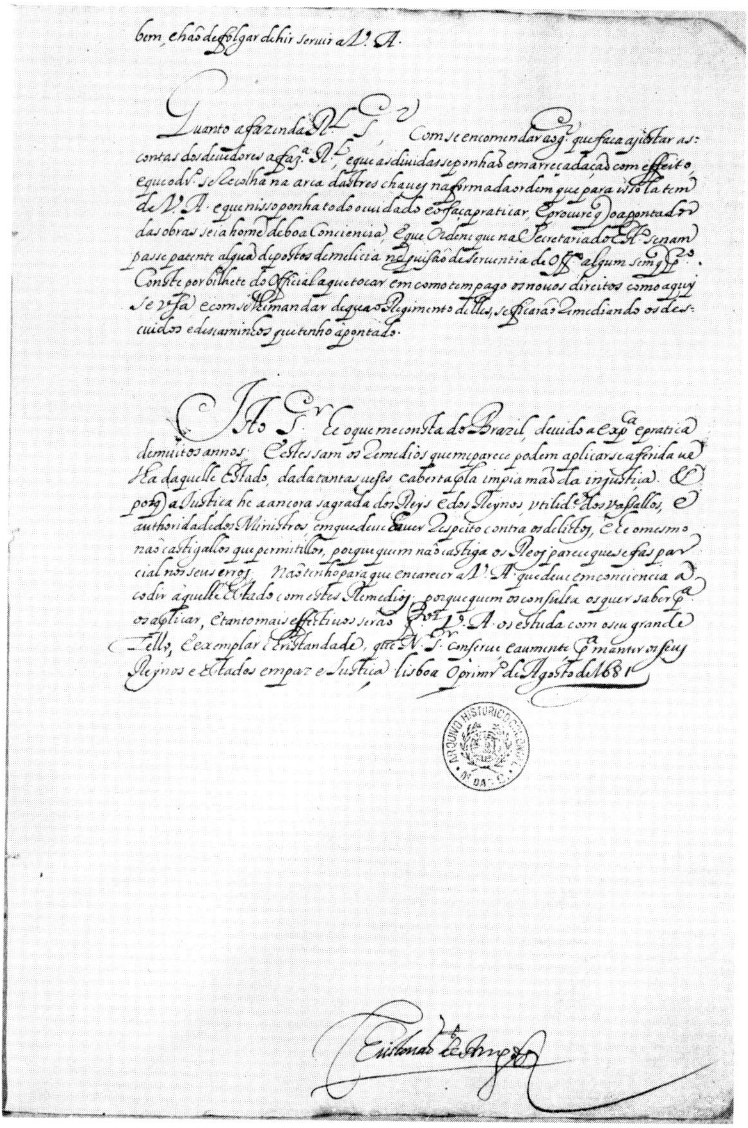

PLATE 9. Report on justice in Brazil with autograph signature of Desembargador Cristóvão de Burgos, 1681. (Bancroft Library Microfilm Collection.)

DESEMBARGADORES, arrivant en Costume au Palais de Justice

PLATE 10. Desembargadores in Rio de Janeiro at the end of the colonial era. (From J. B. Debret, *Voyage pittoresque et historique au Bresil . . .*, Paris, 1834-1839; courtesy of the Newberry Library.)

Pernambuco was by any reckoning the wealthiest captaincy in colonial Brazil. It was still a major area of brazilwood export and contained over 150 *engenhos* around the city of Olinda.[24] From the mid-sixteenth century there was a growing Pernambucan resentment of Bahian political dominance and royal control.[25] Pernambucan colonists resented the investigative and regulatory functions exercised by desembargadores on circuit tour. As we have seen, these tours had caused much hostility in São Paulo and Rio de Janeiro, where colonists had proffered legal and physical opposition to interference by the Relação. In Pernambuco this resistance to royal authority was especially strong since the northern captaincy had prospered under the decentralized donatary system. The Albuquerque Coelho family and the sugar oligarchy held a large amount of political control over local affairs, and they resented any interference from Portugal or from Salvador. The exercise of authority by the Relação in what the proprietor, Duarte de Albuquerque Coelho, and his brother, Matias de Albuquerque, considered their bailiwick was a certain cause of conflict. Moreover, their opposition was supported by the sugar oligarchy of the northern captaincy, who by the early seventeenth century were expressing a growing sense of regional interest.

It is impossible to reconstruct a full list of Pernambucan grievances against the Relação and the central government, but from extant documentation a pattern of hostility and irritation with Bahian control is clear. Pernambucans had taken great profits from legal and illegal trade, and the investigation of André Farto da Costa in 1613 in which the Relação participated had struck at many people. The *câmara* of Olinda, representing local interests, tried by

---

24. Mauro, *Portugal et l'Atlantique*, 193.

25. Francis A. Dutra, "Matias de Albuquerque: A Seventeenth-Century Capitão-Mor of Pernambuco and Governor-General of Brazil" (unpublished Ph.D. dissertation, New York University, 1968), provides an excellent account of the Albuquerque Coelho family and the rivalry between Bahia and Pernambuco. Personal conversations and correspondence with Professor Dutra have been invaluable aids in the writing of this section.

subterfuge and delaying tactics to hinder the investigation.[26] Moreover, periodic judicial investigations probably caused as much hostility in Pernambuco as they did in Rio de Janeiro. In September 1612, for example, Afonso Garcia Tinoco and two other desembargadores were ordered to conduct an investigation of all officeholders in Pernambuco, to hear all cases presently before local judges, and to assist in the distribution of *sesmarias* in the northern captaincy of Rio Grande.[27]

To this normal regional opposition to central control must be added the personal factor. The representatives of Duarte de Albuquerque Coelho ran the captaincy in a rather high-handed manner, and those who opposed the Albuquerque Coelho clique often sought the support of the Relação in their litigation. Matias de Albuquerque, the representative of the family's interests and captain of Pernambuco from 1629, could hardly hide his irritation with the meddling of the High Court in Pernambucan affairs. He complained of the Relação's intervention in his appointment of a treasurer of the captaincy, and on other occasions he quarreled with members of the tribunal.[28] The fact that Matias de Albuquerque never openly criticized the Relação may indicate a healthy respect for its power and a realization that an attack on it would have to be oblique. Once the governorship had fallen to Matias de Albuquerque, his attack on the tribunal was not long delayed.

The final straw appears to have been the refusal of the Relação to suspend criminal justice, a wartime measure suggested by Matias de Albuquerque as a means of enlisting troops against the Dutch. As governor, Matias de Albuquerque had issued a number of

26. "Apontamentos de André Farto da Costa," AHU, Bahia *pap. avul.* caixa 1 (1613), (1st series non-catalogued); king to Provedor da Fazenda of Pernambuco (Lisbon, 8 October 1612), AHU, Pernambuco *pap. avul.* caixa 1; certification of Vasco de Sousa Pacheco, Capitão-mor of Pernambuco (Bahia, 24 February 1616), AHU, Bahia *pap. avul.* caixa 1 (1st series non-cataloged).

27. BI, Correspondencia . . . Gaspar de Sousa, f. 22.

28. Dutra, "Matias de Albuquerque," 247–257.

pardons and suspended the prosecution of certain crimes in an effort to shore up the colony's defenses. This he had done without consultation with the Relação. The magistrates, viewing these measures as an infringement on their powers, refused to obey the governor's orders and reimprisoned some of the pardoned men. Finally, Matias de Albuquerque appealed directly to the crown. His plea won royal support and on 1 April 1626 the crown ordered the Relação to back down from its position. Four days later the High Court was abolished by a royal order.[29]

The connection between the complaints of Matias de Albuquerque and the demise of the Relação is supported not only by a close chronological correlation, but also by contemporary evidence. The unsigned report of c. 1626 submitted by Bahian colonists in support of the Relação provides the key.[30] It noted that in 1625 a certain *donatário*, unwilling to allow desembargadores to interfere in his captaincy, had joined forces with the town council of Salvador to bring about the High Court's abolition. A retainer of the *donatário* was chosen as attorney for the municipal council, and upon returning to Portugal he allegedly presented "false information and reports signed by impassioned people and the retainers of *fidalgos*" in order to bring about the tribunal's abolition. The *donatário* in question was most certainly Duarte de Albuquerque Coelho, the proprietor of Pernambuco, who had come to Brazil in the Luso-Spanish armada of 1625 and was thus in Bahia during the period following the city's recapture. The charge leveled against him is not without some support. Although the papers in question have not been found, a letter from Philip IV to the governors of Portugal noted the reports of Matias de Albuquerque, the *provedor-mór*, and Sergeant-Major Pedro Correia da Gama,

---

29. *Alvará* of 1 April 1626, BGUC, Codice 709; *Provisão* of Matias de Albuquerque (20 July 1626), AMCS, Livro 156; *alvará* of 2 August 1626, *AHNRJ*, Assentos da Relação, Codice 541.

30. Razões q. darão os moradores da Bahya para não se extinguem a Relaçao," BNL, *Col. Pomb.* 647, ff. 69–72.

concerning the garrison; these contained specific suggestions concerning the High Court.[31] These suggestions undoubtedly argued for the abolition of the Relação, and they may be taken as the precipitating cause of its demise.

The abolition of the Relação of Bahia resulted from a combination of factors, some accidental and others born of that institution's history. First, the wartime conditions created by the reopening of the war in the Netherlands and the Dutch seizure of Bahia placed great pressure on the defensive structure of the Iberian empires, which called forth increasing military demands on the crown's fiscal resources. The crown began to look in every direction for money or ways in which to force certain groups to assume financial or military obligations with little additional cost to the crown. Taxation was one method, and increasing tax levies to pay for the war against the Dutch became a major cause of unrest in Portugal and in Spain itself. Attempts were made to paint the war as a religious conflict in order to force the knights of the Spanish and Portuguese military orders to fulfill their ancient obligations as defenders of the faith. The crown put jurists to work finding clauses in the grants to the *donatários* which would require them to pay for the cost of their captaincy's defense.[32] Obviously, the crown sought ways to enlist the full support of groups who could bring military or financial resources to the war effort, and if enlisting this support meant the granting of certain concessions, that would be done.

The Relação made a perfect target. There was already royal concern with the increasing size of the bureaucracy and a general dislike of the legal profession. The High Court of Bahia, with its salaries and extra costs, seemed non-essential for the war effort, and

31. AGS, *Sec. Prov.* 1520 (31 January 1626), f. 6v.

32. BNM, Papeles de Ordem de Christo 938, ff. 202–210, details the crown's attempt to force all *comendadores* of the Portuguese military orders to go to Brazil to combat the Dutch. BNL, Fundo Geral 7627, ff. 41–43v., deals with the legal attempts to force the proprietors to defend their captaincies.

if by its abolition its salaries could be turned over to defense so much the better. Moreover, by acquiescing to the demands of the *câmara* of Bahia and the *donatário*, of Pernambuco, the crown also hoped to gain their full support. Thus, the Relação became a kind of royal sacrifice to colonial interests. Reasons of state and private interests had combined to close the doors of the first Brazilian High Court.

Was there no one, then, to speak in the court's behalf? Such people did in fact exist. Their unsigned plea, "Reasons given by the colonists of Bahia for not abolishing the High Court," argued for the maintenance of the Relação as the one significant check on the excesses of the bishops, *donatários*, and *poderosos da terra*, who intimidated the scribes and ships captains so that the poor were unable to have their suits prepared or even carried to the metropolitan courts.[33] These colonists did not claim that all had gone well while the Relação sat in Bahia, but rather that the personal failings of individual magistrates were not necessarily those of the institution. If justice had been lacking while the High Court sat in Brazil, without it the situation would revert to chaos. As far as the money for the garrison was concerned, they argued that "there is no king however poor whom four or five thousand *cruzados* would enrich or impoverish, how much less so Your Majesty." Again, as in the past, they pointed to the five *audiencias* in the viceroyalty of Peru and the tribunal in the Spanish Canary Islands. Was it proper, they asked, that a few islands with a small population should have a resident court, while Brazil, so large and so far from the metropolis, did not?

The main thrust of their argument, however, centered upon the benefits produced by the presence of a large group of judges who as a body were less subject to the pressures of interest groups and venal officials. Whatever the excesses and abuses of the desembargadores, the situation had been far worse before 1609, when the *ouvidor geral* administered justice in the colony. Then too, why had the Brazilian tribunal been singled out?

33. BNL, *Col. Pomb.* 647, 69–72.

> And if some say that the judges are also thieves and commit injustices, I say that this is not the fault of the Relação but of their bad performance and lack of Christian principles, and that this is no reason to abolish the Relação. Those that are bad should be severely punished as an example and then replaced, for there is no lack of *letrados*. . . . And if the misdeeds of desembargadores were reason to extinguish the courts, there would be none at all because in each there are good men and bad men, and even in the Casa da Suplicação in Lisbon there were some who had gone astray and were dismissed from their positions, but the Casa da Suplicação was not destroyed.[34]

Without a Relação in Brazil, they claimed, the pace of justice had slowed, the jails were full, the Jews went unpunished for their treason, powerful officials worked their illegal will, and things had been turned topsy turvy.

This document presents a point of view that differs greatly from the sources that are traditionally used in evaluating the performance of the Relação of Bahia prior to 1626. This divergence of opinion may be partially explained by the origins of the authors involved. Internal evidence indicates that the author or authors of the unsigned "Reasons given by the colonists," represented poorer folk of orthodox Catholic origins who disliked and feared royal officials, the sugar planters, the local *câmara*, and the New Christians. Perhaps we are dealing here with artisans or tenant farmers who felt that the High Court had offered them opportunities for justice which had not previously existed.

In this context, it is important to remember that the authors of the three traditional accounts of the Relação each represented an interest group with long-standing complaints against the High Court. The Franciscan priest, Frei Vicente do Salvador, had taken umbrage at the magistrates' attack on the authority of the bishop and the prerogatives of the ecclesiastical courts. His *História do Brasil* (1627) reflected his feelings toward the tribunal. The professional soldier, Sergeant-Major Diogo de Campos Moreno, saw in the Relação an unnecessary institution staffed by corrupt

34. *Ibid.*

letrados, a group for whom he had no affection. His *Livro que dá rezão do Estado do Brasil* (1612) expresses the soldier's contempt for the lawyer, a contempt that was certainly heightened by the struggles between the Relação and the garrison discussed in Chapter Nine. The most pungent critique of the Relação can be found in the *Diálogos das grandezas do Brasil* written in 1618 by Ambrosio Fernandes Brandão. Brandão was a New Christian sugar planter connected with Pernambuco, and although much of his criticism of the High Court has a ring of truth, he too perhaps viewed the tribunal with a jaundiced eye. For all its failings, the Relação probably provided justice to a wider range and larger proportion of the colonial population than ever before, and the very complaints of representatives of the Church, the military, and the sugar elite are evidence of its achievements.

It is important to note that the attack on the Relação never questioned its legitimacy as such, but emphasized instead the crown's financial needs. Groups and individuals might dispute points of law and spheres of jurisdiction with the High Court, but the legitimacy of the judges seemed inviolate. Whereas the Jesuits in Brazil and even *ouvidores* were on occasion expelled from communities because their unpopular views so upset the colonists, no such attempt was made against the desembargadores as a body. To have done so would have been tantamount to rebellion against the king, for the magistrates represented the authority of the crown both in reality and in the popular mind. Thus any attempt to control or diminish the authority of the Relação had to be made through established channels of appeal to the metropolis and by playing off the crown's desire for centralized control against its pressing fiscal problems.

Appeal to the metropolis as a means of undercutting the Relação indicates that the attempts to integrate the magistrates into the social and economic fabric of the colony in order to incorporate the power of the tribunal and subvert its independence had not been wholly successful. Magistrates often expressed interest in the colony and the welfare of the colonists as well as in their own personal gain, but in last analysis the Relação remained tied to the crown and often beyond the control of the colonial elite.

The demise of the Relação caused a number of readjustments in the structure of justice. With the High Court gone, the previous system based on an *ouvidor geral* was reinstituted. Antão de Mesquita, married in Brazil and perhaps willing to remain there, was selected to stay in the colony as *ouvidor geral.* In fact, the crown also considered appointing him *provedor dos difuntos*, although these duties were given to Diogo de São Miguel Garces instead.[35] The other desembargadores were instructed to sail for Portugal and the king ordered the governors of Portugal to arrange means of accommodating themselves with positions in the metropolis. The magistrates expected to be awarded places in the Casa da Suplicação or the Relação do Pôrto, as their predecessors had been in 1621, "it being an inviolate custom that magistrates from Brazil receive them before all others."[36] Most of the magistrates were satisfied in their desire and some rose to even greater office. Martim Afonso Coelho became *juiz da Índia e Mina*, Antônio das Póvoas became a member of the Conselho da Fazenda, and Manoel Jácome Bravo attained a seat in the municipal council of Lisbon. Some of the desembargadores became regular advisers on Brazilian matters and were called upon by the governing bodies to offer expert opinion and advice.[37] Thus a tradition was begun that was to be revived in the eighteenth century. The desembargadores, wrote Sebastião da Rocha Pitta in 1724, "returning to Portugal . . . occupy the highest councils of the kingdom and the highest place in letters where at present they can be found exercising most worthily those elevated positions."[38]

On 14 April 1628 the *regimento* of the *ouvidor geral* was re-

35. ANTT, Mesa da Consciência, liv. 29, ff. 130–131v.

36. AGS, *Sec. Prov.* 1475, ff. 247–250.

37. For example, see ANTT, *Chan. Filipe III, Doações*, liv. 1, f. 7v.

38. Sebastião de Rocha Pitta, *História da America portugueza* (1724) (Lisbon, 1880), p. 81.

issued to Paulo Leitão de Abreu.[39] The captaincies of the south had maintained their judicial autonomy under the *ouvidor geral do sul*, but the removal of the Relação from Bahia necessitated appeal to Portugal from his decisions. The old problems of expense and delay once again appeared, but now they were exacerbated by the tenuous communications across a hostile Atlantic infested by enemy ships. Complaints against this situation by the colonists in Rio de Janeiro moved the crown to expand the powers of the *ouvidor geral do sul* in a new *regimento* of 1630, and in the same year a new set of instructions was issued to the *ouvidor geral do Brasil* in Bahia.[40]

From 1630 to 1652 the pressures of the war against the Dutch in Brazil and the war for independence against Spain which began with the Portuguese revolt of 1640 precluded much attention to the judicial system, but the Relação was not a forgotten institution. Although inconvenient to some and hated by others, the High Court had proved its value. Both the crown and the colonists had an interest in the re-establishment of the tribunal, and by 1652 the Relação was once again authorized for Brazil.

---

39. Andrade e Silva, *Coll. chron.*, IV, 124–127.

40. *Câmara* of Rio Je Janeiro to king (1630), BNL, Fundo Geral 7627; AGS, *Sec. Prov.* 1475, ff. 275–289; Andrade e Silva, *Coll. chron.* IV, 177.

PART THREE: THE RELAÇÃO REBORN, 1652-1751

XI. PROBLEMS OF JUSTICE

The captaincies of the State of Brazil and the Kingdom of Angola have suffered almost as much damage from judicial missions (alçadas) *as from the Dutch.*

Salvador Correia de Sá (1673)

Colonial Law and Order

The middle decades of the seventeenth century brought considerable changes to Portugal and her empire. In Europe the Portuguese nobility, convinced that the Spanish connection no longer benefited them, finally threw in with their nationalistic, or at least anti-Spanish, compatriots from the poorer classes. The standard of revolt was raised in December 1640, and a new king proclaimed; he was João, Duke of Bragança, now to become Dom João IV, King of Portugal. Spain, embattled in the Low Countries and facing a serious revolt in Catalonia, could not bring her full force against the Portuguese, who themselves showed considerable determination in the long series of border clashes and sieges that constituted the war for independence. This struggle, usually called the War of Restoration, came to a close in 1668 with Spanish recognition of Portuguese independence.[1]

1. The bibliography of the Restoration is enormous. The classic contemporary work is Luís de Meneses (Conde de Ericeira), *História de Portugal Restaurado*, 4 vols. (Oporto, 1945–1946). The original edition dates from 1678–1698. A good general summary is provided in *Dicionário de História de Portugal*, III, 609–639.

Meanwhile, the imperial structure was also changing. All of the Portuguese colonial areas with the sole exception of Ceuta declared for Dom João IV. The danger of Spanish moves in the colonies as part of the Luso-Spanish struggle was real enough, but in the long run it came to little.[2] Instead, the Dutch continued to be the major threat to the Portuguese colonial stations. The Portuguese war against the Dutch on "three continents and five seas" had been in part the result of Portugal's ties to Spain. Despite Portuguese hopes to the contrary, the conflict continued even after the separation from Spain in 1640, carried on by its own momentum and becoming in many ways a purely colonial war.

The struggle ended, as C. R. Boxer has pointed out, with a Dutch victory in Asia, a standoff in Africa, and a Portuguese triumph in Brazil. Luso-Brazilians drove the Dutch from Angola in 1648 and liberated the northern captaincies of Brazil by 1654.[3] Dutch victories at Malacca, Colombo, and on the Malabar coast struck heavy blows at the Portuguese imperial dream, but by the mid-seventeenth century the Indian Ocean was no longer the empire's strength. The sugar and slaves of the Atlantic had surpassed the spices of the East in imperial reckoning. Thus, in terms of value, Portugal had retained the core of its colonial power.

During the period of restoration in Portugal the major administrative reform which affected the colonies was the creation of a new overseas council, the Conselho Ultramarino. This body supplanted the Conselho da Fazenda and now assumed control over all colonial matters of a civil and military nature with the exception of *letrado* appointments to the colonial magistracy, which remained in the hands of the Desembargo do Paço. Established in 1642, the Conselho Ultramarino remained an important organ of government into the nineteenth century, but the creation of a Colonial

2. On the Restoration in the colonies, see *A Restauração e o império colonial português* (Lisbon, 1940).

3. C. R. Boxer, *Four Centuries of Portuguese Expansion, 1415–1825: A Succinct Survey* (Berkeley, 1969), pp. 48–55. (This is a reprint of the original edition published in Johannesburg in 1961.)

Secretary in 1736 and the development of a powerful Colonial Ministry in the 1760's severely circumscribed its power.[4]

Within a year of the Conselho Ultramarino's birth, its councilors received a petition for the re-establishment of the Relação of Bahia. Curiously, the *câmara* of Salvador, which in 1626 had played a major role in the High Court's demise, now became an agitator for its rebirth.[5] In 1642 it suggested that the Relação be reinstituted in Bahia, and as the Dutch War drew to a close later in the decade the city fathers once again complained of expensive legal appeals to the metropolis. These petitions finally took effect in 1651, when the crown began to select magistrates for a new High Court. The final appeal of the *câmara* came in January 1652. In a list of grievances and desiderata, the re-establishment of the Relação ranked first among them.[6] On 12 September 1652 a new *regimento* was issued for the Relação, and in March 1653 the judges took their oath of office in Bahia. At their head as chancellor came Jorge Seco de Macedo, a former desembargador in Goa and a judge in the Casa da Suplicação.[7]

Not everyone in Brazil held fond memories of the Relação and rumblings against its rebirth came from various quarters. Perhaps the most trenchant expression of dissent came from a *letrado* who

---

4. Alden, *Royal Government*, pp. 9–10. There is no adequate study of the Conselho Ultramarino. Marcelo Caetano, *De Conselho Ultramarino ao Conselho do Imperio* (Lisbon, 1943), is only a beginning. A study of this body's factions and membership might open whole new vistas of Brazilian history and illuminate the nature of metropolitan patronage and colonial influences on Portugal. Men with Brazilian experience were sometimes chosen to serve on this council. Salvador de Sá provides a famous example, but there were others. Five desembargadores of the Relação who served in Brazil prior to 1754 eventually became members of the Conselho Ultramarino. By far the best survey to date is presented in Boxer, *Salvador de Sá*, pp. 160–163, 214–222.

5. Varnhagen, *História geral*, III, 143–144; Afonso Ruy, *História política e administrativa da Cidade do Salvador* (Salvador, 1949), pp. 206–207.

6. "Particulares de q. necessita o Povo da Cidade da Bahia," ANTT, Mss. da Livraria 1116, f. 175.

7. *Consulta* of the Conselho Ultramarino (hereinafter abbreviated in the notes as CU), AHU, Bahia *pap. avul.*, caixa 10 (1st series non-catalogued).

later became a member of the High Court. Luís Salema de Carvalho, a magistrate already in Brazil on a judicial mission, noted colonial misgivings about the High Court. He wrote to the Conselho Ultramarino that sending the Relação to Brazil amounted to "protecting the sheep from the wolves by sending more wolves." [8] It was in some ways a prophetic statement.

Bahia in the century between 1650 and 1760 was a growing and maturing colonial settlement. By 1700 urban Salvador contained over 40,000 people, and by the 1770's the total population of the captaincy was calculated at 288,848 souls.[9] Visitors to Salvador in the eighteenth century usually commented on the preponderance of blacks and mulattos on the city's streets. The French traveler Amédée Frézier probably exaggerated when he placed the ratio at twenty black to every white man in Salvador, but an ecclesiastical census from the same decade reveals that even an urban parish like Conceição had 2,820 slaves in a total population of 4,938, or 57 per cent slave, to say nothing of free blacks and mulattos.[10] That same census revealed an even higher ratio of slave to free in some of the sugar growing parishes of the Recôncavo, where after 1700 Africans from the coast of Mina began to appear in large numbers as a result of a Bahian-centered cross-Atlantic trade.

The patterns of life established in the city's first hundred years matured and flourished in baroque effusion during the next century. Religion and sex seem to have been the major pastimes of the urban population. Many observers commented on the devotion of the Bahians, their lavish holy processions, and the beauty of their

---

8. Luís Salema de Carvalho to CU (Bahia, 27 January 1655), AHU, Bahia *pap. avul.*, caixa 6 (1st series non-catalogued).

9. See C. R. Boxer, *The Golden Age of Brazil, 1695–1750* (Berkeley, 1962), pp. 126–161, and Russell-Wood, *Fidalgos*, for the good accounts of eighteenth-century Bahia. The population figures are given in Tales de Azevedo, *Povoamento*, pp. 181–200.

10. Gonçalo Soares da França, "Dissertações de historia ecclesiastica de Brazil (1724)," SGL, res. 1-C-147. Cf. A. Frézier, *A Voyage to the South Sea and along the Coasts of Chili and Peru, 1712–1714* (London, 1716), p. 301.

churches. In fact, this religiosity found expression between 1650 and 1750 in intense architectural activity. William Dampier, who visited the city in 1699, reported thirteen churches and chapels in the city, among them a convent of Poor Clares which dated from 1677.[11] The magnificent Jesuit church, completed by 1672, set the tone of construction which others followed. One of the loveliest of these temples was the convent of Santa Thereza (1686), built by Descalced Carmelites on a beautiful site overlooking the bay. This architectural fervor was matched by institutional activity. In the late seventeenth and early eighteenth centuries the religious brotherhoods of Salvador flourished. The upper-class Misericórdia and the Third Order of St. Francis continued as the most prestigious lay organizations, but they were joined by black brotherhoods like Our Lady of the Rosary (1685) and St. Anthony of Catagerona (1699), and by others which welcomed the growing mulatto population. A secular reaction, revealed in a decline in charitable bequests, began to set in during the mid-eighteenth century, but Bahians maintained their reputation for piety.[12]

The residents of Salvador also had a reputation for lasciviousness and lechery. While foreign observers may have exaggerated the extent of prostitution and the availability of even "decent ladies," there is no doubt that opportunities for sexual license were virtually unlimited. The large mix-blood population indicated the high level of miscegenation. "A black woman to work, a white woman to marry, and a mulatta for sex," was the fantasy of the Bahian male. Virginity, dowries, brides, mistresses, and bastards were topics of great popular interest and common concern.

The economy also occupied a high place among Bahian concerns. After 1650 increasing competition from sugar islands in the Caribbean and the vissisitudes of that agriculture in Brazil seriously impeded the growth of the Brazilian sugar industry. A crisis was reached in the 1680's and although the industry made some re-

---

11. William Dampier, *A Voyage to New Holland (1699)* (London, 1939), p. 35.

12. Russell-Wood, *Fidalgos*, pp. 146–172.

covery thereafter it suffered a second shock in the late 1690's. The discovery of gold in Minas Gerais in 1695 drew many men from the coastal regions and drove the price of slaves skyward. This situation, coupled with a falling price for sugar in European markets, struck hardest at the marginal producers and the *lavradores de cana.* Many of them were eliminated from the industry or suffered a loss in status and economic position. The great planter families survived and continued as the most powerful socio-economic group in the captaincy, and while Brazilian sugar no longer controlled the European market, sugar and the sugar planters remained regionally dominant.

The importance of other economic activities grew in the eighteenth century. Tobacco was an important item in the regional economy. Its cultivation was centered around the Recôncavo towns of Cachoeira and Maragogipe. By the mid-eighteenth century Bahian tobacco was exported to Europe, to the other captaincies of Brazil, and to the Mina coast, where it became a major commodity of exchange in the African slave trade.[13] Tobacco was the "small man's" crop. It did not call for the great operating capital of a sugar mill, and the tobacco growers were neither as wealthy nor as politically powerful as the sugar planters. The same could not be said of the men involved in Bahia's other growing economy, stockraising. By the early eighteenth century large catle ranches had been established in the interior of the captaincy, especially along the southern margins of the São Francisco River. Herds were periodically driven across the backlands to towns just beyond the Recôncavo, where the cattle were then sold for meat and hides or for use as plantation oxen. The ranchers, some of whom had thousands of head on their enormous tracts of land, differed very little from the sugar planters in their social origins or aspirations. Occasionally ranchers also owned *engenhos* and many who did not were tied by blood or marriage to the planter families

13. Pierre Verger, *Flux et reflux de la traite des Nègres entre le golfe de Bénin et Bahia de todos os santos du XVIIe au XIXe Siècle* (Paris, 1963).

of the coast. The "potentates of the backlands," as ranchers like Antônio Guedes de Brito and João Peixoto Viegas were called, did not constitute a threat to the political dominance of the planter class, but represented instead another sector within the landed elite and an enlargement of the Bahian aristocracy.

The diversification of the Bahian economy, the continued export of sugar, and the growing trade in tobacco and hides stimulated the expansion of Salvador's mercantile community and the role of that city as the major Brazilian commercial port. Trade with Portugal was organized after 1649 in a yearly convoy system which operated irregularly until 1765.[14] Some of the vessels which made up these fleets were constructed in the shipyards of Bahia, which by the early eighteenth century built ships for the coastal trade and the India trades as well.[15] By 1759 Salvador had over one hundred merchants engaged in trade with Portugal, Africa, and other Brazilian ports. Perhaps the most important development in the export-import sector was the rise of trade with the Mina coast in Africa, where Bahian rum and tobacco gave the merchants of Salvador considerable advantage over their competitors from Portugal. The port of Whydah alone supplied Bahia with 10,000 to 12,000 slaves a year by 1731.[16]

Of course not all the merchants in Salvador engaged in the trans-Atlantic trade. Some specialized in finance and investment in the captaincy, where the demand for credit was always great. Others found considerable profit in the legal and illegal gold trade which developed after the opening of Minas Gerais. The merchants, as we saw in Chapter Five, had been firmly established in Salvador from its early days. In the century after 1650 the mercantile sector grew in size and expanded its social and political roles. Between

---

14. Alden, *Royal Government*, p. 9.

15. José Roberto de Amaral Lapa, *A Bahia e a carreira da India* (São Paulo, 1968).

16. José Antonio Caldas, *Noticia geral de toda esta capitania da Bahia desde o seu descobrimento até o presente ano de 1759*, facsimile edition (Salvador, 1951), pp. 527–533. Boxer, *The Golden Age*, p. 154.

1700 and 1750 it began to acquire a social standing commensurate with its wealth. This was demonstrated by the increasing acceptance of merchants to high positions within the Misericórdia brotherhood.[17] The station of shopkeepers and the numerous artisan population of the city, many of whom were mulattos or free blacks, does not seem to have changed much by the eighteenth century, although their numbers had surely grown.

The problems of justice encountered by the new High Court of Appeals were the same that had confronted its predecessor: an unruly colonial society, great power in the hands of individuals and families, and broad sectors of the population unable or unwilling to comply with the social norms. The pillory which stood in front of the Jesuit College witnessed the punishment of convicted prisoners from all levels of society and of all hues.[18] Aside from the common punishments of monetary fines, penal exile, and the galleys, branding, flogging, hanging, and beheading were also in use.[19] The first High Court's reluctance to issue death sentences did not reappear with the new tribunal. The hangman's rope and the headman's axe did their share of the labor, although the latter was normally reserved for the high-born, since hanging was considered a dishonorable death. Such was the case in 1687 when Fernão Barbalho Bezerra, a wealthy and respected Pernambucan sugar planter,

17. Russell-Wood, *Fidalgos*, pp. 130–136.

18. The *pelourinho* stood in the Terreiro de Jesus until 1718, when the Jesuits complained that the execution of sentences disrupted religious activities in their church (the present Cathedral of Salvador). The pillory was moved at that time to the area near the church of Our Lady of the Rosary, the chapel of the principal black brotherhood. This square thus came to be known as the Largo do Pelourinho, as it is presently called today.

19. There was yet another form of punishment in use in colonial Brazil which does not appear to have been employed by the Relação. This was the *polé*, a tall pole-and-pulley arrangement by which the victim was raised by his arms tied behind his back and then dropped sharply to a few inches off the ground. This resulted in the painful dislocation of the prisoner's shoulders. The *polé* was commonly employed in Pernambuco, especially for military deserters. See the discussion in F. A. Pereira da Costa, *Anais Pernambucanos*, 10 vols. (Recife, 1951–1967), IV, 30–32.

died beneath the headman's axe for having killed his wife, three daughters, and a nephew in the belief that one of his daughters had submitted to illicit relations in his home and thereby dishonored him.[20] Cases of this nature were rare enough to cause contemporary observers to take note of them, something which these observers did not do in the many instances of capital punishment applied to black slaves, mulattos, and foreigners. An exception, however, was the largest mass execution of colonial Brazil, when in 1718 twenty-seven English pirates were sentenced by the Relação and hung in Bahia.[21]

The enforcement of law on the population of non-European origins was still designed more as an object lesson than as the application of justice. Indians remained basically beyond the interest of the civil judiciary, although a law of 1700 gave the *ouvidor geral* appellate jurisdiction in all cases involving them.[22] Indians, however, were considered along with mulattos and blacks as great troublemakers and hence worthy of special judicial attention.[23] In Rio de Janeiro, Pernambuco, São Paulo, and in Minas Gerais *ouvidores* were able to sentence these "criminal types" to death. Fugitive slaves were also the concern of civil authorities. Usually after capture they were simply returned to their owners, although those that had joined *mocambos* (fugitive communities) and had raided farms or molested travelers were sentenced to whipping and the galleys or to penal exile.[24] In 1690 Desembargador Joseph de Freitas Serrão complained that exiling fugitives to Angola or São Tomé was no punishment since it amounted to sending them home.

---

20. Pereira da Costa, *Anais*, IV, 293; Rocha Pitta, *História*, p. 218.

21. Rocha Pitta, *História*, pp. 306–307. Eight others who were minors or against whom there was not sufficient evidence were sentenced to life in the galleys.

22. *DHBNR*, VI (1928), 318–319.

23. Cf. law of 20 October 1735, printed in Pereira da Costa, *Anais*, IV, 50–51.

24. I have discussed the problem of fugitive slaves and their punishments in "The Mocambo: Slave Resistance in Colonial Bahia," *Journal of Social History*, III (Summer 1970), n. 4, 313–333.

He suggested instead that they be employed by the crown in public works.[25] After 1741 all recaptured fugitives were branded with the letter "F." [26]

In their attitudes toward mestiços, mulattos, and blacks the lily-white desembargadores reflected the general prejudices of the colonial Portuguese, but as representatives of the crown they were also called upon to eliminate outrageous violations of the master-slave relationship. Magistrates sometimes found it difficult to overcome their fears and insecurities in this matter. Desembargador Cristóvão de Burgos devoted an entire paragraph of his 1681 report on the state of justice to the problem of free and slave blacks whose skill with poison was such that they could eliminate whole families without leaving a trace of their deed.[27] Burgos' concern probably stemmed from the fact that his relative, Francisco Mendes de Burgos, had been killed by his mulatto slave.[28] Nevertheless, toward the end of the seventeenth century the Relação gave increasing concern to these problems. In 1700 the judges received royal orders to investigate reports that Brazilian slave-owners were cruelly whipping, mutilating, and starving their slaves.[29] From time to time the Relação did force masters to sell slaves who were being abused. There was, however, a certain leniency for masters accused of mistreating their slaves. A case in point was Francisco Jorge, arrested for whipping his bondsman to death. Upon appeal that he was a poor man with many children and that the charge was false, the Relação granted him a pardon.[30]

In fact, the ease with which criminals were released on bail (*fiança*), received permission to remain at liberty (*cartas de*

25. Memorial of Joseph de Freitas Serrão (24 May 1690), APB, *Ord. reg.* 1, n. 78.

26. Livro de Registro da Relação, BGUC, Codice 707.

27. AHU, Bahia *pap. avul.*, caixa 14 (1 August 1681). See below, note 31.

28. APB, Relação 454, f 69v.

29. Accioli, *Memórias*, II, 149. This work is a treasure-trove of information which reprints many documents. It is poorly organized, has no index, and is exasperating to use.

30. *Alvará de perdão* (Salvador, 21 April 1678), APB, Relação 495, f. 75v.

seguro), or were pardoned seriously undercut the authority of the Relação. Curiously, men from opposite ends of the social structure had the most success in securing these writs. Whites often had the power, influence, or wealth needed to obtain release from the civil authorities. Slaves imprisoned for minor crimes, and sometimes for major ones, had the advantage of a master who could plead for their release on the grounds that they were necessary for his livelihood. Those in the middle—poor whites, freedmen, artisans, and manual laborers—had no one to plead their case and lacked the necessary wealth or connections to secure their own release. It was they who greatly suffered from the wretched conditions of the jail of Salvador, which despite various attempts at reform remained by all accounts a hell-hole. Nevertheless, the High Court's leniency in granting pardons brought periodic complaints which moved the crown to action in 1679. In 1681 Desembargador Cristóvão de Burgos deplored the continuing situation, and in 1698 the crown again moved to tighten up the granting of pardons and bail.[31] A glance at the *Livros de perdões e fiança* of the Relação bear witness to the ineffectiveness of this measure.

The *regimento* issued to the Relação did not differ significantly from the previous guidelines of 1609. The jurisdiction of the High Court remained basically unchanged.[32] All other captaincies were once again made judicially subordinate to the Relação at Bahia, while the Estado do Maranhão remained a separate entity over which the Bahian tribunal exercised no control. The Conselho Ultramarino rejected a number of suggestions to establish a separate

31. King to Gov. D. João de Lencastre (Lisbon, 16 January 1699), *DHBNR*, XXXII (1936), 424–425; memorial of Cristóvão de Burgos (Lisbon, 1 August 1681), AHU, Bahia *pap. avul.*, caixa 14. I have used the microfilm copy available in the Bancroft Library, University of California, Berkeley, California.

32. An oversight was corrected in 1724 when Chancellor Caetano Brito de Figueiredo pointed out the failure of the *regimento* of 1652 to provide for a *juiz dos cavaleiros* to hear cases involving those persons holding titles in the military orders and thus exempt from the normal legal process, *DHBNR*, XC (1950), 54.

tribunal in Pernambuco on the ground that Brazil was incapable of supporting so many judges. The councilors argued that it was unwise to permit an increase in the number of *letrados* in Brazil, which sorely needed soldiers, not lawyers, on its soil.[33] These sentiments influenced the composition of the High Court itself, so that instead of ten desembargadores the newly created tribunal had assigned places for only eight judges. Once again the magisterial-military rivalry and general disillusionment with the legal bureaucracy crippled the High Court's performance. In the quarter of a century between the High Court's death in 1626 and its rebirth in 1652 the colony's population had grown and the area of settlement had expanded well beyond the coastal fringe. To recognize these changes by reestablishing the Relação made very good sense, but to do so on a reduced scale made none at all.

Understaffing plagued the High Court of Bahia throughout its history. Magisterial complaints of overwork must be taken with a grain of salt, but the volume and consistency of similar pleadings from a variety of sources cannot be dismissed. The absence of judges from Salvador while on special investigations, extra duties of an administrative nature, and a heavy docket all combined to slow the judicial process. Capital crimes often went without punishment because the necessary quorum of six judges could not be gathered.[34] The crown did authorize the number of places in the High Court to be raised to ten in 1658, but for some reason, probably budgeting, the measure did not take effect.[35] Only a series of complaints in 1698 finally raised the strength of the High Court to ten judges, but the growth of the colony and the ever-increasing commitments of the desembargadores allowed no decrease in the pressures of magisterial office.[36]

---

33. CU to king (31 March 1654), AHU, Pernambuco *pap. avul.*, caixa 4.

34. Report of Joseph de Freitas Serrão (1698), AHU, Bahia *pap. avul.*, caixa 18; *Alvará* (12 April 1720), BGUC Codice 709.

35. King to Gov. Francisco Barreto (Lisbon, 18 June 1658), *DHBNR*, LXVI (1944), 146.

36. AHU, Bahia *pap. avul.*, caixa 18 (9 July 1698); CU to Gov. Dom João de Lencastre (10 November 1698), *DHBNR*, XC (1950), 35–36; *Assento* (3 August 1719), AHNRJ, Codice 540.

The ten judges of the Relação were simply unable to cope with the number of cases on the court's docket. As we have seen in Chapter Four, the volume of litigation far exceeded the available time. Moreover, the High Court often operated at less than full strength because the judges, like everyone else in Brazil, were subject to the high morbidity and poor health conditions in the colony. References to desembargadores too sick or incapacitated to perform their duties can be found throughout the history of the High Court, but the most serious incident was certainly the death of five judges in the yellow fever epidemic of 1685–87, a situation which brought the court's business to a standstill.[37] Magistrates sometimes took advantage of Brazil's unhealthy reputation to cut short their terms of service by pleading that their "aches and pains (*achaques*)" demanded medical attention available only in Portugal. This was the case of Chancellor Manoel Carneiro de Sá, who sought and received permission in 1691 to leave after four years of service instead of a full six-year term.[38] Real or feigned, such illness depleted the manpower available for the High Court.

To worsen the situation, the Relação maintained a strict schedule of procedure in the courtroom in which civil appeals were heard first, criminal cases next, and crown business last.[39] The volume of civil appeals was usually so great that little time remained for the other kinds of cases. As a result, those accused of criminal offenses often languished in the decrepit jail of Salvador for months and even years, suffering extreme privation; some even starved to death. Only the charitable activities of the Misericórdia, which

---

37. Varnhagen, *História geral*, III, 260n.; *DHBNR*, LXXXIX (1950), 54–56. The judges who died were Manoel da Costa Palma, João de Góes e Araújo, João de Couto de Andrade, José da Guarda Fragoso, and Jerônimo de Sá e Cunha.

38. Gov. Antônio Luís Gonsalves da Câmara Coutinho to king (Bahia, 21 June 1691), *DHBNR*, XXXIII (1936), 349; (Bahia, 14 July 1692), 444–445.

39. The Count of Sabugosa wrote in 1735 that the Relação moved very slowly and that the majority of prisoners ended their life in prison; APB, Cartas do Governo 153, f. 9. In 1749 the *juiz da coroa* registered a complaint that crown matters were never attended to because of the lack of time. APB, *Ord. reg.* 35 (May, 1740), 28, 2C.

provided some medical attention and food to these unfortunates, prevented even worse conditions.[40] Certainly, the magistrates bear some of the responsibility for this situation, but the workload of any one of them must have been enormous and the crown's constant use of desembargadores for non-tribunal duties further complicated the problem. It was a matter of bureaucratic accretion in which the crown found it more expedient to increase the powers and responsibilities of the existing bureaucracy than to create new positions and staff.

The judges provided a pool of well-trained bureaucrats, supposedly loyal to the throne, and therefore ideal trouble-shooters and members of new administrative bodies. Whenever a particularly dangerous situation developed in Brazil, a desembargador of the Bahian tribunal was sent to investigate and report. The French attack on Rio de Janeiro in 1710, the urban rioting in Minas Gerais in 1720, and the fighting between sugar planters and merchants in Pernambuco in 1711 (the War of the Mascates) all brought investigations carried out by the royal magistrates. Sometimes the duties were even more hazardous. Desembargador Dionísio de Ávila Varieiro sailed with fifty soldiers in 1692 to Porto Seguro to disperse a band of cutthroats who had terrorized the captaincy. He succeeded in capturing the leaders, who were tried and hung by the Relação.[41]

More time-consuming and less heroic was magisterial service in newly created administrative organs where the institutionalized dignity and status of the judges lent a sense of legitimacy to bodies that lacked the patina of age. The colonial treasury council, the

40. Russell-Wood, *Fidalgos,* pp. 245–250, provides a good description of the situation in the jail of Salvador. A prisoner could qualify for Misericórdia assistance only if he was destitute, had been in prison for thirty days, and was not imprisoned for debt or was awaiting deportation. A law of 8 June 1686 designed to eliminate extortion of prisoners by the jailers and to reinforce previous legislation of 1678 and 1681 had only limited success. See APB, *Ord. reg.* 1, n. 49A.

41. Rocha Pitta, *História,* 224; *Obras completas de Gregôrio de Mattos,* 7 vols. (Salvador, 1969), II, 400–410.

Junta de Conselho da Fazenda, established in 1652, included on its staff the *juiz da cora e fazenda* of the Relação, two *desembargadores dos agravos*, the crown's attorney, and the *provedor da fazenda*. The Casa da Moeda or mint, which dated from 1694, always had the chancellor of the Relação as its superintendent.[42] Desembargador participation in these bodies was natural since, in good Iberian fashion, these boards usually exercised some judicial powers. Here again is an example of the way in which the magistracy assumed other bureaucratic tasks in the colony.

As in the case of the first Relação, royal magistrates were often given special tasks or were placed on ad hoc commissions.[43] Among their most important duties in the late seventeenth and early eighteenth centuries was settling the price of sugar.[44] That commodity remained central to the agricultural life of the captaincy and its price was usually of general concern. Sugar planters had long complained that the merchants of Salvador manipulated the going rate for sugar, deflating the price and ruining the producers. Throughout much of the seventeenth century the *câmara* had undertaken the task of fixing the price of sugar by means of a commission representing consumers, producers, and exporters presided over by a royal magistrate. In 1690 the crown established a commission to meet two weeks before the arrival of the fleet in order to establish a fair price. This body included representatives of both the planters and the merchants with two desembargadores acting as arbiters.[45] In 1697 and 1698 the Relação set the price by itself. Eventually, in 1751, a permanent board, the Mesa da Inspeçcão, was created to regulate prices and control the quality of agricultural exports, especially sugar and tobacco. In Bahia, the

42. Caldas, *Noticia geral*, p. 81.

43. For example, Desembargador Miguel de Siqueira Castelobranco as *ouvidor geral* of the Relação was ordered in 1704 to inspect all ships sailing for the Mina coast in order to prevent dyewood smuggling. AHU, Bahia *pap. avul.*, caixa 21.

44. Boxer, *Portuguese Society*, p. 107.

45. ACS, Livro das Portarias 159, f. 239; APB *Ord. reg.* 7, n. 703; *DHBNR*, LXXVII (1950), 16–17.

presiding official of this body, the intendant general, was always a desembargador.[46] The inclusion of such duties in the daily routine of the High Court magistrates was logical and perhaps even necessary, but its ultimate effects on the administration of justice proved to be detrimental. Whatever the difficulties created by increased responsibilities in Salvador, however, these were far outweighed by the ever-increasing role of the High Court magistrates within the rest of the colony and even beyond.

The extent to which the crown was willing to expand the Relação's responsibilities can be seen in the case of West Africa. By the mid-seventeenth century Brazil had surpassed India as the most important colony in the Portuguese empire. Slowly, the crown began to recognize this fact by extending the jurisdiction of colonial officials in Brazil to include parts of West Africa. The suggestion to place Angola within the appellate authority of the Relação of Bahia rather than directly under the metropolitan Casa da Suplicação had been made as early as 1626, and officials in both colonies restated the idea from time to time.[47] Although the crown never completely implemented such a change, the desembargadores of the Relação did conduct *residências* and *devassas* in Africa. In 1684 Desembargador Antônio Rodrigues Banha was sent from Bahia to Luanda to conduct a *residência* of the governor. Another example was the selection of a judge of the Bahian tribunal to perform an investigation of São Tomé in 1714.[48] In the late seventeenth century the crown often granted the title of desembargador of the Relação of Bahia to judges sent on special missions from Portugal to Africa, even though these men did not take office in Bahia.

46. The Boards of Inspection were soundly hated by both the planters and the merchants. See, for example, their joint complaints in 'Representação dos cultivadores de açucar e negociantes da Bahia (1772)," BNR, II-33, 19, 27.

47. "Rezões q. darão," BNL, Col. Pomb., 647. In 1629 a royal official returning from Angola made a similar suggestion. See Luciano Cordeiro, *Questões historico-coloniais*, 3 vols. (Lisbon, 1935), I, 337.

48. AHU, Bahia *pap. avul.*, caixa 16 (28 April 1688); *Consulta* of CU (26 January 1714), *DHBNR*, XCVI (1952), 114–115.

The High Court of Bahia was not always anxious to increase the area of its responsibility and of its obligations. In 1744, when seven leaders of a slave rebellion that had erupted in São Tomé arrived in Bahia for sentencing by the Relação, the judges balked. They wrote to the crown claiming that the Relação had no formal jurisdiction over Africa.[49] The crown dismissed their objections and ordered that the sentences be handed down. Missions to West Africa, however, never proved to be a major problem. Far more important was Brazil itself.

The slow and sometimes painful expansion of the settled area toward the interior created a number of administrative and judicial problems which ultimately became the responsibility of the Relação. The need to refer constantly to Salvador or other coastal towns for notarized documents, administrative decisions, and police protection became increasingly burdensome for the growing population of the *sertão*. In the Recôncavo, agricultural towns like Cachoeira, Jaguaripe, and São Francisco do Conde grew in the latter half of the seventeenth century to a point at which their incorporation as separate municipalities became necessary. Then too, small communities began to dot the *sertão* along the margins of the São Francisco River and into the captaincies of Sergipe d' El-Rey, Pernambuco, and Piauí. Difficulties of communication and transport and the great distances between settled areas made judicial supervision from Salvador impossible. Desembargadores sent from Salvador to conduct investigations in the *sertão* were often reluctant to leave the comforts of the capital, and when they did embark on such missions, they often found it difficult to obtain food and lodging in the interior.[50] Such conditions contributed to the lawlessness of the interior and made the words "*sertão*" and "hideout" roughly equivalent.

The criminals of the *sertão* came from both ends of the social

---

49. King to Count of Atoguia (Lisbon, 16 March 1751), APB, *Ord. reg.* 48.

50. *Consulta* CU (21 February 1663), AHU, Bahia *pap. avul.*, caixa 8 (2nd series non-catalogued); Report of Pedro Gonçalves Cordeiro Pereira (Bahia, 30 November 1723), *DHBNR*, XC (1950), 90–91.

scale. Robberies and murders committed by mulattos, *mestiços*, and escaped slaves became a constant theme in the *sertão* and in rural areas along the coast. Even a town in the Recôncavo like Maragogipe had a nasty reputation as a "robber's den." [51] In the mining district of Minas Gerais, opened after 1695, all sorts of gold seekers, vagabonds, and camp followers flocked to the gold washings and created in the towns of that region a highly volatile population. The countryside of Minas Gerais, moreover, was continually disrupted by large numbers of escaped slaves who often turned to banditry.[52]

The escaped slaves, vagabonds, and highwaymen who infested the trails of interior Brazil were not the only source of difficulty. The great cattle ranchers who had pushed their herds along the São Francisco River and whose *sesmarias* often included enormous tracts of land reigned in the *sertão* with little or no opposition from royal authority. The threat of violence, kinship ties, and the deference owed to powerful social superiors allowed these backland potentates (*poderosos do sertão*) to favor their allies, destroy their opponents, and escape the penalties of the law. In 1699 the crown took this situation under consideration, but witnesses were often so terrorized that they refused to testify unless royal protection was guaranteed; [53] and even then, in the *sertão*, the protection of a wealthy rancher and his hired toughs was worth far more than a writ of the crown.

This situation remained in many ways unchanged into the present century, but during the energetic administration of Dom João de Lencastre (1694–1702) and his successor Vasco Fernandes Cesar de Meneses (1720–35) a number of interior settlements were officially incorporated as municipalities in an effort to provide them with better administration and a sounder judicial base. Each of

---

51. King to Marquis of Angeja (Lisbon, 26 October 1717), APB, *Ord. reg.* 11, n. 83.

52. See Boxer, *Golden Age*, Chapter VII, *passim*.

53. King to Dom João de Lencastre (Lisbon, 19 January 1699), APB, *Ord. reg.* 5, n. 111.

these towns would have a *juiz ordinário* as a member of the town council and would thus have a resident law officer. In 1698 and again in 1700 the crown ordered that rural parishes in the *sertão* were also to have a resident judge and a captain-major to assist him in the prosecution of criminals.[54] That such measures proved unsuccessful is an understatement to say the least. Not only did the criminals—high and low alike—continue to have their way in most areas, but the officials themselves often left much to be desired and in their totality formed yet another source of lawlessness.

Finding men for office was the first problem. Most of the backwoodsmen and drovers who inhabited the *sertão* were functional illiterates. The crown ruled that as long as his secretary could read and write a judge did not have to be so qualified.[55] But literate scribes were as scarce as literate judges. The captains-major who governed the captaincies proved more a cause than a remedy of trouble. They continually abused their office and power and often clashed with *câmaras*, local officials, and royal magistrates.[56] Because of ignorance, impotence, or kinship, local judges rarely prosecuted the captains-major.[57]

To remedy this situation, the crown introduced professional royal magistrates at the local and regional (*comarca*) levels. In 1696 the first *juiz de fóra* took office in Salvador and in that year an *ouvidor geral do crime* was assigned to the *comarca* of Bahia. As it had been argued in Portugal, these professional magistrates were less subject to local pressures than the elected municipal judges. The Viceroy of Brazil, the Marquis of Angeja, presented such an

54. In 1698 the crown ordered that a *juiz ordinário* be established every five leagues in the *sertão*. In 1700 the idea was repeated in a somewhat different form. King to Dom João de Lencastre (Lisbon, 15 February 1698), APB, *Ord. reg.* 5, n. 38; and again (Lisbon, 11 February 1700), APB, *Ord. reg.* 6, n. 29.

55. APB, *Ord. reg.* 5, n. 38.

56. For example, report of *desembargador sindicante* Belchior Ramires de Carvalho (Olinda ?, 22 July 1689), AHU, Pernambuco *pap. avul.*, caixa 8.

57. Marquis of Angeja to king (Bahia, 4 July 1715), APB, *Ord, reg.* n. 10B.

argument in 1715 when he pointed out the need for *juizes de fóra* in the Recôncavo towns, where local judges had "out of kinship or deference allowed the guilty to continue their crimes." [58] Although the Conselho Ultramarino refused this particular request because of bugetary considerations, royally appointed *juizes de fóra* and *ouvidores* became permanent elements of the judicial-administrative framework of eighteenth-century Brazil.

Juizes de fóra took up residence in major towns like Olinda, Rio de Janeiro, and Salvador. Bahia's *ouvidoria* (jurisdiction of an *ouvidor*), established in 1696, was divided in 1742 in an effort to provide better control of crime. In that year a separate *ouvidoria do sul da Bahia* designed to administer justice in the southern half of the captaincy was created with its seat at Jacobina. Similar offices were created elsewhere. Each captaincy had an *ouvidor geral* who usually served as *provedor da fazenda* and probate judge as well. Nor were newly settled areas forgotten. In the gold mining district of Minas Gerais royal magistrates took up positions in four districts after 1714. There were *ouvidores* in Vila Rica, Sabará, Rio das Mortes, and Serro de Frio. Moreover, a *juiz de fóra* sat in Riberão do Carmo and a royal magistrate served as intendant general in the diamond mining region in western Minas Gerais and Mato Grosso.

These officials did not stem the tide of violent crime in the *sertão*, or anywhere else for that matter. Although there were partial successes, as in Jacobina, where by 1721 the rate of violent crime was cut sharply, too many difficulties remained unresolved.[59] Personal power continued to dominate the interior and highwaymen found that their mobility provided ample protection. Criminals often fled from one jurisdiction to another in order to escape capture. The border between Bahia and Pernambuco formed by the São Francisco River caused some difficulty. Although the crown tried to plug the gap in 1749 by allowing judges to cross in hot pursuit, the boundary was still the cause of contention and

58. *Ibid.*

59. Russell-Wood, *Fidalgos*, p. 244.

difficulty twenty years later.[60] The problem seemed to stem as much from the justice officials as from the men they were supposed to arrest. Reports of venality, favoritism, contrabanding, and ignorance were commonly voiced by colonists against the *ouvidores.*

Attempts to have *ouvidores* to carry out *residências* of their colleagues in neighboring captaincies proved to be an ineffective measure. Shared interests, old school ties, and a tendency toward professional "backscratching" made such evaluations a shallow farce.[61] The laxity of these examinations, and the fact that there was hardly a judge "who did not have some old-timer in the Desembargo do Paço as his protector," caused these magistrates to commonly ignore the decisions of the Relação and to thumb their noses at the governors and other royal officials.[62] In 1725 the Viceroy of Brazil, the Count of Sabugosa, complained to the Conselho Ultramarino about the "disorders" of the *ouvidor geral* of Paraíba, the "absurdities" of the magistrates of Alagoas and Sergipe d'El-Rey, the "excesses" of the *ouvidor geral* of São Paulo, and the illegal marriage of the crown magistrate in Rio de Janeiro.[63] These *letrados,* said the Viceroy, seemed to form "a formidable league against the law of God, the laws of Your Majesty, and the rights of the people." [64] Unfortunately, similar if somewhat less eloquent complaints were constantly voiced in the colonial period.

The crown's response to this situation was to charge the desembargadores of Bahia with the review of these subordinate magistrates. Thus, wheras the creation of the lower jurisdictions had

60. King to Count of Galvêas (Lisbon, 8 August 1749), APB, *Ord.* reg. 47; Count of Azambuja to Francisco Xavier de Mendonça Furtado (Bahia, 29 March 1767), BNR, II-33, 23, 17.

61. King to Vasco Fernandes Cesar de Meneses (Lisbon, 20 October 1722), AHU, CU, 247, f. 326v.

62. Count of Sabugosa to king (Bahia, 22 Jan. 1725), in Luís dos Santos Vilhena, *A Bahia no Seculo XVIII,* 3 vols. (Bahia, 1969), II, 359. This is a new edition edition of *Recopilação do Noticias Soteropolitanas e Brasilicas,* Braz de Amaral, ed. (Bahia, 1922). Hereinafter cited as Santos Vilhena, *Recopilação.*

63. *Consulta* CU (9 July 1725), *DHBNR,* XC (1950), 76–82.

64. See above, note 61.

reduced the responsibility of the Relação in the first instance, the High Court magistrates now become responsible for control of the new judges. To perform these reviews—both the triennial *residências* and the less regular *devassas*—desembargadores had to absent themselves from the halls of the Bahian tribunal. Often these missions would include not only an investigation into the performance of a particular individual, but also a general review of the state of justice and administration within the region. However beneficial for the captaincies of the colony, the absence of the desembargadores from Salvador impeded the operation of the High Court. In fact, the growing role of the desembargadores in the administrative organs of Salvador and their ever-increasing duties of review in other captaincies were tendencies that could not be easily reconciled. The performance of one worked to the detriment of the other. In August 1709 the governor of Brazil wrote to the crown that he had not sent a desembargador to investigate an incident in the *sertão* because there were so few in Salvador and because those who were there held two and three offices.[65] The accretion of administrative duties in Salvador and the use of desembargadores as circuit judges and special investigators in other captaincies were tendencies which had begun in the period of the first Relação. As the colony grew in size and population, these demands became even more burdensome and the effectiveness of the High Court even more questionable.

There was yet another problem: *devassas* were costly. Although the pay scale varied according to time, place, and hardship, Table 1 indicates the extent of variation and the levels of possible cost.

Often the costs were defrayed by collecting fines from the guilty or by securing food and lodging from the local populace, a policy that weighed heavy on the colonials. The problem was also compounded by dishonest desembargadores who inflated their expense accounts or worked so slowly that the cost of their missions reached astronomical sums. Desembargador Diogo Filipe

65. Gov. Luís Cesar de Meneses to king (Bahia, 3 August 1709), APB, *Ord. reg.* 7, n. 583.

TABLE 1

Devassa Costs Per Diem

	To Pernambuco, 1612 (in réis)	To Vila Nova de São Francisco, 1709 (in réis)	To Bahian *sertão*, 1714 (in réis)
Desembargador	1200	2500	5000
Bailiff	600	2000	2000
Scribes	(2 at) 600	2000	(2 at) 1600
Guard	(6 at) 550	(12 at) 320	(24 at) 500
Total	6,300	10,340	22,200

Source: BI, Correspondencia Gaspar de Sousa, f. 117; *DHBNR*, LXV (1944), 154–156; *DHBNR*, XCVI (1952), 128–131.

Pereira had made a judicial inspection of the Recôncavo in 1716 for which he claimed an allowance to cover 435 days of service; it was later revealed that the mission had lasted only 104 days.[66] In 1673 Desembargador Manoel da Costa Palma had drawn 1,000 *cruzados* per month as his stipend while on mission in Paraíba. This brought heated complaint from the colonists of the captaincy, who were forced to foot the bill. Reports of the incident eventually reached the Conselho Ultramarino in Lisbon where Salvador Correia de Sá, an old Brazil-hand and always a defender of local interests in the colony, took up the colonists' cause. With some exaggeration, he claimed that "the State of Brazil and the Kingdom of Angola have suffered almost as much damage from judicial missions as from the Dutch." [67] His solution was to set a time limit on these tours, after which no salary could be drawn. The proposal does not appear to have taken effect.

Inhabitants of the other captaincies occasionally tried to avoid

66. King to Des. Manuel da Costa Moreira (Lisbon, 30 October 1717), AHU, Codice 247, ff. 108–109.

67. *Consulta* CU (7 June 1673), *DHBNR*, LXXXVII (1950), 232–236.

the visitations of the Bahian magistrates and the costs of appealing cases to Salvador by petitioning for the establishment of a Relação in their area. Even a town as small as Serenhaen (Pernambuco) sought this solution.[68] In the southern captaincies, there was, of course, a tradition of some judicial autonomy, since in the seventeenth century this area had been placed under its own *ouvidor geral.* Complaints against the necessity of appealing from his decisions to Bahia were voiced from time to time. In 1658, for example, colonists in Rio de Janeiro asked that officials accused in *devassas* be allowed to present their defense in Rio rather than having to bear the expenses of a hearing in Bahia.[69] The growth of Minas Gerais compounded the problem since the volume of appeals increased in a rough proportion to the growth of population. In 1733 the town councils of Vila Rica and Ribeirão do Carmo reopened the issue and offered to defray part of the costs of a new Relação to be established in Rio de Janeiro.[70] The crown authorized the creation of a new tribunal, but lack of funds apparently kept the plan from taking form.

By mid-century the crown could no longer ignore the demographic and economic shift which had taken place. The burgeoning population of Minas Gerais and the value of the gold taken from its streams gave southern Brazil a new importance. Also, the Portuguese thrust to the far south in the captaincy of Rio Grande de São Pedro and to the banks of the Plate River made the south strategically vital to Portugal's imperial ambitions. Rio de Janeiro, the major port on the southern coast, stood closest to the mines and to the Luso-Spanish military frontier to the south. Its eighteenth-century roles as an entrepôt for Minas Gerais and a staging area for expeditions to the southern marches were added to its former position as the regional administrative center. The creation of the Relação of Rio de Janeiro in 1751 was a step toward recognition

68. AHU, Pernambuco *pap. avul.*, caixa 8 (3 February 1796).

69. *Consulta* CU (10 January 1658), ABNR, XXXIX, 85.

70. Gov. of Rio de Janeiro to CU (17 October 1733), IHGB, 1.1.26; Alden, *Royal Government*, pp. 44–45.

of the city's political importance which would culminate in 1763 with its elevation as the viceregal capital. The creation of this new tribunal in Rio de Janeiro divided the jurisdiction of the Bahian High Court in two, separating it from the captaincies south of Espírito Santo and the new lands to the west.

Administrative Conflicts

Basically, the patterns of conflict between the Relação of Bahia and other branches of colonial government remained little changed throughout the seventeenth and eighteenth centuries. Disputes with the *provedor-mór* remained a constant feature of the High Court's history. Invariably the crown would reprimand the judges for interfering in treasury matters, and just as invariably they would interfere again.[71] Despite a flurry in the 1690's, the bitter battles with the episcopacy which had characterized the history of the first Relação did not reappear after 1652.[72] Perhaps the creation of an archbishopric in Salvador in 1676 contributed in some way to reducing the former tensions. In fact, the Conselho Ultramarino had to intervene in 1679 to prevent Desembargador Pedro Cordeiro de Espinosa from serving as deacon of the cathedral and a member of the ecclesiastical court while also sitting with the Relação.[73] This situation violated the standard practice of maintaining a strict separation between civil and ecclesiastical bureaucracy. Cooperation or at least non-interference replaced the old animosity between the bishop and the judges. Conversely, the High Court found a new opponent in the Alfândega (Customs House) of Bahia, with which it clashed in 1745 over matters of control and

---

71. Copia de provisoens de Smg. sobre os ministros da Relação do Brasil senão intrometerem nas materias da Faz. Real, AHU, Bahia *pap. avul.*, caixa 15; caixa 17 (18 January 1694); APB, *Ord reg.* 37 (Lisbon, 20 July 1740), f. 1.

72. King to Gov. Dom João de Lencastre (Lisbon, 25 November 1695), *DHBNR,* XXXII (1936), 403–405. The dispute concerned the actions of the vicar-general and his violation of the High Court's authority.

73. *Consulta* CU (22 July 1679), *DHBNR,* LXXXVIII (1950), 155–159.

jurisdiction. This incident appears, however, to have been an isolated one.[74]

The relationship between the Relaçâo and the municipal council of Salvador was a curious dialectic of need and rejection.[75] This, of course, had been the historical pattern set in the time of the first High Court. The *câmara* of Salvador had accepted the High Court as an ally in 1609 but had become disillusioned by the Indian legislation which resulted in the law of 1611. Between 1624 and 1626 the *câmara* had played a key role in bringing about the abolition of the Relação. By 1643, however, the city councilors of Salvador had once again petitioned for the establishment of a resident High Court, and by 1652 they had achieved their goal. Often unhappy when the High Court sat in Salvador, the municipal council found that the dfficulties and expenses incurred by judicial pleadings to Portugal outweighed the disadvantages of a resident tribunal. The desembargadores, on their part, had no respect for the elected judges of the town council, whom they felt were ignorant and venal. The general pattern of relations between the two institutions did not change until 1696, when the Relação became directly responsible for the selection of the *câmara's* personnel. In the century after 1652 cooperation broken occasionally by incidents of conflict characterized these relations.

The last major period of conflict between the aldermen (*vereadores*) and the desembargadores took place in the 1670's. The confrontation involved a number of problems of a personal and an institutional nature. Theoretically, justice in Brazil was to be universalistic, applied equally and fairly to all. This goal was rarely achieved and thus the men of the town council sought the next best thing: justice and administration which favored their

74. King to Count of Galvêas (Lisbon, 30 September 1745), APB, *Ord. reg.* 43.

75. Affonso Ruy, *História da Câmara Municipal da Cidade do Salvador* (Salvador, 1953); Afonso Ruy, *História política e administrativa da Cidade do Salvador* (Salvador, 1949); C. R. Boxer, *Portuguese Society*, Chapter III, provides general descriptions of the municipal council of Salvador and its history.

interests, basically those of the sugar-planter, slave-owning aristocracy of the colony. To this end, the Bahian planter elite looked to marriage, friendship, and the placement of their sons on the bench as means to secure a favorable hearing in the halls of the Relação. This policy, however, was not always successful. Those magistrates most closely tied to Bahian society were often the very men who caused the most trouble. Their high official position combined with their local connections and often their personal wealth made them impervious to all legal and social controls. The *câmara*, for example, complained more than once against Cristóvão de Burgos, a wealthy Bahian-born magistrate, who continually refused to comply with municipal ordinances or pay municipal taxes.[76] Another desembargador, Cristóvão Tavares de Morais, who had married in Brazil, became involved in an acrimonious dispute with the *câmara* in 1714 over the question of municipal properties.[77]

By 1670 the *câmara* of Salvador was once again complaining of the activities of the desembargadores and advocating the abolition of the High Court. In response to their complaint the crown ordered an investigation. Desembargador João de Couto had been appointed to act as secretary of the investigating commission, with the result that no witnesses had been willing to testify so long as this "friend and colleague" of the guilty sat with the commission. Nothing had been accomplished and the aldermen continued to complain that "the Relação brings ruin in every way." [78]

The aldermen may have had good cause for complaint, but their previous stance on the High Court and their numerous turn-abouts certainly undercut their credibility. The Conselho Ultramarino proved basically unsympathetic to the *câmara's* position. The crown's representative on the Conselho Ultramarino put his finger on the matter when he pointed out that the *câmara* had not

---

76. *Consulta* CU (10 January 1673), *DHBNR*, LXXXVII (1950), 225–226. Also see below, pp. 353–355.

77. Ruy, *História política*, p. 275.

78. *Consulta* CU (12 December 1678), *DHBNR*, LXXXVII (1950), 150–152.

simply asked for the dismissal of the guilty magistrates, but had sought to have the High Court abolished. This, he said, was nothing more than a test of rights and powers. He suggested that the king make it quite clear to the municipal council of Salvador that the crown did not "share with them the matter of how to govern his kingdom." [79] This rebuff had little effect on the city fathers, who in the following year once again petitioned for the High Court's abolition.[80]

On one matter the Conselho Ultramarino and the *câmara* of Salvador could agree: Brazilian-born magistrates caused a great deal of trouble. After the re-establishment of the Relação in 1652, the crown had recognized the colonial contribution to the victory over the Dutch by allowing Brazilians to serve in the Bahian tribunal. The policy had been restated in 1668 and adhered to by the king, Dom Pedro II, at that time.[81] The *câmara's* hostile letter of 1670 caused the Conselho Ultramarino to reconsider the whole matter of natives serving in the area of their birth, a situation which violated one of the basic tenets of Portuguese bureaucratic organization. It was one thing for the Conselho Ultramarino to decide that no Brazilian-born magistrates would be appointed in Brazil, but quite another to convince the Desembargo do Paço of Lisbon, the body responsible for magisterial appointments, to comply. The two councils had fought over the right of appointment since 1656, and the powers of the latter had been continually circumscribed.[82] The Desembargo do Paço was therefore reluctant to comply with the decision of the Conselho Ultramarino, not so much out of philosophical disagreement as from a desire to maintain its jurisdictional autonomy. Thus in 1677 a Bahian, João da Rocha Pitta, was nominated by the Desembargo do Paço to serve in the Relação of Bahia. The Conselho Ultramarino demurred, asking that Rocha Pitta be sent to some other position "not in his homeland where kinship and

79. *Ibid.*
80. *Consulta* CU (23 Nov. 1679), *DHBNR,* LXXXVIII (1950), 167–168.
81. Accioli, *Memórias,* II, 29.
82. *Consulta* CU (26 April 1661), *ABNR,* XXXIX, 94–95.

friendship pervert that necessary disinterest and where all is subject to love and hate."[83] The Desembargo do Paço ignored the plea and Rocha Pitta gained his promotion, but it now became apparent that royal policy would henceforth exclude Brazilians from the Bahian High Court.

The colonists reacted strongly to this change. The town councils of Rio de Janeiro, Pernambuco, and Paraíba complained that their sons had gone to Coimbra at great expense and risk in the hope of entering the king's employ. To exclude them because the Bahians were too susceptible to private interest made no sense at all, since Pernambuco and Rio de Janeiro were hundreds of miles from Salvador.[84] Their appeal found some support in the Conselho Ultramarino, where the crown's advocate (*procurador da coroa*) argued that permitting Brazilians to serve would encourage them to become *letrados*, a group "without which monarchies cannot rule."[85] The pleas of these captaincies had limited success. In 1680 Francisco da Silveira Sottomayor, a native of Rio de Janeiro, became a judge of the Relação. But for the following thirty-eight years no Brazilian received the coveted gown of the High Court. The *câmara* of Salvador had gained one of its goals by eliminating some of the most potentially difficult royal magistrates, but it had failed to diminish the power of the Relação.

Unable to carry the issue in Lisbon, the *câmara* began to snipe directly at the High Court. Since 1674 the magistrates had been allowed to maintain their own butcher shop in order to avoid the cost of meat purchases. The High Court leased this shop at the standard rate of 150,000 *réis* payable to the municipal council. In 1679, in the midst of the dispute with the Relação, the *câmara* leased the shop to someone else without even informing the royal magistrates of the Relação. The judges complained bitterly, but their remonstrance drew the response that the shop would now

83. *Consulta* CU (23 May 1677), *DHBNR*, LXXXVIII (1950), 97.
84. *Consulta* CU (24 July 1677), *DHBNR*, XCII (1951), 230–233.
85. *Câmara* of Rio de Janeiro to CU (17 November 1678), IHGB, Arquivo 1.1.22.

yield 650,000 *réis* in open auction and thus the former arrangement was void. The incident was minor, but it illustrates the level at which the two institutions were willing to fight.[86]

The whole nature of the relationship changed with the introduction of a *juiz de fóra* as a permanent member and president of the municipal council of Salvador.[87] The idea was born in the heat of the battles of the 1670's. The Relação had suggested to the crown in August 1677 that a resident professional magistrate on the town council would not only be able to improve the administration of justice by eliminating the favoritism and partiality shown by the *juizes ordinários,* but would also be able to prevent the misappropriation of funds by the *câmara.*[88] The crown did not act on this recommendation at that time, but in 1696, as we have seen, the measure was instituted upon the urging of Dom João de Lencastre, the active and imaginative governor-general of Brazil. In fact, the establishment of the *juiz de fóra* in Salvador was in some ways like the establishment of new towns in the Recôncavo and *sertão*—it was a measure designed to increase royal control of the colonial population, and it weakened the power of the coastal municipal councils.[89]

These modifications were accompanied by a new method for the selection of municipal councilors which gave the Relação added powers of control over the *câmara.* Instead of the former system, in which lists of eligible citizens were prepared and then one of the lists selected by chance, members of the Relação were now able to participate in the selection of the next group of *vereadores.* A special board (*Mesa do Desembargo do Paço*) composed of the

---

86. Relação to CU (1681), AHU, Bahia *pap. avul.,* caixa 14; *câmara* of Bahia to CU (29 January 1681), AHU, Bahia *pap. avul.,* caixa 14.

87. The standard account is presented in Varnhagen, *História geral,* III, 267–268.

88. *Consulta* CU (18 July 1678), *DHBNR,* LXXXV (1950), 138–139.

89. *Juizes de fóra* were also established in Rio de Janeiro and Olinda by 1703. One is tempted to see this extension of royal control as a reaction to the discovery of gold in Minas Gerais in 1695, but despite the chronological circumstance there is no direct evidence to support this position.

governor, the chancellor, and the oldest *desembargador de agravos* was given the task of reviewing the triennial lists of eligible citizens, and from them selecting the town councilors. This change obviously placed the Relação in a crucial position and allowed it to determine the personnel of the *câmara*.[90] Although the municipal council was still able to exercise an independent role, as some magistrates and governors-general discovered, relations between the *câmara* and the royal officers of government were relatively placid after 1696. The crown encouraged the aldermen to report on the performance of retiring governors and magistrates as a means of keeping a check on these officers. The *câmara's* occasional letters of evaluation usually praised these officials in the most laudatory terms, recommending their subsequent promotion to the highest positions of government.[91] Although the glowing terms were sometimes deserved, as in the case of Francisco Mendes Galvão, who from all accounts was the fairest judge ever to sit in the Relação, the laudatory remarks became almost a standard procedure.[92] What might have been an effective mechanism of control became instead an empty formula. Disputes and conflicts were still possible, but never again did the municipal council threaten the existence of the High Court.

The governors-general or viceroys, the crown's highest officers in Brazil, were both the main support and the major opponent of the Relação.[93] In the Portuguese imperial system the governor-general was not only the presiding officer in the High Court but also its chief counterweight and opponent. The crown wanted the

---

90. Caldas, *Noticia geral*, 73–77. The Mesa do Desembargo do Paço was also responsible for the granting of *cartas de seguro*, the setting of bail, and the award of pardons.

91. *Documentos históricos do Arquivo Municipal. Cartas do Senado*, 5 vols. (Salvador, 1951–1962), e.g., III, 108–109; IV, 24–26, 52–54.

92. Francisco Mendes Galvão was an exceptional judge. On his retirement the alderman pleaded for more judges in his mold 'pedimos que os menistros q. virem para esta terra tão afastada da Sua Real presença sejão como este. . ."). *Ibid.*, III, 108–109.

93. See Alden, *Royal Government*, pp. 430–434.

wheels of colonial government to spin smoothly, but at the same time it wanted to discourage too close a relationship between the various offices. Wrote the Conselho Ultramarino in 1728: "It is not very helpful to Your Majesty's service that there be great friendships between the Governors and the senior magistrates with whom they serve; for it is very useful that they keep watch on each other."[94] Such an attitude in metropolitan councils contributed to the conflicts that dotted the relatively long periods of cooperation between the judges and the governors-general.

Royal orders instructed the governors-general to take their role as *regidor* of the High Court seriously, and to attend to its business regularly. The *regimento* given to Governor Roque da Costa Baretto in 1677 served as the model; in it he was admonished to guard the king's law and justice, to make sure that the magistrates performed their duties, and to report on each judge's performance.[95] Some took these instructions seriously, others did not. All the governors-general took their oath of office as *regidor* of the High Court, but it is impossible to know how many regularly attended its sessions. The normal duties of the *regidor*—assigning magistrates to special missions, authorizing circuit tours, and making interim appointments—were actually performed by some of these senior officers, as the letter book of Governor Francisco Baretto indicates, but the absence of similar orders in the correspondence of other governors-general probably means that such duties were performed by the chancellor.[96] It would appear that those governors-general who paid little attention to the Relação were able to avoid open conflict, while senior officers who took their judicial duties seriously often ran afoul of the judges.

Gubernatorial evaluations of the High Court's members were

94. *Consulta* CU (30 Oct. 1728), *DHBNR*, XC (1950), 171–173.

95. *DHBNR*, VI (1928), 312–466, especially cap. 37.

96. For example, see the gubernatorial orders (*portarias*) of Francisco Barreto authorizing Desembargador João Vanvecem to make an inspection of all officers in Bahia, or his interim promotion of João de Góes to serve as *ouvidor geral do civel* due to the illness of Afonso Soares da Fonseca. *DHBNR*, VII (1929), 239, 358.

often of so general a nature as to be worthless. On occasion, however, there were real attempts to report magisterial behavior, and as such, these documents provide valuable glimpses into the performance of the Relação and its members. The reports of Governor-General Antônio Luís de Câmara Coutinho were models of this sort, making critical evaluations of each magistrate on the bench and suggesting general reforms.[97] In 1692, for example, he called for older, and presumably wiser, magistrates to be chosen for service in the High Court. He was also highly critical of desembargadores remaining in Brazil after the stipulated term of six years and of magistrates marrying in Brazil, two practices which brought an overinvolvement in local society and a decrease in the High Court's credibility. These evaluations sometimes brought royal action. In 1680, for example, the recommendations of Governor-General Roque da Costa Barreto led to the recall of four magistrates.[98]

The mechanisms of mutual control and the common goals which existed in the time of the first Relação continued to operate after 1652. Cooperation and conflict between the judges and the governors-general cannot be analyzed as a historical process changing over time, but rather as two simultaneous tendencies, each of which could be called into play by a specific event or the congruence of certain personalities in various offices. The commonality of interest between the Relação and the crown's chief officer could be emphasized by an outside threat. Thus in 1658 the High Court and Governor-General Francisco Barreto joined forces against André Vidal de Negreiros, the governor of Pernambuco, who had openly challenged the authority of the central government by refusing to obey orders sent out from Bahia. The High Court showed itself to be jealous of its prestige and consequently of royal power. The governor and the judges agreed that "the authority of this tribunal is offended and despised; the jurisdiction of this government and

97. See his evaluations of 1691 and 1692 in *DHBNR,* LXXXIX (1950), 209–211; and AHU, Bahia *pap. avul.*, caixa 16.

98. Alden, *Royal Government*, p. 434.

captaincy general violently usurped." Under pressure Vidal de Negreiros finally submitted to the authority of Bahia.[99]

Governors-general often found the pocketbook a sure way to magisterial good will. The crown tried to keep magisterial salaries and perquisites in line with the rising cost of living in the colony. In 1699 the basic salary (*ordenado*) was increased to match the pay scale of other Portuguese High Courts, and in 1726 it was raised to 600,000 *réis*, where it remained for the duration of the eighteenth century.[100] The *ordenado* did not, however, represent the actual income of the desembargador's office. Over the years following the reestablishment of the Relação in 1652 the governors-general had established various bonuses as an effective means of maintaining cordial relations with the judges and as a way of muzzling their opposition. Between 1652 and 1740 various governors-general had authorized eleven of these *propinas*, but the pinnacle had been reached under Dom João de Lencastre (1694–1702) and his successor Dom Rodrigo da Costa (1702–1705). These men authorized such special grants as 10,000 *réis* to each judge as an Easter bonus (begun in 1703), 20,000 *réis* for St. Anthony's Day, 50,000 *réis* for St. John's Day, 20,000 *réis* for St. Michael's Day (all begun in 1695), 50,000 *réis* for the festival of Our Lady (begun in 1704), and 10,000 *réis* for the festival of the 11,000 Virgins. In each case the governor-general also authorized his own receipt of these awards, usually at a rate three times that given to the judges.[101] By the mid-eighteenth century, the desembargadores received a salary of 600,000 *réis*, *propinas ordinários* totaling 270,000 *réis*, and another 330,000 *réis* in extra *propinas* (sometimes called *emolumentos*) in honor of such events as royal birthdays. These payments came to a sum of 1,200 *milréis* as the legal earnings of a desembargador without counting his fees for special services

99. *Assento* (22 October 1658), ANRJ, Codice 540, pp. 1–2; see also the documents published in Varnhagen, *História geral*, III, 220–222.

100. *Provisão* (Lisbon, 23 September 1699), APB, *Ord. reg.* 5, n. 133; *Ord. reg.* 21, doc. 31 (Lisbon, 28 February 1726).

101. Count of Galvêas to king (Bahia, 8 June 1741), APB, *Ord. reg.* 37.

or earnings while on special commissions or *visitas*.[102] Such rewards probably did much to ease tensions between the High Court and the governor's palace.

In theory, the Relação should have been a constant adviser to the governor-general on all matters of importance in the colony. The plenary session, or *mesa grande*, presided over by the governor-general in his role as *regidor*, had been designed specifically for this purpose. But although the crown recommended such consultation from time to time, the judges were rarely convoked for this purpose. A notable exception took place in 1669, when Governor-General Alexandre de Sousa Freire called upon the Relação to approve a major military expedition against hostile Indians in southern Bahia and to proclaim this action a "just war" under the terms of the law of 1611.[103] Such policy decisions, however, were extremely rare. One is struck by the number of times the *mesa grande* was convoked to settle disputes over precedence within the court's chambers or the appointment of a new court barber rather than to act on matters of political significance. The High Court remained an enforcer of royal policy, and at times a mediator between that policy and colonial interests, both by its corporate nature as a tribunal and through the personal ties of its magistrates. It did not, however, become a formulator of policy, nor in fact did it ever dispute the governor-general's predominance in this sphere. The magistrates recognized their subordination in this area, and those conflicts which did arise between them and the governors-general did not usually involve questions of political power.

An explanation of this situation probably lies in the relative ease of contact with Portugal and the policy of a Lisbon-oriented centralization sponsored by the crown. The time lag between Bahia and Lisbon was always less than that between Lima or Mexico and Madrid; thus royal decisions could be made and implemented far

---

102. Santos Vilhena, *Recopilação*, II, 334–335, gives a breakdown of desembargador earnings at the beginning of the nineteenth century.

103. *Accordão* of the Mesa Grande (Bahia, 2 May 1676), APB, *Ord. reg.* 30.

more rapidly than in the Spanish empire. The Lisbon orientation, the magistrate's professionalism, and the governor-general's authority all combined to create a situation in which the High Court remained an enforcer, not a formulator, of policy.

Given the fact that imperial theory called for each element of government to guard its prerogatives and thus to limit the excesses of any other element, friction between the governors-general and the magistrates is understandable. Governors-general sometimes generated the ill feeling of desembargadores by simply performing the duties of the *regidor*. Censure of magistrates for failure to meet their professional obligations brought trouble. Chancellor Jorge Seco de Macedo provoked many complaints because of his laxity in handing down judgments, and Governor-General Francisco Barreto threatened to hold back his salary because of it.[104] This, in fact, was the action taken by the Count of Obidos in 1667, when he prevented Desembargador Manoel de Almeida Peixoto from drawing his salary.[105] His reason was ostensibly Almeida Peixoto's absenteeism, but there was another side to the story. Almeida Peixoto claimed that the governor-general had plotted his assassination, and that because of this he had fled to a monastery for asylum, where he remained, unable to attend the sessions of the High Court.[106] The religious institutions of Salvador became, in fact, the usual refuge of magistrates fleeing the power of central authority. Governor-General Pedro de Vasconcelos continually battled the magistrates of the High Court who, in his opinion, failed to show him the proper respect. One, Antônio de Macedo Velho, had to flee to the Franciscan monastery to escape the governor-general's wrath. Interestingly, when the Conselho Ultramarino heard of the incident, it warned the governor-general that he

104. *Portaria* of Francisco Barreto to Chan. Jorge Seco de Macedo (Bahia, 2 March 1662), *DHBNR,* VII (1929), 81–82; AHU, Bahia *pap. avul.,* caixa 8 (1st series non-catalogued).

105. *Portaria* of Count of Óbidos to Provedor-Mór da Fazenda (Bahia, 25 August 1665), *DHBNR,* VII (1929), 229.

106. Manuel Almeida Peixoto to CU (Bahia, 7 February 1667), AHU, Bahia *pap. avul.,* caixa 10 (1st series non-catalogued).

would be held culpable should any harm befall Macedo Velho.[107]

One incident, admittedly an extraordinary one even by Brazilian standards, illustrates the level of conflict and cooperation which could exist between desembargadores and a governor-general. Moreover, it underlines how individual magistrates were pulled into the vortex of family and factional feuds which played a counterpoint in so much of the colony's life. The protagonist in this incident was Antônio de Sousa de Meneses, a doughty old soldier given to command and possessing more valor than sense. His right arm had been lost in a naval battle against the Dutch and in its place he wore a limb of silver, from whence came his nickname, "Braço da Prata."[108] He arrived as governor-general in 1682 and quickly won the dislike of a number of important individuals and powerful local factions, especially the Vieira Ravasco clan. This group included Bernardo Vieira Ravasco, secretary of state for Brazil, his son Gonçalo Ravasco Cavalcanti de Albuquerque, and Vieira Ravasco's brother, Padre Antônio Vieira, the elderly and distinguished Jesuit preacher and missionary who had returned to Brazil in 1681 to pass his remaining years. The family was well-connected to the Relação; its Brazilian lineage began with the arrival of Bernardo's father, Cristóvão Vieira Ravasco, a clerk of the first High Court, and one of Bernardo's sisters had married Desembargador Simão Alvares da Penha, a member of an important Pernambucan family.[109] The presence of the surnames Cavalcanti and Albuquerque in the Vieira Ravasco family tree indicates that ties existed with other Pernambucan clans.

The governor-general, however, had his own supporters and friends on the bench. Desembargadores Manoel da Costa Palma and the Bahian-born João de Góes e Araújo were closely tied to the

107. *Ibid.*

108. The following summary of the "Braço da Prata" incident is based on the accounts in Calmon, *História do Brasil,* III, 868–871, and Varnhagen, *História geral,* III, 279–282. These, in turn, are based on Rocha Pitta, *História,* p. 211; and João Lúcio de Azevedo, ed., *Cartas do Padre Antônio Vieira,* 3 vols. (Coimbra, 1928), especially volume III.

109. See below, pp. 346–349.

governor-general and did his bidding. Góes e Araújo held a prominent place in Bahian society; he was a benefactor of the convent of Desterro, a brother of the Misericórdia, and linked by the marriage of his two sisters to important families in São Paulo.[110] Padre Vieira accused him of being "the hand with which Antônio de Sousa writes."[111] Most important, both Góes e Araújo and the governor-general had become fast friends of Francisco Telles de Meneses, a Bahian gentleman and stepson of Desembargador Cristóvão de Burgos, who had purchased the office of chief constable (*alcaide-mór*) and whose abuse of power and acid tongue had created a host of enemies, including the Vieira Ravascos.[112]

With the arrival of Antônio de Sousa de Meneses in 1682, the chief constable began a campaign of vengeance against his personal and familial enemies, many of whom were the leading citizens of the captaincy. All those linked by family or friendship to these men also stood in danger from the Telles de Meneses faction. The situation was most certainly the culmination of generations of those family rivalries that had long given Bahia the flavor of Shakespeare's Verona.

One desembargador, João Couto de Andrade, opposed the governor-general's roughshod abuse of power, but he was soon forced to seek asylum in the Jesuit College, where he was shortly joined by a number of those persecuted by the Telles de Meneses faction. An attempt at reconciliation was made on Christmas Eve in 1682, when Padre Vieira sought to intercede with the governor-general.

---

110. See the biographical note, "Biographia. João de Góes e Araújo," *Revista do Instituto Histórico e Geografico da Bahia*, IV (March 1897), n. 11, 618–623.

111. Vieira to Marquês de Gouveia (5 August 1684), Azevedo, ed., *Cartas*, III, 499–506.

112. Telles de Meneses had purchased the office in 1667 and had taken the oath of office with Góes e Araújo serving as a witness in the ceremony. By 1672 Telles de Meneses was feuding with the city council, a dispute which caused the governor-general to appoint a desembargador to investigate the matter. The magistrate chosen was none other than Góes e Araújo! See *DHBNR*, VIII (1929), 89.

Harsh words passed between them and the Jesuit was ordered from the chamber and told never to enter the governor's palace again. This he found ironic since, as he said, he had been welcomed in all the royal palaces of Europe.[113]

The feud continued in the streets. Antônio de Brito de Castro insulted a nephew of Telles de Meneses. The nephew retailiated with an ambush that left Antônio de Brito seriously wounded. Seeing the hand of Telles de Meneses in this attack, Antônio de Brito retired to the Jesuit College where, perhaps with the connivance of those in asylum there, he plotted the death of the chief constable. The plot was a badly kept secret and news of it reached the ears of the intended victim, but Telles de Meneses was so sure of his powerful allies and so secure in the belief that his "noble and far-flung" family would protect him that he ignored all warnings. On 4 June 1683, while passing near the cathedral in a litter borne by his slaves, he was attacked by eight masked men.[114] One slave was killed, another wounded, and Telles de Meneses suffered fatal wounds. The culprits, one of whom was Antônio de Brito de Castro, fled to the Jesuit College. Such an attack made in broad daylight on a high functionary was too much even for Bahia. The governor-general, beside himself with rage, quickly surrounded the Jesuit College with the palace guard. A series of arrests followed in which the governor-general sought to apprehend all those who opposed the Telles de Meneses faction. Bernardo Vieira Ravasco was placed in a dungeon and Padre Vieira himself was charged with complicity in the crime.

The venerable Jesuit was no meek opponent, and he now raised his powerful pen in his own and his family's behalf. His long service at the court in Portugal had given him many influential friends and Vieira was not above calling on their aid. To former Governor-General of Brazil Roque da Costa Barreto, Vieira wrote that

---

113. Vieira to Roque da Costa Barreto (25 June 1683), Azevedo, *Cartas,* III, 477–481.

114. *Consulta* CU (5 October 1683), *DHBNR,* LXXXVIII (1950), 262–267.

the unjust charges against him and his family would be easily proved since no one in Bahia dared give testimony which contradicted the governor-general. Said Vieira with his usual eloquence, "Am I such an evil priest, such an evil religious, such an evil christian, and such an evil man that I left Rome and Portugal at the age of seventy-five to come to Brazil to have men murdered?" [115] Yet another metropolitan string which he began to pull led to Diogo Marchão Temudo, judge of the Desembargo do Paço.[116] Vieira's letters to these men indicate clearly that metropolitan connections could be called into colonial disputes and that such personal ties, of a strength impossible to measure, played a role in the government and judicial administration of the colony.

To support his charges, Antônio de Sousa initiated an investigation under the direction of Desembargador Manoel da Costa Palma—hardly a disinterested party. The close and well-known relationship of this magistrate to the Telles de Meneses faction caused an uproar in Salvador which subsided only after he had been replaced by João da Rocha Pitta, a Bahian-born magistrate but one of the few judges uncompromised in the struggle. The investigation dragged through the courts until 1692, when Antônio de Brito de Castro was finally pardoned. The Vieira Ravascos had been exonerated in the interim, although Bernardo remained in peril until the governor-general was replaced in 1684.

The "Braço da Prata" incident is interesting from a number of viewpoints. First, it shows clearly the extent to which personal and family relations influenced the actions of both colonials and royal officials. The personality of the governor-general obviously played a crucial role in determining the intensity if not the course of the dispute. Personal quirks and personality clashes make any attempt to generalize about the nature of relations between governmental institutions extremely tenuous. In this particular dispute it is also obvious that the judges of the High Court did not respond as a body, but were themselves divided and allied to one or another

115. Azevedo, *Cartas,* III, 480.

116. *Ibid.,* 487.

faction. Although it was a corporate body, the Relação was composed of individual magistrates who often pursued individual courses of action. Finally, the incident clearly shows that the judges were not disinterested protectors of the law standing above the dust of local politics, factional feud, and personal interest, but were instead part of colonial society and thus fully enmeshed in the ties of friendship, kinship, and interest which integrated that society.

XII. MAGISTRACY AND BUREAUCRACY

He who to judge the people is elected
Must of the highest qualities be possessed,
By every human tie quite unaffected,
His judgment wise, in noble words expressed;
Courageous, upright, free, by all respected,
Toward rich or poor unswayed by interest.
A friend of truth who will not twist its course
Though urged by plea or threat, by bribe or force.

Rehuel Jessurun, *Dialogo dos Montes* (1624)

The judges of the Bahian High Court not only sought benefits available in the Brazilian colony, but as members of a larger structure, the Portuguese bureaucratic empire, they also pursued certain professional goals intimately connected with its operation. The early struggles of crown and aristocracy, which precipitated the rise of a bureaucratic class, had by the mid-seventeenth century been left two hundred and fifty years in the past. This long period had seen the increasing bureaucratization of the Portuguese monarchy and the extension of the bureaucracy to colonial areas won by Portuguese arms or conquered by Portuguese diplomacy. Despite certain "patrimonial" vestiges of government—positions awarded because of ascriptive status and certain offices sold or granted as rewards—the process of bureaucratization, predicated on the existence of a professional bureaucratic elite, played an ever-increasing role in the administration of government. The crown had fostered the professionalization of the magisterial bureaucrats and the formulation of professional goals, norms, and motivations in an attempt to turn these men into fully compliant servants of royal interest.[1] This was a theory of bureaucratic management with little regard for social reality. In Pavlovian fashion, only the stimuli of bureaucratic advancement were to bring magisterial response.

As we have seen, this theory of bureaucratic control ignored on one hand the existence of strong competing norms and motivations embedded in the relationship of bureaucrats to other social groups through ties of interest, family, and association. Moreover, the emergence of the professional bureaucracy as a class with its own traditions and goals which could at times conflict with those of the crown was another unintended result of the professionalization process. Still, many of the goals and attitudes of the royal bureaucracy were adopted by the magistrates as they constantly sought to rise through the various ranks of office, each of which brought new rewards of status, prestige, and wealth. The desembargadores acted in response to professional motivations, class interests, personal motives, and colonial pressures. To comprehend the importance of the last two factors, it is necessary to examine the operation of the others—the composition and workings of the magistracy both as a social class and as a branch of the royal bureaucracy.

A logical starting point is to present a composite view of the lives and careers of the desembargadores themselves.[2] Materials for prosopographical analysis are widely scattered and difficult to obtain; but by using a list of the Bahian magistrates compiled in 1759 by José Antônio Caldas and by correcting it, filling in its omissions,

1. S. N. Eisenstadt, "Political Struggle in Bureaucratic Societies," *World Politics*, IX (1958), n. 1, 58–76; "Bureaucracy, Bureaucratization, and Debureaucratization," *Administrative Science Quarterly*, IV (December 1959), 302–320.

2. On the nature and problems of collective biography and multiple career line analysis see Lawrence Stone, "Prosopography," *Daedalus*, C (Winter 1971), 46–79.

and adding to it the names of the magistrates of the first Relação (1609–1626), a complete catalogue of these men can be reconstructed. In this new list (Appendix III) are 168 desembargadores who served in the High Court of Bahia in the century and a half between 1609 and 1759. University records, the entrance examinations for royal service (*leitura dos bacharéis*), and royal chancery records then provide a skeletal outline of the professional life of these men.[3] One caveat is in order, however. Because no study of the personnel of the Portuguese bureaucracy or of any of its component sections exists, the following analysis is severely limited in its ability to yield general conclusions, or to set these "Brazilian" findings within the context of the whole imperial structure. With this restriction in mind, however, a composite view of the magistrates and an analysis of the bureaucratic system in which they operated can provide new insights into the colonial regime and its operation in Brazil.

The geographical origins of the Bahian desembargadores seem to reflect the demographic distribution of the Portuguese population rather than any tendency toward regional dominance within the professional bureaucracy.[4] The two most striking aspects of the magistrates' geographical backgrounds are the extremely small

---

3. José Antonio Caldas, *Notícia geral desta capitania da Bahia* (1759), facsimile edition (Salvador, 1951), pp. 161–183. The list which Caldas apparently took from the APB, Livros de Posse of the Relação was later copied by Santos Vilhena in his *Recopilação*. It is, however, incomplete and is marred by some errors of paleographic interpretation. Appendix III is the author's attempt to compile a complete listing up to 1759, and to add to it significant personal and professional information. Santos Vilhena carries the listing up to the 1790's, and for more recent times the present Supreme Court of Bahia, the Forum Ruy Barbosa, maintains an accurate catalogue. An early presentation of this data listed only 167 desembargadores. This should be corrected to 168. See Stuart B. Schwartz, "Magistracy and Society in Colonial Brazil," *HAHR*, L (November 1970), n. 4, 715–730.

4. In the following analysis, much information was gathered from these collections: ANTT, *Leitura dos Bacharéis; Livros de Chancelaria*, Felipe I to José I (usually the series *Doações*); AUC, *Livros e verbetes da matrícula*, BNL, F.G. 1.007, "Catálogo alfabético dos Ministros de Letras."

number of judges from the Algarve and the large number from the city of Lisbon. The Algarve has traditionally been an area of low population density, a fact which may explain the absence of men from that region among the Bahian judges. It should also be noted that the Algarve had very little connection with Brazil or the Brazil trade. Until a study is made of the Portuguese magistracy as a whole, it will be impossible to determine whether the small number of *algarvios* in the Bahian tribunal was proportional to their presence in royal service, or whether through lack of interest or connection in Brazil these men sought service in other areas. Lisbon, on the other hand, is overrepresented. Long the largest city in the kingdom and a traditional center of the professions, crafts, and trades, Lisbon was naturally the birthplace of judges, since many came from bureaucratic, mercantile, or artisan backgrounds.[5] As the bureaucracy grew, so too did the number of offices in Lisbon and thus an increasing number of children of the men who filled these offices were born in that city. Of the 168 desembargadores of Bahia, 28 per cent were Lisbon-born, and if we add to the total those born in the hinterland of Extremadura, that figure reaches 40 per cent.

Other areas appear to be proportionally represented, as shown in Table 2. The more heavily populated regions of Minho and Tras-os-Montes are, after Lisbon-Extremadura, the best represented. They are closely followed by the province of Beira, which contains the city of Coimbra, another bureaucratic center and the seat of the university, where the fathers of some of the desembargadores were studying at the time their sons were born. Noticeable by their complete absence are judges born in the Portuguese State of India or in the colonies of West Africa. During the period under discussion, these areas did not contain a numerically significant European population and, moreover, children born there were

5. Frei Nicolau de Oliveira, in his *Livro das grandezas de Lisboa* (Lisbon, 1627), calculated the city's population in 1620 at 165, 878, of which 114,728 were free resident adults; cited in Fortunato de Almeida, *História de Portugal*, V, 159.

TABLE 2

Geographical Origins of the Desembargadores of Bahia, 1609–1759

Region		No.	Per cent
Lisbon and Suburbs		39	28
Extremadura		16	12
Minho and Tras-os-Montes		27	19
Beira		21	17
Alentejo		16	12
Algarve		2	1
Azores		5	4
Brazil		10	7
Bahia	7		
Pernambuco	2		
Rio de Janeiro	1		
		136	100
Unlocated [a]		7	—
Unidentified [b]		25	—
		168	100

Source: ANTT, *Leitura dos Bacharéis;* AUC, *verbetes de matrícula;* AHU, Bahia *papéis avulsos.*

[a] Town name is available but province cannot be determined. All are in continental Portugal.

[b] No information available.

likely to be "tainted" by mixed blood or religious unorthodoxy. The Azores, however, were a European settlement area and were well represented in the Bahian High Court. Brazil was also a colony of settlement and by the late eighteenth century contained a population of 1,500,000, of which perhaps 20 per cent could trace European origin.[6] Not only did ten Brazilians serve in the Bahian

6. Dauril Alden, "The Population of Brazil." Alden's calculation is for the period circa 1776.

tribunal, despite the rules discouraging this, but Brazilian-born magistrates also held inferior positions in Brazil as well as offices in India, West Africa, and Portugal.[7] The crown apparently had no qualms about using Brazilian-born magistrates in metropolitan positions or in other areas of the empire. The lack of a university in Brazil and the costs of providing for matriculation at Coimbra sifted poorer Brazilians out of the educational process, so that Brazilian-born magistrates were either sons of the colonial oligarchy or of royal officials stationed in Brazil. Nevertheless, those who embarked on a magisterial career did not find colonial birth a handicap to advancement.

The crown recruited professional magistrates from a broad spectrum of Portuguese society but men of certain social origins tended to predominate. The majority of magistrates who served in the Bahian tribunal between 1609 and 1759 were men of middle rank whose presence in the king's service reflected their use of the legal profession as a channel of upward social mobility. The old military and landed nobility neither abandoned their positions in royal councils nor faded into social obscurity. The social history of Portugal was not simply the story of an ever-rising bourgeoisie. While merchants and mercantile interests shaped the state and its policies in many ways, the nobility through their control of landed property, their participation in commercial ventures, and their influence at court continued as a powerful national force. While the rise of mercantile and *letrado* classes closely allied to royal power could not be stemmed, the titled nobility chose to maintain at least the outward manifestations of its traditional functions. The career of arms was still considered more suitable for a *fidalgo* than a career of letters, and while the former might eventually lead to an administrative position, the principles on which it was based differed considerably from those of the *letrado* bureaucrat. Forced

7. Luiza da Fonseca, "Bacharéis brasileiros," 109–406. This article includes a good discussion of the examination process in the Desembargo do Paço and complete transcripts of a few investigations. She lists many Brazilians who entered the magistracy and served in Brazil.

to recognize the power of the *letrados* and the wealth of the great commercial houses, the nobility assumed a stance of social aloofness entrenched in the security of titles, rank, and properties. Whatever the economic or political vissisitudes of the second estate, its system of values permeated the society and set the standard to which others aspired.

Among the Bahian desembargadores, the sons of *fidalgo* families were far and few between. Based on a sample of 100 desembargadores, only 8 per cent descended from noble origins or had inherited claims to *fidalguia*. Moreover, their presence seemed to lessen over time. Of the 96 magistrates appointed between 1700 and 1759, only two can be identified as sons of *fidalgos*.

Many of the desembargadores might be described as the sons of non-noble gentry, men with a father who was identified as "honorable," "living on his holdings," or as "of the principal people of this town." Magistrates of such backgrounds constituted 28 per cent of the total. Another important category were those men whose fathers had been public functionaries, such as tax collectors, market inspectors, and notaries. About 11 per cent of the Bahian judges came from such origins. Thus the sons of non-noble gentry and minor officeholders comprised about 40 per cent of the desembargadores, a fact which indicates that men of these social categories found a career in royal service particularly attractive. This may be partially explained as a search for institutionalized legitimacy in which the title, dignity, and recognition accorded to a royal magistrate tempered the insecurities felt by men whose origins, while not humble, were nonetheless undistinguished. The presence of these men in the magistracy surely indicated that opportunities for social mobility existed. It has been pointed out in another national context, however, that in a society not yet fully stratified by class and in which estates or orders are still used to define social roles, mobility tends to be generational.[8] The data on the Bahian judges tend to support this contention, and there are

---

8. Roland Mousnier, *Peasant Uprisings in Seventeenth-Century France, Russia, and China* (New York, 1970), especially Chapter I.

many examples of magistrates whose grandfathers were merchants or even farmers and whose fathers were "honorable" property-holders or minor officials.[9] For these families, the placement of a son in the magistracy where membership in the Order of Christ or even a grant of *fidalguia* was possible constituted the culmination of three generations of social mobility.

By far the largest single category of magistrates were the sons of university-trained lawyers and bureaucrats. At least 22 per cent of the judges had *letrado* fathers, and many could count at least one grandfather in the *letrado* ranks. Sons followed fathers into the university and then into royal employ, often finding their paths smoothed by parental guidance and nepotism. Such favoritism was considered entirely proper, and was in fact institutionalized. In 1710 Manoel da Costa Bonicho petitioned for a place in the Relação of Bahia as a reward for his father's services to the crown since "the sons of magistrates who have served well should be rewarded and preferred." Despite the fact that he was a bastard and that other men had been waiting for this appointment, the Desembargo do Paço acceded to his plea.[10] The sons and grandsons of *letrados* often married the daughters of other *letrados* so that a penchant toward endogamy and class perpetuation characterized this group. The case of Antônio Rodrigues Banha, who entered the Relação of Bahia in 1729 and whose father, Dionísio de Azevedo e Arevalos, and maternal grandfather and namesake had both preceded him as members of that tribunal, was not uncommon in the Portuguese bureaucracy.[11]

A number of other social categories appear with surprising regu-

---

9. For example, Antônio José de Afonseca Lemos, whose grandfathers were both merchants and whose father was a *licenciado*, indicates this kind of mobility (ANTT, *Leitura dos Bacharéis*, maço 20). An even more striking example was the case of Manoel Ferreira da Silva, whose father was a probate clerk and sometime alderman of Pombal and whose grandfathers were both tailors (ANTT, *Leitura dos Bacharéis*, maço 7, n. 3).

10. *Parecer* of Desembargo do Paço (Lisbon, 28 November 1710), *Cadaval*, II, 67.

11. ANTT, *Chan. da Ordem do Christo*, Liv. 186, f. 147v.

larity in the origins of the desembargadores. In theory, the sons of artisans and merchants could not enter royal service, since these occupations were considered ignoble and the stigma of such backgrounds was passed on from father to son. Nevertheless, these two categories comprised 16 per cent of the occupational sample. As noted in Chapter Four, the sons of artisans who had served in the representative organ of the trade guilds, the Casa do 24, did not suffer the usual disability for royal employ. This was usually the reason why magistrates with artisan ancestors could be found on the bench of the Relação. During the entrance examinations some men encountered serious objections to their backgrounds. Diogo Pacheco de Carvalho was almost refused entry to royal service because his paternal grandfather had been a cobbler and his father had begun to learn the trade as a youth.[12] Similar objections confronted Dionísio de Azevedo e Arevalos when it was discovered that his maternal grandfather had been a muleteer.[13] In both cases the Desembargo do Paço overlooked the "impediment" of birth. Exceptions to the traditional social restrictions do indicate the existence of opportunities for upward social mobility for supposedly unfit subjects of the crown, but the statistical frequency of these exceptions is impossible to determine since the men under consideration here were obviously those who succeeded in circumventing the usual restrictions.

Descendants of men who lived by trade or commerce could not, in theory, enter the magisterial ranks. The Portuguese had great difficulty, however, in reconciling the importance of trade, commerce, and merchants in their empire with social restrictions inherited from an earlier age. Their solution, in effect, was a definition based on success. Portuguese social practice distinguished between men who tended shop or engaged in retail trade and those who were wholesalers or export-import merchants.[14] These latter,

12. ANTT, *Leitura dos Bacharéis*, maço 4, n. 15, 1670.

13. *Ibid.*, maço 1A, n. 21, 1696.

14. Russell-Wood, *Fidalgos and Philanthropists*, pp. 120–121. The merchant class has received very little historical attention until recently. Two

over the course of time, were accepted as living by the law of nobility and thus eligible for royal service. Almost without exception desembargadores whose fathers engaged in commerce came from this category. They were usually described as "merchants of big business (*mercador de grosso trato*)," and sometimes the phrase "without shop or stall (*sem ter tenda nem logea*)" was added. Desembargador João de Sá Sottomayor's father fell into this category because, as a real estate broker owning thousands of houses, he too was considered a "great" merchant.[15] Two magistrates in Bahia were the sons of foreign merchants living in Lisbon—one a Fleming, the other a Venetian. This fact raised no objections against their employment by the crown.[16]

The sons of professional soldiers clearly qualified for royal service since there was nobility in the career of arms, but mariners did not share the same esteem. When Manoel da Costa Palma sought entry into royal service in 1656, a number of *desembargadores do paço* questioned his suitability and pointed out that both his father and maternal grandfather had been ship captains in the India trade.[17] Other members of the Desembargo do Paço noted previous examples that established the eligibility of ship captains. When João Guedes de Sá, whose father had captained a vessel in the Brazil trade, came before the Board of Justice in 1681, no voices were raised against his suitability for service.[18]

The data on social origins become more significant when placed in the context of the size and social distribution of the Portuguese population. In the seventeenth and eighteenth centuries Portugal had between two and three million people. The vast majority of this population labored as peasants or as rural proletariat. The

---

good studies are Frédéric Mauro, *Nova história e nôvo mundo* (São Paulo, 1969), and Virginia Rau, *Estudos de História* (Lisbon, 1968), both of which contain short studies of merchants and commerce in the Portuguese empire.

15. ANTT, *Leitura dos Bacharéis*, maço 2, n. 31, 1697.

16. *Ibid.*, maço 14, n. 58, 1645; maço 3, n. 13, 1714.

17. *Ibid.*, maço 6, n. 21, 1656.

18. *Ibid.*, maço 13, n. 9, 1681.

various restrictions against the entrance into royal service of men from such origins obviously eliminated a large strata of the population. The loophole left for the sons of artisans became the major point of entry for the sons of the *povo* (people). The relatively small number of *fidalgos* by birth among the magistrates is even more significant, for although the *fidalgo* class and titled nobility constituted less than 5 per cent of the total population, the various restrictions worked in their favor. *Fidalgos* had the opportunity to enter the professional bureaucracy in numbers disproportionate to their total. Many who did enter royal service were probably younger sons with no hope of inheritance. It was, however, as Table 3 demonstrates, those groups between the peasants and the

TABLE 3

Social Origins of the Desembargadores of Bahia, 1609–1759 *

Father's Occupation or Social Rank	Number and per cent	Father's Occupation or Social Rank	Number and per cent
Fidalgo	8	Artisan/Shopkeeper	6
Letrado	22	Real Estate	1
Merchant	9	Farmer	1
Physician	2	"Humble"	1
Military	9	Minor Office	11
Sea Captain	2	"Honorable" [a]	17
		"Properties" [b]	11

* Of the 168 magistrates, social origin data are available for 103. I have used a sample of 100.

[a] This category is usually expressed as "honrado," "da governança," or "gente principal da villa." All simply indicate that the man is considered honorable and is thus qualified to serve in the municipal council of his own.

[b] Men in this category are usually described as living on their properties (*fazendas*).

nobility who filled the offices of bureaucracy in numbers which far exceeded their proportion in the total population. The non-noble gentry, minor officials, and especially the *letrados* served the crown and themselves in the magistracy.

Occupational background was not the only criteria for royal service, and other impediments kept men out of the magistracy. If a candidate or any of his male ancestors was found to be illegitimate, there was sufficient cause to deny him entry. The prohibitions against bastardy or mechanic origins were lifted, it appears, far more frequently than cases in which a man was tainted with "the blood of Moor, Jew, mulatto, or other infected race." Few men with this disability even appeared before the Desembargo do Paço. This was due in part to the winnowing process begun when a man sought admission to the university at Coimbra, which occasionally maintained similar restrictions. Many New Christians, the prime targets of these restrictions in the seventeenth century, had been eliminated from possible candidacy long before they ever appeared before the Desembargo do Paço. New Christians, however, were ubiquitous enough that some surely slipped through the net of restrictions, and it would be surprising indeed if a few of the fully orthodox and "racially" pure desembargadores did not have a semitic skeleton in the family closet. The "purity of blood" of only two Bahian judges was formally questioned, but only one can be positively identified as a descendant of New Christians.[19] The specifics of his case provide a curious insight into the workings of the Portuguese bureaucracy.

Afonso Rodrigues Bernardo e Sampaio was the son of a physician from Alcobaça.[20] After completing a course in civil law at

19. See also the file of Ignacio Dias Madeira, ANTT, *Leitura dos Bacharéis*, maço 18, n. 7, 1724. When Francisco Velasco de Gouveia was nominated for the Casa da Suplicação in 1650, some judges objected because he was a New Christian. In his defense, Gouveia pointed to nine New Christians predecessors in that tribunal, among them the great Portuguese jurist Duarte Nunes de Leão. See António José Saraiva, *Inquisição e Cristãos-novos* (Oporto, 1669), p. 172.

20. ANTT, *Leitura dos Bacharéis*, maço 6, n. 18, 1704.

Coimbra, he entered the magistracy and served in Cabo Verde as a circuit judge. The crown had promised to reward successful performance in this post with a promotion to the Relação of Bahia. While he was in Portugal awaiting appointment to Bahia, an enemy claimed that Bernardo e Sampaio's paternal grandmother had been sentenced by the Inquisition for judaizing. An inquest was opened and evidence supporting the accusations came to light. The Desembargo do Paço sought advice from the Mesa da Consciência. The final decision, based on a previous case of 1605, was that the law prohibited New Christians from "reading" for entry into the magistracy, but did not require that those already in office be deprived of their positions, especially if they had performed their duties without fault. The Desembargo do Paço promoted Bernardo e Sampaio to the Bahian tribunal and ordered that the matter be relegated to perpetual silence. One might argue that this case demonstrates a certain degree of toleration and willingness to bend the social restrictions. Since Bernardo e Sampaio never received another post, it is probably more logical to argue that the Desembargo do Paço had swept this case under the rug in an attempt to maintain an image of orthodoxy and racial purity as a support of magisterial authority.[21]

Aside from the various restrictions, recruitment for the magistracy was still not entirely open, but remained limited to men holding a university degree in canon or civil law. Most received only the bachelor's degree, although a few of the desembargadores of Bahia did hold a doctorate. The curriculum concentration of the Bahian judges changed slowly over time. The seventeenth-century preference for a degree in canon law, which enabled the holder to enter either the civil or the ecclesiastical hierarchy, began to fade toward the end of that century. By the early eighteenth century a trend toward civil law can be noted in the degrees of the desembargadores appointed to Bahia. In the half century prior to 1700, only 33 per cent of the magistrates sampled held degrees in civil law. In the period 1701–1758, that proportion rose to 53 per cent.

21. See below, pp. 328–329.

This trend reflects a growing secularization of the state and an increasing disassociation of the royal and ecclesiastical bureaucracies.[22]

Such changing trends and even the university reforms of the late eighteenth century did not significantly alter the nature of Portuguese legal education or jurisprudence. Coimbra maintained a monopoly in this sphere.[23] Study of the law remained basically the reading and explication of the Roman codes and the medieval glossators. One Portuguese jurist characterized his nation's legal writings as "sordid and affected erudition, degenerated into a formal pedantry based on an unbearable profusion of authorities, with which [the authors] fill up and fatten out their books; all of which is a consequence of the lack of good logic, method, and system." [24] The study of such sources was hardly suitable preparation for the ever-growing range of duties placed in the hands of the judicature. Nevertheless, the theory that familiarity with Roman law prepared a man for the magistracy and that magistrates were best suited for the tasks of bureaucracy continued to prevail.[25]

Whatever the failings of legal training as preparation for the tasks of government, the Coimbra experience produced a number of effects which gave the Portuguese bureaucracy its distinctive character. First, since all the magistrates had to secure a law de-

---

22. Manuel Xavier de Vasconcelos Pedrosa, "Letrados do seculo xviii," *Anais do Congresso Comemorativio do Bicentenário da Transferência da Sede do Govêrno do Brasil*, 4 vols. (Rio de Janeiro, 1967), 257–318, notes a decline in the study of canon law after 1760 among Brazilian students at Coimbra.

23. The Jesuit-controlled university at Évora did not grant degrees in civil or canon law. The crown never dominated it to the same extent as Coimbra, and thus was probably reluctant to see magisterial preparation offered there. For a good review of the university system in Portugal, see António José Saraiva, *História da Cultura em Portugal*, 2 vols. (Lisbon, 1950–1955), II, 154–203.

24. Antonio Barnabé de Elescano, *Demetrio moderno ou o bibliografo juridico portuguez* (Lisbon, 1781), p. 132.

25. On the continuing impact of Roman law, see Theresa Sherrer Davidson, "The Brazilian Inheritance of Roman Law," in *Brazil, Papers presented in the Institute for Brazilian Studies, Vanderbilt University* (Nashville, 1953), pp. 59–92.

gree at Coimbra, no matter what their social origin or place of birth, the university served as a centralizing agent. Attempts to establish other universities in the empire, such as that made in 1675 to turn the Jesuit College of Bahia into a university, were unsuccessful. The result was a system of bureaucratic preparation centered on the metropolis and thus more subject to royal control. Second, the common university experience created conditions among the personnel of the magistracy and among the lawyers which were counter-productive in terms of bureaucratic aims but which facilitated the rise of a *letrado* class. Friendships and clientage resulted from the shared experience of Coimbra, so that there was often little social distance between the bar and the bench. This fact may also help to explain the relative ineffectiveness of *residências* which investigated judicial behavior, since these were generally carried out by other magistrates.

The composite biographies of the desembargadores also indicate a general magisterial career pattern within the bureaucracy. After graduation from Coimbra, most of these *letrados* began the examination process, which usually took two years to complete. As we have seen, the young *letrados* entered the service between the ages of twenty-six and twenty-eight. First assignment was generally to a position as *juiz de fóra* in a provincial Portuguese town. Completion of a successful three-year term brought a second appointment, either to another position as *juiz de fóra* or to the next magisterial level as *corregedor* or *ouvidor* of a *comarca.* Other appointments might follow at three or six-year intervals and extension of tenure in the same post was not uncommon. This pattern of service provided a magistrate with considerable experience and seasoning before he might be considered for promotion to one of the three high courts—Goa, Bahia, and Oporto. Men who attained this level of the magistracy were considereed a bureaucratic elite, and the title of desembargador was ardently sought by magistrates as the culmination of a career. The magistrates who served in the Brazilian tribunal had an average of fifteen years previous experience before arrival in Bahia. Typical career patterns are shown in Figure 3.

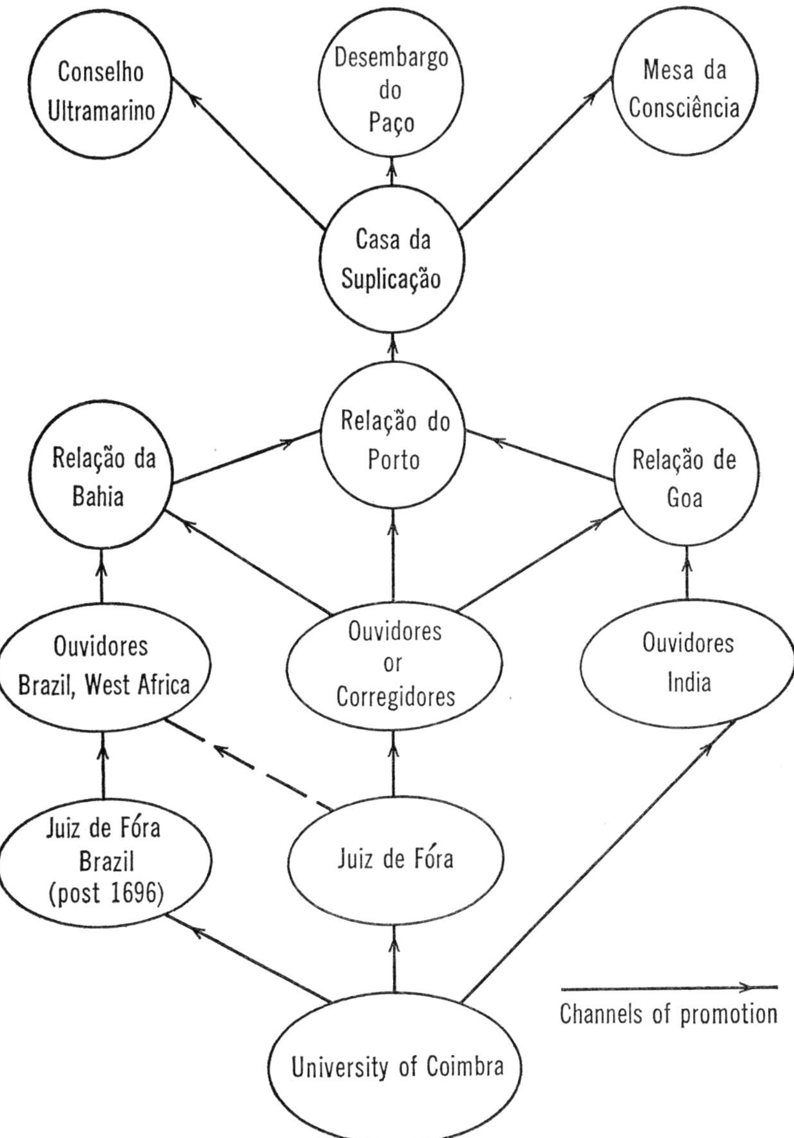

Fig. 3. Typical Career Patterns of the Portuguese Magisterial Bureaucracy.

There were, of course, alternate career patterns. Brazilian-born magistrates seem to have been particularly successful in securing positions in the Relação with less than ten years experience. Some *letrados* apparently took the entrance examination and then preferred to practice law before accepting a magisterial position.[26] João da Rocha Pitta had practiced law in the Relação of Bahia for almost six years before he was given a judicial position in that body in 1678. Paschoal Ferreira de Veras pleaded cases before the Oporto tribunal for six years before his first magisterial position as *ouvidor geral* of Espírito Santo in 1739. He later received a promotion to the Relação of Bahia in 1745.[27] Another pattern can be seen in the careers of men who received advanced magisterial placement after teaching at Coimbra. Manoel da Costa Bonicho went directly from the lecture-hall to the High Court of Bahia in 1695 as did a professor of canon law, Antônio Álvares da Cunha, in 1741.[28] Such placements displayed a deep respect for learning and legal erudition. There was still another pattern set by those men who received assignments to posts such as probate judge, auditor, or customs inspector; in other words, fiscal positions.[29] Such appointments do not appear to correlate with either social origin or university degree of the appointee.

The average age of a desembargador on arrival in Bahia was forty-two. The majority of these men, therefore, spent their mid-forties in the High Court. As a group, the dsembargadores were experienced, middle-aged bureaucrats, seasoned with fifteen years of service. They were men past the impulses of youth who had

26. Recently graduated *letrados* usually practiced law while awaiting their dossiers to be completed for the entrance examination. This fulfilled the requirement for two years of legal practice before entrance into the magistracy.

27. ANTT, *Leitura dos Bacharéis,* maço 17, n. 25 (1668); *Chan. João V Doações,* liv. 100, f. 106; liv. 108, f. 332.

28. ANTT, *Leitura dos Bacharéis,* maço 7, n. 10 (1684); maço 12, n. 15 (1735).

29. A few judges served in the Inquisition tribunals as canon lawyers. None were ecclesiastics, however.

already demonstrated their capabilities, or at least their ability to conform to the regulations and expectations of the royal bureaucracy. Trustworthy, loyal, and experienced, the desembargadores became the ideal bearers of colonial administration.

Although no royal order or decision of the Desembargo do Paço exists which indicates a change in the policy of promotion or of required past service for candidates to the Bahian tribunal, a statistical analysis of magisterial career patterns shows that such was the case. Sometime prior to 1690 a change did indeed take place, and large numbers of magistrates began to arrive in Bahia after previous experience in the colonial judiciary. Before 1690 only 9 per cent (5 out of 54) of the desembargadores had previous colonial experience, but in the period 1690–1758 over 43 per cent (44 out of 105) held previous posts in the overseas empire. Moreover, 23 per cent of all the desembargadores appointed in that period and over 50 per cent of those with colonial experience had served in Brazil prior to appointment in the Relação. Many had held posts as *ouvidor geral* in the captaincies. The explanation of this change may lie in the exclusion of Brazilians from the High Court brought about by the *Câmara*-Relação struggles of the late seventeenth century. The first-hand knowledge of the colony which the Brazilian-born judges had previously supplied was sorely needed, and the Desembargo do Paço may have turned to judges already experienced in the colony as an alternative solution.[30] Certainly Figure 4 seems to support this contention.

Previous Brazilian experience undoubtedly prepared judges for service in the Relação and may have made them more sensitive to colonial interests, but it was not an unmixed blessing. Colonist complaints against lower magistrates in Brazil cast serious doubts on their honesty and competence for any office, to say nothing of the Relação. The promotion of these men to the bench sometimes brought to power those men most closely tied to private interests or moved by venal goals. Take, for example, João Gonçalves

30. See above, pp. 264–266.

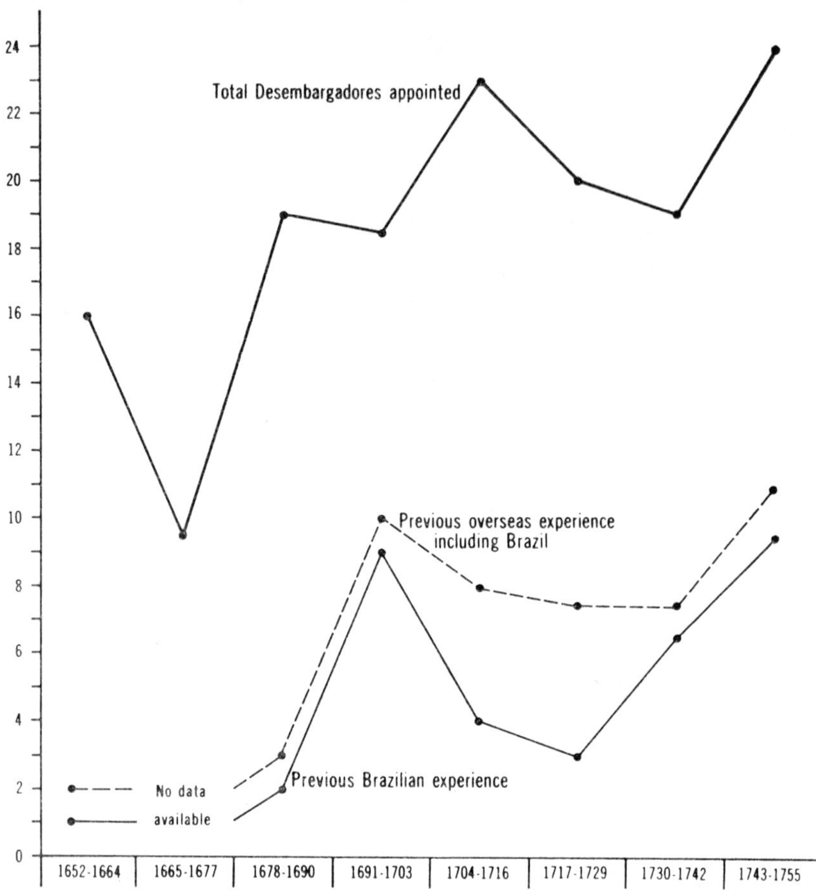

Fig. 4. Previous Overseas Experience of Bahian Desembargadores.

Pereira, a bachelor in canon law who became *ouvidor geral* of Cuiabá in 1735.[31] In that capacity, he fabricated a Spanish threat on the Mato Grosso frontier to camouflage an illicit trading expedition which, according to some, he had organized in cooperation with merchants in Cuiabá. Gonçalves Pereira's illegal moves on the sensitive border between Spanish Chiquitos and Portuguese Mato Grosso moved the captain-general of São Paulo to comment that

31. AUC, *verbete da matrícula;* ANTT, *Chan. João V. Doações,* liv. 88, f. 336; liv. 108, f. 268.

Gonçalves Pereira must have been "demented or blind with ambition" to have attempted this scheme.[32] Such criticism did not prevent the promotion of this venal magistrate to the Bahian tribunal in April 1747. Gonçalves Pereia certainly brought experience to the Relação, but it was not the kind prescribed in bureaucratic regulations.

Despite the royal tendency to employ judges with colonial experience, only in two instances did magistrates who had served in the Portuguese State of India also discharge professional duties in Brazil. Of the 152 judges appointed between 1652 and 1758, only two had been in India, and one, Jorge Seco de Macedo, was appointed as chancellor in Brazil after long service in the Casa da Suplicação—an indication that his India experience was of little concern.[33] Conversely, men who had served in the West African colonies of Angola, Cabo Verde, São Tomé, and Guiné often saw later duty in the Relação of Bahia. In effect, there were two branches of the colonial magistracy, an Indian Ocean corps and an Atlantic Ocean corps. Each had its own personnel and channels of promotion, but both were integrated into the bureaucratic system of the peninsula. Magistrates from either colonial branch might achieve promotion to positions in the metropolis, but there was virtually no contact between the two colonial corps. This pattern of separation did not exist among colonial executives, since in the eighteenth century it was not uncommon for men who had served as viceroy in India to later hold a similar position in Brazil.[34]

---

32. Gonçalves Pereira's career is traced in David Davidson's "How the Brazilian West was Won; Freelance and State on the Mato Grosso Frontier, ca. 1737–1752," in Dauril Alden, ed., *Colonial Roots of Modern Brazil.*

33. Jorge Seco de Macedo held a post in the Goan tribunal and also served in the Inquisition of Goa in the 1630's. While at this post the Viceroy of India denounced him for involvement in trade and for being "mais solicitador de mercadores que inquisidor" (António Baião, *A Inquisicão de Goa*, 2 vols., Lisbon, 1930–1949, I, 227). When nominated for chancellor of Bahia, however, he was described as "noticioso e de bons procedimentos." See AHU, Bahia *pap. avul.*, caixa 6 (Lisbon, 15 April 1654).

34. Alden, *Royal Government*, p. 34.

The present state of research does not permit an assessment of the value of these branches of the magistracy as channels of advancement, nor does it allow a statement regarding their prestige in comparison with wholly metropolitan service. One would imagine that magistrates who did all their junior service in Portugal maintained better patronage ties than those men sent to Brazil or Asia, and thus generally rose higher and faster through the ranks of office. The fact that only 7 per cent of the magistrates who served in the Relação of Bahia eventually attained positions in offices ranking above the Casa da Suplicação indicates that the highest offices in the royal councils were staffed by *letrados* who had risen through the India service or, more likely, had gained all their experience in Portugal itself. If magistrates sent to Brazil realized that they were entering a junior or less prestigious branch of service and that later promotions might be inhibited by this fact, then the bureaucratic codes of behavior would have had much less effect on them. Knowing that even exemplary performance provided no guarantee of professional reward could have led the desembargadores to actions which offered their own rewards.

There is no evidence, however, that Brazilians or magistrates in Brazil perceived their disadvantage for later promotion.[35] Instead, it appears that by the late seventeenth century the Relação of Bahia had become a prized post within the magistracy. Whereas almost all of the original desembargadores of 1609 had sought to be excused from service in Brazil, by the end of that century *letrados* actively petitioned for such appointments.[36] The growth of the colony, its increasing importance within the imperial structure,

35. Rocha Pitta, *História*, pp. 334–336, expresses, in fact, the opposite point of view, noting with pride those Brazilians who had achieved high office in the Portuguese empire.

36. For example, Francisco Cabral de Almada, collector of the special tax (*donativo*) in the Azores, requested and received in 1664 the gown of a desembargador of Bahia and a promise of a position in that tribunal when a vacancy opened. He never took office and became instead chancellor of the High Court of Goa. See ANTT, *Chan. Afonso VI Doações*, liv. 25, f. 432; liv. 29, f. 278–278v.

and, after the gold strikes of the 1690's, its fabled wealth undoubtedly influenced this change of opinion.[37] There are even some references to the Bahian tribunal as more important than that of Oporto. By the eighteenth century such statements may have reflected the actual situation, but in terms of bureaucratic advancement Oporto always stood above Bahia. Nevertheless, appointment to the Relação of Bahia was a highly prized award.

It became a custom of the Desembargo do Paço to promise a place in the Bahian High Court to magistrates sent as *ouvidores* in the captaincies of Brazil and even to judges sent to West Africa. João de Sá Sottomayor went to a post as *ouvidor* of Sergipe in 1704 not only with the promise of a place in the Relação, but with the privilege of wearing a desembargador's robe while serving in the inferior position.[38] Jerônimo da Cunha Pimental was promised a position in the High Court of Bahia as soon as a vacancy opened.[39] In the interim he was sent to Angola. By 1705, a backlog of magistrates who had been promised a place in the High Court and who were unable to assume the position moved a number of men to complain to the crown. The problem became further complicated when, after 1718, the Desembargo do Paço tried to comply with its promise by making supernumerary appointments.[40]

Magistrates actively sought a High Court position, but, although many non-professional bureaucratic offices could be bought, the magisterial posts do not appear to have been available for purchase—at least not publicly. They were reserved for professional bureaucrats who were, in theory, assigned solely on the basis of merit and experience. Sale of such offices would have constituted

37. Luís Botelho de Queirós stated in 1713 that the office of *ouvidor geral* of Rio de Janeiro was worth 2,400,000 *réis* annually, or about twice the amount of its salary and perquisites. Positions in the Relação could probably generate even more than that. See *Cadaval*, II, 359–360.

38. ANTT, *Chan. Pedro II, Doações*, liv. 54, f. 235. Diogo Rangel de Castelobranco was sent to Paraíba in 1687 under similar conditions. ANTT, *Chan. Pedro II, Doações*, liv. 18, ff. 37, 75.

39. *Ibid.*, liv. 18, f. 211v.

40. *Ibid.*, liv. 23, f. 119; liv. 29, f. 236; BGUC, Códice 709, f. 154.

an open violation of the ideology upon which the edifice of royal government had been constructed. Still, in the 1680's a few judges in Bahia are referred to as proprietors (*proprietários*) of their office. In other contexts, this term usually implied that a man could treat his office like a piece of property, sell it, pass it on to a heir, or otherwise dispose of it. In the letters of appointment of the magistrates in question, however, there is no mention of payment for the rights of ownership, nor any other indication that the office had been purchased. It appears that in some instances the term "proprietor" is simply used as a synonym for incumbent.[41] Perhaps a most satisfactory explanation can be found in the appointment of Francisco de Figueiredo Vaz in 1757.[42] His "letter of proprietorship of a place as desembargador" grants him a position for the standard six-year term, but adds that he may hold the post so long as no replacement is sent. In this case proprietorship could constitute a special privilege which allowed a magistrate to maintain some control over his incumbency while leaving ultimate control in the hands of the king.

The crown continued to provide other inducements and privileges to men selected for service in the Bahian High Court. Judges often received a special bonus to pay for the costs of moving to Brazil. This was usually accompanied by the promise to provide for the magistrate's family should some accident befall him. Just as magistrates sent to the captaincies of Brazil might be promised a post in the Relação of Bahia, so too, the desembargadores of Bahia were almost invariably promised promotion to the Relação of Oporto. As a privilege some judges were allowed to take possession of the Oporto office immediately, so that their seniority in that tribunal would begin before completion of their Bahian du-

41. For example, a document of 1681 refers to Antônio Rodrigues Banha, who was serving as interim chancellor by appointment of João Castelinho de Freitas, as "proprietor of the office." AHNRJ, Códice 540 (22 May 1681).

42. AHNRJ, Códice 542, f. 160. It would not be surprising if in times of financial difficulty, cash payments by *letrados* could obtain this privilege from the crown.

ties.[43] Promotion to the rank of desembargador also brought with it certain benefits and privileges (*proes e precalços*) such as exemption from taxation.[44]

The crown continued to award habits in the Order of Christ and grants of *fidalguia* (knighthood) to magistrates in recognition of past service and in order to buttress their authority. The military orders had by the late seventeenth century lost much of their significance as fighting organizations. The outward symbols of chivalry remained, but the military orders had become exclusive clubs whose ranks were filled not only by distinguished soldiers but by those people who had performed some service for the throne.[45] Magistrates fell into this last category. Between 1609 and 1759 at least 22 per cent of the desembargadores of Bahia wore the coverted cross of the Order of Christ emblazoned on their robes.[46] Often these awards fell to men of artisan or gentry backgrounds, men who normally might be excluded from the military orders because of a "defect" in their backgrounds. The case of Domingos Gonçalves Santiago is illustrative. Although his maternal grandfather was an artisan, Gonçalves Santiago was granted membership specifically because he had been appointed to the Relação of Bahia.[47] In other words, the rank of his office had overcome the defect of his birth. Whether the acquisition of these awards by

---

43. Letters of appointment given under these circumstances awarded the Bahian office with *posse tomada* in the Relação of Oporto.

44. *Ord. fil.*, II, t. lix.

45. Francis A. Dutra, "Membership in the Order of Christ in the Seventeenth Century: Its Rights, Privileges, and Obligations," *The Americas*, XXVII (July 1970), n. 1, 3–25.

46. The records of the military orders are presently housed in the ANTT. I have checked all the desembargadores of Bahia in the *habilitações* of the Order of Christ. I have not included those who obtained their habit after service in the Relação. I was unable to carry out a similar search in the records of the orders of Santiago and Aviz. The figure of 22 per cent is therefore probably misleadingly low as an indication of magisterial membership in the military orders, but since the Order of Christ was more prestigious than the others, it is a fair index of magisterial attainments in this area.

47. ANTT, Ordem de Christo, *Habilitações*, maço 13, n. 48 (1726).

men like Gonçalves Santiago reflects an attempt by the crown to bolster their authority and obscure lackluster origins, or whether it was an effort by the judges in question to allay their own sense of social insecurity, is a moot point. Nevertheless, it is clear that in cases such as those of Bento Rabello (1655), Francisco de Figueiredo (1657), and Antônio Rodrigues Banha (1733), entry into the Order of Christ came just before or shortly after appointment to the Relação.[48]

Although the magistracy had developed as a corps of professional bureaucrats with specific functions within the political structure, the magistrates had also, over the course of time, sought to turn their position into the basis of social status. Having emerged under royal tutelage as a counterweight to traditional groups like the titled nobility, the crown judges began to demand the privileges, symbols, and recognition of the very groups whose power they had most inhibited. Portugal shared this historical process with other nations in western Europe, and as in Prussia and France the magisterial bureaucrats did not become the implacable enemies of the aristocracy, but instead sought to penetrate its ranks.[49] Two tendencies in this process can be identified. First, the magistrates justified their social ascendancy by developing a theoretical basis of their own nobility. This theme lay beneath the debates of arms versus letters in the seventeenth century, as the *letrados* sought to prove their utility to the body politic. By the eighteenth century, jurists argued that the study of law by itself literally ennobled an individual, and that by extension all judges should be considered the equals of the landed and military nobility.[50] While justifying

48. *Ibid.*, *Chan. Ordem de Christo*, liv. 33, f. 334v; liv. 43, f. 228v; liv. 186, f. 147v. I found no evidence that magistrates in the military orders ever acquired commanderies (estates with a fixed income). These appear to have been reserved for the traditional nobility.

49. Cf. Hans Rosenberg, *Bureaucracy, Aristocracy, and Autocracy; The Prussian Experience, 1600–1815* (Cambridge, Mass., 1958), pp. 57–74; Franklin L. Ford, *Robe and Sword, The Regrouping of the French Aristocracy after Louis XIV* (Cambridge, Mass., 1953), pp. 59–78.

50. Francisco de Almeida e Amaral Botelho, *Discursos jurídicos em que*

their own positions, however, the magistrates also sought entry into the ranks of the aristocracy through the acquisition of the insignia and privileges traditionally accorded it. This second tendency was to some extent sponsored by the crown, which through the dispensation of these rewards was able to maintain control over the performance of its magistrates.

The crown's control of both the symbols which legitimatized social advancement and the internal rewards of the bureaucracy kept the magistracy tied to royal interests. The magistracy did become to some extent a self-perpetuating class with a tendency toward heredity of profession, though not of office. Its titles became in effect social designations. Once a man held the office of desembargador, he invariably employed his title whether he continued to hold that office or not. But in the Portuguese empire the magistracy did not become a *noblesse de la robe*, an identifiable nobility based on office and function. Individual magistrates might be, and often were, integrated into the traditional nobility by marriage, or they might achieve this position through the action of the crown; but a magisterial class, either in competition with or as an adjunct of the landed and military aristocracy never developed as an autonomous entity with independent class goals beyond those prescribed by the crown.

Once appointed to the Relação, a desembargador might delay as much as two years while he settled his affairs and placed his household in order before leaving for Brazil. Four to six months, however, was a more common interval between appointment and arrival in the colony. The crown tried to stagger replacements, sending out two or three new magistrates at a time and thus maintaining a mixture of experienced judges and recent arrivals on the bench. The obvious goal was bureaucratic continuity. The six desembargadores who took office in February 1710 constituted the largest group of replacements to take office at the same time. This situation was extraordinary and had been caused by the recall of

---

se contém várias matérias úteis aos principantes com os assentos da Caza da Supplicação (Lisbon, 1790), pp. 97–111, states this position clearly.

four desembargadores accused in a *devassa* of 1709.[51] On arrival in Bahia, each judge took his oath of office in the presence of his colleagues and the viceroy. This ceremony formally initiated a desembargador's incumbency.

Since the terminal date of office in the Relação often cannot be ascertained, it is difficult to estimate the average length of service in Bahia. In the period of the first Relação, the judges were sent to Brazil with the promise of promotion after six years of satisfactory service. This formula became standard but there were constant exceptions to it; and some judges served two and even three times the six-year limit.[52] Magistrates whose personal life tied them closely to the colony were prone to violate the six-year regulation. Marriage, of course, created such ties, and the case of Antão de Mesquita de Oliveira, who had married in Brazil and who served there for twenty-one years (1609–1630), illustrates this point. In 1683 the Conselho Ultramarino complained that the virtual perpetuity of overseas positions endangered the very foundations of government, especially when many who remained beyond six years were "natives of the land." Similar complaints were lodged again in 1691 but with little apparent effect.[53]

Brazilian-born magistrates most consistently circumvented the six-year limitation. Cristóvão de Burgos sat in the Relação for twenty-six years (1654–1680); João de Góes e Araújo held his position for eighteen years (1667–1680) and died in office. João da Rocha Pitta served in the High Court for twenty-four years (1678–1702), and although he received appointments to offices in Portugal he refused to leave his native Bahia. Attachments of

---

51. Desembargadores Luís da Costa Faria, Miguel de Siqueira Castelobranco, Manoel Freyre da Silva, and Antônio de Campos e Figueiredo were all charged in 1709 and forced to return to Portugal. All were exonerated. See AHU, Bahia *pap. avul.*, caixa 22 (1st ser. uncatalogued).

52. A suggestion to extend the term to eight years was voted in the Desembargo do Paço but remained ineffective. See Alden, *Royal Government*, p. 33n.

53. *Consulta* CU (23 October 1683), *DHBNR*, LXXVIII (1950), 272–273; AHU, Bahia *pap. avul.*, caixa 16 (25 June 1691).

family, property, and familiarity held these men to Brazil and exercised a stronger influence over them than did professional motivations. The behavior of these magistrates indicates quite clearly that the goals of bureaucratic advancement and the norms of bureaucratic life were never fully adopted by all the magistrates. Alternate sources of income and prestige severely curtailed the force of bureaucratic motivations and contributed to the non-professional behavior of many judges.

The increased financial and personal attractions of Brazil in the eighteenth century gave rise to another type of problem. It became increasingly difficult to force desembargadores to return to Portugal once their term of office in Brazil had expired. Royal magistrates still took their own sweet time in getting to posts in the colony, but by 1706 the crown was also confronted by desembargadores who found excuses to remain there after six years.[54] Although some governors wished to employ them in judicial roles in order to lighten the burden of the legitimate desembargadores, the crown refused to permit such a measure. Some judges became so enamored of the colony that they simply refused further appointments. Bernardo de Sousa Estrela, a magistrate from the Azores who had married in Brazil, served a six-year term in the Relação and then retired in 1730 at the age of sixty. He spent the next thirty years of his life in Bahia, living on his wife's estates and acquiring a reputation for piety. He was finally buried in the Franciscan monastery in a solemn ceremony in which the desembargadores of the Relação served as pallbearers.[55] This last fact emphasizes an interesting phenomenon. The title and rank of desembargador stayed with a man even after he no longer held office. It became a description of social position not merely of function,

---

54. *Alvará* (15 Nov. 1608), AHNRJ, Cod. 541, ordered all officials sent to the colonies to take their positions in eight months. In 1706 and 1709 the crown took steps to hasten the return of magistrates from Brazil. APB, *Ord. reg.* 7, n. 611.

55. Manuel Lopes de Almeida, *Notícias históricas de Portugal e Brasil*, 2 vols. (Coimbra, 1964), II, 75–76.

and the influence a retired magistrate might exercise over his successors must not be overlooked.

For those desembargadores who returned to Portugal, promotion to the High Court of Oporto was normal. Occasionally, *devassas* or *residências* might prevent some magistrate's promotion, but these had relatively little effect. In fact, one member of the Conselho Ultramarino complained in 1728 that ordinary *devassas* in Brazil were worthless since even in notorious cases nobody could be persuaded to testify.[56] The Oporto post, therefore, was assured. Of the 58 per cent (96 of 168) of the desembargadores promoted to another position, 86 per cent (83 of 96) went first to Oporto. About half of them finally reached the Casa da Suplicação. Very few attained positions in the king's councils.

The promotional channels and natural mortality winnowed the magistrates from royal employ and reserved positions at the apex of the bureaucracy for men with the highest degree of competence, the greatest leverage with patrons, the most experience, and the greatest stamina. Ultimately professional success probably depended on a combination of all these elements. The regulated steps of advancement also placed a premium on performance which pleased one's superiors and which conformed with the code of bureaucratic behavior as set down in the *Ordenações filipinas*. The few magistrates who served in Brazil and who later attained high positions in royal councils, such as the Conselho Ultramarino or Desembargo do Paço, appear to have no common characteristic in their personal or professional biographies to indicate why they advanced. Their careers and those of their colleagues depended to a large extent on the operating principles of the imperial bureaucracy.[57]

Four principles cemented the disparate parts of the bureaucracy and guided personnel decisions within it. Seniority, merit, precedent, and nepotism became the pillars upon which promotion and

---

56. *Consulta* CU (7 January 1728), *DH*, XC (1950), 140–141.

57. For example, see in Appendix III, Manoel Carneiro de Sá, Manoel da Costa Bonicho, Manoel Antônio da Cunha e de Sottomayor.

reward rested. Patronage might also be added to this list, but so little overt evidence of it remains for the historian, and so much of that is only by inference, that this principle must remain a recognized but undefinable characteristic of the magistracy. Nepotism, like patronage, was an element of patrimonial administration which lingered on into the eighteenth century, long after the magistracy had become in theory, fully "rational" and professional. The creation of a *letrado* class made the institutionalization of nepotism a desired goal within the magistracy. It insured preferential treatment for the relatives of magistrates and contributed to a sense of occupational and perhaps class solidarity. When Manoel da Costa Bonicho, the son of a former desembargador of Bahia, received his appointment to the Relação, the document made no mention of any past service, the usual formula, but stated instead that the position was awarded because "he is the son of Manoel da Costa Bonicho, *desembargador de agravos* in the Casa da Suplicação."[58] Such awards insured the growth of family traditions within the magistracy and promoted generational continuity.

Merit was a bureaucratic principle which sprang from a different tradition. In theory, as the bureaucracy became increasingly professional and rational in directing all activities toward the resolution of its specific tasks, merit should have become a central principle of bureaucratic advancement. But merit must be equated in this context with competence, not excellence. A magistrate was expected to perform his prescribed duties without serious deviation. Little room existed in his charge of office which allowed innovation or imaginative administration, and the examinations at the termination of incumbency sought infractions of regulations, not outstanding performance. The model magistrate was the man who performed his tasks in such a way that none could complain. Francisco Mendes Galvão had such a reputation. In the 1690's, Governor Antônio Luís Gonsalves da Câmara Coutinho waxed lyrical

58. Cristóvão Salema de Carvalho asked for and received a position in 1655 because his father was a desembargador. See king to Count of Odemira (Lisbon, June 5, 1655), *DHBNR*, LXVI (1944), 88.

over the virtues of this desembargador, who served in his post "with such authority and justice that the most learned senator could envy him." [59] Six years later, in 1697, Câmara Coutinho said: "even those parties against whom he passes sentences leave his house, as I have often heard, saying that if Francisco Mendes Galvão finds no justice in their plea, it is a sign that there is none." [60] The emphasis on impartiality and honesty indicates the basis of magisterial merit. What most judges hoped for was a tour of duty that caused no ripples of complaint. In effect, merit or excellence was a negative principle in that it affected bureaucratic advancement more often by its absence than by its presence.

Seniority, however, was fully employed as a principle of advancement in the Portuguese bureaucracy.[61] It rested on a foundation of belief that length of service and experience naturally resulted in accumulated wisdom. Deference to age was also present in the principle of seniority, but it appears that seniority in service rather than simple age played a more important role. Promotion between ranks and precedence within them depended directly upon seniority. Desembargadores displayed an acute sensitivity to this matter and were extremely zealous in defending their antiquity in rank. Magistrates appointed to the Relação who could not take their posts immediately sometimes had a representative take the oath of office in Bahia so that no time toward seniority would be lost. The view that seniority may have minimized in-group aggression within the bureaucracy by reducing the need for professional competition is not supported by the history of the Relação.[62]

59. AHU, Bahia *pap. avul.* caixa 16 (Bahia, 25 June 1691).

60. Gov. Antônio Luís Gonsalves da Câmara Coutinho to CU (Bahia, 12 July 1697), AHU, Bahia *pap. avul.* caixa 17.

61. Michel Crozier, *The Bureaucratic Phenomenon* (Chicago, 1964), pp. 70–74, discusses the seniority system and suggests that the principle is not simply rejected by younger men and accepted as one grows older. He finds instead that acceptance of seniority is an index of a man's integration into his position, and is in some ways a measure of his socialization by his superiors.

62. Robert Merton, "Bureaucratic Structure and Personality," in Robert Merton, ed., *Reader in Bureaucracy* (New York, 1952), pp. 361–371.

Seniority may have lessened tension and competition in other spheres of activity, but at the same time it concentrated conflict at a particular point, as each magistrate tried to establish his seniority and the prerogatives due him because of it.

Most disputes between the magistrates arose over matters of seniority and precedence within the chambers of the tribunal. Desembargadores were especially careful in asserting their precedence not only for reasons of prestige but also because later promotions and appointments might depend on this criterion. Often the dispute centered on determining the date a particular judge took office, or more exactly, whether his length of service should be calculated from the date of his oath of office or his first day of service. This was exactly the question that arose in 1716 between Tomás Feliciano de Albernás and Manoel da Costa Moreira, and repeated in 1721 by two other judges.[63] A second cause of these squabbles lay in the promotion of desembargadores from one position to another within the Relação. Conflicts resulted over seniority in rank versus seniority in the Relação. In 1675 Cristóvão de Burgos challenged the right of his colleague Agostinho de Azevedo Monteiro to sit in the first seat to the right of the chancellor, the senior position on the bench. Azevedo Monteiro had taken that position because he was serving an interim chancellor, and Burgos felt that as senior *desembargador de agravos* the chair belonged to him. A full meeting of the Relação was called by the governor, and after the two disputants had left the chamber the other judges voted in favor of Burgos.[64] Most disputes of this nature were settled with dignity, but instances of name-calling and even fistfights within the High Court's chambers were not unknown.

Operational precedents became the custom and usage which

63. Assento (22 April 1716) AHNRJ, Códice 540, f. 109. The problem of supernumerary appointments became apparent in 1729, when three desembargadores appeared in Bahia to fill one vacant post. The position was awarded on the basis of the date of appointment. In a later case of 1736, the decision was made on the basis of the date of sailing from Lisbon. See AHNRJ, Códice 540, ff. 122, 135.

64. AHNRJ, Códice 540 (10 December 1675), f. 56.

modified the written statutes of bureaucratic behavior. If a magistrate petitioned for a special favor, an additional stipend, or to be excused from some duty, he usually cited some previous case of a similar nature. How such information became available to judges, or more exactly, how it was transmitted is a particularly interesting problem. Magistrates in Portugal probably had access to the chancellary books where precedents might be sought and found. Men in Brazil, however, could depend only on the registry books of the Relação. Word of mouth probably played an important role in the transmission of such knowledge and a kind of bureaucratic oral tradition developed in which the usages of the magistracy were passed from one generation of judges to the next. Such a situation obviously gave judges who remained in their positions for long periods of time additional power, since they became repositories of information for their colleagues. Brazilians and those most attached to Brazil may thus have wielded an influence in the Relação not fully reflected by their numbers because they tended to remain in office longer than their colleagues.

Service in the Relação of Bahia constituted one step on a ladder of bureaucratic achievement which in theory led from the lecture halls of Coimbra to the councils of the king. Magistrates who gained a position in the Bahian tribunal could not devote all their energy and interest to the resolution of personal and professional problems in a wholly Brazilian context if the hope of bureaucratic advancement had any meaning for them. The desembargadores were part of an imperial system of administration which bound together disparate areas of empire, and as such, their actions sometimes responded to pressures not generated in the colony. The degree to which the various echelons of magistracy were integrated into this system, and the ease with which magistrates moved from positions in Portugal to the colonies and then back again, indicates the amount of bureaucratic continuity which this system provided. A Brazilian sub-system of professional magistracy only developed after 1690, when junior positions in the colony served as preparation for the High Court of Bahia. Even then, later promotion was almost invariably back to Portugal.[65] Although in economic-political terms Brazil stood in a classic colonial position within the Portuguese empire, in bureaucratic terms it was well-integrated with the metropolis. Magistrates sent to Brazil might choose to mobilize certain personal resources in the colony with little regard for the effect of these actions on their professional life, but many judges viewed their service in Brazil as simply a stage in their careers. Such a view obviously influenced magisterial perceptions of role, duty, and professional morality. It tended to isolate the judges from society and forced them into a pattern of formalism in the approach to both personal and professional matters. The most striking aspect of magisterial bureaucracy in colonial Brazil, however, is the extent to which bureaucratic formalism and detachment, despite the strong motives of career advancement and professionalism, broke down in the face of personal goals, non-categorical relationships, and the various attractions of the colony.

---

65. After 1752 some desembargadores went to the Relação of Rio de Janeiro following service in Bahia.

XIII. THE BRAZILIANIZATION OF BUREAUCRACY

Even if we concede to him the merit, capacity, and talent to serve Your Highness, it should be in other parts and not in his homeland, where kinship and friendship pervert the necessary disinterest. Judges are men of flesh and blood, subject to hate and love.
Câmara of Salvador (1 September 1676)

Many ministers of the High Court become patrons of the very cases that come before it.
Conselho Ultramarino (1725)

In the century between the reestablishment of the Relação of Bahia (1652) and the creation of a second Brazilian High Court in Rio de Janeiro (1751), magisterial bureaucrats became part of the everyday life of the colony. As members of the tribunal and as individuals, the desembargadores played an active role in the colony's social, cultural, and economic life, often in ways neither desired nor intended by bureaucratic regulations. The impact of the magistracy on colonial society must be viewed not only in terms of its professional actions, but in light of the life styles and personal motivations of the magistrates and the reactions or initiatives of certain elements of the colonial population in relation to it. Bureaucratic formulas are often written as though the population to be served (or controlled) will have little effect on the bureaucrats. In Brazil this was an unfounded assumption. The most striking aspect of government in Brazil was the interpenetration of two supposedly hostile forms of human organization: bureaucracy and kinship-personal relations. Colonial society displayed a remarkable ability to "Brazilianize" the bureaucrats if not the bureaucracy—that is, to integrate them into existing systems of power and patronage. The inducements offered by colonial groups and individuals and the desires of the magistrates both set the process of interpenetration in motion.

Upon arrival in Salvador, a magistrate's first personal concern was the establishment of his residence. Many judges rented houses in the upper city, near the courthouse and the other administrative buildings. Notary records occasionally supply this sort of information. In 1702, for example, Antônio Rodrigues Banha lived on the street which ran from the Jesuit College to the Carmelite monastery, and his colleague Belchior Ramires de Carvalho resided on the street below the Benedictine church.[1] A census of 1775 reveals six desembargadores living in the parish of São Pedro in the heart of the city. But there were exceptions, especially among men closely tied by family or interest to the colony. Pedro de Unhão Castelobranco, who began his service in the Relação in 1686, built a beautiful seaside mansion at a scenic spot just east of the main port facilities. This building, the Solar de Unhão, became a landmark of the city's prospect and remains so today.[2] Desembargadores who acquired properties in the rural areas of Bahia sometimes spent much time outside of Salvador. Brazilian-born Luís de Sousa Pereira maintained a residence in Cachoeira, although he also owned houses in Salvador.[3]

Magistrates usually brought their families with them to Brazil. Aside from his wife and children, a judge's household might in-

1. APB, Livro de Notas 18A (8 October 1702), f. 128v; 112–113v.

2. The Solar de Unhão presently houses the Bahian State Museum of Folk Art.

3. *Consulta* CU (20 September 1734), *DHBNR*, XCI (1951), 29–30.

clude relatives, godchildren, servants, employees, and slaves; the bondsmen were employed as bearers for the judge's litter, or, in the eighteenth century, as footmen for his coach. The presence of relatives and protégés beneath a magistrate's roof added certain dimensions to the scope and complexity of his social relations, for these people not only exerted some influence on the head of the household, but through their connections with others in society, opened new channels of influence or pressure between individuals and the High Court.[4] Table 4, based on the census of 1775, provides some idea of the internal structure of a magistrate's household. The roles of husband, father, sponsor, and protector were as much a part of a magistrate's life as his professional obligations.

It was perhaps in the spiritual realm, however, that the participation of magistrates in colonial life became most apparent. The Relação employed a chaplain to conduct the mass said before each session of the court, and many judges took their religious obligations seriously. Almost by definition a good servant of the king was also a good Catholic, but the pervasiveness of the Church led the desembargadores into situations which conflicted with their roles as disinterested guardians of the law.

The religious life of colonial Brazil was rich and the opportunities for participation many. Individual magistrates became benefactors of Salvador's churches and convents. As distinguished officials, desembargadores were sometimes called upon to assume leadership roles and financial obligations during major religious celebrations. Such was the case in 1702, when Chancellor Antônio Rodrigues Banha joined the *juiz de fóra* of Salvador and a wealthy merchant as sponsors and directors of the public procession of the Feast of the Resurrection.[5] These individual efforts paralleled the High Court's collective celebration of the Feast of the Holy

---

4. Desembargadores sometimes brought retainers to Brazil. Cristóvão de Burgos (1654) and Antônio Rodrigues Banha (1680) were both accompanied by such men. See AHU, Bahia *pap. avul.* caixa 8 (2nd series uncatalogued); caixa 15.

5. APB, Livro de Notas 18a (8 October 1702), f. 128v.

TABLE 4

Desembargador Households, São Pedro Parish, 1775

Name	Age	Civil Status	Family	Slaves	Dependents	Comments on Dependents
Francisco Manoel da Silva	44	S		5		
Agostinho Alvares da Silva	45	S		4	Angela, 50, B Maria B	Cooks
José da Rocha Dantas	40	S		4	Antônio, 20, W José 26, W	Both unmarried
João Baptista Dacier	43	M	Catherina (wife), 30 José, 19 Maria, 12	6	D. Ana, 24 Petornilha, 55 Francisco, 13 Antônio, 40, B and his wife Mariana de Jesus, 33	
João Ferreira Bittancourt	55	S		9		
Antônio Gomes Ribeiro	28	S		5	Andre de Sousa, 17, W	Unmarried servant

Key: S(ingle), M(arried), B(lack), W(hite).
Source: da Costa, "População da Cidade da Bahia em 1775," *Actas, Colóquio international de estudos Luso-brasileiros*, 4 vols. (Coimbra, 1965), I, 191–274.

Spirit, held annually in the church of the Carmelites. This celebration was usually attended by the highest officials and other members of the elite of the colony and a special sermon on justice, preached by a noted priest or even the archbishop, generally accompanied the mass.[6] Such activities fulfilled the judge's religious obligations, provided certain psychological benefits, and simultaneously reinforced the elevated status of the desembargadores and their tribunal.

Desembargadores were prohibited from joining the prestigious and exclusive Third Order of the Franciscans and the Carmelites, but they consistently sought membership in the Misericórdia of Salvador. This institution, dedicated to social welfare and charitable works, became in Bahia a social club to which the "best" people belonged. The rank and dignity of the judges made them suitable members, excellent candidates for the Misericórdia's annually elected board, and possible choices for its principal office of *provedor*. In fact, between 1711 and 1715 three desembargadores controlled that office, a situation which raised serious complaint in 1716, when critics charged that Dionísio de Azevedo e Arevalos had obtained that office by fraud.[7] These complaints resulted in a royal order excluding desembargadores from the position of *provedor* but allowing them to continue on the governing board of the Misericórdia.

Like many other religious institutions in colonial Brazil, the Misericórdia served as a credit facility, loaning money at a standard 6¼ per cent, for sound ventures such as house construction or land purchases. Membership in the Misericórdia and an active role on its board probably offered certain financial advantages to a magistrate, both through his own access to capital and in the power he

---

6. An example of these sermons can be seen in Antônio de Sá, *Sermão que pregou o P.M. . . . da Companhia de Iesus na Bahia, pregado a Iustiça* (Coimbra, 1672).

7. *Consulta* CU (4 September 1716), *DHBNR*, XCVI (1952), 251–254; Codice 247, ff. 68–69v. See the discussion in Russell-Wood, *Fidalgos*, pp. 111–112.

could wield on behalf of friends or retainers. It is not surprising to find Desembargador Cristóvão de Burgos, *provedor* of the Misericórdia in 1665, still among its list of debtors in 1694.[8] Personal influence in the Misericórdia made loans against insufficient collateral easier to obtain and could even free a man from his debts. Small wonder that desembargadores sought the governing offices of the Misericórdia.

Since a man seeking admission as a brother of the Misericórdia needed a sponsor, the records of that institution also provide some indication of magisterial personal ties. Sponsorship of desembargadores came from two sources: colleagues on the bench or members of the Bahian elite. Thus, Desembargador Pedro de Unhão Castelobranco sponsored the candidacy of two colleagues in 1693. Both were admitted as brothers of superior standing (*maior condição*).[9] The other tendency can be seen in admission of Desembargador Cristóvão Tavares de Morais, who was sponsored in 1705 by his father-in-law, Colonel Cristóvão Cavalcanti de Albuquerque, a wealthy Bahian sugar planter. Cavalcanti de Albuquerque married another daughter to a desembargador, João de Sá Sottomaior, who also joined the brotherhood in 1720.[10] Many of the magistrates who sought entry in the Misericórdia belonged to one of the military orders or were *familiares* of the Inquisition.[11] Thus their racial purity and religious orthodoxy were supposedly assured by previous tests, and their entry went uncontested on these grounds.

In his study of the Bahian Misericórdia, Professor A. J. R. Russell-Wood has made the interesting suggestion that magisterial domination of the *provedor*'s office in the early years of the eighteenth century reflects a period of transition in which the old

---

8. "Lista das Pessoas que devem a esta S. Caza da Miz[a]," AHU, Bahia *pap. avul.*, caixa 8 (Bancroft microfilm).

9. ASCMB, A/1/2 Livro de Termo (29 June 1692), f. 839; (6 September 1693), f. 919, 921.

10. ASCMB, A/1/2 Livro de Termo (21 June 1705), f. 118; (12 July 1720), f. 186.

11. A *familiar* was a lay assistant and informant for the Holy Office.

planter oligarchy was slowly withdrawing from its control of the brotherhood's principal offices while the mercantile sector was not yet able to assume these roles.[12] Close scrutiny of the desembargadores who held the *provedor* position indicates, however, that if the planters were retreating, they knew how to fight a rear-guard action. The eight desembargadores who held the *provedor* position between 1609 and 1716 were, without exception, either Bahian-born or married to a Brazilian woman. In general, the wives of these magistrates were planters' daughters and some of the judges themselves owned plantations and could qualify, as did Cristóvão de Burgos and Dionísio de Azevedo e Arevalos, as *senhor de engenho*. It is difficult to see a planter retreat, therefore, in the presence of these men in the *provedor*'s position. Instead, it becomes clear that no matter what the rank or prestige of a desembargador, only those closely linked to the colony could gain access to high positions in the Misericórdia. Furthermore, this situation also underlines the integration of the magisterial elite and the sugar oligarchy in ways which defy their classification as distinct and competing groups.

Desembargadores were, of course, more than participants in sociological relationships, for like all men they also acted according to ideas, principles, and prejudices. The lack of magisterial personal correspondence prevents any individual analysis of these phenomena, and various porfessional principles and motivations have been outlined above. It is important, however, to recall that the judges were men of learning, whose very training inspired careful study and considered thought in the making of decisions. Their schooling and intellectual proclivities drew them into closer contact with each other and with the small group of Brazilians who formed the small intellectual community of the colony.

The colonial status of Brazil placed limitations on its intellectual life. Frontier conditions, the lack of a printing press, and the failure to establish a university in the colony, all combined to stifle

12. Russell-Wood, *Fidalgo*, pp. 111–112.

intellectual pursuits or to direct them toward the metropolis. The Portuguese system of colonial administration, which made each area dependent on Lisbon and centralized administration under the crown, leaving little power to intermediate institutions, found parallels in cultural and intellectual matters. Authors in Brazil had to seek licenses for publication, and even publishers, in the metropolis. Students wishing to attend a university made the long trip to Portugal. Little wonder, then, that Brazil long reflected the intellectual trends of Portugal. Men of learning in Brazil, or at least those with some education, could be found primarily among the clergy and the liberal professions. Of the clerics, the Jesuits surely led the list both in quality and quantity, although distinguished Franciscans and Benedictines also made contributions to the colony's intellectual life. Among secular authors, the vast majority were *letrados,* which literally meant "men of letters." The names of the poet Gregório de Matos e Guerra (1636–1696) or later Desembargador Tomás Antônio Gonzaga (1744–1809), a poet and essayist, come most readily to mind, but other more obscure figures can also be found among the *letrado* intellectuals.

The desembargadores all had a university education, yet in the period prior to 1760 they seemed little inclined toward intellectual or at least literary pursuits. The absence of desembargador authors does not mean that the judges lacked interest in learning and ideas, but probably reflects the absence of an atmosphere which might have generated more overt activity in this area. Unlike Lima or Mexico City, where the Spanish American magistrates often divided their time between the court and the university, at times even holding lectureships in the latter, Bahia had no university and no local printing press. No Solórzano Pereira, Matienzo, or Morga developed among the Brazilian magistrates, no desembargador whose writings on contemporary matters, law, statecraft, or history are remembered today, much less read.[13] But when men did gather

13. Many of the Spanish American *oidores* published important works in these areas. For example, Juan de Solórzano Pereira, *Política Indiana,* 5 vols. (Madrid, 1647); Juan de Matienzo, *Gobierno del Perú* (1567), Guillermo

for intellectual discussion in Brazil, magistrates and *letrados* were always among them.

In 1724 the Viceroy of Brazil, Count of Sabugosa, established in Salvador the Academia dos Esquecidos, a learned society founded in part to aid the Portuguese Royal Academy of History to write the nation's history. Among the seven original members, two were desembargadores and a third was *juiz de fóra* of Salvador.[14] Of these three *letrados*, Chancellor Caetano Brito de Figueiredo stands out. This learned judge read to his fellow members of treatise on the natural history of Brazil, which included long sections on Indian origins, climate, insects, birds, and other natural phenomena.[15] This still unpublished manuscript is filled with references not only to the standard classical authorities but also to Portuguese authors like Francisco de Brito Freyre, who wrote on Brazil, and to Spaniards like Padre José de Acosta and Antonio de Herrera, who studied Spanish America.[16] Obviously, this desembargador had read widely in literature not included in the legal curriculum of Coimbra.

Even more interesting is the extent to which Brito de Figueiredo had consciously or unconsciously absorbed a nativist outlook. Like the other members of the group, this peninsula-born magistrate sang the praises of Brazil, that "most precious jewel of the Lusitanian sceptre, the most valuable stone of the Portuguese crown." [17] Moreover, prevailing colonial attitudes also appear in this work. Slavery he considered a positive benefit to the colony, although he

---

Lohman Villena, ed. (Paris, 1968); Antonio de Morga, *Sucesos de las islas filipinas*, W. E. Retana, ed. (Madrid, 1909).

14. Calmon, *História de Brasil*, III, 1042–1043; Accioli, *Memórias*, II, 373.

15. Caetano Brito de Figueiredo, "Dissertaçoes academicas e históricas nas quais se trata da historia natural das cousas do Brasil (1724)," SGL, MS. 1-C-148.

16. Francisco de Brito Freyre, *Nova Lusitania ou guerra Brasílica* (Lisbon, 1675); José de Acosta, *Historia Natural y Moral de las Indias*, 2nd ed. (Mexico, 1962); Antonio de Herrera y Tordesillas, *Historia general de los hechos de los Castellanos en las islas y tierra firme del mar oceano*, 8 vols. in 4 (Madrid, 1725–1730).

17. As translated in E. Bradford Burns, *History of Brazil* (New York, 1970), p. 95.

argued that prior to the arrival of Africans in Brazil, there had been little sickness and the first colonists had lived to ripe old ages. Thus with the "utility and convenience" of slavery had come the evils of disease. The chancellor's description of the Indians represented the colonists' traditional position, and not the stance of the Jesuits. He called the Indians: "Rational beasts, without Faith, Law, nor Religion, shadows and brutal caricatures of human nature. It is said that those of Florida, Mexico, Peru, and Chile display civility, order, and very different customs, but the writers who describe those discoveries and conquests employ hyperboles to make their deeds seem the greater." [18]

Such attitudes reflect the extent to which peninsula-born judges could acquire colonial attitudes and a colonial outlook. Brito de Figueiredo's work seems no less nativist than the more famous *História da America Portugueza* of Brazilian-born Sebastião da Rocha Pitta, another member of the group. Little else can be said of the intellectual pursuits of the desembargadores in the period before 1750. The Academia dos Esquecidos met only eighteen times and its very name "Esquecidos" (the Forgotten Ones) reflected its relationship to the general community. It would appear that most judges devoted their energy to personal and professional matters.[19]

Once established in Salvador, the desembargadores became part of the captaincy's everyday routine. Caps were doffed in respect as the judges passed through the streets on their way to and from the courthouse. People addressed them in respectful terms and with deference to their rank. But, like most men in high office, the idiosyncrasies and personal characteristics of the judges became objects of public criticism and ridicule. Some acquired nicknames like "Busy" (*Ocupado*), while others received less respectful

---

18. Brito da Figueiredo, "Dissertações," 22, 46.

19. Caetano Brito de Figueiredo is the only desembargador who served before 1750 that published any of his writings. His *Diario panegyrico das festas que na famosa Cidade da Bahia se fizerão em applauso da fausto e feliz Natalicio do Exmo Senhor D. Pedro de Noronha* was published in Lisbon in 1718. See Barbosa Machado, *Biblioteca*, I.

sobriquets. It is unlikely that many people used Joseph de Freitas Serrão's nickname, "Rabo da Vaca" (Cow's Tail), in his presence. Needless to say, very little information of this type has survived to the present, but official reports on magisterial performance often cite the *vox publica* as a source of information, and given the often-cited colonial pastime of tale-telling, it would be surprising indeed if the magistrates escaped without notice.

Perhaps the best source of contemporary opinion of the desembargadores and the Relação is found not in traditional historical materials but in the poetry of the Bahian satirist Gregório de Matos e Guerra.[20] A Coimbra-trained *letrado,* Matos served as a royal magistrate in Portugal before returning to his native Bahia. His often scandalous and always pungent verses won him some admirers and a host of enemies, and he was eventually deported to Angola as a result of his writings. While in Bahia, however, Matos maintained close if not always cordial relations with a number of desembargadores, and as former magistrate himself, he took particular interest in the nature and state of the Brazilian judiciary.

Matos' writings reveal the desembargadores not as faceless officials isolated from the society in which they served, but as men of flesh and blood whose exploits and foibles became matters of public comment and concern. His treatment of individual magistrates varied according to his personal relationships to them. Some he praised, others he damned. Dionísio de Ávila Varieiro became the subject of laudatory poems which described his exploits and eulogized him at his death.[21] Desembargador Pedro de Unhão Castelobranco, owner of a great mansion, married to a Bahian

20. *Obras completas de Gregório de Matos,* 7 vols. (Salvador, 1969), is a new edition of the poet's works. All further references are to the volume and page in this edition. Gregório de Matos has never received adequate biographical treatment. At present the Bahian scholar Fernando da Rocha Peres has undertaken this task. See this "Gregório de Matos e Guerra: seu primeiro casamento," *Universitas,* I (1968), 135–149; "Documentos para uma biografia de Gregório de Matos e Guerra," *Universitas,* II (1969), 53–65.

21. *Obras completas Matos,* II, 400–414.

woman, and *provedor* of the Misericórdia, must have been a well-known figure in Bahian society when Matos penned a somewhat sarcastic poem about him.[22] For some judges Matos could dip his pen in more acidic ink, and his verses on the faults of "Rabo da Vaca" left little unsaid.[23]

Gregório de Matos organized his criticism of the Relação and the judicature around the themes of power and corruption. The authority of the magistrates was not to be questioned nor were their lives to be threatened, for the judges possessed the power to destroy a man or to issue sentences which far exceeded the severity of his crime. In a poem concerning three mulattoes who threatened some desembargadores and who were hung, drawn, and quartered for their misdeed, Matos made his point clear. Using the allegory of a card game, he warned that gambling with the judges was a dangerous sport, since "the three clubs of the Relação is always trump." [24] The power of the legal authorities often exceeded the force of the law. Offending a desembargador or falling afoul of the High Court left a man with little recourse but flight. Once sentenced, little could be done; and a miscarriage of justice usually remained unredeemed. The case of Domingos da Costa Guimarães, sentenced unjustly by the Relação to a public flogging and whom the crown later supported by forcing the desembargadores to pay damages, clearly stands as an exception.[25] The populace of Brazil viewed the Relação with a wary respect.

That respect had nothing to do with admiration, for if the poems of Gregório de Matos are any index, the venality and malfeasance of justice officials, even the professional magistrates, had reached uncontrollable levels by the end of the seventeenth century. Although Matos may have overstated his case, his own legal training and supporting evidence drawn from collateral sources generally

22. *Ibid.*, II, 418–419.
23. *Ibid.*
24. *Ibid.*, II, 265.
25. King to *Câmara* of Salvador (Lisbon, 8 July 1716), APB, *Ord. reg.* 12, n. 21.

lend credence to his criticism. He claimed that all levels of the judicial bureaucracy—judges, *letrados*, clerks, and notaries—appeared to be "cut from the same cloth." At the top, members of the Desembargo do Paço, that guardian of the king's justice, acted like "haughty villains" with "hearts of steel," while in Bahia judges took bribes from both the plaintiff and the defendant in a judicial process so prolonged that "death and universal judgment arrived before the court's final sentence." Justice, said Gregório de Matos, was "bastardized, sold, and unjust." [26]

Although Matos had identified corruption as a major flaw in the judicial system, he made no distinction between various types of corruption and their relative effects on the judiciary or the society. Abuse of office to serve personal goals might violate a judge's professional obligations, but from a social viewpoint it had much less impact than forms of corruption which involved an exchange of favors and rewards between a magistrate and some other member of society. The "Brazilianization" of the magistracy was the "corruption" of the purely bureaucratic goals by a variety of personal, class, monetary, and ascriptive criteria. The result of this process was not wholly dysfunctional to the effective operation of the colonial system, since the penetration of nonbureaucratic standards and criteria into the rigid imperial structure created a resiliency and flexibility which allowed government to continue in the face of constantly changing historical and social circumstances.[27]

In the broadest sense, corruption covered a wide range of deviations from the laws and bureaucratic rules. Throughout the history

---

26. *Obras completas Matos*, I, 6; I, 32; VII, 1675, 1679.

27. For a functional approach to corruption, see Robert O. Tilman, "Emergence of Black-Market Bureaucracy: Administration, Development, and Corruption in the New States," *Public Administration Review*, XXVIII (September–October 1968), n. 5, 437–444; David H. Bayley, "The Effects of Corruption in a Developing Nation," *Western Political Quarterly*, XIX (December 1966), n. 4, 719–732; O. P. Dwivedi, "The Case for Bureaucratic Corruption," in Michael T. Dalby and Michael S. Werthman, eds., *Bureaucracy in Historical Perspective* (Glenview, Ill., 1971), pp. 88–95.

of the Portuguese empire, observers, both foreign and domestic, remarked upon the venal nature of the magistracy and the ease with which justice could be subverted. The comment of Lord Tyrawley, England's envoy to Lisbon in the 1730's, can serve here as an example; "The Portuguese more than any other people adhere to that rule of Scripture that a gift maketh room for a man, and it is incredible how a present smooths the difficulties of a solicitation; nay they even expect it and though the presents necessary are not considerable, since a few dozen bottles of foreign wine, or a few yards of fine cloth will suffice, yet this often repeated amounts to money." [28] Tyrawley's observations on Portugal could be transferred with little change to the Portuguese colonies. In fact, although the evidence is fragmentary and impressionistic, it appears that the level of colonial corruption had increased over time, so that the complaints registered against magistrates in eighteenth-century Brazil exceeded those of the previous century.

The increasing bureaucratization of the empire and the continual accretion of duties and powers by the desembargadores created ever-greater opportunities for corruption. Magistrates not only controlled the High Court and the lower courts, but as senior officials they also wielded considerable influence on institutions such as the treasury and the mint and the appointative functions of the viceroy. Anyone applying for a clerking or notarial post usually sought a letter of recommendation from a desembargador. Moreover, after 1678 no lawyer could practice in Bahia without certification by the Relação, so that once again the powers of the judges were increased.[29] One need not cite Lord Acton's dictum on power in order to understand how ever-greater responsibilities led to an increase in corruption.

It is important to remember that not all acts considered corrupt

---

28. Cited in Boxer, *Golden Age*, p. 209; C. R. Boxer, "Lord Tyrawley in Lisbon," *History Today*, XX (November 1970), n. 11, 791–798.

29. For examples of desembargador recommendations, see *DHBNR*, XLV (1944), 209–216. On control of lawyers, see AHNRJ, Codice 540 (18 March 1679).

among the bureaucracy were necessarily illegal. Magistrates and other royal officers served under standards designed to improve their efficiency as royal bureaucrats, and thus certain activities might be prohibited to them which while not illegal were considered detrimental to their professional performance. Chief among these restrictions stood the royal legislation forbidding any crown official to trade or carry on commerce in the area of his jurisdiction. This law always proved difficult to enforce, especially among the governors and captains-major, who often viewed their posts as patrimonial positions rather than bureaucratic offices.[30]

Magistrates in Brazil continually disobeyed the restrictions on trade and often carried on business, either in their own name or by using front-men as agents. Laws against such activities stood on the books from the inception of the Relação, but they proved virtually impossible to enforce. In 1720, the crown moved against continual violations of the law by issuing a restatement of the restrictions called the *lei novíssima*.[31] Shortly thereafter, a major investigation was launched by the crown and four Bahian desembargadores were implicated. Two were punished by dismissal from royal service for "doing business in their own name." [32] The two desembargadores, Manoel Ferreira de Carvalho and Afonso Rodrigues Bernardo e Sampaio, had both done previous service in Africa and may have been involved in the slave trade. Bernardo e Sampaio was the New Christian judge discussed in the previous chapter, and there is reason here to suspect that punishment had fallen heavily on him because of his background as well as his crime.[33] Certainly, his punishment did not impress his colleagues,

30. William Delany, "The Development and Decline of Patrimonial and Bureaucratic Administration," *Administrative Science Quarterly*, VII (March 1963), n. 4, 485–501.

31. BGUC, Codice 711, f. 134.

32. *Carta régia* (9 November 1725), "manda riscar do serviço os Dezores Afonso Roiz de São Payo e Manoel Ferreira de Carvalho por se deixarem vencer por Intereses e Respeitos com pouca limpeza de maos e negociarem em seu proprio nome." BGUC, Codice 709, f. 164–164v.

33. See above, pp. 291–293.

for by 1728 the *ouvidor geral* of Bahia complained that the desembargadores continued to conduct business. Little could be done, and as late as 1799 desembargadores were still contrabanding.[34]

Two aspects of magisterial business activities call for some comment. First, a survey of the notary records of Salvador makes it quite clear that the lending and borrowing of money did not violate the anti-commerce legislation. Examples of desembargadores involved in such activities can be found throughout the history of the High Court. Desembargador Francisco Rodrigues da Silva borrowed 250,000 *réis* at the standard 6¼ per cent from the great Bahian financier João de Matos de Aguiar, who made this loan in 1699 against the collateral of the judge's cane fields in Passé.[35] Or, in another case, in 1728 Cosme Rolim de Moura lent 4,000 *cruzados* to Desembargador Luís de Sousa Pereira. In the same year and month Sousa Pereira also lent 2,000 *cruzados* to Colonel Bernardino Cavalcanti de Albuquerque against the collateral of a cattle ranch with 250 head and eight slaves. Both transactions were made at the 6¼ per cent interest rate, the highest figure possible under ecclesiastical definitions of usury, but it is difficult to believe that Sousa Pereira did not intend from hidden interest rates to make a good profit from all this wheeling and dealing.[36] It is significant, however, that these contracts were made in public before an authorized notary. Had they been considered illegal, such would not have been the case.[37]

---

34. *Consulta* CU (7 January 1728), *DHBNR*, XC (1950), 140–141. The revealing report of 1799 is printed in Accioli, *Memórias*, III, 221–222.

35. APB, Livro de Notas 15 (28 May 1699).

36. APB, Livro de Notas 52 (20 October 1728), ff. 104–105v; 51 (10 Oct. 1728), 202v–204.

37. A rather suspicious-looking contract was made in August 1731 between two men, Luís de Mello da Silva and Diogo Pais Pereira, and the Benedictines of Bahia under which the friars leased their fishing smacks, warehouses, slave quarters, and a small farm to the two contractors. In all the contracts of lending and borrowing the magistrates always used their title, Desembargador. In 1731 there was a desembargador named Luís de Mello da Silva and another named Diogo Felipe Pereira. Were they contractors? Did they simply drop the title and make a slight change in

It appears that some forms of commerce were permitted or condoned among the magistracy and that the crown chose to apply the bureaucratic standards selectively. Once again we can turn here to the distinction between law and acceptable behavior. The crown was willing to allow a certain amount of business so long as it did not elicit strong objections from other officials or the colonial population, and so long as it did not prove disruptive to bureaucratic operations. When objections were raised the crown could enforce the existing statutes. Although desembargadores underwent frequent scrutiny and on some occasions were even recalled, only the two above-mentioned magistrates suffered severe punishment for their infractions.[38] Obviously, the frequency of chastisement did not coincide with the incidence of the abuse.

Magistrates often used the power and influence of their office for personal gain, convenience, or to protect their families and dependents. Examples of such behavior can be found throughout the history of the Relação. In 1676 Joseph de Freitas Serrão refused to vacate the houses he rented, despite a notice of eviction, and then prevented his landlord from a hearing in the courts.[39] Caetano Brito de Figueiredo, after borrowing large sums of money to finance his purchase of a sugar mill, cane fields, and jewelry, refused for nine years to pay the debt. When his creditor tried to bring suit, the desembargador used his office to prevent any legal action.[40] Perhaps more serious was the use of magisterial influence

---

the name to cover up their illegal activity? See APB, Livro de Notas 57, ff. 127–131.

38. For example, Desembargadores Luís da Costa Faria, Miguel de Siqueira Castelobranco, Manoel Freyre da Silva, and Antônio Campos de Figueiredo were all recalled to Portugal in 1710. All were acquitted. AHU, Bahia *pap. avul.*, caixa 22 (1st series non-catalogued). Investigations into magisterial behavior always included questions on illicit trade as part of the interrogatório. These exams became so *pro forma* that such abuses were seldom revealed. See APB, Livro de Devassas (1759–1783).

39. Prince regent to Gov. of Brazil (Lisbon, 26 January 1677), APB, *Ord. reg.* I, 37, 37A. For a similar case involving Desembargador Tomás Feliciano de Albernás, see APB, *Ord. reg.* 17 (Lisbon, 6 April 1723).

40. APB, *Ord. reg.* 21, n. 24c.

to undermine the court in instances of felonies committed by a judge's relatives or dependents. We have already seen an example of this procedure in the case of Balthesar Ferraz, but the problem continued after 1652. Jorge Seco, a nephew of Chancellor Jorge Seco de Macedo, murdered a man in Bahia and then fled to the Carmelite monastery in Salvador. Because of his uncle's power and influence, no one would bring him to justice.[41] In 1716 the slaves of Cristóvão Tavares de Morais became involved in a street brawl in front of the desembargador's house. When the local constabulary interceded, one of the officers was wounded in the scramble. At this point the desembargador stepped from his home, staff of office in hand, not to aid the arrest of his slaves, but to free them. The viceroy arrested Tavares de Morais and he was only freed after appeal to the crown.[42]

Often the abuse of office was for direct personal gain. The charges brought by Francisco de Estrada against Desembargador Antônio Rodrigues Banha in 1692 demonstrate the techniques a judge could use to increase his own fortune.[43] Estrada had inherited an *engenho* from his father, but unable to meet his creditors' demands, he placed the mill, its equipment, four dependent cane farms, and forty slaves on the auctioneer's block. When the bidding began, Rodrigues Banha, as magistrate in charge of the auction, insisted that all bids be made in cash. Since there was always very little ready specie in the colony, this extraordinary requirement eliminated most competitors, so that Rodrigues Banha's mother-in-law acquired the property for him at a price far below its market value. Estrada tried to bring suit, but since Rodrigues Banha sat in the Relação nothing could be done. The desembargador, claimed Estrada, had even hired toughs to attack a lawyer working on the case. Not content with this success, Rodrigues Banha then proceeded to pressure Estrada's other creditors to en-

---

41. *Consulta* CU (30 October 1663), AHU, Bahia *pap. avul.*, caixa 8.

42. King to Marquis de Angeja (Lisbon, 8 May 1716), AHU, Codice 247, f. 63v; APB, *Ord. reg.* 10, n. 48.

43. Petition of Francisco de Estrada (undated), BNRJ, II-34, 5, 24.

force payment of his outstanding debts. Estrada, unable to meet these demands, fled to the "bowels of the *sertão*" in order to avoid arrest. There was little else he could do.[44]

The reasons for such behavior varied, but financial pressures and status aspirations contributed to the magistrates' abuse of office for personal gain. Although salaries and perquisites were substantial in relation to those of other officials, desembargadores expected to maintain themselves in a style befitting their rank. The crown had envisioned sober and frugal paragons of simple living, but in a colonial society already known for its ostentation and profligacy, such a life style seemed impossible. Desembargadores often incurred heavy financial burdens. Upon appointment in Portugal, the magistrate had to arrange transport for himself and often for his household as well. After arrival in Salvador, he had to buy or rent lodgings, purchase a sedan chair and a number of slaves, and hire a few domestic servants. After these initial costs, the pressures of maintaining a certain image which reflected his elevated position, and perhaps the pressure exerted by a judge's wife who wished to appear no less affluent than the colonial ladies, drove him into certain abuses.

The story of Agostinho de Azevedo Monteiro provides a thumbnail sketch of the process.[45] He arrived in Bahia in 1659 accompanied by his wife, seven children, a slave woman, and a servant lad. By no means a wealthy man, he was described at the time as not having "eighteen shirts to call his own." Azevedo Monteiro's yearly income as a desembargador came to 400,000 *réis* from which he paid 60,000 *réis* in rent. The remainder did not suffice to support his family for more than half a year. Under such pressure he launched into financial activity. He forcibly sequestered some house sites in Salvador at a price below their market value. Turning then to the Recôncavo, he rented land, slaves, and livestock.

44. Gov. Antônio Luís Gonsalves da Câmara Coutinho to king (Bahia, 15 July 1692), *DHBNR*, XXXIV (1936), 57–60. This letter supported Rodrigues Banha and dismissed the incident.

45. *Consulta* CU (8 August 1675), *DHBNR*, LXXXVIII (1950), 48–50.

He held this property for six years without paying a cent, and when the owner initiated a suit, Azevedo Monteiro used his influence to delay proceedings. This practice worked so well that he decided to do it again, renting cane fields, harvesting a sugar crop, and then refusing to pay rent to the owner. By 1675, the *câmara* of Salvador complained that this once poor magistrate now owned twenty-seven slaves worth 1,200 *milréis*, to say nothing of horses, oxen, and tools. Little wonder that Azevedo Monteiro never sought promotion in Portugal and was content to remain in his Brazilian post for sixteen years.

Azevedo Monteiro's career indicates that graft was not simply a response to financial pressures, a result of low salaries and high expenses. Even when such pressures had lessened and when a magistrate could live comfortably, he continued to use his office for personal gain. The position of the desembargadores at the fulcrum of power offered opportunities which few men—whether well or poorly paid—could ignore. The judges saw the disparity between their rank and their income. Magisterial class aspirations lay not only in achieving status equal to that of the nobility, but in acquiring the material benefits and symbols which traditionally accompanied that status.

Although desembargadores engaged in business and sometimes owned fee-earning minor offices, their primary goal was the acquisition of landed property.[46] Landed wealth rather than noble lineage created the Brazilian aristocracy, and it is, therefore, not surprising to find magistrates in Brazil driving for the ownership of a sugar plantation or cane farm. Some desembargadores held *sesmarias*, but the majority obtained their lands through purchase, inheritance, or dowry. They seem to have preferred Recôncavo sugar lands. Luís de Sousa Pereira owned sugar lands in Cachoeira and Iguape; Pedro de Unhão Castelobranco in São Francisco do Conde; and Dionísio de Azevedo e Arevalos in Paripe. This last

46. For example, João Elizeu de Sousa owned a treasury office in Cachoeira. ANTT, *Chan João V, Doações*, liv. 78, f. 63v.

judge eventually managed his mother-in-law's plantation, Engenho Jacarancanga, which had belonged to her husband, Desembargador Antônio Rodrigues Banha.[47] Brazilian-born judges like João de Góes e Araújo usually exceeded their colleagues in property ownership, acquiring land through grant, inheritance, and purchase.[48] Land gave the magistrates wealth and status equal to their aspirations.

The acquisition of an independent source of income, however, weakened the force of professional motivations and bureaucratic restrictions. A magistrate who made a fortune in Brazil might have little interest in an eventual promotion. Graft created its own closed circle. A desembargador violated the bureaucratic regulations in order to obtain wealth or land, and having done this, the laws designed to prevent such behavior and channel him toward professional goals became decreasingly important. Bureaucratic constraints weakened as a man accumulated more wealth and property, and consequently each venal act facilitated its successor.

Brazilians rarely complained against magisteral ownership of land or accumulation of wealth, for society's standards were not those of the bureaucracy. Many of the colonists had come to Brazil to seek their fortunes and they did not object to magistrates doing the same. What concerned the colonists, however, was the outright misuse of office for personal ends, the subversion of justice through bribery and favoritism, and the selfish abuse of power. Such activities were unjust by colonial and bureaucratic standards alike.

Of all magisterial abuses, the one that drew the most severe contemporary condemnation was the outright sale of justice. Gregório de Matos had written against the subversion of justice through bribes and the manner in which venal judges could sell the High

47. APB, Livro de Notas 100, f. 240–243; Livro do Notas 30, f. 119v.–122v.; Livro de Notas 99, ff. 233–38v.; Livro de Notas 25, f. 168.

48. João de Góes e Araújo owned sugar lands in the Recôncavo. He also received at least two *sesmarias*. See the grants of 1679 and 1683 in *Publicações do Arquivo Nacional*, XXVII (1931), 69, 77. On his *engenhos*, see ANTT, *Chan. Afonso VI, Doações*, Liv. 20, f. 250.

Court's integrity. Rumors about such behavior became common coin but evidence was hard to come by. It was said that Fernão da Maia Furtado accepted bribes and gave legal council to the same people on whom he passed judgment.[49] An investigation of his activities made in 1655 revealed nothing, and he remained in office until his retirement in 1663. The pervasiveness of this type of corruption is suggested in a letter of 1799 which casts some light on earlier times. The Governor of Bahia reported that a local sugar planter annually sent all the desembargadores a few crates of sugar "as has been done in all times past, and is now being done by others in this city." [50]

Colonials particularly objected to the fact that very little could be done to stop or to punish these magisterial abuses. Although competition and enmity existed among the desembargadores, friendship and cooperation created the more usual pattern. Royal ordinances sponsored social interaction among the judges by placing limitations on other social options. Moreover, shared professional attitudes, common backgrounds, and similar interests all drew the magistrates toward cooperation with their colleagues on the bench. How could a local merchant or planter sue a desembargador when the judge's friends, colleagues, and *compadres* all sat in the tribunal which heard the case? One example should suffice. In 1681 João Rodrigues dos Reis brought charges against the actions of a desembargador but a year and half had passed without any decision. Rodrigues dos Reis claimed that the chancellor had not acted, nor would he act, because of "the particular friendship with which he treats the accused, ordinarily going about in his company." In fact, he asked that the *provedor-mór* conduct the investigation since the "other judges are ill-disposed to the plaintiff because the accused is a desembargador." [51]

49. *Consulta* CU (4 March 1655), AHU, Bahia *pap. avul.* caixa 6 (1st series uncatalogued).

50. APB, Cartas do Governo 39, f. 154v. The author wishes to thank M. Daniel Teysseire for this reference.

51. AHU, Bahia *pap. avul.*, caixa 14 (30 June 1681).

Judges considered "suspect" or personally involved in a case were sometimes removed, but such measures must have been ineffective in a situation in which the ties of interest and friendship were many and the number of judges few. Frustration with this situation and jealousy sometimes led to violent attacks on the desembargadores. In 1693, seven men were charged with laying an ambush for Desembargador João de Sousa. The accused men pleaded for a change of venue, claiming that de Sousa and another desembargador were their personal enemies, and had trumped up these charges.[52] In 1734, an assassin murdered Desembargador Luís de Sousa Pereira while he dined at his estate in Iguape.[53] Such attacks constituted the ultimate form of colonial criticism.

Bribery, graft, and malfeasance drew both royal and colonial censure, but such activity was not the only form of magisterial behavior that violated the bureaucratic code of performance. As we noted in Chapter Eight, primary relationships linked the desembargadores to society and created pressures which could impinge on their professional performance. The tendencies already noted in the period 1609–1626 continued to prevail after 1652. The myriad associational and ritualized primary relations of the desembargadores were limited only by the often-disregarded prohibitions and by existing social distinctions which concentrated these contacts among certain strata of society. Shared interests, cooperation in some task, a business arrangement, mutual membership in an organization, and even a common life style created a web of associational contact which violated the theoretical isolation of the magistracy. In addition, a second layer of primary relations formed by consanguinity, affinal kinship, marriage, and ritual god-parentage were usually ritualized within the Church.[54] These tended to

52. APB, *Ord. reg.* 2 (7 February 1693).

53. *Consulta* CU (20 September 1734), *DHBNR*, XCI (1951), 20–30.

54. The literature on kinship is extensive but generally ahistorical in nature. Aside from the work of Wagley, cited above, three articles have proven most helpful. They are: S. N. Eisenstadt, "Ritualized Personal Relations," *Man*, N. 96 (July 1936), 90–95; Conrad Kottak, "Kinship and

become accumulative, so that once one such connection had been established, others almost invariably followed. Ritualized relationships also had a tendency to extend across generations, giving them a permanency not found in the associational connections. Both associational and ritualized contacts exerted strong pressures on the operation of government in colonial Brazil.

One example can perhaps reveal the whole universe of these ties, and by doing so demonstrate not only their existence, but their complexity as well. In 1681, Manoel Pais de Costa married Isabel d'Avila, but the girl's mother, the widow Catherina Fogaça, claimed that her daughter had been carried off unwillingly.[55] An investigation was begun but da Costa complained that he had little hope of a fair hearing since there were "great reasons to suspect the judges of that state because of the affinity and family ties (*affinidade e parentesco*) between Catherina Fogaça and Tomé Pereira Falcão who [had] many desembargadores of that Relação as his supporters and friends (*parciaes e amigos*)." Here we see not only the threat of personal relations in the judgment of a case, but also that this influence could be transmitted to relatives, so that direct contact with the desembargadores was not even necessary so long as some friend or relative had access to the "resource" of influence.

This example also indicates the level of society in which these relations were most likely to be found. Catherina Fogaça was no destitute widow, but a member of the Dias d'Avila family, owners of great tracts of land north of Salvador and also the São Francisco River and one of the most powerful clans of colonial Brazil.[56] Tomé Pereira Falcão was her brother-in-law. This Bahian gentle-

---

Class in Brazil," *Ethnology*, VI (1967), n. 4, 427–443; Sidney W. Mintz and Eric R. Wolf, "An Analysis of Ritual Co-Parenthood (*compadrazgo*)" *Southwestern Journal of Anthropology*, VI (Winter 1950), n. 4, 341–368.

55. *Parecer* of CU, AHU, Bahia *pap. avul.* caixa 14 (30 January 1680); (17 March 1681).

56. On Catherina Fogaça and the Dias d'Avila family see Pedro Calmon, *História da Casa da Tôrre*, 2nd ed. (Rio de Janeiro, 1958).

men, so well-connected with the desembargadores of the Relação, was the son of a sugar planter, captain of Iguape in the Recôncavo, and as alderman of the *câmara* of Salvador in 1671 had defended the right of Brazilians to serve in the Relação.[57] Undoubtedly the most common and effective personal contacts were those established between the magistrates and the sugar-planter and cattle-rancher elite of Brazil, especially those in the captaincy of Bahia. Certainly such relations also existed between the judges and people of lower social rank, but since there could be little exchange of "favors" in a superior-inferior relationship, one suspects that these had far less impact on judicial behavior.

It is only fair to note the reverse of these primary relations: dislike, competition, and enmity could result as easily from them as could friendship and cooperation. There was no guarantee that kinship or mutual participation in the Misericórdia always bred respect or amity. Nevertheless, a desembargador who acted professionally out of spite or hate, in contradiction to the laws and merits of the case, introduced nonbureaucratic criteria into the operation of government just as surely as a judge who acted out of friendship.

The extended family lay at the heart of these relations. In Brazil the number of elite families—those of noble origins, descendants of first colonists, and the wealthy sugar or cattle oligarchy—remained limited. Frei Antônio de Santa Maria Jaboatão's eighteenth-century genealogy of Bahian families listed only 148 separate lineages, and at any given point in time the number was always less than that.[58] The infusion of suitable new blood from Portugal did not really present a viable alternative; the metropolitan population

57. *Ibid.*, 79–81.

58. Genealogical analysis in this chapter is based on Jaboatão's *Catalogo genealógico* as reorganized and presented by Afonso Costa in "Genealogia baiana," *RIHGB*, CXCI (1946), 1–279, hereafter cited as Costa, "Genealogia;" and "Achegas genealógicas," *Revista do Instituto Histórico e Geográfico da Bahia* LXI (1935), 69–460. For Pernambuco see Borges da Fonseca, "Nobilarchia pernambucana," *ABNR*, XLVII (1925), XLVIII (1926).

was small, and those Portuguese who did migrate to Brazil usually came from social categories with which the vainglorious Brazilians would have no truck. Thus the total of possible unions was small, and the genealogical trees of the colony became gnarled and twisted in a thicket of constant cousin marriages. Indicative of these familial convolutions is the manner in which names began to lengthen. A simple "João de Sousa" of the sixteenth century had become a "João de Sousa Pacheco de Carvalho" by the eighteenth century, as patronyms were employed to distinguish family branches and avoid possible confusion. Because wealth, property, power, and influence often became available to an individual as a direct result of these ties, it became imperative that members of this social stratum be able to identify relatives to a distant degree. It is an art not entirely dead in Brazil today.

Marriage served as the principal link between families and the most effective method of incorporating magistrates into local society on a permanent basis. The attractions of bringing a desembargador into the family were many. First, increasing limitations on the number of possible family combinations imposed by existing ties of blood and inter-family feuds made the desembargadores especially welcome, for unlike many Portuguese immigrants the judges were socially acceptable by virtue of their position. The robe of the desembargador obscured his origins. Of the fifteen Portuguese-born magistrates who married in Brazil and for whom we have information on their social origins, none were *fidalgos;* seven came from *letrado* backgrounds, and five were the sons of merchants or soldiers. Certainly, the judges' peninsular origins cannot have played a role in attracting the Bahian oligarchy. Instead, the judges seemed to offer power and prestige of direct benefit to the family while they sat in the colony, and on return to Portugal might even bring a Brazilian family new metropolitan ties, property, and influence.

The desembargadores, for their part, could view a colonial marriage as an opportunity to acquire wealth and property concomitant to the social rank to which they aspired. Did Antônio Rodrigues Banha marry Maria Francisca de Vasconcellos because she would inherit the Engenho Jacarancanga? How much influence did the enormous dowry of 24,000 *milréis* exert on Desembargador Tomás Feliciano Albernás' selection of Colonel João Teixeira de Sousa's daughter as his wife? [59] These are questions that cannot be answered, but they point out the plausible reasons of such unions. Love cannot be dismissed, but in this social system women brought additional resources into the kindred and were therefore carefully secluded and manipulated for family goals, a situation which tended to preclude amorous matches.[60]

Although the law of 1610 prohibited these marriages and despite the fact that most desembargadores came to Brazil as mature men already married, almost 20 per cent (32 of 168) of the magistrates wed Brazilian women. Most judges obtained the necessary permit before marrying in the colony, but the increase in these unions at the beginning of the eighteenth century caused considerable royal concern. In 1706 the crown ordered the Desembargo do Paço to refrain from seeking these permits for overseas magistrates. This policy was soon discarded, however, when the crown discovered that magistrates would marry with or without permission. This became clear in 1728 when two judges of the Relação did just that.[61] Bernardo de Sousa Estrela married in Bahia against the expressed wishes of the crown, and the Conselho Ultramarino wanted him publicly disgraced as an example to others. The judge escaped this punishment, but his retirement in 1730 may have been due to recognition that his superiors did not favor his advancement.[62] Francisco de Santa Barbara e Moura had been granted a permit to marry while on service in Angola, and he had claimed that it was

59. APB, Livro de Notas 37 (20 August 1722), f. 220, deals with the Engenho Jacarancanga. The dowry arrangements of Albernas are recorded in Livro de Notas 59 (18 June 1734).

60. William Goode, "The Theoretical Importance of Love," *American Sociological Review*, XXIV (1959), 38–47.

61. King to Desembargo do Paço (Alcântara 16 August 1706), *Cadaval*, II, 58–59; Pereira de Costa, *Anais*, IV, 514; BGUC, Cod. 711, f. 330.

62. *Consulta* CU (30 October 1728), *DHBNR*, XC (1950), 171–173.

valid for Brazil as well.[63] Although some of his colleagues wanted him dismissed, his later promotions indicate that the crown took no action against him. In 1734, the crown, realizing the difficulties of controlling this situation, threatened to expel any judge who married in Brazil without the special permit.[64] Similar marriages can be found into the nineteenth century, but their frequency appears to have decreased after the 1740's.

While the social origins of all the brides cannot be determined, the existing sample (12 of 34) indicates that these women came from two elements of the colonial population. The daughters or widows of other royal officials were theoretically unencumbered by colonial ties and thus suitable as brides for the desembargadores. But, because royal officials constantly participated in colonial life, marriage to their daughters created the same complications as marriage to the child of a sugar planter, the other group from which the judges chose their spouses. The social origins of the brides, listed in Appendix II, should be of little surprise if we view these unions as an exchange of magisterial prestige and power for access to the wealth and property of colonial families. It should also be noted that a number of the brides were widows. Given the average age of the desembargadores, it is likely that many were marrying for a second time. Second marriages raise questions as to the possible influence and linkages of a magistrate to his step-children, but there are presently no answers for these.

Another area which defies analysis is the existence of illicit sexual relations. Obviously such information is difficult to obtain, but occasional references to concubinage and homosexuality among the desembargadores, reports of magisterial "donjuanism," and the recognition of illegitimate children all point to the existence of these relations.[65] The extent to which these ties influenced pat-

63. *Assento* (27 November 1728), AHNRJ, Codice 540; BGUC, Codice 708, f. 27.

64. BGUC, Codice 711, f. 330.

65. Desembargador Belchior de Sousa Villas Boas fathered an illegitimate son who was born to a single woman of good family. ANTT, *Chan. João V*,

terns of influence and patronage is difficult to determine, for while lacking legal recognition, they might be more intimate and lasting than formal relations. One thing is certain: the desembargadores could maintain an active sex life in the colony, and the arms of mulatto girls, young cadets, and lonely dowagers opened to them.

In Portuguese society the number of linkages could be increased by creating ties of fictive kinship. This was normally done through the Church-sanctioned institution of ritual kinship (*compadrio*). By serving as godparents at a baptism or witness at a wedding, an individual created a series of ties not only between himself and his godchild or the wedded couple, but with their natural parents as well. Ties of *compadrio* placed genuine obligations on the parties involved, and were in fact considered to create degrees of affinity which prohibited sexual union.[66] *Compadrio* could establish primary relations between an inferior and a superior, such as between a sugar planter and his tenant, but often they were used to create ties between people of similar social standing, or to reinforce existing ties of consanguinity or friendship. Unlike the marriage tie which directly linked a judge to only one family, or at least to one family at a time, fictive relations were theoretically unlimited. A desembargador could become *compadre* as often as he was asked, if he so desired. Thus fictive kinship presented in quantative terms an even greater threat to judicial disinterest than did ties of blood and marriage. But if judges were to live within a society, to marry, and to have children, then Church doctrine called for, and the crown had to permit, the creation of these ties.

The social genealogy of a desembargador, the web of both kin and other primary relations, simply constitutes a series of possible

---

Legitimações, 133, f. 30–30v. For an example in the 1780's, see Wanderley Pinho, *História*, p. 111. Gregório de Matos criticized "Rabo da Vaca's" skirt-chasing (*obras completas*). The damning report of 1799 on the Relação contains a Sodom and Gomorrah-like description of magisterial sex life (Accioli, *Memórias*, III, 221–222).

66. Francis X. Wahl, *The Matrimonial Impediments of Consanguinity and Affinity*. The Catholic University of America, Canon Law Studies, n. 90 (Washington, D.C., 1936).

primary influences on his professional behavior.[67] In most cases it is impossible to determine the motivations of a particular decision even when evidence exists which points to primary relations. The desembargadores, like most men, acted in response to a mixture of motivations which, because of certain subconscious assumptions and rationalizations, they did not fully grasp themselves. Thus, the identification of primary relations simply adds another variable, albeit an important one, to the mixture. Kinship analysis has other limitations. As descendants of Adam, all men are, at least allegorically, related. In colonial Brazil, where the number of settlers was limited, family ties eventually connected all the elite clans, so that even the bitterest rivals might find a common ancestor in their family trees. Thus each individual chose from the total of blood, marriage, and ritual ties a certain number of individuals whom he considered to be his relatives. The extended kindred, therefore, was an "ego-oriented construct," an individual's calculation of those bonds which he considered operative. Thus, genealogical description can, at best, establish only a range of possibilities.

In view of these limitations, it is still possible to note some tendencies in the linkages between desembargadores and Brazilian society. Certain Bahian families seemed to favor connections to the magistracy almost, it would seem, as a matter of policy. Thus, in the social genealogies of three important families, the Cavalcanti de Albuquerques, Rocha Pittas, and Ferrão Castelobrancos, most of the distinguishing characteristics of a magisterial connection can be seen.

---

67. This term is used and explained by Anthony Leeds in "Brazilian Careers and Social Structure: An Evolutionary Model and a Case History," *American Anthropologist*, LXVI (December 1964), 1329. This excellent study of informal groupings in contemporary Brazil suggests approaches to the historian, but Leeds admits: "one can discover this informal organization only through field work, not through published sources. But without knowing this organization, one cannot understand how Brazil functions, economically or politically." The historian, unable to interview the subjects of his study, cannot reconstruct the operative kindred or group by sociometric analysis. (See J. L. Moreno, *Who Shall Survive*, Washington, D.C.,

The Cavalcanti de Albuquerque family was among the most powerful and largest in northern Brazil, and among the most prestigious. Its lineage could be traced to the donataries of Pernambuco, to a Florentine gentleman, Felipe Cavalcanti, who fled to Brazil to escape the wrath of Cosmo de Medici, and to a Flemish nobleman, Arnau de Holanda, who was among the first settlers of Pernambuco. The family had spread throughout the northern captaincies of Brazil and one branch had been established in Bahia since the period of the Dutch War. Cavalcanti connections to the High Court had existed during the period of the first Relação through the marriage of Manoel Pinto da Rocha to a girl of the Pernambucan branch, and as Figure 5 demonstrates, these ties also developed after 1652.[68]

Colonel Cristóvão Cavalcanti de Albuquerque, a wealthy and distinguished Bahian landowner, married Isabel de Aragão, the daughter of a *senhor de engenho* who counted among her aunts and uncles the *alcaide-mór* and the wife of Jerónimo Sodré Pereira, another wealthy plantation owner, military man, and sometime *provedor* of the Misericórdia of Salvador.[69] The union of Cristóvão Cavalcanti de Albuquerque and Isabel de Aragão produced three children: Antônio Cavalcanti, Ana de Aragão, and Joana Calvalcanti de Albuquerque. Antônio owned properties in Cachoeira but earned a reputation as a high-living and tough young blade who sired a number of bastards. His misadventures apparently lay behind his murder, which some said had been ordered by his father to protect the family name. The other children lived more orderly lives. Ana de Aragão married Sebastião da Rocha Pitta, the noted historian. Joana married three times: she first wed Colonel Francisco Pereira Botelho, and after his death she married Desembargador José de Sá de Mendonça in 1690. Upon his death, she married one of his colleagues, Desembargador Bernardo de Sousa

---

1934.) The best he can do is to establish probabilities and present examples based on sound data.

68. See above pp. 178–180.

69. Costa, "Genealogia," 17–24.

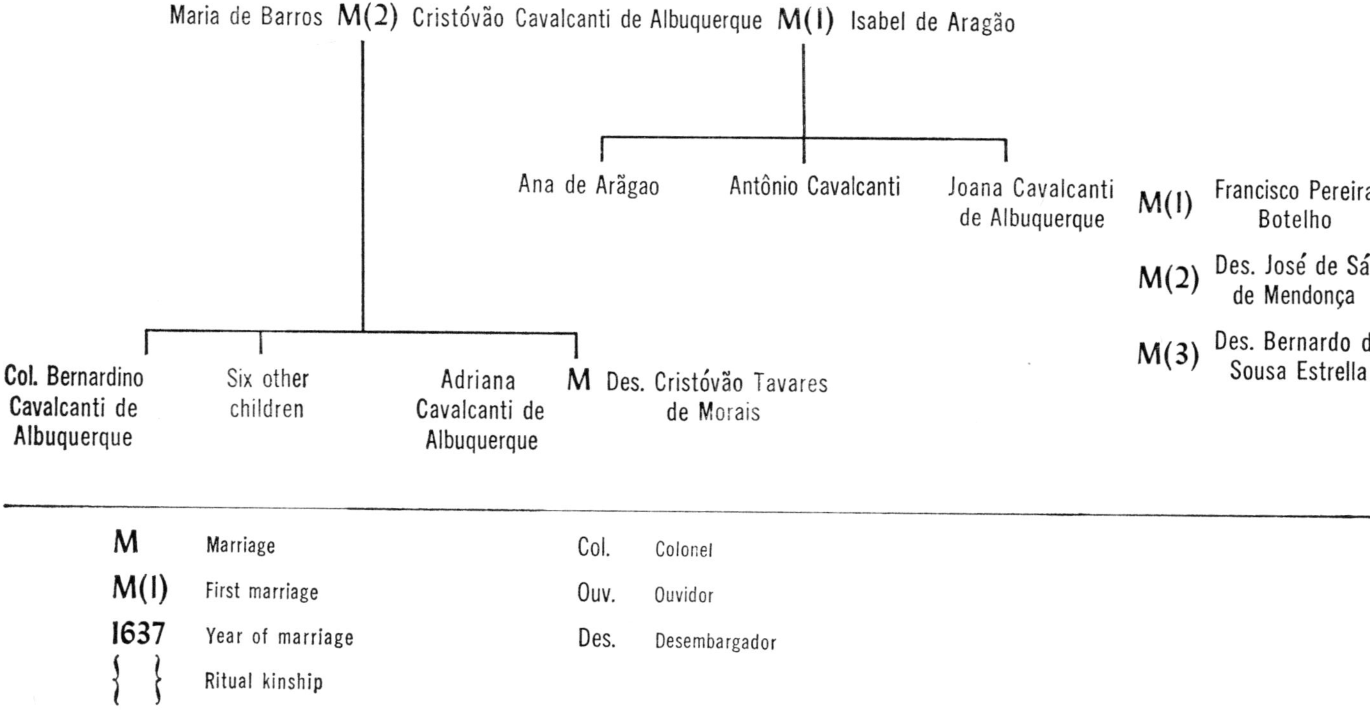

Fig. 5. The Cavalcanti de Albuquerque—Magistracy Connections.

Estrela in 1721. This third match produced two children, both of whom owned properties and held military posts in Cachoeira.

Meanwhile Isabel de Aragão had died and Cristóvão Cavalcanti de Albuquerque had remarried. This second union resulted in eight children, among them Adriana Cavalcanti de Albuquerque, who married Desembargador Cristóvão Tavares de Morais, and Colonel Bernardino Cavalcanti de Albuquerque, a wealthy plantation owner.[70] Thus, three desembargadores were linked by marriage to the kinship group of the Cavalcanti de Albuquerques and through them to other notable Bahian families such as the Rocha Pittas, the Vieira Ravascos, and the Araújos. It is impossible to determine to what extent the ties of kinship influenced the actions of the judges or to what degree of distance kinship ties remained in force; but given the importance of the family and the many references to the influence of ascriptive roles on bureaucratic behavior, it seems safe to assume that the influence was considerable. Not only did kinship influence bureaucratic performance, but through ties of association and friendship, the links of blood and marriage could stimulate other relations. It is not surprising, therefore, to find Colonel Bernardino Cavalcanti de Albuquerque, brother-in-law of a desembargador, borrowing money in 1728 from Luís de Sousa Pereira,[71] another desembargador.

The Rocha Pitta genealogy reveals multiple magisterial connections through birth or marriage to the Brazilian planter class and also provides an example of how these ties could reach back to the metropolis. The Rocha Pitta lineage defied even the efforts of contemporary genealogists, and the exact relationship of the three branches of the family remains cloudy. Of particular interest is that branch linked to the Pernambucan family of da Penha Deusdará. During the Dutch War, Manoel Álvares da Penha had earned the nickname "Deusdará" (God will provide) for the supplies he pro-

70. ASCMB, A/1/3 Livro de Termo (21 June 1705), f. 118.
71. APB, Livro de Notas 51 (10 October 1728), 202v.–204.

vided to the Luso-Brazilian forces in Pernambuco.[72] His efforts earned him not only this soubriquet, which he incorporated into the family name, but also the crown's gratitude as expressed in a title of nobility with coat of arms and ownership of the lucrative office of *provedor* of the Customshouse of Pernambuco. The crown's appreciation of these services probably lay behind the appointment in 1653 of Manoel's son, Simão Álvares da Penha Deusdará, as the first Brazilian-born desembargador. In 1637, Simão had married Leonarda Vieira Ravasco, who as we have seen above was the sister of Padre Antônio Vieira. Simão, his wife, children, and sister moved to Bahia, where he took up his duties as desembargador of the Relação, holding at the same time the customs house office which his father had passed on to him.[73]

In Baia, Simão Álvares arranged a suitable marriage for his sister, Francisca da Penha Deusdará, with Simão da Fonseca de Siqueira, the owner of Engenho Caboto in the Recôncavo parish of Matoim. Shortly thereafter, the desembargador, his wife, mother, and children died in a shipwreck, leaving only his sister to carry the family name through her daughter, Aldonça da Penha Deusdará.[74]

Aldonça wed the widower Antônio da Rocha Pitta, whose story is a colonial epic in itself. He had come out from Portugal at the request of a childless uncle who owned some cane fields in Iguape. These lands may have been attached to the plantation of Tomé Pereira Falcão. While there, he fell in love with the owner's niece and in 1678 eloped with the girl against her family's wishes, being shot at and wounded in the process. Through inheritance of his uncle's lands and by some good fortune, Antônio soon became one of the wealthiest men in the captaincy of Bahia and one of the five largest landowners in the whole Northeast. His properties included

72. Costa, "Genealogia," 832; ANTT, Lectura dos Bachareís, maço 5, n. 40 (1645). See Wanderley Pinho, *História,* pp. 91–102, for a discussion of the Rocha Pittas.

73. ANTT, *Chan. João V., Doações,* liv. 26, f. 112.

74. Wanderley Pinho, *História,* p. 97.

sesmarias north of Salvador, cane fields in Iguape, at least one ship in the slave trade, and the Engenho Freguesia in Matoim which bordered Fonseca de Siqueira's Engenho Caboto. Bahian society recognized his success by granting him entry into the prestigious Third Order of the Franciscans and by electing him *provedor* of the Misericórdia in 1700.[75]

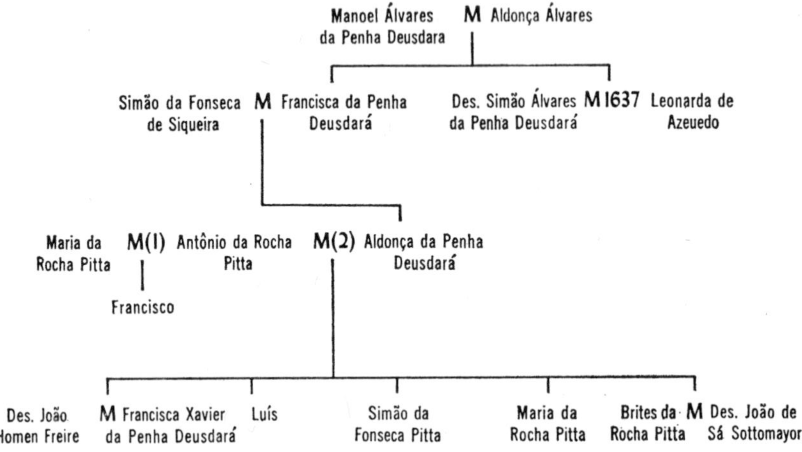

Fig. 6. The Penha Deusdará—Magistracy Connections.

From his impetuous marriage to Tomé Pereira Falcão's niece, Maria de Rocha Pitta (probably a distant cousin), one son was born. This boy, Francisco, later married his mother's uncle's daughter—that is, the child of Tomé Pereira Falcão—indicating perhaps that a family reconciliation had been reached. Upon the death of his first wife, however, Antônio da Rocha Pitta sought a second marriage, choosing as his bride Aldonça da Penha Deusdará, the daughter of the Engenho Caboto's owner. It is from this second match that new magisterial connections can be traced. (See Figure 6.)

75. Costa, "Genealogia," 133; Russell-Wood, *Fidalgos*, pp. 110, 118–119; Wanderley Pinho, *História*, pp. 91–95; Calmon, *História da Casa da Tôrre*, pp. 79–80, 139–140.

Aldonça da Penha Deusdará and Antônio da Rocha Pitta had five children. Two of the daughters married desembargadores of the Bahian tribunal, who were undoubtedly attracted by the wealth and social position of their father-in-law. One of these judges, João Homem Freire, married Francisca Xavier in 1723. He later returned to Portugal accompanied by his wife and his unmarried sister-in-law, Maria da Rocha Pitta. There, he arranged her marriage to his nephew, who held an entailed estate near Coimbra. The ties established in Brazil could and did reach back to the metropolis.[76]

By tracing, through Figure 7, the primary relations of the third family, the Ferrão Castelobrancos, it is possible to see how the marriage of a desembargador and his establishment in Brazil might forge a series of horizontal ties with others of his own generation as well as creating vertical links through his descendants. A magistrate's marriage could result in the creation of a new elite family subject to alliance or competition with other colonial kindreds, and which might at some future date seek once again the magisterial connection.

Pedro de Unhão Castelobranco had entered the Relação in 1686 after serving as *ouvidor geral* in Rio de Janeiro, where he had been denounced by the Governor of the Captaincy in a traditional executive-judiciary squabble. These charges had not prevented Castelobranco's promotion to the High Court.[77] In Salvador, he wed Lisbon-born Damiana Francisca da Silva and settled down in his seaside mansion as a dominant figure in Bahian society at the close of the seventeenth century. His marriage produced two children and through their lives we can begin to understand the dynamic interaction of kinship, power, and wealth.

Pedro de Unhão Castelobranco's daughter, Maria Francisca, contracted an excellent marriage to Antônio Gomes. The bridegroom was a knight of the Order of Christ, *moço fidalgo*, the brother-in-

76. ASCMB, A/1/3 Livro de Termo (21 February 1723); Costa, "Genealogia," 136–137.

77. *Autos de Correições*, I, 74–77; Coaracy, 196.

law of Salvador Correia de Sá of Rio de Janeiro, and son of Pedro Gomes, a distinguished soldier and provisional governor of Rio de Janeiro (1681–1682).[78] Desembargador Unhão Castelobranco's experience in the southern captaincies had probably led to this connection, and here we see the network of primary relations extending from region to region. The wedding was a social event of some importance. The Governor of Brazil, Matias de Cunha, and the wife of *carioca* Desembargador Francisco da Silveira Sottomayor served as witnesses to the ceremony, thus establishing ties of ritual god-parentage to both the newlyweds and their parents.[79] Eventually, Maria Francisca married again, this time to a desembargador of the Casa da Suplicação in Portugal.

Maria Francisca's brother, Antônio Ferrão Castelobranco, pursued a career of arms, eventually becoming a lieutenant-general and governor of São Tomé. While in Bahia, Antônio Ferrão became a wealthy and respected gentleman whose social rank was such that he was a leading candidate for the office of *provedor* of the Misericórdia in the period 1717–1720, a position hotly contested by his major opponent, Gonçalo Ravasco Cavalcanti de Albuquerque. The competition of Antônio Ferrão and Gonçalo Ravasco was in some ways representative of the struggle of two major Bahian families, both of which had close ties to the magistracy. Antônio Ferrão won the office in 1718, the same position his father had won in 1693. Using his influence in the Misericórdia, Antônio Ferrão began to provide for his family.[80]

Antônio Ferrão's marriage produced six children. One son, João Ferrão, entered the Jesuit Order; another died at an early age; one daughter married; and three others entered convents in Portugal. In order to supply the dowries needed to place these daughters in religious institutions, Antônio Ferrão had obtained 300 *milréis* from the Misericórdia. Since the Misericórdia was supposed to provide

---

78. Costa, "Genealogia," 195–196.
79. *Ibid.*
80. Russell-Wood, *Fidalgos*, pp. 112, 189.

dowries only for poor girls, complaints were made and in 1728 the governing board tried to revoke the grants.[81] Antônio Ferrão, in Portugal at this time, brought the case before the Casa da Suplicação, which ruled in his favor and forced the Misericórdia to stand by its previous arrangement. The decision of the Lisbon tribunal should not be surprising, since Antônio Ferrão's brother-in-law, Jerônimo da Costa de Almeida, was a judge in that court.

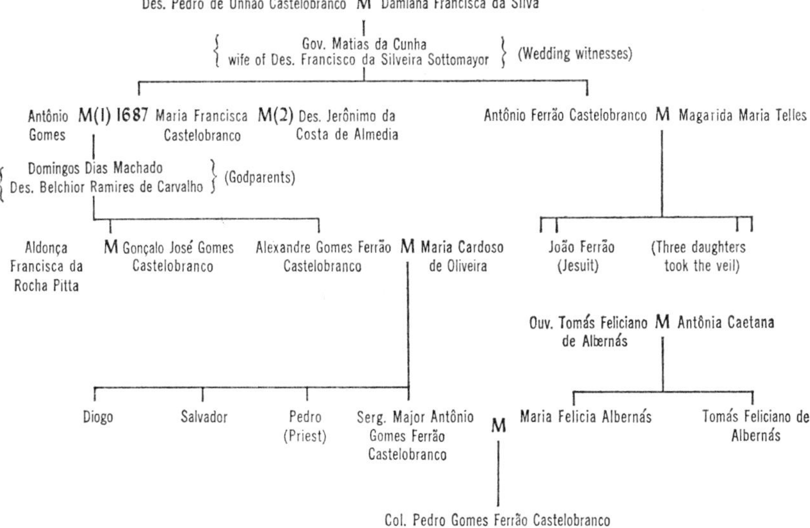

Fig. 7. The Family of Desembargador Pedro de Unhão Castelobranco.

Desembargador Pedro de Unhão Castelobranco's grandchildren through his daughter established the Castelobranco name as a permanent element in Bahian society. Maria Francisa bore Antônio Gomes two sons. The elder, Alexandre Gomes Ferrão Castelobranco, held the *fidalgo* title and became a knight in the Order of Christ. He served as a colonel of militia and eventually established his extensive holdings on the São Francisco River as an entailed estate. The younger son, Gonçalo José Gomes Castelobranco, also had *fidalgo* rank. His baptismal sponsors had been Desembargador

81. *Ibid.*, pp. 189–190.

Belchior Ramires de Carvalho and Domingos Dias Machado, the bastard son and only heir of Antônio Pais de Aragão, a fabulously wealthy scion of the powerful Garcia de Aragão family.[82] Ritual godparentage now tied these men to the Unhão Castelobranco family. Gonçalo José later married Aldonça Francisca da Rocha Pitta, from a family with its own magisterial connections.

The fourth generation can be traced through the four sons of Alexandre Gomes Ferrão Castelobranco. Little information remains on the lives of his sons Diogo and Salvador, but Pedro became a priest. Antônio, the eldest son, inherited the entail on the São Francisco and became a true *poderoso da terra* as sergeant-major of a colonial regiment and alderman of the *câmara* of Salvador in 1755. Antônio chose as his wife Maria Felicia de Albernás, the daughter of Tomás Feliciano Albernás, *ouvidor* of Sergipe and eventually desembargador of Bahia—once again, the magisterial connection. These ties of kinship eventually enabled Tomás Feliciano de Albernás' son and namesake to rent from his brother-in-law the Engenho Paporiu in São Francisco do Conde at a very reasonable rate.[83] The story can be brought to the end of the eighteenth century in the person of Pedro Gomes Ferrão Castelobranco, the son of Antônio and Maria Felicia, who inherited the entail, became a militia colonel, alderman of Salvador in 1785 and a powerful man at the close of the century.[84] Here was a colonial clan with both magisterial origins and connections.

If any one group of desembargadores consistently violated the bureaucratic prohibitions against local involvement, it was surely the ten Brazilian-born magistrates. These men came to the High Court with pre-existing ties of familiarity, friendship, and family in the colony. Four married Brazilian women, thereby increasing the range of their personal contacts. The fathers of the Brazilian-born magistrates belonged either to the colonial landed elite or had

82. Arquivo da Curia Metropolitana do Salvador, Paroquia de Vitória, Batizados (1630–1713); Costa, "Genealogia," 116.

83. APB, Livro de Notas 100, f. 240–243 (1758).

84. Costa, "Genealogia," 116.

served as royal officials in Brazil. As we have seen, it was impossible to distinguish between these two categories in many cases. The difference in their fathers' social standing or occupation had no appreciable effect on the performance of these judges. Desembargador Antônio Rodrigues Banha, son and grandson of desembargadores, and Luís de Sousa Pereira, son of Desembargador Luís de Sousa, participated in the colony's social and economic life with the same vigor as João de Góes e Araújo or João Rodrigues Campelo, sons of the sugar elite.

The extent of magisterial involvement with colonial society fostered by the appointment of Brazilians to the Relação can be seen in the fascinating story of Desembargador Cristóvão de Burgos Contreiras.[85] Born in Bahia probably between 1615 and 1618, Burgos was the son of Maria Pacheco and Jerônimo de Burgos, a *letrado* who held various minor bureaucratic posts in the colony. Moreover, Jerônimo de Burgos was a respected member of Bahian society, a brother of the Misericórdia and in 1633 an alderman of the town council.[86] Young Cristóvão was sent to Coimbra, where he received a bachelor's degree in civil law; in 1644 he entered the royal employ. After a tour of duty as *juiz de fóra* of Ponta Delgada in the Azores, he returned to Brazil where in November 1651 he married the widow Helena da Silva Pimentel. This lady was the daughter of Bernardo Pimentel de Almeida, a planter and sometime member of the town council of Salvador. Moreover, her former husband had been a widower with seven children and thus Cristóvão de Burgos now became linked not only with the Pimentel family, but also to these children, one of whom was Francisco Telles de Meneses, chief constable of Salvador.[87]

Shortly after his wedding, Burgos petitioned the crown for a position in the newly created Relação of Bahia, and in 1654 he joined the High Court as a replacement for Simão Álvares da

85. Cristóvão de Burgos Contreiras, ANTT, Leitura dos Bacharéis maço 2, n. 55.

86. Afonso Ruy, *História da Câmara Municipal do Salvador* (Bahia, 1953).

87. See above pp. 276–279.

Penha Deusdará.[88] In the years following the expulsion of the Dutch from Brazil, the crown seemed willing to allow Brazilians the right to serve in high colonial positions. It would appear that the Desembargo do Paço had consciously selected Burgos for this reason but members of the Conselho Ultramarino were not in favor of the policy. They complained that Burgos should not be appointed in Bahia, "where he is a native and after he had married there very well and without license to do so." [89]

For the next twenty-six years Cristóvão de Burgos served in the Relação to the mixed reactions of his fellow colonials. On one hand, there was a certain pride and satisfaction in having a Brazilian on the High Court, but on the other, Burgos caused much complaint. The *câmara* of Salvador constantly accused him of tax evasion and using his office for private advantage. In 1675 the town council pointed out that Burgos' failure to pay certain taxes set a bad example, and that in his case it was especially reprehensible since he was "the wealthiest man in the country." [90]

Such a statement may have been hyperbole, but investigation in the notary portfolios and land grants of Bahia indicate clearly that Cristóvão de Burgos was no pauper. He had received a large land grant on the São Francisco River in 1659 but his major property holdings were in the Recôncavo parishes.[91] Besides land which he owned in Santo Amaro de Pitanga, Burgos controlled three sugar mills, two in the parish of Paripe and the other in Passé. One of the these *engenhos* had been acquired as part of his wife's inheritance. At least two of these mills had dependent cane growers and tenants. Thus Cristóvão de Burgos was not only a judge of the High Court

88. *Consulta* CU (2 October 1651), AHU, Bahia *pap. avul.* caixa 6.

89. *Consulta* CU (8 August 1656), AHU, Bahia *pap. avul.* caixa 8 (2nd series non-catalogued).

90. *Câmara* of Salvador to Conselho Ultramarino (Bahia, 20 July 1662), AHU, Bahia *pap. avul.* caixa 8 (1st series non-catalogued); king to *Câmara* of Salvador (Lisbon, 18 March 1675), ACMB, Livro 159, f. 161.

91. *Sesmaria* (27 October 1659) in *Publicações do Arquivo Nacional*, XXVII, 17.

of Bahia, but a wealthy, well-connected *senhor de engenho* with slaves and dependents.[92]

Here was a man linked by interest, family, birth, and association to the colony in a manner never intended by the crisp prohibitions of the law and the regulations of his profession. His social position was recognized by membership in the Misericórdia and election to its governing board in 1691.[93] He could count among his relatives other members of the planter elite and among his colleagues the highest royal officers in the colony. And in 1680, when a promotion raised him to the Casa da Suplicação, Burgos became an influential consultant on Brazilian affairs in the metropolis.

Other examples of this pattern are easily found, but perhaps a counter example, a Brazilian-born judge who avoided these connections, can be even more revealing. João da Rocha Pitta was continually singled out in the 1690's as an exemplary magistrate, "living *as if* he were not a native," and "not *even* having a farm" (emphasis mine).[94] Such statements indicate that personal connections and ownership of land were expected characteristics of the Brazilian-born judges, and that one who did not participate in such activities was surely a rare exception. A gubernatorial description of João da Rocha Pitta's performance underscores not only his virtues, but the usual practices of the desembargadores as well:

---

92. References to Burgos' property can be seen in APB, Livro de Notas 2 (13 July 1674), f. 64–67v; Livro de Notas 18 (12 May 1701), f. 124v; Livro de Notas 25 (23 March 1715), ff. 208–210v. This last item refers to the sale of the Engenho Cruz das Tôrres in Passé, which was sold in 1715 to Desembargador Dionísio de Azevedo Arevalos by Jerônimo Rodrigues de Castro, who had purchased it previously from Cristôvão de Burgos. He also owned the five largest cane fields in Paripe. See *Cartas do Senado*, III, 30.

93. Burgos had received permission to return to Brazil in 1682 in order to settle his estate. Either he never returned to Portugal or he later retired to Brazil, for when he was elected to the Board of th Misericórdia he must have been in his seventies. Cf. Andrade e Silva, *Coll. cron.* IX (10 January 1682), 85; ASCMB, Elleções A/1/34 f. 66.

94. *Consulta* CU (9 November 1692), *DHBNR*, LXXXIX (1950), 209–211.

"João da Rocha Pitta, being a son of this land and living here so many years, does not marry although he is fifty-five years of age, and it seems as though he has no relatives because of the notable isolation in which he lives; and he owns no land in this State, existing only on his salary with great honesty and with great credit as an officer of His Majesty." [95]

João da Rocha Pitta was the exception that proved the rule.

---

95. Gov. Antônio Luís Gonsalves da Câmara Coutinho to CU (Bahia, 25 June 1691), AHU, Bahia *pap. avul.* caixa 16.

XIV. CONCLUSION

Twixt good and bad there is great difference
As is the judge, so shall be the sentence.
Epitaph from Portuguese Diu (1580)

There are not courts enough to protect the law when duty is absent from the conscience of the judges.

Ruy Barbosa

The decade of the 1750's provides a convenient point from which to glance back at the process we have traced. The accession of Dom José I to the Portuguese throne in 1750 was soon followed by the political dominance of his chief minister, Sebastião José de Carvalho e Melo, later the Marquis of Pombal. This iron-willed autocrat ushered in a period of profound reform in the administrative and economic structure of the Portuguese empire. Based on his observation of England's ascendancy and employing virtually despotic powers, Pombal launched a policy of state intervention in the agricultural, manufacturing, and commerical sectors of the economy. Accompanying these measures were a number of administrative changes designed to provide tighter royal control of the empire and a more efficient way of extracting the taxes needed for the programs of national reconstruction.[1]

1. On Pombal's policies in Brazil see, Alden, *Royal Government;* Kenneth Maxwell, "Pombal and the Nationalization of the Luso-Brazilian Economy," *HAHR*, XLVII (May 1968), 608–631. Both of these works incorporate the extensive bibliography on this subject.

The measures Pombal took in Brazil must be seen against a background of that colony's crisis of declining revenues and the threat of military confrontation with Spain on the southern and western frontiers. As Dauril Alden has pointed out, the two problems were related, for Brazilian revenues were falling off at exactly the time that military expenses were increasing.[2] By the 1750's the volume of gold and diamond production had begun to flag, and so had the royal revenues. Sugar and tobacco agriculture suffered from natural conditions and from unfavorable market conditions in Europe. Against this tapestry of gloom Pombal wove a design of reform. He altered the system of taxation in the mining areas, established monopoly trading companies, created boards of control to regulate agricultural exports, reorganized fiscal administration, and stimulated agricultural developments in regions like Maranhão. The creation of the Relação of Rio de Janeiro was one of the earliest Pombaline changes in Brazil. It marked the end of an era in the history of the colony's judicial and administrative structure, and was the first step in the shift of government from the Northeast to the South. This movement recognized the economic realities of a declining sugar complex on the northeastern coast and the need to extract more revenues from the mineral producing areas of Minas Gerais and Goias. At the same time the growing population of the southern captaincies and the military threat of Spain in the Plate region called for closer royal control. The establishment of Rio de Janiero in 1763 as the viceregal capital simply completed a process begun in the preceding decade.

Institutions might be created and capitals moved with relative ease, but the nature of colonial government was more difficult to alter. After two hundred and fifty years of colonial rule, the relationship between state and society in Brazil had been established as a dynamic equation of interests and powers. Economic considerations, royal absolutism, bureaucratic goals, professional motivations, class and personal interests all determined the nature and operation of government in the colony although the influence of each

2. Alden, *Royal Government*, pp. 9–13.

varied in accordance with specific historical situations. In this study we have tried to identify and analyze the institutional structure of magisterial government, the nature and functions of the bureaucracy, the career patterns and objectives of the bureaucrats, and the interests of various sectors of colonial society. The political system of the colony resulted from the interaction of each of these elements.[3]

The Relação of Bahia, with the governor or viceroy as its president, was the apex of the colonial administrative structure and as such best represented the institutional basis of royal government. In judicial matters, as the highest tribunal in Brazil its authority was unquestioned, and only after 1751 did it share that status with the High Court in Rio de Janeiro. The politico-administrative powers of the Relação of Bahia, while great, were to a large extent negative. Many aspects of colonial government lay in the hands of other institutions, but the High Court's ability to check, limit, or delay the policies and actions of virtually everyone else in the colony placed it at the fulcrum of power. The power to prevent something was as crucial as the power to act, and it gave the Relação enormous leverage in the conduct of government. Through the course of its history, there was hardly an aspect of government in which the High Court did not at some time intervene.

In a system of countervailing powers, jurisdictional overlap, and multiple standards or goals, the Relação held a central position. Through its powers of review the crown looked to the High Court as a guardian of royal interest and standards. The many disagreements and conflicts between the desembargadores and other officers in the colony brought appeal to the metropolis and eventual decision by the crown. Such a system was well-suited to the establishment and maintenance of colonial dependency, for it made the councils in Lisbon the ultimate arbiters of colonial life and it impeded the development of decision-making in the colony.

The Relação was powerful at its creation in 1609 and at its

---

3. I have already presented some of these conclusions in Schwartz, "Magistracy and Society." 715–730.

recreation in 1652, and the crown continually expanded its responsibilities and the duties of its magistrates. This process was fully understandable, given the historical role of the judiciary as allies of the crown, representatives of royal authority, and professional bureaucrats. But the crown's dependence on the magistracy's loyalty and skill placed an insupportable burden on its professional and personal capacities, and this in turn had a deleterious effect on the enforcement of law. Each new task assigned to the desembargadores detracted from their performance of other obligations, and their courtroom duties seemed to suffer worst of all. The expansion of other branches of the bureaucracy and an increase in the number of subordinate magistrates did not alleviate the situation. As the ultimate guardian of royal interests, the Relação and its judges found that whatever duties were lightened by such measures were outweighed by new regulatory and investigative responsibilities which the High Court assumed over the new officers. Undoubtedly, corruption, neglect, and personal limitations contributed in some part to the notorious reputation of the colonial judicial system, but much of the problem lay in the structure of a bureaucracy, which fused the various powers and responsibilities of government in the same institutions and men who performed them.

The failures of the Relação and the subordinate magistrates in administering justice were to some extent compensated, in the crown's view, by the political functions they performed. As Brazil moved from the rule of proprietary captaincies to direct royal control, the judicial officers—first the *ouvidor geral* and later the desembargadores, *ouvidores*, and *juizes de fóra*—assumed important administrative and political roles. The colonial relationship of Brazil to the Portuguese metropolis developed around Brazil's ability to supply agricultural products and minerals to Portugal within a controlled commercial system. Despite the economic reality the contours of colonial organization were not primarily economic. For reasons of history and political philosophy, the structure of judicial administration became also the structure of empire. Just as in Portugal, where *letrados* had been the strong right arm of royal absolutism, so in Brazil they were employed to control the centripetal forces generated by specific class interests. Without the sugar planters and later the "donos de gado e gente," the cattlemen of the *sertão*, Brazil as a colony had no meaning; but the power of these men also threatened the operation of colonial government. The crown always sought to eliminate or at least control those interests, institutions, or groups which stood between the monarch and his subjects. Bureaucratic government based on the crown's judicial prerogatives and administered by the magistracy became a means to this end.

While the ranks of bureaucracy were many, the magistrates clearly constituted an administrative patriciate, the most respected and privileged officials of the crown, exceeded in rank and honors only by the noble viceroys and ambassadors whose preeminence derived as much from their social standing as from their services. The magistracy represented all that was rational and professional in the bureaucracy of empire, but we should not confuse them with civil servants. While the concept of service to the state or the community was embedded in the king's obligations to the realm, the magistrates remained royal servants. Still, it was not uncommon for those who served in Brazil to represent colonial interests or to reconcile royal legislation with Brazilian realities.

Drawn from a variety of social backgrounds but representing to a large extent non-titled gentry, bourgeoisie, and functionary origins, the magistrates shared the common experience of legal training at Coimbra. The halls of the university became the preparation for imperial government. There students learned the principles of law, the theories of government, and the standards of performance which would make them loyal and competent servants of the crown. The Coimbra education shared by all the magistrates was in reality a process of bureaucratic socialization which readied a man for the robe of office. After entry into the magistracy advancement through the channels of promotions could lead eventually to the High Court of Bahia and beyond that to the councils of the king. The men who served in the Bahian tribunal usually came after fifteen years of professional experience, as veterans of bureaucratic life.

Common university training, career goals, and professional experience created a sense of class consciousness among the magistracy. The crown's policy of promotion, privilege, and reward, which was designed to bolster the authority of the magistracy, also fed the ambition and pride of the bureaucrats, who at times assumed the attitudes and aspirations of the nobility or of the colonial elite. Once created, the bureaucracy had a life of its own, and magistrates sometimes sought collective or individual goals beyound those prescribed by the law. The crown, however, maintained control over the state and the bureaucracy. Through the system of education and promotion, rotation in office, and institutional checks, the magistracy remained tied to royal interest and dependent on the crown. This was a major feature of the Portuguese administrative and social structure. Despite family traditions of bureaucratic service, we cannot properly speak of a nobility of magisterial office, a *nobreza da toga*, which came to regard bureaucratic posts as their exclusive domain or office as an extension of social rank. The magistracy was in theory open to all (Jews, New Christians, blacks, and mulattoes excluded). Desembargadores and lower magistrates did not own their offices nor could they pass them to others of their choosing. Any magistrate was always subject to review, dismissal, and replacement. While grants of nobility or memberships in the honorific military orders might be given to reward or encourage bureaucratic service, high office did not automatically confer nobility on the incumbent. Thus, unlike the French nobility of the robe or the Prussian judicial nobility, the Portuguese magistrates remained a professional elite rather than a distinct social class, although there was always a tendency for them to become one.[4]

The crown used promotion, honors, privileges, and ample stipends to lift the magistrates above selfish interests or the influence

4. Cf. Ford, *Robe and Sword*, pp. 202–252; and Rosenberg, *Bureaucracy, Aristocracy, and Autocracy*.

of others. The creation of officials who can approach their tasks and decisions *sine ira et studio* is a classic goal of bureaucratic government.[5] But the very measures designed to reinforce the authority and dignity of the desembargadores did not isolate them from an awed society. The prestige and power of the magistracy attracted the colonial elite into alliance with them, and the magistrates for their part were not slow to use their position for personal or familial benefit. Disinterested magistrates were the guardians of the formal structure of empire envisioned by the crown. At the same time, these men often pursued individual or collective goals which openly conflicted with the standards of their office. This was the paradox of colonial government, but it was a paradox which gave the regime its life by reconciling the interests of metropolis and colony.

Bureaucracy and society in colonial Brazil formed two interlocking systems of organization. The metropolitan-directed administration, characterized by categorical and impersonal relations, served as the basic outline of imperial government, the structure of sovereignty which politically tied colony to crown as flesh to bone. Like an anatomical drawing in a medical textbook, however, the skin of formal governmental structure could be peeled back to reveal a complex system of veins and nerves created by interpersonal primary relations based on kinship, friendship, patronage, and graft. Here the diagrammatic analogy ends, for the network of personal relations constantly altered as personalities, forces, and alliances sought ever-greater resources of power and influence. The dynamic nature of this process provides at least a partial explanation of the colonial regime's resiliency and the longevity of the Brazilian elite. By making social alliances with bureaucrats, colonial groups, families, and individuals acquired powerful supporters who could affect the implementation of policy or the application of law —and these were especially important areas because colonials did not often participate in the formulation of either law or policy.

5. Peter M. Blau, *The Dynamics of Bureaucracy*, 2nd ed. (Chicago, 1963), pp. 82–99.

Although government might expand and new offices might be created, the formal table of imperial organization and its underlying principles remained basically static. The penetration of the governmental structure by primary relations provided a certain flexibility which facilitated the accommodation of new political, social, and economic forces and allowed the resolution of problems at the local level.

The magistracy played a crucial role in the formal table of organization. Despite its partial development as a social class, the magistracy continued to represent centralized royal government and all that was professional, rational, and categorical in the bureaucracy. If desembargadores, the highest-ranking and supposedly most competent professional magistrates, could be suborned by kinship and graft, what hope was there for lower magistrates, governors, tax collectors, and clerks whose concept of office was far more akin to ownership of a profit-generating property? According to the bureaucratic norms, a magistrate's links to society violated the standards of his profession, but this situation was not wholly inimical to the operation of government. It was perhaps the best that could be expected of an authoritarian regime in which the bureaucratic apparatus had never supplanted the strongly particularistic nature of Iberian society. This situation persists in contemporary Brazil, where the use of *pistolão* (pull or influence) is almost a way of life. Its roots, however, extend far back into the colonial heritage.[6]

The colonial regime in Brazil has long puzzled historians, for while complaints against its inefficiency and decay were common coin, it succeeded in binding the colony to the mother country for more than three centuries. Even after political ties were severed in 1822, many dynastic, commercial, cultural, and personal bonds persisted. The reasons for the success of the colonial regime lie in both its accomplishments and its failures, and in the peculiar contours

6. See Lawrence Graham, *Civil Service Reform in Brazil* (Austin, 1968); Raymundo Faoro, *Os Donos do poder* (Porto Alegre, 1958).

of the colony's society and economy. On almost every level, the thrust of colonial government pointed toward constant dependence on the metropolis and the integration of Brazil into the larger imperial structure. The relatively limited powers of the viceroy over subordinate governors, the multiple institutional checks, the incorporation of Brazilian posts into the hierarchy of office and the channels of promotion, and the constant need to refer matters to Portugal—all these bound the bureaucracy to the crown and the colonial government to the metropolis. The absence of a university or even a printing press in Brazil meant that higher education, professional training, and even intellectual pursuits led each generation of the colonial elite back to the mother country. The absorption of bureaucrats into colonial society served a similar function. This flaw of rational administration was a failure with a purpose.

The crown established its authority in Brazil on the philosophical identification of sovereignty and law and the administration of that law by a government of magistrates. Even in times of crisis or revolt threats to royal sovereignty were rare, and colonial displeasure was usually directed against specific men or laws rather than against the principles of royal government. Similarly, through much of the colony's history the crown recognized that the economic investments and efforts of the private sector made Brazil a valuable possession. Thus, so long as royal sovereignty was recognized, taxes collected, and the outline of administration maintained, the planters and ranchers exercised relatively free rein over the colony's social and economic life with little interference from the crown. The Relação and its subordinate magistrates, moved by principle, professional goals, and loyalty, came the closest to the ideal of impartial application of the law, but given the geographical and social realities of colonial life, this ideal was rarely achieved. For many Brazilians, especially those in rural areas, justice came at the end of a planter's whip or a rancher's boot. This situation existed to some extent because the crown allowed it and because the colonial elite was able to integrate the officers of the crown into a system of primary relations. The colonial regime endured because powerful interests in both Brazil and Portugal derived sustenance from it.

It has been argued that the deficiencies of Portuguese rule in Brazil stemmed from the transplantation of European government and institutions, with little adaption, to the realities of the New World.[7] While this is true in part, in an institutional sense, it is just as true that the faults of colonial government sprang from the recognition and satisfaction of certain colonial demands. Since the lower echelons of government provided the crown with an area of patronage, the bureaucracy at this level tended to grow in response to its own demands for office or the crown's need to reward, rather than to the size of the task. The men who held these offices, and there were many colonials among them, often demanded more from society than they provided, and the burden of government, both fiscal and psychological, fell on those who had the most need of its protection. The magistrates, who were the men most likely or able to provide this protection, generally failed to do so.

Brazilians often complained of bureaucratic abuses, but they rarely criticized the nature of government or the fact that officials amassed fortunes and became linked to local society. Instead, Brazilians aspired to place their sons in royal service or marry their daughters to the king's officers. These opportunities may have been more ephemeral than real, but so long as the bureaucracy remained theoretically open to colonials and so long as it could be "Brazilianized," the Brazilian elite accepted it as its own. Government in the colony was often ineffective, sometimes oppressive, and usually corrupt, but it was rarely viewed as a tool of foreign domination.

In sum, the integration of magistracy and society linked the economic elite to the governmental elite in a union of wealth and power. The corruption of the bureaucracy, whether by family or

7. See Alden, *Royal Government*, pp. 486–494, for a discussion of this and other evaluations of the colonial regime.

money, still left the vast majority of the colony's inhabitants unable to share in controlling their own destinies. To the plantation slave, the cobbler, and the cowboy it mattered little whether oppression came from Lisbon or Bahia, from royal officials or local potentates. The integration of state and society, with whatever benefits it brought to certain elements in the colony, was bought at the expense of most Brazilians.

REFERENCE MATERIAL

APPENDIX I.

RULERS OF PORTUGAL AND BRAZIL

RULERS OF PORTUGAL AND HER EMPIRE, 1495–1777

Dom Manoel I (1495–1521)
Dom João III (1521–1557)
Dom Sebastião (1557–1578)
Cardinal Henrique (1578–1580)
Philip I (II of Spain) (1580–1598)
Philip II (III of Spain) (1598–1621)
Philip III (IV of Spain (1621–1640)
Dom João IV (1640–1656)
Dom Afonso VI (1656–1667)
Dom Pedro II (regent 1667–1683, monarch 1683–1706)
Dom João V (1706–1750)
Dom José (1750–1777)

VICEROYS AND GOVERNORS OF PORTUGAL UNDER THE SPANISH HAPSBURGS, 1580–1640

Cardinal Alberto, Archduke of Austria, January 1583–February 1593
Junta of Five Governors, July 1593–January 1600
  Miguel de Castro, Archbishop of Lisbon
  João da Silva, Count of Portalegre
  Francisco de Mascarenhas, Count of Santa Cruz
  Duarte de Castelobranco, Count of Sabugal
  Miguel de Moura, *escrivão de puridade*

Viceroy Cristóvão de Moura, Marquis of Castel Rodrigo, January 1600–July 1603
Viceroy Afonso de Castelobranco, Bishop of Coimbra, August 1603–December 1604
Viceroy Pedro de Castilho, Bishop of Leiria, May 1605–February 1608
Viceroy (second term) Cristóvão de Moura, February 1608–February 1612
Viceroy (second term) Pedro de Castilho, March 1612–June 1614
Viceroy Aleixo de Meneses Archbishop of Braga, July 1614–July 1615
Viceroy Miguel de Castro, Archbishop of Lisbon, July 1615–March 1617
Viceroy Diogo da Silva e Mendonça, Count of Salinas and Marquis of Alenquer, March 1617–August 1621
Junta of Three Governors, 1621–1631
  Martinho Afonso Mexia, Bishop of Coimbra
  Diogo de Castro, Count of Basto
  Nuno Alvares Portugal
  Later replacements were: Afonso Furtado de Mendonça, Archbishop of Lisbon and later Archbishop of Braga; and Diogo de Castro, Count of Portalegre.
Junta of Two Governors, 1631–1633
  Antonio de Ataide, Count of Castro D'Ayro e Castanheira
  Nuno de Mendonça, Count of Val de Reis
Viceroy João Manoel, Archbishop of Lisbon, April 1633–July 1633
Viceroy Diogo de Castro, Count of Basto, July 1633–December 1634
Vicereine Magarida, Princess of Parma and Duchess of Mantua, December 1634–1640

VICEROYS AND GOVERNORS OF BRAZIL, 1549–1760

Tomé de Sousa, 1549–1553
Duarte da Costa, 1553–1558
Mem de Sá, 1558–1572
Luís Brito de Almeida, 1573–1578
Lourenço da Veiga, 1578–1581
Interim government of *câmara* and *ouvidor geral* Cosme Rangel, 1581–1583
Manuel Telles Barreto, 1583–1587
Interim government of the bishop, *provedor-mór*, and *ouvidor geral*, 1587–1591

Francisco de Sousa, 1591–1602
Diogo Botelho, 1603–1607
Diogo de Meneses, 1608–1612
Gaspar de Sousa, 1613–1617
Luís de Sousa, 1617–1621
Diogo de Mendonça Furtado, 1621–1624
Matias de Albuquerque, 1624–1625 (held this position officially while the Dutch were in Bahia; he appointed Francisco de Moura Rolim, 1625–1627, to conduct government in Bahia)
Diogo Luís de Oliveira, 1627–1635
Pedro da Silva, 1635–1639
Fernando Mascarenhas, Count of Tôrre, 1639
Vasco Mascarenhas, Count of Óbidos, 1639–1640
Viceroy Jorge Mascarenhas, Marquis of Montalvão, 1640–1641
Interim junta, 1641–1642
Antônio Telles da Silva, 1642–1647
Antônio Telles de Meneses, Count of Vila-Pouca de Aguiar, 1647–1650
João Rodrigues de Vasconcellos e Sousa, Count of Castelo Melhor, 1650–1654
Jerônimo de Altaíde, Count of Atouguia, 1654–1657
Francisco Barreto de Meneses, 1657–1663
Viceroy Vasco Mascarenhas, Count of Óbidos, 1663–1667
Alexandre de Sousa Freire, 1667–1671
Afonso Furtado de Castro do Rio de Mendonça, Viscount of Barbacena, 1671–1675
Interim junta of Chancellor of the Relação, Agostinho de Azevedo Monteio, and others. Upon his death, Azevedo Monteiro was replaced by Desembargador Cristóvão de Burgos.
Roque da Costa Barreto, 1678–1682
Antônio de Sousa de Meneses, 1682–1684
Matias da Cunha, 1687–1688
Interim junta of Chancellor of the Relação, Manoel Carneiro de Sá and the Archbishop, 1688–1690
Antônio Luís Gonçalves da Câmara Coutinho, 1690–1694
João de Lencastre, 1694–1702
Rodrigo da Costa, 1702–1705
Luís Cesar de Meneses, 1705–1710
Lourenço de Almeida, 1710–1711
Pedro de Vasconcellos e Sousa, Count of Castelo Melhor, 1711–1714
Viceroy Pedro de Noronha, Count of Vila Verde and Marquis of Angeja, 1714–1718

Sáncho de Faro e Sousa, Count of Vimieiro, 1718–1719
Interim junta of Chancellor of the Relação, Caetano de Brito de Figueiredo, and others
Viceroy Vasco Fernandes Cesar de Meneses, Count of Sabugosa, 1720–1735
Viceroy André de Mello e Castro, Count of Galvêas, 1735–1749
Viceroy Luís Pedro Peregrino de Carvalho Meneses de Ataíde, Count of Atouguia, 1749–1755
Interim junta of Chancellor of the Relação, Manoel Antônio da Cunha Sottomayor, and others
Viceroy Marcos de Noronha e Brito, Count of Arcos, 1755–1760

APPENDIX II.

DESEMBARGADOR MARRIAGES IN BRAZIL

Desembargador	Wife and Birthplace	Comments
Manoel Pinto da Rocha [a]	Catherina de Frielas (Pernambuco)	m. 28 June 1612 in Olinda. Wife a widow with family ties to the Cavalcanti Albuquerques and the Bezerras. See p. 178.
Antão de Mesquita de Oliveira	Antônia Bezerra (Pernambuco)	Wife a daughter of Paulo Bezerra, SdE and alderman of Olinda. See p. 179.
Simão Álvares da Penha Deusdará	Leonarda de Azevedo Ravasco (Bahia)	Daughter of a Relação clerk and sister of Padre Antônio Vieira, thus linked to this powerful clan. See p. 347.
Cristóvão de Burgos	Helena da Silva Pimentel (Bahia)	m. 1 November 1651 in Paripe. Wife a widow, the daughter of Bernardo Pimentel de Almeida, a relative of Gov. of Brazil, Luís de Brito de Almeida. Mother's family had New Christian connections. Antônio da Silva Pimentel was great landowner in Jacobina and chief constable of Salvador for sixteen years.

Desembargador	Wife and Birthplace	Comments
Agostino de Azevedo Monteiro [b]	Catherina de Brito	Monteiro a widower when marriage took place.
João de Góes e Araújo	Catherina de Sousa (Bahia)	Daughter of Ruy Carvalho Pinheiro, secretary of the *câmara* of Salvador and a *moço fidalgo*. One of her brothers was a *fidalgo*, sergeant-major, and married a daughter of Cristóvão Vieira Ravasco.
Antônio Rodrigues Banha [c]	Maria Francisca de Vasconcelos (Bahia)	Jaboatão provides no information. She owned Engenho Jacarancanga in Bahia.
Pedro da Unhão Castelobranco	Damiana Francisca da Silva (Lisbon, but married in Bahia)	See p. 350.
Antônio da Cunha Sottomayor [d]	Rosa Maria de Sequeira (São Paulo)	
Belchior da Cunha Brochado [e]	Maria Francisca de Paula e Almeida (Bahia)	Daugh. of Capt. Sebastião Barbosa of an infantry regiment in Bahia. Cunha Brochado was related to the Portuguese ambassador to France.
José de Sá e Mendonça	Joana Cavalcanti de Albuquerque (Bahia)	m. 5 May 1690 in Maragogipe. She was a widow, daugh. of Col. Cristóvão Cavalcanti de Albuquerque, SdE and alderman of Salvador.
Bernardo de Sousa Estrela	Joana Cavalcanti de Albuquerque (Bahia)	m. upon the death of José de Sá e Mendonça.
Cristóvão Tavares de Morais	Adriana Cavalcanti de Albuquerque (Bahia)	Daugh. of Col. Cristovão Cavalcanti de Albuquerque and half-sister of Joana. See p. 344.
Luís da Costa Faria [f]		

Desembargador	Wife and Birthplace	Comments
João de Sousa [g]	Mariana Pereira de Siqueira (Bahia)	m. *ca.* 1719, daugh. of Domingos Lopes de Siqueira.
André Leitão de Mello [h]	Maria Ferreira de Carvalho (Bahia)	
João de Sá Sottomayor	Brites da Rocha Pitta (Bahia)	Daugh. of Antônio da Rocha Pitta, wealthy SdE.
João Homem Freire	Francisca Xavier da Penha Deusdarà (Bahia)	Daugh. of Antônio da Rocha Pitta and sister of Brites.
Dionísio de Azevedo e Arevalos [i]	Isabel Theresa Maria da Vasconcelos	Daugh. of Desembargador Antônio Rodrigues Banha. See de Sousa, note g.
Tomás Feliciano de Albernás [j]	Clara Maria de Lima (1) (Sergipe) Antonia Caetana (2) de Sousa	(1) daugh. of Francisco Gomes de Abreu of Sergipe d'El-Rey; m. while Albernás served as *ouvidor geral* in that captaincy. See p. 352.
Luís de Sousa Pereira [k]		
Diogo Mendes Duro Esmeraldo [l]	Luísa Barbosa (Bahia)	Daugh. of José de Góes de Sequeira of Santo Amaro.
Luís Siqueira de Gama [m]	Catherina Álvares da Cunha (Santos)	m. while da Gama was serving as *juiz de fóra* of Santos (c. 1714).
Antônio do Rego e Sá Quintanilha [n]		
Francisco de Santa Barbara e Moura [o]		
Luís Machado de Barros [p]	Joana Doria de Meneses	
Antônio José da Fonseca Lemos [q]	Maria de Araújo e Aragão (Bahia)	m. in Maragogipe, daugh. of Francisco de Araújo e Aragão, alderman of Salvador, 1686.

Desembargador	Wife and Birthplace	Comments
João Álvares de Figueiredo Brandão [r]		
Antônio Pires da Silveira [s]		
Ignacio Dias Madeira [t]		
Bento da Silva Ramalho [u]	Maria de Sá	
Manoel Vieira Pedrosa	Luísa de Queirós Araújo (Bahia)	Widow of the captain of a fort on Itaparica island; she was a member of the Araújo Góes family, well-placed and extended.
Bernardino Falcão de Gouvea	Luísa Clara de Argolo e Querós (Bahia)	Daugh. of Paulo de Argolo, *fidalgo* and wealthy owner of Engenho Cinco Rios.
Jorge Salter de Mendonça [v]	Antonia Francisca Pessoa de Lima (Pernambuco)	
Francisco Antonio Berco da Silveira [w]		Had married in Rio de Janeiro while serving there as *ouvidor geral.*

* Information has been obtained from Jaboatão, "Catalogo," unless otherwise noted. Marriages and genealogies discussed in the text are indicated by the appropriate pages. Abbreviations used: daugh(ter); SdE(senhor de engenho); m(arriage).

[a] Petition of Francisco Bezerra, BI, Correspondencia Gaspar de Sousa, f. 297.

[b] ANTT, Leitura dos Bacharéis, maço 9, n. 51 (1697).

[c] APB, Libro de Notas (? January 1715), ff. 119v.–122v.; Livro de Notas 37 (21 May 1722) ff. 91–92v.

[d] ANTT, Leitura dos Bacharéis, maço 17A, n. 31.

[e] *Obras completas Matos,* II, 413, wrongly attributes this person to Dionísio de Ávila Varieiro. See Fonseca, "Bacharéis brasileiros," 180.

[f] License to marry in Bahia, ANTT, *Chan. Pedro II, Doações,* liv. 62, f. 27.

[g] ANTT, Leitura dos Bacharéis, maço 7, n. 6 (investigation of Luís de Sousa Pereira).

[h] License to marry in Bahia, ANTT, *Chan. Pedro II, Doações,* liv. 44, f. 254v.; Fonseca, "Bacharéis brasileiros."

[i] APB, Livro de Notas 37 (20 Aug. 1722), f. 220.

[j] License to marry in Brazil, ANTT, *Chan. João V, Doações,* liv. 34, f. 135v. APB, Livro de Notas 59 (18 June 1734); Livro de Notas 100, f. 240–243.

[k] ANTT, *Chan. João V., Doações,* liv. 56, f. 224 (28 August 1719).

[l] *Ibid.,* liv. 66, f. 19v.

[m] ANTT, *Chan. João V., Doações,* liv. 39, f. 169; Fonseca, "Bacharéis brasileiros," 203.

[n] License to marry in Brazil, ANTT, *Chan. João V, Doações,* liv. 62, f. 285 (2 March 1723).

[o] *Assento* (27 November 1728), AHNRJ Codice 540; BGUC Codice 708, f. 27.

[p] AHU, Con. Ultramarino 249, f. 68.

[q] ACMB, V, 42; ANTT, Leitura dos Bacharéis, maço 20A, n. 26.

[r] License to marry in Brazil, ANTT, *Chan. João V., Doações,* liv. 99, f. 77v. (21 September 1739).

[s] ANTT, *Chan.* João V, Doações, liv. 90, f. 5.

[t] License to marry in Brazil, ANTT, *Chan. João V, Doações,* liv. 105, f. 54v.

[u] AHNRJ, Codice 542 (17 June 1743).

[v] Fonseca, "Bacharéis brasileiros," 264–265, 374.

[w] ANTT, *Chan. João V, Doações,* liv. 118, f. 292.

APPENDIX III.

DESEMBARGADORES OF THE RELAÇÃO OF BAHIA, 1609-1758

The following table has been compiled from a wide variety of sources, including the *Leitura dos Bacharéis* and *Chancelarias* of the ANTT, the *Livros e verbetes de matricula* of the AUC, and the *Catálogo alfabético dos Ministros de Letras* in the BNL. Other archives, such as the AHU, APB, and BGUC, supplied information to fill gaps in the record. The list in Caldas, *Noticia geral*, has provided the names of judges in the period 1652 to 1758 and served as a starting point, but I have emended it in a number of places and added to it the judges who served prior to 1652. The following categories of classification have been used:

1. Name. Orthography has been modernized.

2. Date and place of birth. At the time of the examination before the Desembargo do Paço certain documents provided the candidate's age. I have used this figure to calculate his birthdate by subtracting it from the date of examination. My calculation of birthdate should be within a one-year margin of error. Brazilian birthplaces have been placed in italics.

3. Father's occupation. This category includes status as well as occupation. The reader should refer to the discussion in Chapter Twelve for an explanation of these terms.

4. University degree. I have indicated here receipt of a degree in canon (C) or civil (L) law. When possible the degree of doctor (Doutor) and licenciate (Lic) have also been indicated, as has a teaching position at Coimbra (Prof).

5. Entry in service. This column indicates the date of examination by the Desembargo do Paço.

6. and 8. Prior and posterior service. Indicates the principal bureaucratic offices held by a desembargador before and after his service in Bahia. Colonial service has been indicated by the inclusion of place names. Offices not accompanied by place names indicate service in metropolitan Portugal. Reappointment at the same bureaucratic level is indicated by a number, e.g. (2). The principal abbreviations used are: Aud ger (Auditor geral); CdS (Casa da Suplicação); Conso (Conselheiro, member of a royal council); CU (Conselho Ultramarino); Corg (Corregedor); DdP (Desembargo do Paço); Goa (Relação de Goa); J Alfama (Juiz de Alfama, level similar to juiz de fóra); J Alfan (Juiz da Alfândega); J. Cível (juiz do Cível in Lisbon); JF (Juiz da Fóra); J. India (Juiz da India); J. Órfãos (Juiz dos órfãos); MdC (Mesa da Consciência); OG (Ouvidor geral); *Oporto* (Relação do Pôrto); Ouv (Ouvidor); Prov (Provedor); Rio (Relação do Rio de Janeiro); Sup (Superintendente de Diamantes).

7. Entry in Relação. Up to 1626 the year of entry is noted. After 1652 the day, month, and year of the official oath-taking is used. Naturally, this date is posterior to the date of appointment.

9. Comments. The following abbreviations have been used: F. (Fidalgo by birth); St. (Knight of Order of Santiago); M (Married in Brazil); I (Brother in the Misericórdia); X (Knight of the Order of Christ); P (Provedor of the Misericórdia); FC (Fidalgo by appointment).

Name	Birthplace and Date	Father's Occupation	Univ. Deg.	Entry in Service	Prior Service	Entry in Relação	Posterior Service	Comments
1. Antão de Mesquita de Oliveira	Guarda		C			1609	CdS	M
2. Antônio das Póvoas	Midões	Fidalgo	C			1609	Oporto CdS	F
3. Gaspar da Costa					Oporto CdS	1609		X
4. Francisco da Fonseca Leitão	1572	Fidalgo			JF (2)	1609	Oporto CdS	
5. Manoel Jácome Bravo	Vianna		C	1600	JF	1609	Oporto CdS	
6. Pero de Cascais de Abreu	Olivença		L			1609	Oporto	
7. Manoel Pinto da Rocha	Mesão Frio		C		JF Corg (2) Ouv	1609		M, P
8. Sebastião Pinto Lobo	Leiria		C		J Orfãos Prov (2)	1609	Oporto	
9. Ruy Mendes de Abreu		Letrado			JF (4)	1609		X, FC
10. Afonso Garcia Tinoco	1556			1589	JF (2) Corg	1609	CdS	
11. João de Sousa Cardenas	Evora	Letrado	C			1621		
12. Diogo de São Miguel Garces					OG Angola	1621	Oporto	
13. Martim Afonso Coelho	Lisbon	Fidalgo	C			1621	Oporto J India	
14. Nuno Vaz Fialho	Vianna do Alentejo		L		JF (2) Corg	1621	Oporto CdS	

15.	Francisco Mendes Marrecos	Alvito		L			1621		
16.	Pedro Casqueiro da Rocha						1621		
	[Relação abolished 1626–1652]								
17.	Francisco de Figueiredo	Coimbra	Letrado		1628		3 III 1653	Oporto	X
18.	Luís Salema de Carvalho	Moura			1628	Prov	3 III 1653	Oporto	
19.	Simão Álvares da Penha	*Pernambuco*	Prov da Faz. Pernambuco		1645		3 III 1653	Died in office	M
20.	Francisco Barradas de Mendonça					OG Maranhão	3 III 1653		
21.	Fernão de Maia Furtado	Evora	"humble"		1630	J Orfãos	3 III 1653		
22.	Afonso Soares da Fonseca	Moura	Physician	L Doutor	1627	Corg	16 I 1654		
23.	Cristóvão de Burgos	*Bahia*	Letrado	L	1644	JF	22 I 1654	CdS	M, I
24.	Jorge Seco de Macedo	Lisbon		C		Goa CdS	22 VIII 1655		X FC
25.	Bento Rabello		Letrado			Corg	1 IV 1656	Oporto	X
26.	Agostino de Azevedo Monteiro					Corg	11 IV 1659		M
27.	João Vanvecem	Lisbon	Great merchant Flemish	C	1645	JF	11 IV 1659	CdS Conso	

Continued

Name	Birthplace and Date	Father's Occupation	Univ. Deg.	Entry in Service	Prior Service	Entry in Relação	Posterior Service	Comments
28. Leandro de Castro da Silveira	Odemira (Beija)	"gente principal da vila"	C	1643	JF J Orfãos	8 II 1661		
29. João Velho de Azevedo	Lisbon			1644	JF J Alfan	30 III 1662		
30. Tomé da Costa Homem	Arganil (Coimbra)	"honrado"		1647	JF	8 IV 1662	Oporto	
31. Manoel da Almeida Peixoto	Aveiro		C	1645	Aud. ger.	25 VIII 1663		
32. Bernardo de Macedo Velho	Lisbon	Letrado		1646		22 III 1664	CdS	
33. João de Góes e Araújo	*Bahia*	escrivão da Miseri-córdia		1663		18 IV 1667		M, P
34. Pedro Cordeiro de Espinosa	Azores	"honrado"	Doutor	1661		24 IV 1668		
35. Manoel da Costa Palma	Palma	Pilot in the India trade		1656		7 XII 1669		
36. Pedro da Rocha Gouveia	Guimarães	"da-gov-ernança da vila"		1669		7 XII 1669	Oporto	
37. João Velozo de Brito	Alcobaça	"da-gov-ernança da vila"		1660		7 XII 1669	Oporto	
38. Antônio Nabo Pesanha						7 XII 1669		
39. José de Freitas Serrão	Lisbon		C			23 III 1675		

40. Francisco Craveiro de Almeida	Viseu	Fidalgo		1659	Corg	II V 1675	Oporto	
41. João da Rocha Pitta	*Bahia* 1637	Letrado	L Prof	1668	JF	17 III 1678		
42. João do Coito de Andrade	Lisbon	Fidalgo		1671		17 III 1678		
43. José de Almeida Machado	Lisbon		C			24 V 1678		
44. João Castelinho de Freitas	Obidos	da governança de Obidos"		1658	JF (2) Corg	30 V 1679	CdS	
45. Antônio Rodrigues Banha	Evora Monte		L			8 VI 1680		M, P, X
46. Bento de Barros Bezerra	Vianna		C	1666	JF (2) Corg	8 VI 1680	Oporto	
47. Francisco de Pugas e Antas						8 VI 1680		X
48. Francisco da Silveira Sottomayor	*Rio de Janeiro*		C Lic			26 IX 1680		X
49. João de Sepulveda da Matos	Lisbon	Market inspector	C	1658	Corg OG Pernambuco	26 V 1682	Oporto Con Ultra	
50. Francisco Pereira	Azambuja	Elected judge	C			14 II 1686		
51. Pedro da Unhão Castelobranco	Lisbon	Letrado			Ouv Rio de Jan.	23 IV 1686	Oporto	P, X, M
52. Belchior da Cunha Brochado		Master of castle of São Jorge		1679		17 V 1687	Oporto CdS	M

Continued

Name	Birthplace and Date	Father's Occupation	Univ. Deg.	Entry in Service	Prior Service	Entry in Relação	Posterior Service	Comments
53. Jerônimo de Sá e Cunha		Clerk (illegitimate birth)		1674	JF (2)	7 VI 1687		
54. José da Guarda Fragoso	Leiria					7 VI 1687	Oporto	
55. Jerônimo da Cunha Pimental	Provezende	Merchant	C	1683	JF	25 V 1688	Oporto	
56. Manoel Carneiro de Sá	Vila do Conde	"honrado"		1681	J Alfan	26 V 1698	Oporto CdS DdP MdC Conso	
57. Francisco Mendes Galvão	Arco de Valdeves					1 VI 1688		X
58. Belchior Ramires de Carvalho	Vila Nova de Foscoa			1668	JF Ouv Mazagão Corg	24 V 1689		I
59. João de Sousa	Lisbon					6 V 1690		
60. Dionízio de Ávila Varieiro	Matozinhos 1648	Captain		1673	JF (2) J Alfama OG Pernambuco	6 XI 1691	Oporto	M, I
61. Estevão Ferraz de Campos	Setúbal 1661	Tithe collector "fazendas"	L	1688		25 V 1694	Oporto CdS	
62. Miguel de Siqueira Castelobranco	Covilhã	"da governança"		1679	OG Rio de Janeiro	7 VII 1694		
63. Manoel da Costa Bonicho	Coimbra 1654		L Doutor Prof	1684		9 VI 1695	Oporto CdS DdP	

64. José de Sá e Mendonça	Guarda	Letrado		1674	OG Pernambuco	20 X 1696	Died in office 1721	M, P
65. Diogo Rangel Castelobranco	Paço de Luminar	Fidalgo			JF OG Paraíba	5 III 1699		
66. Francisco Lopes da Silva	Vila do Conde	"da governança"		1680	OG Angola	14 III 1697	Oporto	X
67. Manoel Nunes de Magalhães						21 V 1697		
68. Luís da Costa Faria	Vila Cova	"fazendas"		1679	JF (2) Ouv Prov	9 V 1699	Oporto CdS	M
69. Antônio de Campos Figueiredo	Vizeu	"avaliador dos órfãos"		1679	JF	9 V 1699	Oporto CdS	
70. Manoel Ferreira da Silva	Pombal	"da governança" "escrivão dos órfãos"	C	1687	JF (2) Ouv	9 V 1699		
71. Cristóvão Tavares de Morais	Azores	Letrado		1681	JF (2) Corg	16 III 1700		I, M St
72. Ignacio Morais de Sarmento	Miranda 1688	"fazendas"		1690	OG Pernambuco	1 III 1701	Oporto CdS	
73. Belchior de Sousa Vilas Boas	Lisbon 1654			1680	J Orfãos JF Corg Prov Bahia	28 I 1701		
74. João Guedes de Sá	Lisbon	Ship captain in Brazil trade		1681	OG Pernambuco	28 V 1701	Oporto CdS MdC	

Continued

Name	Birthplace and Date	Father's Occupation	Univ. Deg.	Entry in Service	Prior Service	Entry in Relação	Posterior Service	Comments
75. José da Costa Correia	Lisbon 1658	"da governança da Bragança"		1682	JF JF Bahia	20 IX 1701		FC
76. Diogo Pacheco de Carvalho	Trancoso	Artisan	C	1670	Ouv Sergipe Prov Bahia	18 III 1702		
77. João de Sousa	Refoios (Oporto)	Alferes		1691		6 XII 1703	Oporto CdS Con Ultra	M
78. Diogo Mendes	Tomar 1657	"fazendas"		1696		12 III 1705	Oporto CdS	
79. João de Pugas de Vasconcelos	Lisbon 1656		L	1692	OG Angola	2 XI 1706	Oporto	
80. André Leitão de Melo	Tavira	Captain	L	1694	JF JF Bahia Prov Bahia	18 VI 1707	Oporto Cd3	M
81. Manoel de Azevedo Soares	Oporto	Shopkeeper	L		JF OG Cabo Verde	18 VI 1707	CdS	
82. Carlos de Azevedo Leite	Guimarães			1691	JF (2)	21 VI 1707	Oporto	
83. João de Sá Sottomayor	Ponte de Lima	Real estate		1697	Ouv Sergipe	28 VII 1708		P, M
84. Gregório Pereira Fidalgo da Silveira	Estremoz		L	1686		22 IX 1708		
85. Diogo Filipe Pereira	Oporto 1667	"fazendas"		1691		13 II 1710	Oporto	
86. João Vieira de Macedo	Oporto		C	1690	Ouv Bahia	13 II 1710		
87. Alexandre Botelho de Moraes	Torre de Moncorvo		L		JF	13 II 1710	Oporto CdS	

88. Antônio de Macedo Velho	Lisbon	Clerk		1693	JF (2)	13 II 1710	CdS Con Ultra	
89. Cristóvão Gomes de Azevedo	Evora			1703		13 II 1710	Oporto	
90. Rodrigo Rabelo da Silva	Bracarena (Lisbon)	Captain of the Torre de Belem	L	1693	OG Angola	13 II 1710	Oporto	
91. Antônio da Cunha Sottomayor	Vila Viçosa 1674	"fisco mor"		1696	Ouv Alfan Ouv	27 X 1711	Oporto CdS	FC, M
92. Luís de Mello da Silva	1669	Chief constable		1696		20 X 1711		
93. Antônio Sanches Pereira						20 VI 1713	CdS	X
94. Manoel da Costa Bonicho	Coimbra	Letrado	C	1708		20 VI 1713	Oporto CdS DdP	
95. Dionísio de Azevedo e Arevalos	Odemira	"da governança"		1696	OG São Tomé	8 VIII 1713		P, M
96. Manoel de Lima Barreto	Coimbra			1682	JF (2) Corg	I VI 1715	Oporto	X
97. Caetano de Brito de Figueiredo	Lisbon 1672	"escrivão da fazenda"	C	1698	JF (2) Ouv	I VI 1715	Oporto	X
98. João Homem Freire	Vizeu	Letrado	L	1715		I IV 1715	Oporto	M, I
99. Tomás Feliciano de Albernás	Lisbon		L	1694	OG Sergipe	7 XI 1715		M, X

Continued

Name	Birthplace and Date	Father's Occupation	Univ. Deg.	Entry in Service	Prior Service	Entry in Relação	Posterior Service	Comments
100. Manoel da Costa Moreira	Belem (Lisbon) 1666	"mestre de obras do ofício de pedreiro"	L	1691	J Alfama	23 XI 1715	Oporto	
101. Luís de Sousa Pereira	*Bahia* 1691	Letrado	L	1716		18 IV 1718		X, M
102. Luís Siqueira da Gama	Lisbon		C		JF (2)		Oporto CdS	M
103. Afonso Rodrigues Bernardo e Sampaio	Alcobaça	Physician	L	1704	OG Cabo Verde	27 VI 1719		
104. José de Acunha Soares					OG Alagoas	20 V 1720		
105. José de Caminha Falcão	Coimbra 1668	Letrado	L Doutor	1705		8 VI 1720	Oporto	X, FC
106. Diogo Mendes Duro Esmeraldo	Oporto 1675	Letrado		1699	Prov	26 VI 1720	Oporto	M
107. Antônio de Rêgo e Sá Quintanilla	Lisbon 1674	"honrado"	C	1697	Ouv	26 VI 1720	Oporto	M, X
108. Manoel Ferreira de Carvalho	Setúbal 1665	"fazendas"	C	1695	OG Angola	20 XII 1720		
109. Bernardo de Sousa Estrela	Azores 1670	"person of substance"	C	1699	JF (2) Corg	21 VIII 1723	retired in 1730; d. 1759	M
110. João Veríssimo da Silva Torres Cordeiro	Lisbon 1694	Letrado		1716	Corg	21 VIII 1723		
111. Xavier Lopes Vilela	Oeiras			1708	OG Cabo Verde	23 XI 1724		

112. Francisco de Santa Barbara e Moura	Lisbon		C		OG Angola	3 IV 1724	Oporto CdS	M
113. Domingos Gonçalves Santiago				1716	JF (2)	14 VI 1727	Oporto	X
114. João Leal de Gama de Ataide	Tavira	Merchant		1717	JF	3 IV 1727	Oporto CdS	
115. Pedro Velho do Lagar	Lisbon	Merchant Venetian	L	1714	JF (2)	14 VI 1727	Oporto CdS	
116. André Ferreira Lobato Lobo	Puralete			1710	Corg	14 VI 1727	Oporto CdS	
117. Luís Machado de Barros	Vila do Conde			1719		5 VII 1727	CdS MdC	M
118. Pedro de Freitas Tavares Pinto	Lisbon 1687	fazendas"		1712	J Orfãos	5 VII 1757	Oporto	FC
119. Pedro Gonçalves Cordeiro Pereira	Ourique 1684	"honrado"			Oporto Ouv Bahia	6 IX 1727	CdS	
120. Antônio Rodrigues Banha	*Bahia* 1714	Letrado			JF Ouv Vila do Principe (Minas)	3 III 1729		X
121. Teotônio Ferreira da Cunha	Lisbon 1689	Artisan	C	1716	JF (2)	23 VII 1729	Oporto CdS	
122. Caetano Alberto de Osuna		Goldsmith			Practicing law in CdS	23 XII 1730	Oporto CdS MdC	X
123. Francisco Lopes de Carvalho	Lisbon	(Fidalgo)	C		JF OG Pernambuco	5 XII 1731	Oporto CdS	X, FC

Continued

Name	Birthplace and Date	Father's Occupation	Univ. Deg.	Entry in Service	Prior Service	Entry in Relação	Posterior Service	Comments
124. Antônio Marques Cardoso	Lisbon 1686	"tailor for clerics"	L	1716	JF OC Moucha (Piauí)	19 VIII 1733	Oporto	
125. Francisco Pereira da Costa	Lisbon				OG Paraíba OG Angola	6 IV 1734		X
126. Antônio José da Fonseca Lemos	Lisbon 1696	Letrado	L	1721	JF J Civel	9 XI 1734	Oporto CdS DdP	M
127. Sergio Justiano de Oliveira	Lisbon 1699	"honrado"	C	1725		9 XI 1734	Oporto CdS	
128. João Alvares de Figueiredo Brandão	Vila Cova		L		JF Corg	19 IV 1735	Oporto	M
129. Antônio Pires da Silveira	Bragança 1688	Farmer	C	1716	Corg	19 IV 1735	Oporto CdS	
130. Francisco de Sá Barreto	Assequins de Agueda		L	1718	JF (2) Corg	19 IV 1735	Oporto	X
131. Ignacio Dias Madeira	Tondella 1697	Letrado	L	1724	JF Goa	22 VI 1737	CdS	M
132. Bento da Costa de Oliveira e Sampaio	Oporto 1702	Merchant	C Doutor	1724	JF (2)	13 III 1739	Oporto CdS	
133. Antônio Rodrigues da Silva	Vila do Conde 1690	"fazendas"	L	1710	Aud. ger. OG Pernambuco	18 VI 1739	Oporto	
134. Manoel Luís Pires	Lisbon	Custodian of the Casa da India "propretario"			JF (2)	11 VI 1741		X

135. Manoel Antônio da Cunha e de Sottomayor	Vianna 1708	Fidalgo	C	1732		11 VI 1741	Oporto CdS Con Ultra	FC
136. Antônio Alvares da Cunha	Oporto	"fazendas"	C Prof	1735		11 VI 1741	Oporto CdS	
137. Bento da Silva Ramalho	Vieira		C		OG Pernambuco	9 V 1741	Oporto	M
138. Venceslão Pereira da Silva	Alenquer 1692	"fazendas"	L	1717	JF Bahia	9 V 1741	Oporto	
139. Manoel Vieira Pedrosa						9 V 1741		M
140. Francisco de Campos Limpo	Vizeu 1698	Letrado		1720	JF Corg Oporto CdS	22 IX 1742		X
141. Carlos Antônio da Silva Franco	Sacavém (Lisbon) 1707	Letrado	C	1730	JF (2)	4 III 1745	Oporto	
142. Pascoal Ferreira da Veras	Oporto		C	1720	OG Espírito Santo	2 XII 1745	Oporto	
143. Acursio José de Magalhães	Coimbra		L			5 VII 1746		
144. João Gonçalves Pereira	Medeiros		C		JF OG Cuiabá	11 IV 1747		
145. Agostinho Felix dos Santos Capello	Alcafozes (Castelo Branco) 1709	"da governança"	C	1732	OG Sergīpe	19 IX 1747		
146. Jorge Salter de Mendonça	Lisbon		L		OG Paraíba	18 XI 1747	Oporto	M

Continued

Name	Birthplace and Date	Father's Occupation	Univ. Deg.	Entry in Service	Prior Service	Entry in Relação	Posterior Service	Comments
147. João Cardoso Pinheiro	Oporto 1702		C	1731	JF (2)	18 I 1748	Oporto	
148. Luís Cunha Varela		Letrado	C	1733	JF Corg	18 I 1748		
149. Manoel da Fonseca Brandão	Torrozelo		L		JF Ouv Bahia	14 III 1748	Rio CdS	
150. João Rodrigues Campelo	*Pernambuco* 1697	Sargento-Mór	C	1721	JF Ouv São Paulo	23 IX 1749	Oporto	X
151. Cristóvão Alvares de Azevedo Osorio	*Bahia* 1708	Sargento-Mór	L Doutor	1738	JF OG São Tomé	25 I 1752		X
152. Francisco Marcelino de Gouveia			C	1734	JF Ouv Bahia	13 IV 1752		X
153. Francisco Xavier de Carvalho	Santarem		C		JF	16 IV 1752	Oporto	X
154. Raimundo Coelho de Melo	Lisbon 1718	Courtier	C	1738	Ouv	16 IV 1752	Oporto	FC
155. João Elizeu de Sousa	*Bahia* 1695	Captain	C	1721	JF (3) Corg	18 I 1753		
156. Diogo Vieira de Sousa	Ourique 1718	Estates and business	C	1751		18 I 1753		
157. Francisco Antônio Berco da Silveira	Fayal (Azores) 1702	Merchant	C		JF OG Rio de Janeiro	6 IV 1754	Oporto CdS	*M*
158. Antônio Ferreira Gil	Lisbon	Artisan	C	1730	OG Paraíba	27 IV 1754	Oporto	
159. Bernardo Ribeiro Velho	Vila Franca de Xira	Captain	C	1730	JF (2)	27 IV 1754		

160. Bernadino Falcão de Gouvea						27 IV 1754		M
161. Fernando José da Cunha Pereira	Vizeu 1711	Letrado		1736	OG Angola	27 IV 1754	Oporto CdS	
162. Luís Rabelo Quintella	Lisbon	Merchant	L	1749	JF	27 IV 1754	Oporto	
163. Ciríaco Antônio de Moura Tavares	Estremos 1712	Treasury officer in army		1736		8 IV 1755	Oporto	X
164. Sebastião Francisco Manoel	Óbidos	"fazendas"	L	1739	JF	8 IV 1755		
165. João Pedro Henriques de Silva					OG Moucha (Piauí)	9 VIII 1757		
166. Francisco de Figueiredo Vaz						18 III 1758	Oporto	
167. Tomás Rubi de Barros Barreto	Vianna 1714	da governança"		1740	Sup. Serro do Frio	24 X 1758	CdS	
168. Joaquim José de Andrade	Lisbon				JF (2) Ouv Bahia parte do Sul	7 XI 1758		X

GLOSSARY

Accordão. Sentence or resolution of a court of justice.
Advogado. Lawyer.
Alçada. Jurisdiction; sometimes used as a synonym for *devassa.*
Alcaide. Chief constable of a city.
Aldeia. A village; used in Brazil especially for Indian villages under Jesuit control.
Alfândega. Customs house.
Alferes. Lieutenant; ensign.
Almotacel. Inspector of weights and measures.
Alvará. Royal decree to remain in force for one year, but usually issued with provision for indefinite extension.
Arroba. A unit of weight equal to 32 lbs.
Assento. Memorandum or resolution taken in a high court.
Bacharel (pl. *Bacharéis*). Holder of a bachelor's degree; also a synonym for a lawyer or a judge.
Caixa. A box or crate.
Câmara (*senado da Câmara*) Municipal council.
Canones. Canon law.
Capitania. Captaincy, a territorial division.
Capitão-mór. Captain-major.
Carta régia. A royal order intended to be permanent.
Casa de Vinte-quatro. Representative body of the artisan guilds in Portugal.
Chanceler. Chancellor of a High Court.
Comarca. A territorial division or district, sometimes equated with a province.
Compadrio, Compadresco. Ritual co-parentage; someone involved in these relationships becomes a *compadre* (masc.) or a *comadre* (fem.) or a *padrinho*(*a*), a godparent.
Conselho. A council.
Consulado. Merchant guild.
Consulta. Record of a discussion in council, and by extension a council's decision.
Corregedor. A superior crown magistrate in charge of a *correição.*
Correição. A judicial district; *fazer correição*, to make a circuit tour of a judicial district.
Couto (*homizio*). An area in which those charged with crimes were exempt from prosecution.

Cruzado. Monetary unit equal to 400 *réis.*

Degredado. A penal exile.

Desembargador. A high court magistrate; *dos agravos*, assigned to appellate cases; *extravagantes*, without specific assignment.

Desembargo do Paço. Royal council of justice and the judiciary.

Devassa. Any judicial review or inquiry, especially one brought about by extraordinary circumstances.

Dízimo. Church tithe.

Donatário. Donatary; in Brazil the holder of a *capitania.*

Doutorado. The doctorate.

Engenho. A sugar mill or plantation.

Escrivão (pl. *escrivães*). Clerk, scribe.

Encomienda (Sp.). A grant of Indian labor or tribute in Spanish America.

Engenho. A sugar mill and by extension a sugar plantation.

Entrada. An expedition of exploration or for military purposes.

Familiar. A lay informant of the Inquisition.

Fazenda. Property of any kind; a farm; the treasury; *fazenda de canas* or *partido de canas*, a sugar cane farm.

Fiança. A security, bail.

Fidalgo. A nobleman or gentleman; *fidalguia*, nobility.

Guarda-mór. Chief custodian.

Interrogatório. A questionnaire.

Irmandade. A brotherhood; sodality.

Juiz da coroa e fazenda. High court judge responsible for hearing cases involving royal interests.

Juiz de fôra. The lowest rank in the professional judiciary.

Juiz ordinário; Juiz da terra. Elected magistrate; justice of the peace.

Juiz dos órfãos. Probate judge.

Junta da Fazenda. Treasury board.

Lavrador. A farmer; *de cana*, a sugar cane grower.

Leis. Laws; the course of civil law.

Leis extravagantes. Uncodified legislation.

Letrado. A university graduate, often a synonym for lawyer or judge.

Licenciado. Licenciate degree or its holder.

Maço. A bundle of documents.

Mamposteiro. In Portugal an official who collected funds to ransom prisoners; in Brazil, a layman who acted as protector of Indians.

Meirinho. Bailiff.

Mercê. A royal award or gift.

Mesa. Board or chamber; *mesa grande*, plenary session of the High Court.

Mestiço. A half-breed of Indian and European parentage.

Milrei (*Milréis*). 1000 réis; in the mid-seventeenth century a coin worth about 12s. English.

Morador. A colonist, a householder.

Muscavado. Lower grade of sugar.

Ouvidor. Judge with appellate jurisdiction; *ouvidor geral,* superior crown magistrate in a *comarca.*

Parecer. An opinion, usually given in a council.

Pelourinho. Pillory, symbol of royal control.

Poderosos da terra. Local potentates.

Povo. People; often used to denote the common folk.

Procurador. Legal representative.

Procurador da coroa. Crown's attorney.

Provedor. Superintendant, usually with financial responsibilities; *d'alfandega,* of customs house; *de defuntos,* of intestate property; *dos órfaõs,* of orphans; *provedor-mór da fazenda,* chief financial officer, Treasurer-general.

Regidor. Regent; presiding officer in a High Court.

Regimento. Standing order or instruction.

Réis (sing. *real*). Smallest monetary unit, existed only as money of account.

Relação. A High Court of Appeal.

Residência. Examination of an official's performance held at the end of his term of office.

Senhor de engenho. A plantation owner.

Sertão (pl. *sertões*). The bush, interior, back country.

Sesmarias. Land grants; *sesmeiro,* in Brazil the holder of a *sesmaria.*

Tabelião (pl. *tabeliães*). Notary.

Tenção (pl. *tenções*). A written judicial opinion.

Tostão (pl. *tostões*). A copper coin, a penny.

Vereador. Alderman of a municipal council.

BIBLIOGRAPHY

Most of the preceding story has been reconstructed from a large number of published documents and an even larger number of unpublished manuscripts drawn from the archives and libraries of Brazil, England, Portugal, and Spain. No one archive houses the papers of the Relação or the magistracy, and thus materials for this study have come from a wide range of sources. Portuguese repositories were essential to almost all parts of this study, and the Spanish archives proved especially valuable for the period 1580–1640. Archives in Brazil hold very little for the period prior to 1626, but the history of the High Court after 1652 cannot be written without them. In the following discussion I have listed by country the archives and collections which yielded the materials used in this study. Published guides that proved especially valuable have also been listed. Following this discussion is a list of the books and articles which proved useful. Since virtually none of them deal directly with the Relação, I have not included annotations. Many are discussed, however, in the bibliographies of C. R. Boxer's books, in Dauril Alden's *Royal Government in Colonial Brazil,* and in A. J. R. Russell-Wood, *Fidalgos and Philanthropists.* The reader is directed to these works for judicious remarks on many of the items cited here.

I. MANUSCRIPT SOURCES

Brazil

The archives of Salvador and Rio de Janeiro provided material both on the Relação and on Brazilian society in general. Aside from the normal problems of understaffing, and lack of funds, which are usually overcome by the hospitality and goodwill of the archival staffs, the student also faces the ravages of time, climate, and assorted insects. The documents from the early colonial period have suffered the most from these conditions. Many documents which do remain in Brazilian archives are copies of correspondence which was forwarded to Portugal and can be seen there. On the other hand, records of local institutions in the colony were not sent to the metropolis and must be seen in Brazil. Eight Brazilian archives were consulted in the preparation of this study.

A. *Arquivo da Câmara Municipal da Bahia.* This archive holds the papers of the municipal council of Salvador. The collection is quite large and my research in no way exhausted its possibilities. There are a number of series but numeration is consecutive for the entire collection. I used:

Actas da Câmara (Council minutes)

Nos. 25 (1702–1708); 26 (1708–1711); 27 (1716–1718); 28 (1716–1718). The *Actas* from 1626 to 1700 have been published.

Provisões reaes

Nos. 34 (1641–1680), 135 (1641–1680).

Portarias

Nos. 155 (1624–1642); 156 (1626–1642); 157 (1642–1648); 158 (1648–1657).

B. *Arquivo da Curia Metropolitana da Bahia.* This is the archive of the archbishopric of Bahia, where the old parish registers have been gathered. For the most part their condition is precarious and some are simply illegible. I made use of the following:

Paroquia da Conceição da Praia

1631–1691 Óbitos.

1649–1676 Baptizados (This codex actually records baptisms as early as 1596).

1631–1694 Casamentos

Paroquia da Vitória

1630–1713 Baptizados

C. *Arquivo Histórico da Itamaraty.* This is the archive of the Brazilian Foreign Office. The manuscripts consulted here were actually kept in the Library section since they were in the process of being transcribed in preparation for publication. The papers consulted were: "Cartas do Conde de Torre"; and "Cartas d'El Rey escriptas aos Senhores Alvaro e Gaspar de Sousa," which I have cited as "Correspondencia . . . Gaspar de Sousa." This latter is the letter book of the governor of Brazil for the period 1613–1617.

D. *Arquivo Histórico Nacional de Rio de Janeiro.* This great archive presently houses the records of the Relação do Rio de Janeiro but it has very little on the Bahian tribunal. Codex 311 is a copy of the "Livro Dourado," the register of laws and royal orders kept by the High Court of Bahia. Other copies exist in Evora and Coimbra. Codices 540, 541, and 542 are registers of royal orders and *alvaras.* Codex 540 is especially important since it contains many *assentos* of the plenary session of the Bahian Relação.

E. *Arquivo Público do Estado da Bahia.* The Bahian State Archive contains a significant collection of colonial materials in its historical and judicial sections. A good guide to the collection is *Guia do Arquivo do Estado da Bahia* (Salvador, n.d.). Parts of the series *Ordens régias* have been catalogued in the *Anais do Arquivo Publico da Bahia.* In the Historical Section *(secção historica)* little exists for the period prior to 1626, and thus the APB provided no material for parts I and II of this study. For the period after 1652 the APB was essential. The documents in the historical section are organized by type but the entire collection is numbered consecutively. Most helpful in this study were:

Ordens régias 1–44 (1648–1747)
Cartas do Governo 174 (1726–1758); 175 (1755–1765)
Termos de Posse e Juramentos 123 (1653–1889); 124 (1661–1805)
Devassas 572 (1759–1783); 573 (1741–1822)
Relação 494, 495 (1677–78); 496 (alvaras, 1681–1693); 497 (1693–1699); 498 (Livro de Registro, 1700–1704); 501 (1707–1712); 502 (1712–1715); 503 (1715–1718); 504 (1718–1720)

In the judicial section *(secção judiciaria)* the series Livros de Notas de Escrituras provided much material on the lives of the desembargadores. Unfortunately, the series for Salvador begins in the 1660's, and thus the private lives of the earlier judges cannot be traced.

F. *Arquivo da Santa Casa da Misericórdia da Bahia.* Here too there were very few documents which antedated 1626. Three series proved especially useful: Livros de Tombo (1612–1849); Termos de Irmãos (1613–1772); and Elleições de Provedores e Irmãos (1667–1791). There is no published catalogue of the collection, although a checklist is available in the archive. The student should consult the catalogue and discussion of sources provided in Russell-Wood, *Fidalgos and Philanthropists,* for the best description of this rich depository.

G. *Biblioteca Nacional de Rio de Janeiro.* Many of the pertinent documents housed in this institution have been published in the series *Documentos Históricos*. Others of interest to this study were:

1, 2, 35 Papeis vários
7, 3, 1 Carta de El Rey a Baltesar Ferraz (1588)
II—33, 23, 17 Papeis vários
II—34, 2, 1 Noticia de Jerônimo Sodré Pereira
II—34, 5, 24 Peticão de Francisco de Estrada
II—34, 9, 6 "Portaria sobre a construção, alugel, e venda dos predios pertencentes a Casa da Relação da Bahia (1685–1761)"

H. *Instituto Histórico e Geográfico Brasileiro.* Although the manuscript collection of the IHGB is extensive, there were only a few items of direct interest. The nineteenth-century copies of correspondence sent to the Conselho Ultramarino in the colonial period proved helpful. These documents are catalogued under the heading "Arquivo Ultramarino."

1.1.17 Consultas Conselho Ultramarino (Bahia)
1.1.19 Correspondencia do Gov. da Bahia, Conde de Atouguia.
1.1.22 Consultas Conselho Ultramarino (Bahia)
1.2.11 Conselho Ultramarino Varios

In the section of loose documents kept in tin cases (*latas*) the following items were used:

Lata 37, doc. 6 "Lista dos assentos encadernados em pergamino tomados na Relação da Bahia."
Lata 37, doc. 15 "Catalogo de todas as ordens registradas nos livros 1, 2, 3, 4 de registro da Relação da Bahia feito no ano 1795."
Lata 96, doc. 6 "Copia do Livro Dourado da Relação."

Portugal

Despite the Lisbon earthquake of 1755, the archives and libraries of Portugal still hold the richest collection of historical materials relating to Brazil's colonial past, and especially for the sixteenth and seventeenth centuries. Copies of many documents lost or destroyed in Brazil have survived in Portugal. Moreover, the minutes of metropolitan councils such as the Conselho da Fazenda and the Mesa da Conciência are available only in Lisbon. These archives are a treasure trove and the researcher needs only patience, diplomacy, *sitzfleisch*, and good luck to profit from them.

A. *Academia das Ciências de Lisboa.*

Ms. 133 "Historia da capitania da Parahíba pelo Ouvidor q. foi da mesma provincia"

Ms. 98 "Livro Verde da Relação de Goa"
Ms. 416 "Noticia Sumaria do que sucedio em Portugal desde o tempo do Cardeal D. Henrique . . . ate D. João IV"

B. *Arquivo Histórico da Câmara Municipal de Lisboa.*
Livro 63, 64

C. *Arquivo Histórico Ultramarino* (AHU). By far the most important archive for this study, the AHU houses the papers of the colonial councils, the Conselho da Fazenda and the Conselho Ultramarino. Governmental correspondence, private petitions, cases involving crown interests, and various supporting documents were remitted to Lisbon and are now kept in the boxes (*caixas*) of loose papers (*papeis avulsos*). These are supplemented by the discussions and decisions of the councils (*consultas*) kept in the series of minute books (*Livros de Consultas*). The *caixas* of Brazilian documents are arranged chronologically by captaincy. For Bahia there are three separate series of *caixas* with overlapping dates. The "catalogued series" has been inventoried in Eduardo Castro e Almeida, "Inventário dos documentos relativos ao Brasil existentes no Arquivo da Marinha e Ultramar de Lisboa," *ABNR* (1913–1914, 1916–1918). There are two "uncatalogued" series, the first of which has actually been very well inventoried by Luiza da Fonseca in a two-volume typescript guide entitled "Bahia, Índice dos documentos do seculo xvii," available at AHU. The date is still the surest way of locating the Bahian documents. Some of these documents are available on microfilm at the Bancroft Library of the University of California at Berkeley. Unless otherwise noted I have used the original. The best guide to the codices is presented in H. Fitzler and E. Ennes, *A secção ultramarina da Biblioteca Nacional* (Lisbon, 1928). The principal documents used were:

Papéis avulsos
Bahia, catalogued series, caixas 1–5 (1591–1652)
Bahia, 1st uncatalogued series, caixas 1–13 (1599–1679)
caixas 14–18 (1680–1700), Bancroft microfilm
Bahia, 2nd series uncatalogued, caixa 1 (1642)
Ceará, caixa 1 (1618–1645)
Espírito Santo, caixa 1
Maranhão, caixa 1 (1616–1637)
Pará, caixa 1 (1616–1642)
Paraíba, caixa 1 (1593–1679)
Pernambuco, caixa 1, 2, 3 (1599–1651)
Rio de Janeiro, caixa 1 (1614–1639)
São Paulo, caixa 1 (1618–1719)

Sergipe d'El-Rey, caixa 1 (1619–1725)

Codices of the Conselho da Fazenda

31 (1618); 32 (1620); 33 (1621–1622); 34 (1622); 35 (1623); 35A, 35B consultas de partes; 36 (1624–1625); 37 (1627); 38 consultas de partes (1629); 39 (1631); 40 (1634–1635); 41 (1635–1636) 42 (1636); 172 (1619–1631); 173 (1630's); 1164 Livro de despezas (1613–1622); 1192 Registro de 1164 Libro de despezas (1613–1622); 1192 Registro de consultas (1615).

D. *Arquivo Municipal de Coimbra.* The holdings of this archive are rich in local materials and for representative documents on the contacts between crown and town. Research has been aided by the useful guide by José Branquinho de Carvalho e Armando Carneiro da Silva, *Catálogo dos manuscritos do Arquivo Municipal* (Coimbra, 1964). I used:

"Documentos avulsos" 1464–1826.

"Provisões e capítulos das Cortes" 1426–1660.

E. *Arquivo Nacional da Torre do Tombo (Lisbon).* The riches of this depository still remain only partially revealed despite the ardent researches of both Portuguese and foreign scholars. Each collection has a catalogue but these are of very unequal value and in some cases virtually useless. The staff of the ANTT is presently preparing an inclusive guide and index that will greatly facilitate research. The published volumes that proved most useful were: Pedro d'Azevedo and António Baião, *O Arquivo da Torre do Tombo* (Lisbon, 1905); A. Mesquita de Figueiredo, *Arquivo Nacional da Torre do Tombo* (Lisbon, 1922).

Many collections in this archive provided some material, but a few were indispensable. The Leitura dos Bacharéis contained materials for the magistrates' biographies, and the registers of awards, offices, and privileges (*chancelarias*) outline the professional life of the judges. The enormous Corpo cronológico collection contains letters from royal officials and town councils in Brazil. The Jesuit portfolio (Cartório dos Jesuitas) contains the papers of the Engenho Sergipe do Conde, which shed some light on the Recôncavo and occasionally on the High Court. The following collections proved most helpful:

Cartório dos Jesuitas, maços 5–17 (papers of the engenho of Sergipe do Conde)

Chancelarias Filipe I, II, III, Doações, Privilégios

Chancelarias João IV, Doações

Chancelarias Afonso VI, Doações

Chancelarias Pedro II, Doações

Chancelarias João V, Doações
Chancelarias Ordem do Cristo
Colecção de São Vicente, Livros 10, 12, 13, 14, 17, 19, 22, 23
Convento da Graça, Pecúlios 2, 3
Corpo cronológico, part 1, maços 111, 112, 113, 114, 115, 116, 117, 118, 119, 120; part 3, maços 20–23, inclusive.
Leitura dos Bacharéis (documents located by name of the letrado under investigation).
Manuscritos da Livraria 844, 1104, 1109, 1113, 1116
Mesa da Consciência e Ordens, Livros de registros de consultas 16–36, inclusive (1594–1640).

F. *Arquivo da Universidade de Coimbra.* Here I consulted the records of matriculation of the members of the Relação. The researcher is aided here by a card index (*verbetes*) of this collection.

G. *Biblioteca da Ajuda* (Lisbon). This is the former royal library created in 1756. The manuscripts in this collection which proved especially helpful were the letterbooks of the viceroys of Portugal during the Spanish period, papers of the Desembargo do Paço, and copies of royal correspondence. To assist the researcher there is an excellent guide by Carlos Alberto Ferreira, *Inventário dos manuscritos da Biblioteca da Ajuda referentes a América do Sul* (Coimbra, 1956). This guide is organized chronologically and the interested reader is referred to it for a description of the sources used in this study.

H. *Biblioteca Geral da Universidade de Coimbra.* There are a number of published guides to this rich collection, which is often overlooked by Brazilianists. Best among them are *Catálogos de manuscritos da Biblioteca da Universidade de Coimbra,* 15 vols. to date (Coimbra, 1931 ff); and Francisco Morais, *Catálogo dos manuscritos da Biblioteca da Universidade de Coimbra relativos ao Brasil* (Coimbra, 1931). The most important mss. for this study were copies of the High Court's registry of laws.

Ms. 457 "Cartas regias, 1591–1633"
Ms. 460 "Consultas do Conselho (da Fazenda)"
Ms. 666 (Das Póvoas geneaology)
Ms. 673 Various papers containing appointment lists
Ms. 695 Relação do Porto
Ms. 707, 708, 709 Laws and provisions recorded by the High Court of Bahia. Codex 708 is a copy of the High Court's register.

I. *Biblioteca Nacional de Lisboa.* The Reservados or manuscript section of this library contains an important collection of documents. Of direct interest were:

Fundo Geral, 251, 1555, 7627

Coleção Pombalina, 249, 471, 474, 475, 495, 647, 733, 738

J. *Biblioteca Pública de Évora.* Many of the most interesting mss. have already been published. See, for example, Frédéric Mauro, *Le Brésil au XVII siècle, Documents inédits relatif à l'Atlantique portugais* (Coimbra, 1961). An excellent published catalogue is J. H. Cunha Rivara, *Catalogo dos manuscritos da Biblioteca Publica Eborense,* 4 vols. (Lisbon, 1850). Of particular interest were:

CXV/2–3 "Livro Dourado da Relação"

CV/2–6 "Versos satiricos da Bahia"

CXVI/1–33 "Resolução que o Bispo e ouvidor geral do Brazil tomaram sobre os injustos cativeiros dos Indios"

CXVI/1–25 "Sumario das armadas que se fizerão e guerras que se derão na Conquista do Rio Parahiba em 1584"

CV/2–19 "Papel secreto que se deu a Rey de Castella em q. se lhe da conta da qualidade, partes, e sufficiencia dos principais ministros de Portugal. . . ."

K. *Biblioteca Pública Municipal do Pôrto.* The Brazilian holdings of this library are not numerous but some are of great interest. There are also some items on the High Court of Oporto that were useful.

Ms. 126 Livro do Rezão do Estado do Brasil

Ms. 686 Domingos Alves Branco Muniz Barreto, "Observações sobre a fortificação da Cidade da Bahia"

Ms. 795 "Colleção do que mais essentialmente contem os livros da esfera e dos Assentos da Relação do Porto (1773)"

Ms. 1114 José Luis Ferreira Nobre, "Compendio da Antiguidade e estabelecimento das Relações de Lisboa e Porto"

Ms. 1155 P. Manuel Baptista, "Petição da Provincia do Brasil (1654)"

L. *Sociedade de Geografia de Lisboa.*

Caetano de Brito Figueredo, "Dissertações Academicas e historicas nas quais se trata de historia natural das cousas do Brasil (1724)"

Gonçalo Soares de Franca, "Dissertações da Historia eclesiastica do Brasil (1724)"

"Documentos dirigidos a Fernão Telles de Meneses, Governador das Armas e da Relação do Porto (1648–1652)"

Spain

The Biblioteca Nacional de Madrid, the Archivo Nacional de Madrid, and the Real Academia de la Historia all held a few useful items, as did the Archivo General de Indias in Seville. The most important Spanish archive for the history of Brazil is the Archivo General de Simancas, which preserves the papers of the Conselho de Portugal, the supreme advisory council on Portuguese affairs during the union of the Iberian crowns. Matters discussed by the Conselho da India, the Conselho da Fazenda, Desembargo do Paço, and Mesa da Consciência were eventually submitted for review to the Conselho de Portugal, and hence its record books (Secretarias Provinciales, Portugal) are rich in Brazilian materials. Moreover, the Spanish reform of justice in Portugal is documented in the collection Estado: Negociaciones de Portugal.

A. *Archivo General de Indias* (Seville). I found no materials relating directly to the Relação, but there are many documents concerning Brazilian history in this archive. There is now a large but imperfect guide by João Cabral de Mello Neto, *O Arquivo das Indias e o Brasil* (Rio de Janeiro, 1966). The bundles (*legajos*) from the Audiencia de Charcas and the Audiencia de Lima contain materials on the Portuguese in Spanish America in the 1580–1640 period.

B. *Archivo General de Simancas.* Research in this archive was greatly facilitated by the following indices and guides: Angel de la Plaza, *Guia del Investigador* (Valladolid, 1962), Francisco Manuel Alves, *Catalogo dos manuscritos de Simancas respeitantes a historia portuguesa* (Coimbra, 1933). Most valuable were the guides published in the *Boletim da Filmoteca Ultramarina Portuguesa,* Nos. 14, 15, 16.

Secretarias Provinciales (Libros)

1456, 1457, 1458, 1459, 1460, 1461, 1463, 1466, 1467, 1468, 1469, 1470, 1471, 1472, 1474, 1475, 1476, 1477, 1480, 1481, 1483, 1484, 1485, 1489, 1490, 1491, 1492, 1493, 1494, 1495, 1496, 1497, 1506, 1511, 1513, 1522, 1527, 1529, 1531, 1532, 1533, 1534, 1535, 1536, 1537, 1539, 1550, 1551, 1552, 1553, 1554, 1555, 1577, 1579, 1581, 1583

Secretarias Provinciales (legajos)

2634 2635, 2637

Estado: Negociaciones de Portugal

427, 428

Guerra Antigua

690, 904, 906, 930, 967, 1100

C. *Archivo Historico Nacional de Madrid.* The student can orient himself with Luís Sanchez Belda.

D. *Archivo Historico Nacional* (Madrid, 1958). Of some use to this study were:

Sección del Estado: Virreinato de Portugal

Libros 76, 77, 78, 79, 80, 81

Consejo de Portugal

728, 729

E. *Biblioteca Nacional de Madrid.* The extensive holdings of the BNM are not yet fully catalogued. The best printed inventories are Julián Paz, *Catalogo de Tomos de Varios* (Madrid, 1938), and his *Catalogo de manuscritos de América existentes en la Biblioteca Nacional* (Madrid, 1933). Most complete is *Inventario general de manuscritos de la Biblioteca Nacional*, 8 vols. to date (Madrid, 1953 ff). Of particular interest were:

Ms. 938 "Papeles de Orden de Christo de Portugal"
Ms. 1439 "Correspondencia del Conde de Portalegre"
Ms. 1749 "Papeles de Felipe II"
Ms. 18719 (36) "Relación de los servicios de Diego Luís de Oliveira"
Ms. 2292 "Carta del Conde de Portalegre e descripción de Portugal"
Mss. 2845, 2846, 2848 "Ministerio Real de Portugal (1623–1626)"
Ms. 3014 "Cartas tocante a la India Oriental"
Ms. 4162 André Para, *Información en la causa de los estudios de Portugal* (Madrid, 1633)
Ms. 8686 "Advertencias dadas a Philipe II para la buena administración de la justicia en Portugal"

F. *Real Academia de la Historia de Madrid.* Although there was nothing on the High Court itself, there is much material on Brazil and Portugal under the Hapsburgs. There is a published guide to the Salazar collection. See *Índice de la Colección de Don Luís de Salazar y Castro*, 32 vols. (Madrid, 1949–1963).

England

A. *British Museum* (London). The most reliable guides to the Portuguese materials at the BM are: Francisco F. Figanière, *Catálogo dos manuscritos portugueses existentes no Museu Britanico* (Lisbon, 1853); Conde de Tovar, *Catálogo dos manuscritos portugueses ou relativos a Portugal existentes no Museu Britanico* (Lisbon, 1932). I consulted:

Landsdown 145, 154, 160
Edgerton 319, 320, 323, 324, 1131, 1132, 1133, 1134
Additional 13974, 13975, 13977, 20846, 20848, 20897, 20898, 20933, 20934, 20935, 22830, 28426, 28427, 28428, 28429, 21357

B. *Public Record Office* (London). Although the PRO had no material on the Relação, there were a number of manuscripts that cast light on various events and customs in Portugal and that were useful for this study.

State Papers, Miscellaneous, 9/207

State Papers 94, vols. 9, 11, 13, 22, 28, 33

II. AIDS TO RESEARCH: BIBLIOGRAPHIES, CATALOGUES, GUIDES

Barbosa Machado, Diogo. *Biblioteca Lusitania.* 4 vols., 2nd ed., Lisbon, 1933.

Bishko, Charles J. "The Iberian Backgrounds of Latin American History: Recent Progress and Continuing Problems," *Hispanic American Historical Review*, XXXVI (February 1956), 50–80.

Boxer, C. R. "Some Notes on Portuguese Historiography," *History*, XXXIX (1954), 1–13.

Branquinho de Carvalho, José, and Armando da Silva. *Catálogo dos Manuscritos do Arquivo Municipal.* Coimbra, 1964.

Burns, E. Bradford. "A Working Bibliography for the Study of Brazilian History," *The Americas*, XXII (July 1966), 54–88.

Burrus, E. J. "An Introduction to Bibliographical Tools in Spanish Archives and Manuscript Collections Relating to Hispanic America," *Hispanic American Historical Review*, XXXV (November 1955), 443–483.

Castro e Almeida, Eduardo de. "Inventário dos documentos relativos ao Brasil existentes no Archivo da Marinha e Ultramar de Lisboa," *Anais da Biblioteca Nacional de Rio de Janeiro*, XXXI (1909); XXXIX (1917).

Costa, Américo. *Dicionário Corográfico de Portugal Continental e Insular.* 11 vols. Oporto, 1929–1948.

Diccionario de Historia de España: desde sus orígenes hasta el fin reinado de Alfonso XIII. 2 vols. Madrid, 1952.

Diffie, Bailey W. "Bibliography of the Principal Published Guides to Portuguese Archives and Libraries," *Actas do I Colóquio internacional de estudos Luso-brasileiros* (Nashville, 1953), 181–88.

"Indices de documentos relativos ao Brasil," *Anais da Biblioteca Nacional de Rio de Janeiro*, LXI (1939), 59–238.

"Inventário dos documentos relativos ao Brasil existentes na Biblioteca Nacional de Lisboa," *Anais da Biblioteca Nacional de Rio de Janeiro*, LXXV (1957).

Machado de Faria, António. *Amorial lusitano.* Lisbon, 1961.

Peña y Cámara, José Maria de la. "La participación portuguesa en la obra colonizadora de España en América segun la documentación del Archivo General de Indias," *Actas. Congresso internacional dos descombrimentos*, V, part ii (Lisbon, 1960).

Pinto Ferreira, J. A. (ed.). *Índice chronologico dos documentos mais notaveis que se achavão no illustrissima Câmara da Cidade do Porto.* . . . Oporto, 1959.

Rau, Virginia. "Arquivos de Portugal: Lisboa," *Actas do I Coloquio internacional de estudos Luso-brasileiros* (Nashville, 1953), 189–213.

—— and Maria Fernanda Gomes da Silva. *Os manuscritos do Arquivo da Cadaval respeitantes ao Brasil* (Coimbra, 1955), 2 vols.

Rodrigues, José Honório. *Historiografía del Brasil. Siglo XVI.* Mexico City, 1957.

——. *Historiografía del Brasil. Siglo XVII.* Mexico City, 1963.

——. *Historiografia e Bibliografia do domínio holandês no Brasil.* Rio de Janeiro, 1949.

——. *Teoria da História do Brasil.* 2 vols. São Paulo, 1957.

Serrão, Joel. *Dicionário da História de Portugal.* 4 vols. (Lisbon, 1963–1971).

Law: Collections, Indexes, Commentaries

Almeida e Amaral Bottelho, Francisco de. *Discursos jurídicos em que se contém várias matérias úteis aos principiantes com os assentos da Caza da Supplicação.* Lisbon, 1790.

Altimira y Crevea, Rafael. *Diccionario castellano de palabras jurídicas y technicas tomadas de la legislación indiana.* Mexico City, 1951.

Andrade e Silva, José Justino. *Collecção chronlogica da legislação portugueza (1603–1700).* 10 vols., Lisbon, 1854–1859.

Elescano, António Barnabé de. *Demetrio moderno ou o bibliografo juridico portuguez.* Lisbon, 1781.

Leite, Serafim (ed.). *Estatutos da Universidade de Coimbra (1550).* Coimbra, 1963.

Mello Freire, Pascoal José. *Dissertação histórico iuridica sobre os direitos e iurisdicção do grão-prior do Crato e do seu provisor.* Lisbon, 1808.

Mendes de Almeida, Candido (ed.). *Codigo Phillipino ou Ordenações e leis do reino de Portugal.* Rio de Janeiro, 1870.

Ordenações e leis do Reino de Portugal recopiladas por mandado del Rei D. Filippe o primeiro. 10th ed. 5 vols. in 3. Coimbra, 1833.

Ordenações do Senhor Rey D. Manuel. 5 vols. in 4. Coimbra, 1797.

Pereira e Sousa, José Caetano. *Esboço de um dicionário juridico teorético e practico remissivo ás leis compiladas e extravagantes.* Lisbon, 1825.

Ribeiro, João Pedro. *Dissertações chronologicas e criticas sobre a historia jurisprudencia ecclesiastica e civil de Portugal.* 5 vols., Lisbon, 1825.

——. *Indice chronologico remissivo da legislação portugueza posterior à publicação do Codigo filippino.* 6 vols., Lisbon, 1805–1830.

Solórzano Pereira, Juan de. *Política Indiana.* Madrid, [1647] 1648.

Thomás, Manuel Fernandes. *Repetorio geral ou indice alphabetico das leis extravagantes do reino de Portugal.* 2 vols. Coimbra, 1815–1819.

III. PRINTED DOCUMENTS AND CONTEMPORARY ACCOUNTS

Abranches Garcia, José Ignacio. *Archivo da Relação de Goa (1601–1640).* Nova Goa, 1872.

Abreu e Brito, Domingos. *Um ínquerito à vida administrativa e econômica de Angola e do Brasil.* Alfredo de Albuquerque Felner, ed. Coimbra, 1931.

Acosta, José de. *Historia Natural y Moral de las Indias.* 2nd ed., Mexico, 1962.

Actas da Câmara da Villa de São Paulo. 47 vols. São Paulo, 1914–1938.

Acuerdos del extinguido Cabildo de Buenos Aires. Archivo General de la Nación, 1st series, Buenos Aires, 1907 ff.

Afonso, Gaspar. "Relação da viagem e successo que teve a Nao S. Francisco (1596)" in Bernardo Gomes de Brito, *História tragico-maritima.* 3 vols., Lisbon, 1935, II. 315–436.

Albuquerque Felner, Alfredo de. *Angola. Apontamentos sobre a ocupação e ínicio do estabelecimento dos portugueses no Congo, Angola, Benguela.* Coimbra, 1933.

Antonil, André João, Andreoni, João Antonio. *Cultura e opulencia do Brasil por suas drogas e minas.* Alfonso de E. Taunay, ed. São Paulo, 1923.

Archivo do Estado de São Paulo. *Inventários e testamentos.* 27 vols., São Paulo, 1917–1921.

Archivo portugues-oriental. Nova Goa, 1857.

As gavetas de Torre do Tombo. 5 vols. to date, Lisbon, 1960 ff, in progress.

Azevedo, João Lúcio, ed. *Cartas do Padre Antonio Vieira.* 3 vols. Coimbra, 1928.

Borges da Fonseca, Antônio José Victoriano. "Nobiliarchia Pernambucana," *Anais da Biblioteca Nacional do Rio de Janeiro*, XLVII (1925), 164, 419, 470, and XLVIII (1926), 207, 220, 469.

[Brandão, Ambrósio Fernandes]. *Diálogos das grandezas do Brasil.* José Antônio Gonsalves de Mello, ed. 2nd complete edition. Recife, 1966.

Braśio, Antônio. *Monumenta missionaria africana: Africa ocidental.* 2nd series, 3 vols., Lisbon, 1958–1964.

Brito Freyre, Francisco de. *Nova Lusitania ou guerra brasilica.* Lisbon, 1675.

Burns, E. Bradford. *A Documentary History of Brazil.* New York, 1966.

Caldas, José Antônio. *Notícia geral desta capitania da Bahia desde o seu descobrimento até o presente ano de 1759.* Facsimile edition, Salvador, 1951.

Calendar of State Papers, Foreign Series of the Reign of Elizabeth . . . 1558–1589. 23 vols., London, 1863–1950.

Calendar of State Papers and Manuscripts relating to English Affairs, existing in the Archives and Collections of Venice. . . . 38 vols., London, 1864 ff.

Campos Moreno, Diogo de. *Livro que dá rezão do Estado do Brasil (1612).* Hélio Vianna, ed. Recife, 1955.

Castillo de Bovadilla, Jerónimo. *Politica para corregedores y señores de vassallos en tiempo de paz e de guerra.* 2 vols., Barcelona, 1616.

Cervantes Saavedra, Miguel de. *The Adventures of Don Quixote.* Baltimore, 1950.

"Correspondencia de Diogo Botelho (1602–1608)," *Revista do Instituto Histórico e Geográfico Brasileiro*, LXXIII (1910), part 1, vii–xxxiv; 1–258.

"Correspondencia do Governador D. Diogo de Meneses, 1608–1612," *Anais da Biblioteca Nacional do Rio de Janeiro*, LVII (1935), 29–87.

Cortesáo, Jaime. *Paulіceae Lusitana Monumenta Histórica.* 3 vols. in 4, Lisbon, 1956–1961.

Dampier, William, *A Voyage to New Holland* (1699). London, 1939.

Dias, Eduardo. "Inspeções do Capitão e Sargento-Mór Diogo de Campos Moreno e aventuras do pau-brasil em Ilhéus," *IV Congresso de história nacional* (Rio de Janeiro, 1951), XI, 7–24.

Documentação ultramarina portuguesa. 5 vols. to date. Lisbon, 1960 ff, in progress.

Documentos históricos da Biblioteca Nacional do Rio de Janeiro. 120 vols. to date. Rio de Janeiro, 1928 ff, in progress.

Documentos para a história do açúcar. 3 vols., Rio de Janeiro, 1954–1963.

"Documentos relativos a Mem de Sá, governador-geral do Brasil," *Anais da Biblioteca Nacional do Rio de Janeiro,* XXVII (1905), 127–280.

Dussen, Adriaen van der. *Relatório sobre as capitanias conquistadas no Brasil pelos holandeses (1639).* José Antônio Gonçalves de Mello, trans. and ed. Rio de Janeiro, 1947.

[Ericeira, Conde de] Luís de Meneses. *História de Portugal Restaurado.* 4 vols., Oporto, 1945–1946.

Flores, Xavier A. *Le "Peso político de todo el mundo" d'Anthony Shirley ou un aventurier anglais au service de l'Espagne.* Paris, 1963.

Frézier, A., *A Voyage to the South Sea and the Coasts of Chili and Peru: 1712–1714* (London, 1716).

Garcia, Rodolfo. "Livro de denunciações que se fizerão na Visitação do Santo Officio á Cidade do Salvador da Bahia de Todos os Santos do Estado do Brasil no ano de 1618," *Anais da Biblioteca Nacional do Rio de Janeiro,* XLIX (1927), 75–198.

Gomes de Brito, Bernardo. *História Trágico-maritima.* 3 vols., Lisbon, 1735, II, 328–329.

Gonçalves Pereira, Carlos Renato. *História da administração da justiça no Estado da India.* 2 vols., Lisbon, 1964.

Helmer, Marie. "Comêrcio entre Bahia e Potosí," *Revista de História,* VII (1953), 195–212.

Herrera y Tordesillas, Antônio de. *Historia general de los hechos de los castellanos en las islas y tierra firme del mar oceano.* 4 vols., Madrid, 1726–1740.

"*Historia dos collegios do Brasil,*" *Anais da Biblioteca Nacional do Rio de Janeiro,* XIX (1897), 74–144.

Index das notas de vários tabeliães de Lisboa entre os anos de 1580 e 1747. 3 vols., Lisbon, 1931–1944.

Index das notas de vários tabeliães de Lisboa seculos XVI–XVII. 3 vols., Lisbon, 1949.

Konetzke, Richard (ed.). *Collección de documentos para la historia de la formación social de Hispanoamerica, 1493–1810.* 3 vols. to date. Madrid, 1953 ff, in progress.

Laval, François Pyrard de. *Voyage of François Pyrard de Laval.* Hakluyt LXXX. 2 vols. in 3. Albert Grey, trans. and ed. London, 1890.

Leite, Serafim. *Cartas do Brasil e mais escritos do P. Manuel da Nóbrega (opera omnia).* Coimbra. 1959.

Leite, Serafim. *Monumenta Brasiliae.* 4 vols., Rome, 1956–1960.

——. "Os Capitulos de Gabriel Soares de Sousa," *Ethnos*, II (1941), 5–36.

Ligon, Richard. *A True and Exact History of the Island of Barbadoes.* London, 1657.

Livro primeiro do governo do Brasil, 1607–1633. Rio de Janeiro, 1958.

"Livro segundo do governo do Brasil," *Annaes do Museu Paulista*, III (1927), 5–128.

Livro Velho do Tombo do Mosteiro de São Bento da Cidade do Salvador. Salvador, 1945.

Lopes de Almeida, Manuel. *Noticías históricas de Portugal e Brasil.* 2 vols., Coimbra, 1964.

Malheiro Dias, Carlos (ed.). *História da colonização portuguesa do Brasil.* 3 vols., Oporto, 1924–1926.

Mansuy, André (ed.), André João Antonil. *Cultura e opulencia do Brasil por suas drogas e minas.* Paris, 1968.

Matos, Gregório de. *Obras completas de. . . .* 7 vols., Salvador, 1969.

Mauro Frédéric. *Le Bresil au xvii siècle.* Coimbra, 1951.

Nunes de Leao, Duarte. *Descripção do Reino de Portugal.* Lisbon, 1610.

Oliveira França, Eduardo d' and Sonia Siqueira (eds.). "Confissões da Bahia, 1618," *Anais do Museu Paulista*, XVII (1963).

Oliveira Freire, Felisberto Firmo. *História de Sergipe.* Rio de Janeiro, 1891.

Pereira, Estevam. "Descrezão da fazenda que o collegio de Santo Antão tem no Brasil e das suas rendimentos," *Annaes do Museu Paulista*, IV (1931), 773–794.

Pinto Ribeiro, João. *Preferencia das Letras as Armas.* Lisbon, 1645.

Prefeitura Municipal do Salvador. *Documentos históricos do Arquivo Municipal: Atas da Camara, 1625–1700.* 6 vols. Salvador, 1949–5?.

——. *Documentos históricos do Arquivo Municipal: Cartas do Senado, 1638–1692.* 5 vols., Salvador, 1951–1953.

Prestage, Edgar and Pedro d'Azevedo (eds.). *Registro da Freguesia da Se desde 1563 até 1610.* 2 vols. Coimbra, 1927.

Primeira visitação do Santo Officio ás partes do Brasil. Confissões Bahia, 1591–92. J. Capistrano de Abreu (ed.). Rio de Janeiro, 1935.

Primeira visitação do Santo Officio ás partes do Brasil. Denunciações da Bahia, 1591–1593. J Capistrano de Abreu (ed.). São Paulo, 1925.

Primeira visitação do Santo Officio ás partes do Brasil. Denunciações de Pernambuco, 1593–1595. São Paulo, 1929.

Publicações do Arquivo Nacional, XXVII (Rio de Janeiro, 1931).

Purchas, Samuel. *Hakluytus Posthumous or His Pilgrims.* 5 vols., London, 1625.

Registro geral da Câmara municipal de São Paulo. 20 vols., São Paulo, 1917–1923.

"Regimentos diversos," *Revista do Instituto Histórico e Geográfico Brasileiro*, LXVII (1906), part 1, 189–241.

Revah, I. S. "Le Plaidoyer en faveur des 'Nouveaux-Chrétiens' Portugais du licencié Martin Gonzalez de Cellorigo," *Revue des Etudes Juives*, CXXII (July–December, 1963), 279–398.

Riba, Garcia, Carlos (ed.). *Correspondencia privada de Felipe II con su secretário Mateo Vázquez, 1567–1591.* Madrid, 1959.

Sá, Antonio de. *Sermão que pregou o P.M. . . . da Companhia de Jesus na Bahia, pregado a Iustica.* Coimbra, 1672.

Salvador, Vicente do. *História do Brasil, 1500–1627.* 5th ed., São Paulo, 1965.

Santos Vilhena, Luís de. *A Bahia no Seculo XVIII.* 3 vols., Salvador, 1969.

——. *Recopilação de Noticias Soteropolitanas e Brasilicas*, Braz do Amaral, ed., 3 vols. Bahia, 1922, 1935.

Silveira, Francisco Rodrigues. *Memórias de um soldado da India (1585–1634).* A. de S. S. Costa Lobo (ed.). Lisbon, 1877.

Sluiter, Engel. "Report on the State of Brazil, 1612," *Hispanic American Historical Review*, XXIX (1949), 518–562.

Soares, Pero Rodrigues. *Memorial.* Manuel Lopes de Almeida (ed.). Coimbra, 1953.

Soares de Sousa, Gabriel. *Notícia do Brasil.* 2 vols., São Paulo, 1940.

Souza, João Francisco de. "Documentos inéditos relativos ao Rio de Janeiro," *Revista de Historia*, XXVI (1965), 422–445; XXXIII (1966), 209–230.

Tourinho, Eduardo (ed.). *Autos de correições de ouvidores do Rio de Janeiro.* Prefeitura de Distrito Federal. 3 vols., Rio de Janeiro, 1929–1931.

Vázquez de Espinosa, Antonio. *Compendio y descripción de las Indias occidentales.* Charles U. Clark (ed.). Smithsonian Miscellaneous Collections 108. Washington, 1948.

Veríssimo Serrão, Joaquim. *O Rio de Janeiro no século XVI.* 2 vols., Lisbon, 1965.

Vieira, Antônio. "Annua da provincia do Brasil 1624–1625," *Anais da Biblioteca Nacional do Rio de Janeiro*, XIX (1897), 175–217.

[Vieira, Antônio]. *Arte de Furtar.* Amsterdam, 1657.

Wanderley Pinho, José de. "Testamento de Mem de Sá. Inventário de seus bens no Brasil," *III Congresso de História Nacional,* III (1941).

IV. SECONDARY SOURCES: BOOKS, ARTICLES, AND UNPUBLISHED WORKS

Accioli de Cerqueira e Silva, Ignacio. *Memórias históricas e políticas da província da Bahia.* Annotated by Braz do Amaral. 6 vols., Salvador, 1919–1940.

Albuquerque, Martim de. *O poder político no renascimento português.* Lisbon, 1968.

Alden, Dauril. "Black Robes versus White Settlers: The Struggle for 'Freedom of the Indians' in Colonial Brazil," in Howard Peckham and Charles Gibson, eds., *Attitudes of Colonial Powers Toward the American Indian.* Salt Lake City, 1969, 19–46.

——. "The Population of Brazil in the Late Eighteenth Century: A Preliminary Survey," *Hispanic American Historical Review,* XLIII (May 1963), 173–205.

——. *Royal Government in Colonial Brazil, with Special Reference to the Administration of the Marquis of Lavradio, Viceroy, 1769–1779.* Berkeley, 1968.

——. "Yankee Sperm Whalers in Brazilian Waters, and the Decline of the Portuguese Whale Fishery (1773–1801)," *The Americas,* XX (January 1964), n. 3, 269–270.

Almeida, Fortunato de. *História de Portugal.* 6 vols., Coimbra, 1922–1929.

Almeida, Luís Ferrand de. *A diplomacia portuguesa e os limites meridionais do Brasil.* Coimbra, 1957.

Almeida Costa, Mario Julio de. "Romanisme et Bartolisme dans le droit portugais," *Bartolo da Sassoferato. Studi e documenti per il VI Centenario.* 2 vols., Milan, 1962.

Almeida Prado, J. F. *A Bahia e as capitanias do centro do Brasil.* 3 vols., São Paulo, 1945.

Amaral Lapa, José Roberto de. *A Bahia e a carreira da India.* São Paulo, 1968.

Andrews, Kenneth R. *Elizabethan Privateering. English Privateering during the Spanish War, 1585–1603.* Cambridge, 1964.

Azevedo, Thales de. *Povoamento da Cidade do Salvador.* Salvador, 1949.

Baião, António. "O Bispo D. Marcos Teixeira," *I Congresso do mundo portugues*, IX (1940), 251–260.

——. *A Inquisição de Goa*. 2 vols., Lisbon, 1930–1949.

Beneyto, J. "La gestación de la magistratura moderna," *Anuario de la Historia de Derecho Español*, XXIII (1953), 55–82.

Boxer, C. R. *The Dutch in Brazil, 1624–1654*. Oxford, 1957.

——. *The Golden Age of Brazil, 1695–1750*. Berkeley, 1962.

——. "Lord Tyrawley in Lisbon," *History Today*, XX (November 1970), n. 11, 791–798.

——. "English Shipping in the Brazil Trade 1640–1645," *Mariner's Mirror*, XXXVII (July 1951), 197–230.

——. "Portuguese and Dutch Colonial Rivalry 1641–1661," *Studia*, II (July 1958), 7–43.

——. *The Portuguese Seaborne Empire*. London, 1969.

——. *Portuguese Society in the Tropics. The Municipal Councils of Goa, Macao, Bahia, and Luanda*. Madison, 1965.

——. *Race Relations in the Portuguese Colonial Empire*. Oxford, 1963.

——. *Salvador de Sá and the Struggle for Brazil and Angola, 1602–1686*. London, 1952.

—— (ed.). *The Tragic History of the Sea*. Haklyut Society. 2nd series, CXII, Cambridge, 1959.

Brooks, Mary Elizabeth. *A King for Portugal. The Madrigal Conspiracy, 1594–1595*. Madison, 1964.

Buarque de Holanda, Sérgio (ed.). *História geral da civilização brasileira*. 4 vols. to date. São Paulo, 1960 ff, in progress.

——. "Os projectos de colonização e comércio toscanos no Brasil ao tempo de Grão Duque Fernando I (1587–1609)," *Revista de História*, XXXV (1967).

—— (ed.). *Visão do paraíso. Os motivis edénicos no e colonização do Brasil*. Rio de Janeiro, 1959.

Burns, E. Bradford. *History of Brazil*. New York, 1970.

Butler, Ruth L. "Duarte da Costa, Second Governor-General of Brazil," *Mid-America*, XXV (1943), 163–179.

——. "Mem de Sá, Third Governor-General of Brazil, 1557–1572," *Mid-America*, XXVI (1944), 111–137.

——. "Thomé de Sousa, First Governor-General of Brazil, 1549–1553," *Mid-America*, XXIV (1942), 229–251.

Caeiro, Francisco. *O Arquiduque Alberto de Austria*. Lisbon, 1961.

Caetano, Marcelo. "As Cortes de 1385," *Revista Portuguesa de História*, V (1951), vol. 2, 5–86.

——. *De Conselho Ultramarino ao Conselho do Imperio.* Lisbon, 1943.

Calmon, Pedro. *Espírito da sociedade colonial.* São Paulo, 1935.

——. *História da Casa de Torre.* 2nd ed., Rio de Janeiro, 1958.

——. *História da fundação da Bahia.* Salvador, 1949.

——. *História do Brasil.* 7 vols., Rio de Janeiro, 1959.

——. *O segredo das minas da prata.* Rio de Janeiro, 1950.

Camara, José Gomes B. *Subsídios para a história do direito patrio.* 3 vols., Rio de Janeiro, 1954–1965.

Canabrava, Alice P. "A força motriz; um problema de técnica da industria do acúcar colonial," *Anais. I. Congresso da História da Bahia* (1950), I, 337–350.

——. "A lavoura canaveira nas Antilhas e no Brasil," *Anais. I Congresso da História da Bahia* (1950), I.

——. *O comércio português no Rio da Prata: 1580–1640.* São Paulo, 1944.

Capistrano de Abreu, João. *Caminhos antigos e povoamento do Brasil,* ?, 1930.

Cardozo, Manoel S. "The Lay Brotherhoods of Colonial Bahia," *The Catholic Historical Review,* XXXIII (April 1947), 12–30.

Carvalho Morão, J. M. "Orgãos administrativos e judiciários da colonia do período decorrido de 1500 a 1763," *IV Congresso de Historia Nacional,* IX, 408–460.

Chamberlain, Robert S. "The Corregedor in Castile in the Sixteenth Century and the Residencia as Applied to the Corregedor," *Hispanic American Historical Review,* XXIII (1943), 222–257.

Chaunu, Pierre. "Brésil et Atlantique au xvii siècle," *Annales Economie, Sociétés Civilisations,* XVI (November–December 1961), 1176–1207.

Coaracy, Vivaldo. *O Rio de Janeiro no século dezasete.* 2nd ed., Rio de Janeiro, 1965.

Costa, Afonso. "Achegas genealógicas," *Revista de Instituto Histórico e Geográfico da Bahia,* LXI (1935), 69–460.

——. "Genealogia Baíana," *RIHGB,* CXCI (1946), 1–279.

Costa, Avelino de Jesus da. "População da Cidade da Baía em 1775," *Actas. V. Colóquio internacional de estudos Luso-brasileiros.* 4 vols., Coimbra, 1963.

Costa Porto, João. *Estudo sobre o sistema sesmarial.* Recife, 1965.

Crozier, Michel. *The Bureaucratic Phenomenon.* Chicago, 1964.

Dalby, Michael T. and Michael S. Werthman. *Bureaucracy in Historical Perspective.* Glenview, Ill., 1971.

Dánvila y Buguero, Alfonso. *Don Cristóbal de Moura.* Madrid, 1900.

Davidson, David. "How the Brazilian West Was Won. Freelance and State on the Mato Grosso Frontier, *ca.* 1737–1752," in Dauril Alden, ed., *Colonial Roots of Modern Brazil: Papers of the Newberry Library Conference.* Berkeley and Los Angeles, 1973.

Davidson, Theresa Sherrer. "The Brazilian Inheritance of Roman Law," *Brazil, Papers Presented on the Institute of Brazilian Studies.* Vanderbilt University, Nashville, 1953.

Delany, William. "The Development and Decline of Patrimonial and Bureaucratic Administrations," *Administrative Science Quarterly,* VII (March 1963), n. 4, 458–501.

Diffie, Bailey W. *Latin American Civilization.* Harrisburg, 1945.

Duffy, James. *Shipwreck and Empire.* Cambridge, Mass., 1955.

Dutra, Francis A. "A New Look into Diogo Botelho's Stay in Pernambuco," *Luso-Brazilian Review,* IV (June 1967), 27–34.

——. "Matias de Albuquerque: A Seventeenth-Century *Capitão-Mór* of Pernambuco and Governor-General of Brazil." Unpublished Ph.D. Dissertation, New York University, 1968.

——. "Membership in the Order of Christ in the Seventeenth Century: Its Rights, Privileges, and Obligations," *The Americas,* XXVII (July 1970), n. 1, 3–25.

Eisenstadt, S. N. "Bureaucracy, Bureaucratization, and Debureaucratization," *Administrative Science Quarterly,* IV (December 1959), 302–320.

——. "Political Struggle in Bureaucratic Societies," *World Politics,* IX (1958), n. 1, 58–76.

——. *The Political Systems of Empires.* New York, 1963.

——. "Ritualized Personal Relations," *Man,* 96 (July 1956), 90–95.

Elliott, John H. *Imperial Spain.* New York, 1964.

Ellis, Myriam. *Aspectos da pesca da baleia no Brasil colonial.* São Paulo, 1958.

Elton, G. R. *The Tudor Revolution in Government.* Cambridge, 1962.

Esmein, A. *A History of Continental Criminal Procedure.* Continental Legal History Series. V, John Simpson trans. London, 1914.

Faoro, Raymundo. *Os Donos do poder.* Porto Alegre, 1958.

Fernandes, Florestan. *A organização social dos Tupinambá.* São Paulo, 1948.

Ferreira, Waldemar Martins. *História do direito brasileiro.* 4 vols., São Paulo, 1956 ff, in progress.

Flach, Jacques. *Cujas, les glossateurs et les Bartolistes.* Paris, 1883.

Fonseca, Luiza da. "Bacharéis Brasileiros—Elementos biográficos (1635–

1800)," *Anais. IV Congresso de História Nacional.* Rio de Janeiro, 1951.

Ford, Franklin L. *Robe and Sword. The Regrouping of the French Aristocracy after Louis XIV.* Cambridge, Mass., 1953.

Freyre, Gilberto. *The Masters and the Slaves.* 2nd ed., New York, 1956.

Galvão, Eneas. "Juizes e tribunais no período colonial," *I Congresso de Historia Nacional,* III, 319–340.

Gama Barros, Henrique da. *História da administração pública em Portugal.* 2nd ed., 11 vols., Lisbon, 1945–1954.

Garcia, Nilo. *Aclamação de Amador Bueno. Influência espanhola em São Paulo.* Rio de Janeiro, 1956.

Garcia, Rodolfo. *Ensaio sobre a história política e administrativa do Brasil.* Rio de Janeiro, 1956.

Gomes da Silva, Nuno J. Espinosa. *Humanismo e direito em Portugal no século XVI.* Lisbon, 1964.

Gonçalves Pereira, Carlos Renato. *Tribunal da Relação da Goa.* Lisbon, 1964.

Góngora, Mario. *El estado en el derecho español.* Santiago de Chile, 1951.

Gonsalves Salvador, José. *Cristãos-Novos, Jesuitas e Inquisição.* São Paulo, 1969.

González de Echávarri y Vivanco, J. M. *La justicia y Felipe II. Estudio historico-crítico em vista de diezysiete reales cédulas y cartas acordades del Consejo ineditas.* Valladolid, 1917.

Goode, William. "The Theoretical Importance of Love," *American Sociological Review,* XXIV (1959), 38–47.

Goulart, José Alipio. *O cavalo na formação do Brasil.* Rio de Janeiro, 1964.

Graham, Lawrence. *Civil Service Reform in Brazil.* Austin, 1968.

Greenlee, William B. "The First Half Century of Brazilian History," *Mid-America,* XXV (1943), 91–120.

Hall, Richard. "The Concept of Bureaucracy: An Empirical Assessment," *American Journal of Sociology,* LXIX (July 1963), 32–40.

Hamilton, Bernice. *Political Thought in Sixteenth-Century Spain.* Oxford, 1963.

Hanke, Lewis. "The Portuguese in Spanish America with special reference to the Villa Imperial de Potosí," *Revista de Historia de America,* LXI (June 1961).

——. *The Spanish Struggle for Justice in the Conquest of America.* Philadelphia, 1949.

Harris, Marvin. *Patterns of Race in the Americas.* New York, 1964.

Herculano, Alexandre. *History of the Origins and Establishment of the Inquisition in Portugal.* John C. Branner, trans. Stanford University Publications: History, Economics, and Political Science, I, no. 2. Stanford, 1926.

Jones, A. *Studies in Roman Law and Administration.* Oxford, 1960.

Kagan, Richard L. "Education and the State in Hapsburg Spain." Unpublished Ph.D. thesis, Cambridge University, 1968.

Kellenbenz, Hermann. "Der Brasilienhandel der Hamburger Portugiesen zu Ende der 16 und in der Ersten Hälfte des 17 Jahrhunderts," *Actas. III Colóquio internacional de estudos Luso-brasilieros,* II, 277–296.

——. "O projecto duma 'Casa da Contratação' em Lisboa," *Actas. Congresso internacional de história dos descobrimentos.* V, part 2, 233–249.

Kieman, Mathias. *The Indian Policy of Portugal in the Amazon Region, 1614–1693.* Washington, 1954.

Kirkpatrick, F. A. *The Spanish Conquistadores.* Cleveland, 1946.

Koenigsberger, Helmut. *The Government of Sicily Under Philip II of Spain.* London, 1951.

Kottak, Conrad. "Kinship and Class in Brazil," *Ethnology,* VI (1967), n. 4, 427–443.

Lahmeyer Lobo, Eulalia Maria. "Alguns aspectos ha história da Mesa do Bem Comum dos Mercadores," *V Colóquio internacional de estudos Luso-brasileiros,* II, 383–387.

——. *Aspectos da influência dos homens de negocio na política comercial Ibero-americana.* Rio de Janeiro, 1963.

——. *Processo administrativo Ibero-americano.* Rio de Janeiro, 1962.

Laseros, Mateo. *La Autoridad civil en Francisco Suárez.* Madrid, 1949.

Leeds, Anthony. "Brazilian Careers and Social Structure; An Evolutionary Model and a Case History," *American Anthropologist,* LXVI (December 1964), 1321–1347.

Leite, Serafim. "As raças do Brasil perante a ordem teológica, moral e jurídica portuguesa nos séculos XVI a XVIII," *Actas. V. Colóquio internacional de estudos Luso-brasileiros,* III, 7–28.

——. *Os governadores gerais do Brasil e os Jesuitas no século XVI.* Lisbon, 1937.

——. *História da Companhia de Jesus no Brasil.* 10 vols., Lisbon, 1938–1950.

Lipiner, Elias. *Os judizantes nas capitanias de cima.* São Paulo, 1969.

Litwak, Eugene. "Models of Bureaucracy which Permit Conflict," *American Journal of Sociology*, LXVII (September 1961), 177–184.
Livermore, Harold V. *A History of Portugal*. Cambridge, 1947.
Lockhart, James. *Spanish Peru*. Madison, 1968.
Lynch, John. *Spain Under the Hapsburgs*. 2 vols., New York, 1964–1969.
Machado, Alcântara. *Vida e morte do bandeirante*. São Paulo, 1943.
Malagón-Barceló, Javier. "The Role of the *Letrado* in the Colonization of America," *The Americas*, XVIII (July 1961), 1–17.
Manchester, Alan K. "The Rise of the Brazilian Aristocracy," *Hispanic American Historical Review*, XI (May 1931), 146–168.
Maravall, José Antonio. "Los 'hombres de saber' o letrados y la formación de su consciencia estamental," *Estudios de historia de pensamiento español*. Madrid, 1967.
Marchant, Alexander. "Colonial Brazil as a Way Station for the Portuguese India Fleets," *The Geographical Review*, XXXI (July 1941), 454–465.
——. *From Barter to Slavery. The Economic Relations of Portuguese and Indians in the Settlement of Brazil, 1500–1580*. The Johns Hopkins University Studies in Historical and Political Science, series IX, no. 1. Baltimore, 1942.
——. "Feudal and Capitalistic Elements in the Portuguese Settlement of Brazil," *Hispanic American Historical Review*, XXII (1942), 493–512.
Mauro, Frédéric. *Le Portugal et L'Atlantique au XVII siècle, 1570–1670*. Paris, 1960.
——. *Nova história e novo mundo*. São Paulo, 1969.
Maxwell, Kenneth. "Pombal and the Nationalization of the Luso-Brazilian Economy," *Hispanic American Historical Review*, XLVII (November 1968), 608–631.
Mello, Alfredo Pinto Vieira de. 'O poder judiciario do Brasil," *I Congresso de História Nacional*, IV, 97–148.
Mendes da Luz, Francisco Paulo. *O Conselho da India*. Lisbon, 1952.
Mendes de Almeida, Candido. *Memórias para a história do extinto Estado do Maranhão*. 2 vols., Rio de Janeiro, 1860–1874.
Mendes dos Remedios, J. *Os judeus em Portugal*. Coimbra, 1895.
Merêa, Manuel Paulo. "Da minha gaveta—os secretários do Estado do antigo regimen," *Boletim da Faculdade do Direito da Universidade de Coimbra*, XL (1964), 173–89.

——. "A solução tradicional da colonização do Brasil," in C. Malheiro Dias (ed.). *História da colonização portuguesa do Brasil,* III, 165–188.

Merton, Robert. "Bureaucratic Structure and Personality," in Robert Merton, *et al. Reader in Bureaucracy* (New York, 1952), 361–371.

Métraux, Alfred. *Migrations historiques des Tupiguarani.* Paris (?), 1927.

Mintz, Sidney W. and Wolf, Eric R. "An Analysis of Ritual Coparenthood (Compadrazgo)," *Southwestern Journal of Anthropology,* VI (Winter 1950), n. 4, 341–362.

Monteiro da Costa, Luiz. *Na Bahia colonial. Apontamentos para a história militar da Cidade do Salvador.* Salvador, 1958.

Moreno, J. L. *Who Shall Survive?* Washington, D. C., 1934.

Mousnier, Roland. *Peasant Uprisings in Seventeenth-Century France, Russia, and China.* New York, 1970.

——. *La vénalité des offices sous Henri VII et Louis XIII.* Rouen, 1948.

Nobreza de Portugal. 3 vols., Lisbon, 1960–1961.

Novinsky, Anita. "A Inquisição na Bahia (Um Relatório de 1632), *Revista de História,* XXXVI (1968), n. 74, 417–423.

Nuñez Arca, P. *Brasil restituido. Os 3 Felipes da Espanha que foram reis do Brasil.* São Paulo, 1957.

Oliveira, Oscar de. *Os dízimos eclesiásticos do Brasil nos períodos da colonia e do imperio.* Belo Horizonte, 1964.

Oliveira França, Eduardo d'. "Engenhos colonização e cristãos novos na Bahia Colonial." *Anais do IV Simpósio Nacional dos Professores Universitários de História* (São Paulo, 1969), 181–241.

Oliveira Vianna, Francisco José. *Populações meridionais do Brasil.* São Paulo, 1938.

Ott, Carlos. *Formção e evolução étnica da cidade do Salvador.* 2 vols., Salvador, 1955–1957.

Paes Barreto, Carlos Xavier. *Os primativos colonizadores nordestinos e seus descendentes.* Rio de Janeiro, 1960.

Pagano, Sebastião, "O Brasil e suas relações com a corôa da Espanha ao tempo dos Felipes," *Revista do Instituto Histórico Geográphico de São Paulo, LIX* (1960), 215–233.

Pantaleão, Olga. "Um navio ingles no Brasil em 1581: A viagem do *Minion of London.*" *Estudos Históricos,* I (1963).

Parry, J. H. *The Audiencia of New Galicia in the Sixteenth Century, A Study in Spanish Colonial Government.* Cambridge, 1948.

——. *The Sale of Public Office in the Spanish Indies Under the Hapsburgs.* Berkeley, 1963.

Parsons, Talcott (trans. and ed.). *Max Weber: The Theory of Social and Economic Organization.* New York, 1947.

Pena, Afonso. *A Arte de furtar e o seu autor.* 2 vols., Rio de Janeiro, 1946.

Perdigão Malheiro, Agostinho Marques. *A escravidão no Brasil.* 3 vols. in 1. Rio de Janeiro, 1866.

Pereira da Costa, F. A. *Anais Pernambucanas.* 10 vols., Recife, 1951? 1967.

Peres, Damião (ed.). *História da Portugal.* 7 vols. in 8 with supplement and indices. Barcelos. 1928–1966.

Petrie, Charles. *Philip II of Spain.* London, 1963.

Phelan, John L. "Authority and Flexibility in the Spanish Imperial Bureaucracy," *Administrative Science Quarterly*, V (June 1960).

——. *The Kingdom of Quito.* Madison, 1968.

Pinheiro da Silva, José. "A capitania da Baía. Subsídios para a história da sua colonização na 2ª metade do século XVII," *Revista Portuguesa da História*, VIII (1959), 44–284, IX (1960), 211–245.

Poppino, Rollie. "Cattle Industry in Colonial Brazil," *Mid-America*, XXXI (October 1949), 219–247.

Prestage, Edgar. *The Chronicles of Fernão Lopes and Gomes Eannes de Zurara.* Watford, 1928.

——. *The Royal Power and the Cortes in Portugal.* Watford, 1927.

Ramos, Artur. *Introdução á antropologia brasileira.* 2 vols., Rio de Janeiro, 1947.

Rau, Virginia. *A Casa dos Contos.* Coimbra, 1951.

——. *Estudos de História.* Lisbon, 1968.

Rebello da Silva, L. A. *História de Portugal nos séculos xvi–xvii.*

Rêgo Quirino, Tarcizio do. *Os habitantes do Brasil no fim do século XVI.* Recife, 1966.

Ricard, Robert. "Algunas enseñanzas de los documentos inquisitoriales del Brasil (1591–1595)," *Anuario de Estudios Americanos*, V (1948), 705–715.

Rocha Peres, Fernando da. "Documentos para una biografia de Gregório de Matos e Guerra," *Universitas*, II (1969), 53–65.

——. "Gregório de Matos e Guerra: Seu primeiro casamento," *Universitas*, I (1968), 135–149.

Rocha Pitta, Sebastião da. *História da America portugueza.* Lisbon, 1724.

Rodney, Walter. "Portuguese Attempts at Monopoly on the Upper Guinea Coast," *Journal of African History*, VI (1965), 307–322.

Rosenberg, Hans. *Bureaucracy, Aristocracy, and Autocracy. The Prussian Experience, 1600–1815.* Cambridge, Mass., 1958.

Russell-Wood, A. J. R. *Fidalgos and Philanthropists. The Santa Casa da Misericórdia of Bahia, 1550–1755.* Berkeley, 1968.

Ruy, Alfonso. *História de Câmara Municipal da Cidade do Salvador.* Salvador, 1953.

——. *História política e administrativa da Cidade do Salvador.* Salvador, 1949.

——. *A Relação da Bahia.* Bahia: Centro de Estudos Bahianos, 1968.

Sampaio Garcia, Rozendo. "Contribuição ao estudo do aprovisionamento de escravos negros da America Espanhola (1580–1640)," *Anais do Museu Paulista*, XVI (1962).

Saraiva, António José. *História da Cultura em Portugal.* 2 vols., Lisbon, 1950–1955.

——. *Inquisição e cristãos-novos.* Oporto, 1969.

Scelle, Georges. *La traite négriere aux Indes de Castillo. Contraits et traités d'assiento.* 2 vols., Paris, 1906.

Schwartz, Stuart B. "Free Labor in a Slave Economy: The *Lavradores de Cana* of Colonial Bahia." in Dauril Alden, ed., *Colonial Roots of Modern Brazil: Papers of the Newberry Library Conference.* Berkeley and Los Angeles, 1973.

——. "Luso-Spanish Relations in Hapsburg Brazil, 1580–1640," *The Americas*, XXV (July 1968), 33–48.

——. "Magistracy and Society in Colonial Brazil," *Hispanic American Historical Review*, L (November 1970), 715–730.

——. "The Mocambo: Slave Resistance in Colonial Bahia," *Journal of Social History*, III (Summer 1970), n. 4, 313–333.

——. "Toward a New Interpretation of Government and Society in Colonial Spanish and Portuguese America." Paper presented to the XXXIX International Congress of Americanists, Lima, 1970.

Scott, James C. "The Analysis of Corruption in Developing Nations," *Comparative Studies in Society and History*, XI (June 1969), 315–341.

Senna Barcelos, José Christiano. *Subsídios para a história de Cabo Verde e Guine.* 7 vols. in 3. Lisbon, 1899–1911.

Sherman, William L. "Indian Slavery and the Cerrato Reforms," *His-*

panic American Historical Review, LI (February 1971), 25–50.

Silva Rego, António de. *Portuguese Colonization in the Sixteenth Century*. Johannesburg, 1959.

Silveira, Luis. *Ensaio de iconografia das cidades portuguesas do ultramar*. 4 vols., Lisbon, 1957.

Simonson, Roberto. *História económica do Brasil 1500–1820*. 4th ed., São Paulo, 1962.

Simpson, Lesley B. *The Encomienda in New Spain*. Berkeley, 1950.

——. *Studies in the Administration of the Indians of New Spain*. Ibero-Americana no. 13. Berkeley, 1938.

Sluiter, Engel. "Dutch Maritime Power and the Colonial Status Quo, 1585–1641," *Pacific Historical Review*, XI (1942), 29–41.

——. "Dutch-Spanish Rivalry in the Caribbean Area, 1594–1609," *Hispanic American Historical Review*, XXVIII (1948), 179–87.

Smith, Robert C. "The Arts in Brazil: Baroque Architecture," in *Portugal and Brazil, An Introduction*, Harold V. Livermore (ed.). (Oxford, 1963), pp. 349–384.

Smith, Robert S. *The Spanish Guild Merchant: A History of the Consulado, 1250–1700*. Durham, 1940.

Stone, Lawrence. "Prosopography," *Daedalus*, C (Winter 1971), 46–79.

Sussman, Marvin B. "Some Conceptual Issues in Family-Organizational Linkages." Paper read to the American Sociological Association. Mimeo., 1969.

Swart, K. W. *Sale of Public Offices in the Seventeenth Century*. The Hague, 1949.

Taunay, Afonso de E. *História sesicentista da Villa de São Paulo*. 4 vols., São Paulo, 1926–1929.

Thomas, Georg. *Die portugiesische Indianerpolitik in Brasilien, 1500–1640*. Berlin, 1968.

Tilman, Robert O. "Emergence of Black Market Bureaucracy: Administration, Development, and Corruption in New States," *Public Administration Review*, XXVIII (September–October 1968), n. 5, 437–444.

Trevor-Roper, H. R. "The General Crisis of the Seventeenth Century," *Past and Present*, XVI (November 1959), 31–64.

Vance, John Thomas. *The Background of Hispanic-American Law*. Washington, 1937.

Varnhagen, Francisco Adolfo de. *História geral do Brasil*. 5 vols. in 3. 7th complete edition. São Paulo, 1962.

Vasconcelos Pedrosa, Manuel Xavier de. "Letrados do seculo XVIII," *Anais do Congresso Comemorativo do Bicentenário da Transferência da Sede do Govêrno do Brasil.* 4 vols., Rio de Janeiro, 1967.

Verger, Pierre. *Flux et reflux de la traite des nègres entre le golfe de Bénin et Bahia de todos os santos du xvii*[e] *au xix*[e] *siècle.* Paris, 1963.

Veríssimo Serrão, Joaquím. *Do Brasil filipino ao Brasil de 1640.* São Paulo, 1968.

——. *O reinado de D. António Prior do Crato 1580–1582.* 1 vol. to date. Coimbra, 1956.

Vidago, João. "Unidos Sim, Sujeitos Nao. Ensaio sobre a independencia e continuidade de Portugal durante a dinastia dos Filipes," *Ocidente,* LXX (May 1966), 205–220; (June 1966), 240–259.

Wagley, Charles. *The Latin American Tradition.* New York, 1968.

Wanderley de Araújo Pinho, José. *História de um engenho de Recôncavo.* Rio de Janeiro, 1946.

Wanderley de [Araújo] Pinho, José. *D. Marcos Teixeira quinto bispo do Brazil.* Lisbon, 1940.

Wiznitzer, Arnold. *The Jews in Colonial Brazil.* New York, 1960.

——. "The Jews in the Sugar Industry of Colonial Brazil," *Jewish Social Studies,* XVIII (1956), 189–198.

Woolf, Cecil N. S. *Bartolus of Sassoferato, His Position in the History of Medieval Political Thought.* Cambridge, 1913.

Zimmerman, Arthur F. *Francisco de Toledo.* Caldwell (Idaho), 1938.

Zorroquín Becú, Ricardo. "Orígenes del comercio rioplatense, 1580–1620," *Anuario de historia argentina,* IV (1943).

INDEX